SOCIALIST REGISTER 2025

THE SOCIALIST REGISTER

Founded in 1964

To get online access to all Register volumes visit our website
http://www.socialistregister.com

SOCIALIST REGISTER 2025

OPENINGS AND CLOSURES
SOCIALIST STRATEGY
AT A CROSSROADS

Edited by GREG ALBO and STEPHEN MAHER

THE MERLIN PRESS
MONTHLY REVIEW PRESS
FERNWOOD PUBLISHING

First published in 2025
by The Merlin Press Ltd
Central Books Building
Freshwater Road
London
RM8 1RX

www.merlinpress.co.uk

© The Merlin Press, 2025

British Library Cataloguing in Publication Data is available from the British
Library

ISSN. 0081-0606

Published in the UK by The Merlin Press
ISBN. 978-0-85036-792-8 Paperback
ISBN. 978-0-85036-793-5 Hardback

Published in the USA by Monthly Review Press
ISBN. 978-1-68590-115-8 Paperback

Published in Canada by Fernwood Publishing
ISBN. 978-1-77363-703-7 Paperback

CONTENTS

CONTRIBUTORS

Michael Calderbank is Co-Director of Solidarity Consulting, lobbying on behalf of trade unions in the UK Parliament.

Greig Charnock is Professor of Global Political Economy at the University of Manchester.

Ruth Felder teaches in the Political Science Program, Faculty of Social Science and Humanities at Ontario Tech University.

Nick French is an associate editor at *Jacobin*, a member of the *Dollars & Sense* editorial collective and a member of the Democratic Socialists of America.

Arun Gupta is an investigative reporter who has written for *The Nation*, *The Guardian*, *The Intercept*, *Jacobin* and many others.

Feyzi Ismail teaches global policy and activism at Goldsmiths, University of London, and is active in the British anti-war and trade union movements.

Ayyaz Mallick is a lecturer in human geography at the University of Liverpool.

Jose Mansilla is a professor in the Department of Social and Cultural Anthropology at Universitat Autònoma de Barcelona.

Thomas Marois is Canada Research Chair in Public Banking in the Department of Political Science, McMaster University, Hamilton.

David A. McDonald is Professor of Global Development Studies at Queen's University, Canada, and Director of the Municipal Services Project.

Şebnem Oğuz is a retired professor of political science and a member of Ankara Solidarity Academy.

Umut Özsu is Professor of Law and Legal Studies at Carleton University, Ottawa.

Viviana Patroni is Professor Emerita of International Development Studies, Department of Social Science at York University, Toronto.

Catarina Príncipe is a PhD candidate in political economy. She is a contributing editor at *Jacobin*, co-editor with Bhaskar Sunkara of the book *Europe in Revolt* and a long-time political activist from Portugal.

Touré F. Reed is a professor of 20th century US and African American history at Illinois State University.

Ramon Ribera-Fumaz is Professor of Economic and Urban Geography at the Universitat Oberta de Catalunya.

Ingar Solty is Senior Research Fellow in Peace, Foreign and Security Policy in the Institute for Critical Social Analysis at the Rosa Luxemburg Foundation.

Panagiotis Sotiris works as a journalist and editor in Athens, Greece, and is an editorial board member of *Historical Materialism*.

Susan Spronk is an associate professor in the School of International Development and Global Studies, University of Ottawa.

Hilary Wainwright is co-editor of *Red Pepper* and Senior Research Associate at the Institute of Development Studies working on a worker-led transition to a low carbon economy.

Jeffery R. Webber is a professor in the Department of Politics at York University, Toronto.

PREFACE

The sixty-first volume of the *Socialist Register* arrives at a transitional moment. Such periods, as we know, are often marked by 'morbid symptoms'. It is difficult to escape the conclusion that 'now is the time of monsters' as we await the return of Donald Trump to the presidency of the American empire, and any realistic hopes of limiting planetary warming to 1.5C are dashed as states from all regions of the world retreat from previous commitments to phase out fossil fuels at COP 29. Meanwhile, the inability of neoliberalism to provide a framework for macreconomic stability, ideological legitimacy and global political order has only become more apparent. Yet, even as this is increasingly recognized by policy elites themselves, no coherent alternative has emerged to take its place. And while the American state remains the indispensable anchor of global capitalism, mounting tensions and challenges are driving the fragmentation of power within the structure of its empire – fuelling a surge of insecurity and militarism that now includes genocidal violence and an escalating risk of nuclear conflict.

Against this background, the left is in retreat – from the capitalist core in western states, to the regional centres of power in emerging economies like China and South Africa, to the struggling peripheries of the 'global south' – and for the most part unable to offer leadership to defeated subaltern classes. The sense of powerlessness is amplified by the fact that this follows a period of optimism amidst the unexpected emergence of what seemed to be a major opening for socialist politics, particularly in the advanced capitalist countries but also more broadly. For a moment, it appeared that the ideas developed across decades of *Socialist Register* volumes would take on a powerful and immediate relevance. The 'democratic socialist' moment in the US and UK, the 'new parties' in Europe – Syriza, Bloco, Podemos, Die Linke – and the 'pink tide' wave in Latin America seemed to offer a route to develop a new politics, different from both the vanguardist approaches tied to the events of 1917 as well as the trajectory of postwar social democratic parties whose mass working class bases were steadily eroded as, one after the next, they embraced so many 'varieties of neoliberalism'. Despite their successes in achieving democratic reforms earlier in the century, rather than *transforming* their states these social democratic parties were *transformed by* capitalism.

Seemingly out of nowhere, the surge of popular energy surrounding the candidacy of Bernie Sanders for the Democratic Party nomination in 2016 appeared to present a way out of both the crisis of social democracy and the marginality of far-left parties. The explosive growth of the Democratic Socialists of America that followed, as a new generation of activists flooded that organization to build grassroots support for 'democratic socialists' running for office across the country and develop the political power of the working class, seemed to put the possibility for *something different* on the agenda for the first time in generations. This energy was reinforced soon thereafter by the meteoric rise of Jeremy Corbyn to the leadership of the UK Labour Party, overcoming intense resistance from the Labour establishment even as the influx of young people attracted to his openly – if vaguely – socialist message made that party the largest in Europe. For some, the conclusions drawn by Ralph Miliband and later Leo Panitch (often writing with his co-editor Colin Leys) across the pages of *Socialist Register* about the limits of 'parliamentary socialism' were cast into doubt: could the British Labour Party become a vehicle for socialism after all?

Of course, this democratic socialist conjuncture had in fact emerged from a wider and longer-term political sequence. The explosion of the Occupy Wall Street protests and the formation of the anti-austerity group UK Uncut following the 2008 financial meltdown had been essential for creating the political and ideological terrain upon which Sanders' and Corbyn's campaigns could blossom. And these were themselves significantly inspired by the historic events of the Arab Spring, as the world witnessed the power of mass mobilization to topple dictators, foremost among them Egypt's Hosni Mubarak, a major US ally. The 'pink tide' of Latin America, which saw leftist governments come to power in Venezuela, Ecuador and Bolivia, was also a significant inspiration for the possibilities of a 21st century socialism, as were the new mass 'people's movements' emerging across Asia insistent on democratic and social reforms.

The more immediate context was framed, however, by the emergence across the advanced capitalist countries of new party formations and popular movements. Of particular significance was Syriza, which in 2015 became the only socialist party to come to power in the capitalist core since the 2008 crisis. Even more promisingly, it did so with the support of energetic social movements and a dynamic approach to state power that sought to break with both the communist and social democratic strategies, while offering an alternative to the insurrectionist platforms of smaller Leninist groups.

Suddenly, after decades of defeats and the steady lowering of expectations, with no alternative in sight, there appeared to be a historic opening for a renewal of left politics, supported by the possibility of winning real, tangible victories on the terrain of the state. A new range of tactics and strategies seemed to offer a generational opportunity to rebuild fractured and weakened left forces and attract mass support for socialist politics. Debates swirled among a left that had to grapple seriously with big political questions: How, if at all, could electoral campaigns and elected officials contribute to building wider working-class forces? What political forms were called for to address the challenges of sustaining the struggles of these forces on the hostile terrain of center-left parties and capitalist states? How could they play a role in regrouping fragmented and diminished social movements, and bring them together to form a broader socialist politics? What was the proper balance between electoral politics and base-building, and through what means could this be achieved and sustained? How much could be achieved through electoral and parliamentary means, and how – if at all – could these limits be transcended? What would a socialist transition ultimately entail?

And then, just as quickly, these hopes were dashed. The opening, it seemed, was illusory. The confidence of the resurgent democratic socialist left evaporated as quickly as it had appeared, as the defeat of Sanders, and then Corbyn, facilitated the consolidation of the stranglehold over these parties by centrist coalitions under Joe Biden and Keir Starmer respectively. This followed the crumbling of the European new parties, as Syriza buckled in the face of the iron straitjacket imposed by EU institutions, and Podemos fractured under the weight of its ideological and institutional weaknesses. Bloco fared no better, and even Die Linke has fallen into a potentially existential crisis. To make matters worse, the decomposition of these forces left even fewer checks on the resurgent hard right, which took ground from the collapse of the political centrism of the liberal and social democratic parties. A weakened left offered little in the way of an alternative to supporting the coercive response to far-right forces by increasingly authoritarian neoliberal states, which it dubiously framed as constituting anti-fascist 'popular fronts'. Some on the left, in contrast, turned to the workplace, and trade union organizing, to build the working-class base for radical politics whose absence seemed so directly responsible for yet another round of defeats.

The political terrain had shifted once again. The historic crashing of this global wave of left forces should, if we are sober, force a deep reconsideration of the strategies and ideas that animated these forces. Reckoning with the failures and limitations of past experiments is essential for uncovering whatever possibilities may exist within the present. This is the essence of what Panitch called 'the optimism of the intellect': a commitment to rigorous, unflinching analysis grounded in the determination to create a better future for humanity. It was in grappling with this commitment that we conceived this volume of the *Socialist Register*, the first since 1984 in which Leo had no part in planning or executing. Not only had another cycle of left politics come to a close, but so too had the life of a towering figure of the international left, whose dedication and intellect were central to maintaining the integrity and quality of the *Register* for nearly half a century. Confronting the question of 'what next for the left' in this context was, for us, inseparable from considering the future of the *Register* itself. If the *Register* had played a unique intellectual role for the left since its founding in 1964 by Miliband and John Saville, what would it mean to sustain this role now, in the wake of the closure of the democratic socialist conjuncture?

In this context, we aimed to pull together a volume that confronted directly the impasses and the opportunities – the openings *and* the closures – facing the left internationally. And we have come away from the experience more convinced than ever of the vital role for the *Register* as a space for independent socialist analysis. The scale of the challenges we now face does not diminish but rather amplifies the importance of the political vision that has animated the *Register* from its inaugural volume. Miliband's distinct contribution was to carve out a political space that was neither attached to Leninist parties nor beholden to social democratic illusions. The former had failed, for over a half-century by the time Miliband launched the *Register*, to build a substantial base in the working class that could allow it to come anywhere near taking power. Importantly, Miliband also saw that social democratic politics was not leading toward a gradual transition to socialism, but instead integrating workers more deeply into capitalist states, lowering expectations, marginalizing socialist ideas and constraining political imagination – undermining more than aiding the socialist movement.

That the new left parties, as well as socialist forces within center-left parties, have to such a significant degree succumbed to the pressures of social democratization highlights the continued power of this critique – which hinges not on seeing the limits of these projects as 'betrayals' of the working class, but rather as experiments to learn from. Similar conclusions could be drawn in relation to the radical projects in the global periphery. What these experiences demonstrate above all is the overwhelming gravitational pull of capitalist states and parliamentary institutions, as they absorb political forces operating on this terrain and blunt their mobilizational and radical potential. Far from succumbing to a 'realistic' reformism, these experiences underscore the necessity of connecting strategies for reform to the broader project of socialist transition. No reforms are intrinsically 'non-reformist'; they are only so, as Andre Gorz insisted in the 1968 *Register*, when they challenge capitalist needs and criteria – 'a socialist strategy of reforms must aim at disturbing the balance of the system, and profit by this disturbance to prepare the (revolutionary) process of the transition to socialism'. Building such popular political power requires developing strategic capacities to maintain momentum toward something greater, to counteract the tendency of elected leaders to be absorbed within a narrow parliamentarism, to address and transform the constraints of the capitalist state.

This only makes sense if left politics is explicitly directed toward the goal of socialist transition. Without such an orientation, the relentless pressures of electoral timetables and parliamentary logics inevitably narrow political horizons, reducing reform to an end in itself. Broader transformative goals are perpetually deferred and ultimately abandoned or simply rendered impossible. Miliband argued that it was the height of fancy to imagine that socialists could simply inhabit parliamentary institutions and thereby wield state power in the interests of working classes. Despite the misguided accusation that he held an 'instrumentalist' view of the state, whereby it was directly controlled by dominant capitalists, Miliband's entire work was dedicated to illustrating how badly such a view obscured the deeper structural interconnections between state and society which made it a *class* state. Not only parliamentary institutions, he showed, but the entirety of the state apparatus was structurally implicated in the reproduction of class rule. Even though the dominated classes were able to participate in elections, the state nevertheless remained a capitalist one, bound to facilitate the accumulation of capital and the exploitation of workers.

Of course, this wasn't to say that reform was impossible or pointless, or that the state was merely a machine for the domination of one class by another, as more rudimentary Marxian theories of the state tended to claim. Indeed, the very existence of social democracy, an outcome of hard-fought working-class struggles, pointed to the need for a much more sophisticated understanding. The state, Miliband held, allowed definite but limited possibilities for reform: while it *must* organize reforms to legitimate the system and deflect challenges, elections alone would never be sufficient to allow a socialist transition to commence. On the other hand, it is politically remote that a call to insurrection would ever find mass appeal in a decisive moment of revolt; and even if it did, the idea of directly confronting the terrifying coercive powers of the modern state was unthinkable. If socialism was to be achieved, it could only come about through the combination of struggles of parliamentary and extra-parliamentary forces to 'transform the state'. This would require that working classes and socialists transform, in the process of struggle, their collective capacities and organizations so as to promote radical new forms of democratic participation in political and economic management inside and outside the state.

It was the failure to build organizations capable of connecting a radical struggle on the terrain of the state with the capacity for extra-parliamentary mobilization in the streets that was – and is – at the heart of what Panitch called, in the 1985/86 *Register*, the 'impasse of social democratic politics'. This was necessary both to sustain the dynamic of popular mobilization as well as to sustain the radicalization of forces operating within the state, lest they succumb to social democratization. Limiting the political horizons of the left to working 'from inside' the state inevitably reproduces the limitations of social democratic politics that have surfaced again and again over the twentieth century, as parliamentary forces become absorbed within capitalist states and thereby lose the interest, imagination and capacity to push forward a deeper transformation of society. Conversely, abandoning the state to focus solely on union politics and militant protest is bound to run up against the need for a political vehicle that can serve as the 'organizational and strategic fulcrum' linking class formation and state transformation – bringing together and transcending isolated struggles to address the root causes of inequality, imperial wars and environmental devastation.

Thus, for Miliband, as well as Panitch and Leys, it wasn't that electoral politics and the struggle for reforms were pointless. The problem, rather, was that the British Labour Party, like other social democratic parties, was by no means up to the *necessary* fight for socialism. Its hopelessly top-down and bureaucratic structure and control by risk-averse technocratic leaders, reinforced by its embeddedness within parliamentary politics, meant that it lacked both the means and desire to develop the democratic capacities of the working class or to undertake radical mass mobilization. Despite momentary glimmers of hope, the search for a new politics, oriented around and grounded in 'a party of a different kind' as Hilary Wainwright put the task in the 1996 *Register*, went unfulfilled. The historic defeat of working classes in the core countries following the 1970s crisis – to which social democratic politics offered no meaningful alternative – and the subduing of anti-colonial liberation movements on the global periphery seemed to cast doubt on the relevance of such questions for the 'skeptical age' that followed, as Miliband framed it in his final book. Though the skepticism was disrupted by the post-2008 'opening', its 'closure' today means the search continues.

Where does this search for a more creative and dynamic approach to left organizing, struggle and party building than that of the two primary alternatives thrown up in the twentieth century now stand as the democratic socialist conjuncture comes to a close? Is it possible to wage a struggle 'within and against the state' without succumbing to social democratization? Where does this leave strategic notions of workplace and community 'base building'; of 'dual power'? As an unstable moment of political equilibrium tilting toward a spontaneous moment of workers' rebellion, or a sustained process of political ruptures with the existing complex of ruling class power? Was this 'closure' simply another case of the failure of social democracy to move left, repeated again and again across the twentieth century – thus replaying the cycle of Francois Mitterrand in France through the 1980s? What strategic lessons had been learned as 'democratic socialist' activists turned from protest to politics, and then to the workplace? Were these shifts guided by coherent strategic lessons and principles, or was this simply a matter of jumping from one form of activism to another? Was the left simply 'starting over' once again, or had forces been developed, and lessons learned, over the democratic socialist conjuncture in which new 'openings' and future struggles could still be built?

The framing above draws extensively, although not exclusively, from the organizational trials that the left confronts in the western centres of capitalism. But other zones of the world face the same questions in similar if unique ways. As important has been the search in the global South for exits from western imperialism and colonialism, as political forces in these states defined their own projects for 'de-linking' from the disciplines of the capitalist world market to chart paths for egalitarian development and socialism. From the inaugural issue onwards, the *Register* never wavered in its support for decolonization and anti-imperialist struggles, understanding them as absolutely vital to the global socialist movement.

The questions above are just some of those facing the global left. There are no ready-made answers to sorting through the strategic crossroads that the socialist movement is facing. It is crucial, then, to avoid falling back on old political recipes and investigate carefully, without turning away from harsh conclusions, the current period confronting socialist and progressive movements. Indeed, an initial close empirical mapping of a variety of political flashpoints, issues and struggles seems in order. And this is the challenge we put to our contributors to this volume, with the additional onus of addressing the theoretical and political implications of their contentions. Several of the initial essays help frame this political moment and the concerns that motivated our building of this volume. Panagiotis

Sotiris provides a penetrating overview of socialist debates since the 1970s on the question of the left 'taking power' and the dilemmas of transforming the state, not as an objective in itself, but by shifting the correlation of social forces and developing the collective capacities of the working classes and movements outside the state. Umut Özsu, and Michael Calderbank and Hiliary Wainwright, each provide quite distinct examples of the continual resonance of these debates. Özsu, through the context of the Israeli genocide of Palestinians in Gaza and the Occupied Territories, outlines the failure of postwar international legal and security institutions to contain imperialist and colonial states, and illustrates the geopolitical conflicts still enclosing national politics. And Calderbank and Wainwright take a careful – at times with an edge of dismay – reading of Keir Starmer and the new Labour government in Britain as part of the crisis of social democracy as any kind of an alternative, leaving the British left in a series of political dilemmas and uncertainties that are unique in their context but far from unfamiliar elsewhere.

If these essays address long-time preoccupations of the *Register*, they also bridge to the bulk of the volume's investigation of concrete case studies, from different parts of the world, of the political conjuncture of the crisis of social democratic and liberal centrism, traditional conservative forces holding up but increasingly accommodating a far right still gaining electoral and cultural ground, and a left still fledgling in various efforts at renewal of the labour movement and socialist parties. It may indeed be necessary to recall Gramsci's old comment, however overused and abused, that 'the old world is dying and the new world struggles to be born. Now is the time of monsters.' This is indeed a caution that runs across these essays and their reflections on socialist strategy: Şebnem Oğuz on 'late fascism' and the Turkish state; Ingar Solty on the electoral rise of the fascistic AFD running in parallel to the crisis of Die Linke; Ayyaz Mallick's warnings on core authoritarian features in the governing bloc and state of Pakistan; and Ruth Felder and Viviana Patroni on the strangest of beasts in the emergence of an 'anarcho-capitalist road' in Argentina. In these cases, combating the rise of the far right has prominence in the discussion of the organization of fronts, defensive struggles in the protection of social rights and electoral tactics, and the task of rebuilding a leftwing alternative. In other cases, these struggles are less immediate. Yet the impasse of the left moving ahead remains, even when holding power, as a preoccupation in the essays focused on strategic debates in particular locations: Greig Charnock, Jose Mansilla and Ramon Ribera-Fumaz on the closures of the 'Barcelona En Comú' project and thus a certain passing of the 'right to the city' movement in Europe; Catarina

Príncipe on the cautionary tale of the left governing bloc that has held power in Portugal in the context of the complexities of the European Union; and Jeffery Webber's disentanglement of the 'left populisms' of Latin America through the lens of Bolivia.

The last third of the volume turns first to specific vectors of political struggle and organization that have been crucial terrains for checking – at times even overturning – the neoliberal policy regime. A few sectors of struggle raise the question of 'structural reforms' that provide 'permanent inroads' to the capitalist obsession with exchange value over social need, and alternative distributional logics to the market and prices. These questions and departures are taken up by Davd McDonald in terms of struggles over public service provisioning through a canvas of efforts at the 'remunicipalization' of utilities, including through new forms of democratic control, after the failures of their neoliberalization; by Thomas Marois and Susan Spronk in looking at the possibilities of making public banking institutions vehicles for socialization and community-building rather than private asset accumulation; and Touré F. Reed in providing a forceful assessment of the limits and possible futures of different – even antagonistic – approaches to addressing race and class inequalities in the US.

We close the volume with three essays that focus on the pivot of political agency for the question of strategy, in this case via investigatory essays, written partly in the form of participant observation and partly as activist-theorists of strategy, of leading struggles today where the left has a prominent place. Nick French reviews the past decade or so of the so-called 'rank-and-file strategy' that has held a prominent place in key sections of the American left, especially since the upsurge that came with Bernie Sanders' national leadership bid; Feyzi Ismail develops an innovative comparison of the historical suffragette movement with today's climate justice movement, and the roles of civil disobedience and mass popular action in the repertoires of activists and the building of a socialist politics; and Arun Gupta provides a sweeping account of US social movement actions from Occupy to the Palestine solidarity encampments, reflecting on their successes and where US Palestine solidarity movement organizing may yet need to evolve. Although not given as prominent a place in these accounts, the form, position and practices of socialist political parties after classical Leninism and the end of social democratic ambitions beyond governing nevertheless hovers in the background of all them. These are issues we will necessarily have to return to in future volumes of the *Register*.

The contributors to this year's volume deserve special thanks for taking up the challenge we posed to them on socialist strategy today. With the confluence of events and geopolitical conflicts at hand, which we surveyed in last year's *Socialist Register 2024: A New Global Geometry?*, this was not an easy task. None of us, essayists and editors alike, will be in line with all the positions taken. But disagreements, and different emphases in understanding the current setting and the routes to take, is crucial to debating the responsibilities laying ahead of us. We also want to signal our special thanks to Adrian Howe for his efforts on this volume and his years of contribution to the *Register* and Merlin Press. This is our last volume working together with Adrian as he begins his well-earned retirement. We also want to thank, once again, Tony Zurbrugg for his support and coordination on our behalf with our co-publishers, Fernwood Press and Monthly Review Press. Louis Mackay again delivered a superb cover to capture the themes of the volume and the political crossings we wanted to stress. Alan Zuege and Chris Little, our supporting editorial team, provided invaluable efforts in bringing the volume together. Finally, on a sadder note, we want to acknowledge the passing of Stephen Hellman, comrade and colleague of Leo Panitch and Greg at York University, and a long-time contributor to the *Register* on the transformations in socialist politics in Italy, and notably the experiences of the Italian Communist Party since the 1960s.

GA
SM
December 2024

ON THE (IM)POSSIBILITY
OF A 'LEFT GOVERNMENT':
SOME STRATEGIC QUESTIONS REVISITED

PANAGIOTIS SOTIRIS

The question of a possible 'government of the left' returned to the fore in the 2010s after a long period when it was not part of the discussion of the broader Marxist or Marxist-inspired anti-capitalist left. In fact, the return of radical politicization that accompanied the rise of the anti-globalization movement and a little later the anti-war movement was articulated in terms very hostile to the politics of social democratic or centre-left parties. This particular form of anti-capitalism was mainly articulated in connection with the more revolutionary traditions of the Marxist left. After all, most of this politicization took place in political organizations and groupings that referred to the legacy of what can be described as the May 1968 anti-capitalist left, which was in principle hostile to the idea of government and was formed in rupture with both social democracy and communist reformism, in particular Eurocommunism.

However, this seemed to change after the financial crisis of 2008, in particular following the large global wave of protest after 2010-11 and the signs of an acute political crisis in various countries that were combined with almost tectonic shifts in relations of political representation on the left. This created a situation where a series of political developments – such as the rise of SYRIZA to power, the electoral ascent of PODEMOS, Jeremy Corbyn's successful bid for the leadership of the Labour Party, Jean-Luc Melenchon's elevation to the position of the leading figure of the French left, and even Bernie Sanders' campaigns to win the Democratic nomination – which, despite their different characteristics and dynamics, were all discussed and debated under the same thematic of the possibility of a left government. And this despite the fact that the actual experiences of this participation of the left in governments in Greece and Spain were more than disappointing and in fact represented cases of defeat and capitulation to neoliberal exigencies rather than successful experiments. What was missing was a more strategic political and theoretical discussion. To return to these debates, it's important to first revisit the debates around governance in the history of Marxism before returning to discuss the specific contemporary conjuncture.

MARXISM AND GOVERNMENT: THE OPEN QUESTIONS

A large part of the Marxist tradition, or at least what we could call the tradition of revolutionary Marxism, has always been very skeptical of any form of governance, especially one elected through a traditional parliamentary process. However, this skepticism did not necessarily lead to very clear answers. This is evident already in the Communist Manifesto:

> We have seen above, that the first step in the revolution by the working class is to raise the proletariat to the position of ruling class, to win the battle of democracy. The proletariat will use its political supremacy to wrest, by degrees, all capital from the bourgeoisie, to centralise all instruments of production in the hands of the State, *i.e.,* of the proletariat organised as the ruling class; and to increase the total of productive forces as rapidly as possible.[1]

As we can see, there are no specific indications of what form this 'political supremacy' of the proletariat would take, and the same goes for the 'despotic inroads on the rights of property, and on the conditions of bourgeois production'.[2] This is something that Marx and Engels would admit to when, after the experience of the Paris Commune, they would suggest that the one correction they would make to the Communist Manifesto would be the insistence that the working class cannot use the existing capitalist state apparatus as it is.

> In view of the gigantic strides of Modern Industry in the last twenty-five years, and of the accompanying improved and extended party organization of the working class, in view of the practical experience gained, first in the February Revolution, and then, still more, in the Paris Commune, where the proletariat for the first time held political power for two whole months, this programme has in some details become antiquated. One thing especially was proved by the Commune, *viz.,* that 'the working class cannot simply lay hold of the ready-made State machinery, and wield it for its own purposes'. (See *The Civil War in France. Address of the General Council of the International Working Men's Association,* German edition, p. 19, where this point is further developed.)[3]

At the same time, even in the texts on the Paris Commune, one could find only starting points, such as the following: 'The Commune was to be a working, not a parliamentary, body, executive and legislative at the same time.'[4] However, how exactly this combination of universal suffrage – but not in the sense 'of deciding once in three or six years which member of the ruling class was to misrepresent the people in Parliament'[5] – and the replacement of the standing army by a militia and the abolition of the distinction between executive and legislative would work was not answered.

These ambiguities were also evident in how the classical social democracy of the Second International would view such questions, as exemplified by Kautsky's call for both a revolution and a 'democratic republic', an ambiguity that also led to his rather gradualist approach and insistence on a long period of mainly peaceful struggles that take advantage of bourgeois democratic institutions.[6] And although there has recently been an attempt to reinstate Kautsky's position in the tradition of revolutionary Marxism, in particular by Eric Blanc[7] (and to a certain extent also by Lars T Lih.[8]), it seems to me that even in Kautsky's 'revolutionary period' the contradictory coexistence between the insistence on the need for revolution, especially in places like Russia, and for a different road in countries with developed bourgeois institutions was already evident.[9]

At the same time, most social democrats would remain opposed to any participation in government until World War I (with exceptions such as Alexander Millerand in France being broadly condemned). In contrast, Lenin, within the context of the Russian Revolution, would use the Commune as an example of an antagonistic form for the exercise of power, moving beyond the limitations of parliamentarism:

> The Commune substitutes for the venal and rotten parliamentarism of bourgeois society institutions in which freedom of opinion and discussion does not degenerate into deception, for the parliamentarians themselves have to work, have to execute their own laws, have themselves to test the results achieved in reality, and to account directly to their constituents. Representative institutions remain, but there is no parliamentarism here as a special system, as the division of labour between the legislative and the executive, as a privileged position for the deputies. We cannot imagine democracy, even proletarian democracy, without representative institutions, but we can and must imagine democracy without parliamentarism, if criticism of bourgeois society is not mere words for us, if the desire to overthrow the rule of the bourgeoisie is our earnest and sincere desire, and not a mere 'election' cry for catching workers' votes,

as it is with the Mensheviks and Socialist-Revolutionaries, and also the Scheidemanns and Legiens, the Semblats and Vanderveldes.[10]

Moreover, for Lenin the Paris Commune was indeed the first experiment towards a new, non-bureaucratic and non-'parasitic' functioning of a state form, and of 'smashing' and 'replacing' the bourgeois state:

> The Commune is the form 'at last discovered' by the proletarian revolution, under which the economic emancipation of labour can take place. The Commune is the first attempt by a proletarian revolution to smash the bourgeois state machine; and it is the political form 'at last discovered', by which the smashed state machine can and must be replaced.[11]

It was in this sense that Lenin attempted to offer a redefinition of the democratic republic, through the notion of the dictatorship of the proletariat:

> Engels realised here in a particularly striking form the fundamental idea which runs through all of Marx's works, namely, that the democratic republic is the nearest approach to the dictatorship of the proletariat. For such a republic, without in the least abolishing the rule of capital, and, therefore, the oppression of the masses and the class struggle, inevitably leads to such an extension, development, unfolding, and intensification of this struggle that, as soon as it becomes possible to meet the fundamental interests of the oppressed masses, this possibility is realised inevitably and solely through the dictatorship of the proletariat, through the leadership of those masses by the proletariat.[12]

Lenin pointed to an antagonistic practice of politics and an antagonistic form of exercising power. At the same time, he linked the persistence of the state to the very exigencies of the transition period:

> Now the question is put somewhat differently: the transition from capitalist society—which is developing towards communism—to communist society is impossible without a 'political transition period'.[13]

Moreover, he would insist on the importance of the class aspects of any state apparatus as the determining aspect:

> The point is not at all whether the 'ministries' will remain, or whether 'committees of specialists' or some other bodies will be set up; that is

quite immaterial. The point is whether the old state machine (bound by thousands of threads to the bourgeoisie and permeated through and through with routine and inertia) shall remain, or be destroyed and replaced by a new one. Revolution consists not in the new class commanding, governing with the aid of the old state machine, but in this class smashing this machine and commanding, governing with the aid of a new machine. Kautsky slurs over this basic idea of Marxism, or he does not understand it at all.[14]

Lenin attempted to think more thoroughly that any Marxist of his generation the question of how an antagonistic form of governance could emerge, but it is nevertheless obvious that in his texts we find questions rather than answers in this regard.

The harsh realities of the Russian Civil War and the exigencies of New Economic Policy meant that the Soviet system gradually stopped being a democratic process, most appointments were made from the top, and in fact the whole system looked more like a particular form of a communist-led exceptional state. Lenin's insistence that the crucial aspect was the class character of the government left open the question of what political forms and concrete practices would make possible such proletarian control of the state. Consequently, despite the Bolsheviks' confidence that political power was in the hands of the proletariat, the question of the form of this power remained open. However, at least in the beginning, the desire to put in place a form of government that was antagonistic to the bourgeois bureaucratic mode of politics was more than obvious. Lara Douds' *Inside Lenin's Government* offers a vivid image of the Bolsheviks' attempts towards such a different practice of government:

> All in all, the apparatus of the Sovnarkom Administration Department exemplified the type of revolutionary state machinery envisaged by Lenin as necessary for proletarian democracy. In its internal structure, personal composition and organizational culture, Soviet leaders and state activists strove to create a revolutionary, anti-bureaucratic, responsive apparatus directly connected to the masses. In this it differed from much of the state machinery inherited by the commissariats from the imperial government.[15]

Moreover, Douds shows that the introduction of the 'one-party-state' was not something that was implemented immediately. Instead, a series of organs continued to include representatives of other currents and also remained open to a certain degree of debate, as exemplified by both the composition of the All Russian Central Executive of the Soviets and the collegiate system in the commissariats. However, the exigencies of the Civil War meant an increasing control by the Party over the state, exemplified by the rise of the Politburo as the main decision-making body. Douds explains that this had to do with the main contradiction running through early Soviet attempts towards a radically novel form of governance, which was the existence of 'dual bases of legitimacy for the early Soviet government: from the pyramid of ostensibly elected local and regional Soviets culminating in the Congress of Soviets, VTsIK and the Sovnarkom on the one hand, and from the vanguard Communist Party with its historic mission, on the other'.[16]

This tension is also evident in Lenin's last attempts towards dealing with increasing bureaucratization, as discussed by Moshe Lewin in *Lenin's Last Battle*. Here, Lenin is seen both defending the central role of party organs and suggesting a fruitful collaboration between party and soviet organs, while at the same time insisting on education and maintaining the proletarian character of the organs.[17]

Recently, Eric Blanc has attempted to suggest that there were alternatives to the road chosen by the Bolsheviks through his study of the experience of Finnish social democracy and other movements in the former Russian Empire from 1917-1918.[18] Without denying the important historical insights of Blanc's research, I do not think that it points to an alternative in that particular, singular historical sequence. Nor do I think that the alternative to a certain 'canonization' of the Bolshevik tactics in Russia is to search for 'roads not taken' in that particular moment and project them onto contemporary questions. Nevertheless, from the discussions at the Fourth Congress of the Communist International on the questions of the United Front and the 'Workers' Government',[19] to Gramsci's unfinished research in the *Prison Notebooks*, there was indeed a growing realization of the complexity and difficulty of a plausible revolutionary strategy in countries with developed political and ideological apparatuses.

However, we know that in the end, and in particular after Lenin's death, these concerns about democratization were set aside in favour of the strengthening of this particular state-party form. Moreover, the forms of governance introduced in subsequent waves of revolutions were more or less dependent on this evolution of the Soviet model, especially after the practical abandonment in all but name of the Soviet system. This was also evident in the very introduction of the notion of 'people's democracy' as a model of government. Of course, not all 'people's democracies' were identical and one could point to different experiences of participation or even workers' control. Yet the basic form was that of a government based on the power of the Communist Party that dominated both institutions of representation and ministries – a kind of a 'single-party parliamentarism' with very limited public debate.

Even the most extensive 'rethinking', in practical form, of this model of revolutionary governance – the Chinese Cultural Revolution – offered an example of a revolution inside a revolution but not a set of institutions that would offer a different democratic configuration. By this I mean that there was a dynamic unleashed by the Red Guards, an intensification of struggles that was by itself a democratic process, but with the exception perhaps of the Shanghai Commune no new institutions emerged.[20] The subsequent abandonment of the Cultural Revolution, within the context of the Party's simultaneous turn towards capitalism as the only means to 'develop the productive forces' and even greater, authoritarian Party control of society led to a completely different trajectory.

At the same time, beginning with the Front Populaire in France, already in the 1930s communist parties had begun to accept the possibility of a process of socialist transition that could begin with a progressive government based on a parliamentary majority. This was something that after World War II became close to an article of faith for Western communist parties, especially after the basic acceptance of a 'democratic road to socialism'.[21]

There was of course a series of revolutions that would open important debates on the possibility of a different road than the one taken in the 'people's democracies', but still the question of the particular form of governance remained open. The question of an institutionality that would be antagonistic to the dominant bourgeois one would of course be prominent in all debates in the revolutionary left after May 1968. Particular historical sequences such the Portuguese Carnation Revolution seemed to suggest the continuing pertinence of a dual power strategy, but without providing an example of such a process being victorious.[22] Even the last successful revolution to attract the interest of the global left, the Sandinista revolution in Nicaragua, opted to accept a parliamentary model and held multi-party elections, eventually leading to the defeat of FSLN. They later returned to government through elections, but as a rather different party.[23]

The last great debate on these questions was in the 1970s, when Western European communist parties, in particular the Italian, French and Spanish ones, insisted on the possibility of governmental power being part of a 'democratic road to socialism'. This debate included the criticism by Étienne Balibar[24] and Louis Althusser[25] of the French Communist Party's abandonment of the notion of the dictatorship of the proletariat and the discussions between Althusser and Italian intellectuals around the question of the state and politics.[26] It also included, of course, the debates prompted by Nicos Poulantzas' suggestion that it is possible to have an elected government of the left combined with autonomous movements from below, movements which, as part of Poulantzas' relational conception of power and the State (the state as the material condensation of the relation of forces in the class struggle), are always in a sense inside the state.

> In the democratic road to socialism, the long process of taking power essentially consists in the spreading, development, reinforcement, coordination and direction of those diffuse centres of resistance which the masses always possess within the state networks, in such a way that they become the real centres of power on the strategic terrain of the State.[27]

Poulantzas was fully aware that he was describing a limited situation, with many aspects contingent on the dynamics of the conjuncture. He also tended to take for granted the strength of the movements, a strength that is now absent. At the same time, his shift towards accepting the rules of the parliamentary process was also part of his late preoccupation with the question of totalitarianism, an aspect of his research project that is often not taken into account.[28] The retreat of the left since the early 1980s, the rise of neoliberalism, the right-wing turn of social democracy and the crisis of the communist movement in all its varieties put an end to these debates.

THE RETURN OF THE QUESTIONS OF LEFT GOVERNMENT

The questions of left government emerged again as a 'strategic hypothesis'[29] in the 2010s after a very specific sequence which is worth revisiting. It was part of the broader emergence of important movements since the late 1990s that seemed to bring anti-capitalism back as the order of day. The sense that there was a 'movement of movements' coincided with the idea that there can be broad fronts, or 'united fronts of a new type', where the revolutionary left could work with reformists to create broad anti-neoliberal alliances. This was very evident in the debates that took place in the early 2000s around the potential of the new anti-capitalism, the experience Rifondazione Comunista in Italy, those in Greece that led to tendencies of the anti-capitalist left joining SYRIZA, as well as in the way European Social Forums (and the Word Social Forum) were considered to be the terrain that could enable such convergences. The question of government was not initially central, since it was obvious that it was a process of recomposition of the left, but it is no accident that the crisis of Rifondazione Comunista would start after its participation in the Pronti government.

It was in this context that Latin America seemed for a period to offer an alternative, in the form of a wave of left-wing or progressive governments based on the 'protagonism' of the popular classes.[30] However, some were contradictory, such as the Lula governments in Brazil, which soon moved to the right even while also engaging in experiments in collective planning.[31] The Venezuelan and Bolivian experiments included a revolutionary dynamic by means of involving strong movements and decisive intervention from below at critical junctures, but in terms of governance they also remained to an extent within a certain parliamentary context.[32]

Despite the many returns of anti-capitalism – including the emergence of an impressive new generation of radical theorists and some important defenses of the possibility of a post-capitalist social configuration – strategic questions, in particular how such broad fronts could actually enable the formation of a new revolutionary transformative dynamic, and the problem of power, remained open. There were of course some significant attempts to suggest that Latin America offered the possibility to rethink the open question of a strategy for power, such as Álvaro Garcia Linera's well known text on the creative tensions of the revolution in Bolivia (although to a certain extent it is a defense of the tactics adopted by the Morales governments),[33] George Cicciarelo-Maher's writings on Venezuela,[34] Marta Harnecker's writings, and the echoes of such experiences in the work of Michael Lebowitz.[35] But still, the questions remained open.

At the same time, a great part of the debate around the 'idea of communism' did not move beyond treating an insistence on the 'communist hypothesis' more as a regulatory notion rather than a fully elaborated strategy, at least for advanced developed capitalist formations.[36] To make things more complicated, a significant part of the discussion on the dynamics of movements took a horizontalist approach[37] that was very radical in both its anti-capitalist and egalitarian-participatory tropes, but refused to even touch the strategic question of power.

Nevertheless, there were various important attempts to theorize the new elements. For example, even in the work of Michael Hardt and Antonio Negri one could see an important creative attempt to rethink the ontology of contemporary labour and the potentiality for change.[38] As their Empire project evolved up to the third volume, *Commonwealth*,[39] as well as in their more recent *Assembly*,[40] Hardt and Negri increasingly offered an acknowledgement of the importance of questions of political organization, leadership and power, but still in a strategic void.

THE APORIAS OF LEFT GOVERNMENT

The consequences of the absence of a more strategic debate, despite the urgent calls by figures such as Daniel Bensaïd,[41] were evident when the crisis of the Eurozone erupted, which shifted the focus of the debate from Latin America to Southern Europe. It was a situation where one could witness social and political dynamics without precedent, in particular in some 'weak links of the chain', namely countries such as Greece and Spain. Here, we saw elements of a crisis of hegemony, the implosion of political configurations that had lasted for decades, and social protests that took almost insurrectionary dimensions – not in only in the visible forms of mass protest and rioting but also, and more importantly, of the profound changes people were willing to accept in their lives.

At the same time, new waves of radicalism emerged in North America. Fueled not just by the watershed moment of the 2008 crisis but also through collective experiences such as Occupy! and the movements against racialized police violence, these waves led to an impressive turn to the left, especially by a younger generation, culminating in the Bernie Sanders campaign. Similarly in Britain, the crisis of post-Blair Labour and a previous wave of student (and in some instances trade union) radicalism opened a window of opportunity for Jeremy Corbyn to become Labour Party leader, offering for the first time the possibility that someone from the left of Labour could become prime minister

However, most of tendencies of the left were strategically unprepared for this, as was evident in the fact that there had been no serious debate on the very possibility or impossibility of such a situation. Even some of the more interesting attempts towards rethinking demands that could act as strategic nodes for processes of rupture and transformation, such as by Stathis Kouvelakis, remained at least ambiguous on the question of the form of governance that could make them possible:

What is meant by this? Neither the 'maximum' nor the 'minimum' programme, neither the cry for utopian 'impossibility' nor the management of the existing order of things, but a cohesive set of concrete demands strategically designed to hit the adversary in the heart, where the contradictions of the situation tend to concentrate, in order to create the necessary lever to change the overall balance of forces. Questions such as the default on sovereign debt, the dismantlement of the EMU and confrontation with the authoritarian fuite en avant of the EU are the contemporary equivalent of the demands of peace, bread, land and popular self-government on which depended the outcome of the first assault on Heaven of the twentieth century. Urgently posed as issues of immediate relevance where the current crisis has hit the hardest – that is, in the europeriphery and more particularly in Greece – they are central to the strategic debate of the Left in the Old Continent as a whole.[42]

This can explain why, in the end, the possibility of a left government based on a strong movement was more or less taken for granted without any strategic elaboration. The challenge was articulated, but with the question of strategy not necessarily answered, as can be seen in the writing of Richard Seymour:

It is essential to get this right, therefore, because the question of governmental power in the context of austerity will come up again. Austerity is fundamentally a political question, pertaining to budgets, laws and the role of the state in securing social reproduction. It is perfectly natural that we should consider the question of what to do about holding office. There are more than enough bad examples to learn from: the fate of the Italian Rifondazione Comunista after its participation in a centre-left government, during which its elected representatives supported privatisation and war, is well known. The successes are largely exceptional – the Chavez experience in Venezuela. But unless the Left simply defaults to backing a social democratic (or just Democratic) lesser evil, with the obvious drawbacks which that entails, it needs to develop a strategy for dealing with the dilemmas of wielding governmental power, and doing so in a way that strengthens the hand of workers and social movements against their class opponents.[43]

The challenges were presented, but not the way of dealing with them in a strategic manner, as in Seymour's encapsulation of the difficulty inscribed at the heart of any attempt towards a left government:

It is not just that to govern effectively requires a minimum of cooperation on the part of businesses and investors, as well as international trade institutions, ratings agencies, treaty organisations, and other powerful economic actors, which use what clout they have to veto reforms implemented by national governments. It is that there is an almost seamless circulation of power between them all. A radical government finds it difficult to wield power precisely because, if left to itself, it is rapidly encircled by those who actually hold power and who are accustomed to exercising it. Should it find a way to win time and space for its own agenda, the next obstacle it faces is that it somehow has to administer capitalism, while making it work for reform. That is, it has to find a growth formula that both makes capitalism grow, and profitably, while also transferring wealth and power to workers and the poor. In the twentieth century, the solution to this dilemma was a 'mixed economy', with public ownership, price and incomes policies, and a mildly redistributive welfare state. But that solution, insofar as it ever worked for radical ends, no longer works at all.[44]

At best this was thought in the 2010s as more like a possibility to use state power not as a means to induce social transformation, but rather to help social movements fight from a better starting point:

> The constitutional entrenchment of social rights and ecological duties (as planned by France Insoumise); moves against media monopolies in Britain and super pacs in the United States; and the introduction of (re) nationalized health care and education services can all seriously curtail capital's hold on our imaginations. These together with moves to unshackle trade unions and reverse restrictions on civil liberties can in turn prepare the ground for a broader perspective of advancing working-class power in society ... This is not simply a question of 'holding leaders accountable', as if they were only faltering allies for an idealized 'real' movement from below. Rather, the fight is to use their power to make changes that last beyond them: to impose reforms that push back capital's power and guarantee a basis on which working people can build their lives and their struggles.[45]

It is no accident that there has been a recent resurgence of interest in André Gorz's notion of 'non-reformist reforms'.[46] For Gorz, such reforms were 'not based on what is possible within the framework of a given system and management, but on what must be made possible based on human needs and requirements',[47] and that is why he preferred to call them 'structural reforms'.[48] However, this dialectic of structural reforms and broader transformation is often absent in contemporary debates.

These strategic deficiencies were more than evident in the case of the political currents that played a major role in this cycle of left mobilization. One could see this, for example, in how in the case of Podemos the leading group opted to read the conjuncture through the lens of theories of left populism.[49] As such, they integrated a top-down communicative electoralism that in fact ran counter to the very processes that had led Podemos to become an important force in the political landscape of the Spanish state, processes that had a lot to do with big movements from below.

Similarly, SYRIZA was catapulted to second place in the 2012 Greek elections as a symptom of deep political crisis and tectonic shifts in political representation that made the very signifier 'left government' into a 'point de capiton' for broader political dynamics without this resulting in any actual strategic elaboration on how to deal with state power. This was particularly pronounced given the political culture of SYRIZA did not go beyond a stagist conceptualization of left governance, coming from the traditions of both 'orthodox' communist and Eurocommunist currents of the 1960s and 1970s. And although one could find in the intellectuals around SYRIZA, such as Costas Douzinas, the insistence that the 'task of the Greek Left is to develop the idea of communism' for an age of capitalist crisis and violent social rearrangement',[50] in the end this was not transformed into actual strategizing apart from constant references to the difficulties of the process.[51] There were, however, voices inside SYRIZA, like Christos Laskos and Euclid Tsakalotos, which insisted that the party had a 'transitional programme' which:

> relied on three pillars: firstly, measures to respond to the humanitarian crisis, such as access to energy for heating, social housing and food coupons; secondly, measures to kickstart the economy through increasing the minimum wage and addressing people's inability to pay back their mortgages and tax arrears; and thirdly, a set of institutional interventions aiming to begin the transformation of the Greek state: to address corruption and the lack of transparency, to limit the ability of Greek elites to pay taxes only on a voluntary basis, and to introduce elements of social accountability and direct democracy. If we add to this the commitment to redistribute income, to begin to reverse the commodification of social services especially in the areas of health and education, and support the initiatives discussed in the previous section, then we can see that the concept of a transitional programme is a fair description of the overall approach in question.[52]

But despite such aspirations, SYRIZA in practice lacked both the necessary strategic horizon and also the more extensive thinking of questions of political power and governmental practice, while at the same time underestimating the extent of the ability of the institutional framework – and social violence – of the Eurozone to block any such path. Moreover, the assumption of Laskos and Tsakalotos that 'the "common sense" of the age continued to be affected by ruling ideas about the inefficiency of the state and the importance of the competitiveness of the private sector economy'[53] also led to an underestimation of the extent of the changes people were willing to accept in order to get out of the vicious circle of austerity.

In some cases, the evolution of state apparatuses and the functioning of parliamentary democracy has been presented as evidence of the impossibility of a strategy of ruptures in favour of a more gradualist approach, exemplified in the following passage from Vivek Chibber:

> Our strategic perspective has to downplay the centrality of a revolutionary rupture and navigate a more gradualist approach. For the foreseeable future, left strategy has to revolve around building a movement to pressure the state, gain power within it, change the institutional structure of capitalism, and erode the structural power of capital—rather than vaulting over it. This entails a combination of electoral and mobilizational politics. You build a party based in labor, you strengthen the organizational capacity of the class, you take on employers in the workplace and create rings of power in civil society, and you use this social power to push through policy reforms by participating in electoral politics. The reforms should have the dual effect of making future organizing easier, and also constraining the power of capital to undermine them down the road. There are many names for a strategy of this kind—non-reformist reforms, revolutionary reforms, etc. But whatever you call it, it entails a more gradualist approach than the ones that were available to the Bolsheviks.[54]

While I do not want to deny the validity of any position that stresses the important differences in state apparatuses, their functioning, and the evolution of ideologies, I think that such positions miss an important point. In the current conjuncture, which is characterized by neoliberalism remaining the dominant paradigm in economic policy, by the current form of authoritarian statism, and of course by the increased interlinkages between the national and the international levels, rupture, however difficult it might be, is the necessary condition for reform. Implementing reforms today can only be an institutionally violent process: think of what would be entailed by rupture with the Eurozone, doing away with the independence of central banks, implementing nationalizations and dealing with the scaling down of extremely militarized, repressive apparatuses of the state.

Similarly, some important contemporary debates, such as those on acceleration versus degrowth and the urgent task of combating the impending climate catastrophe have not been articulated in terms of the question of political power, government and a potential revolutionary strategy, something evident in the work of Kohei Saito, for example.[55]

At the same time, we have had Andreas Malm's insistence on an 'ecological Leninism' as opposed to calls for a 'Green New Deal', but this is more like a 'line of demarcation' rather than a fully articulated proposal. It is also interesting that, given the urgency of the question, Malm tends to think in terms of using existing state apparatuses:

> Ecological Leninism leaps at any opportunity to wrest the state in this direction, break with business-as-usual as sharply as required and subject the regions of the economy working towards catastrophe to direct public control. It would mean that 'one part of the population imposes its will upon the other part', to speak with Engels …
>
> But what state? We have just argued that the capitalist state is constitutionally incapable of taking these steps. And yet there is no other form of state on offer. No workers' state based on soviets will be miraculously born in the night. No dual power of the democratic organs of the proletariat seems likely to materialise anytime soon, if ever. Waiting for it would be both delusional and criminal, and so all we have to work with is the dreary bourgeois state, tethered to the circuits of capital as always. There would have to be popular pressure brought to bear on it, shifting the balance of forces condensed in it, forcing apparatuses to cut the tethers and begin to move, using the plurality of methods already hinted at […]. But this would clearly be a departure from the classical programme of demolishing the state and building another – one of several elements of Leninism that seem ripe (or overripe) for their own obituaries.[56]

I believe that the aporetic character of the first phrase of the second paragraph points to the difficulty of strategizing. And the reason is that even if we treat this process as some form of 'use' of existing state apparatuses, it's obvious that such 'use' implies new institutional arrangements and represents an actual rupture, a process of profound transformation, even if presented as emergency use of existing apparatuses.

THE OPEN QUESTIONS

There are two sets of questions that have emerged in this debate: one has to do with how we define the social forces that could support a strategy for political power, the second with the transformations within contemporary states. Regarding the first question, we have seen different approaches.

One is the insistence on the classical Marxist position that the working class, because of its very class position, is more open to social change and transformation, as exemplified by Chibber:

> Why develop a political strategy around the labor movement? There are three basic reasons. First, and this is often lost in intellectual debate— workers happen to be the majority of society. In the United States, the working-class accounts for something like two-thirds of the population. Any political movement that claims to fight for social justice had better represent the interests of more than just a small section of the population. It should be fighting for things that most people want and need, not just some chosen few, no matter how badly off that particular small group is. One of the Left's most compelling attributes has always been that it can claim to be fighting for the needs of the *vast majority*. Second, these masses of working people have good reason to *want* change. And third, they have a unique capacity for bringing about progressive change.[57]

However, one could point to the many questions about this idea that the working class is the vast majority of the population and, by definition, progressive or even revolutionary. On the one hand, we have all the debates around the existence (and role) of salaried social strata that cannot be counted as working class, beginning with Poulantzas' theory of the new petty bourgeoisie. Despite its shortcomings (such as identifying the working class with productive labour), this theory did point to the fact that segments of the collective labour power also perform functions related to the reproduction of capitalist social relations of production and exploitation.[58] On the other hand we have all the questions of the divisions inside the working class induced by racism and nationalism, and the political projects that could overcome them.[59] Such questions point to the fact that although labour as a common condition of exploitation and oppression can be a unifying factor for all these segments of contemporary capitalist societies that depend, one way or the other, upon selling their labour power, at the same time actual unity based on this common condition requires overcoming these various divisions. Therefore, unification is not 'automatic', but rather requires political and ideological work that enable a new 'hegemonic project'.

Apart from this classical Marxist perspective, one could also point to approaches that focus on the contemporary ontology of labour, something more evident in the research project of Hardt and Negri – although there is the open question of whether notions such as the 'multitude' and its creative potential actually point to class analysis or to something that could be described as a 'post-class' analysis.[60] However, a certain ontology of living labour as resistance has also been used to point towards a strategy of social change that does not include taking power, such as in the work of John Holloway.[61] At the same time, a certain interpretation of the value form and the dialectic between labour and social domination has been presented by Moishe Postone as pointing to how 'the proletariat is not, in Marx's analysis, the social representative of a possible noncapitalist future'.[62]

The disintegration of traditional forms of working-class concentration, the transformation of previous 'strong' forms of working-class identity and the gradual distancing of working-class voters from the parties that were supposed to represent them, exemplified in the crisis of both traditional social democracy and communist reformism, has made connecting the working class and transformative politics more difficult. This is despite the persistence of working-class struggles and the fact that wage labour has actually continued to expand. It is here that one can find the appeal of the approach of left populism.[63] Although proponents of left populism have repeatedly insisted on the importance of social movements, demands and aspirations, the very logic of their approach focuses not on class analysis or class composition, but on the discursive interpellation that has the potential of transforming grievances into a mobilized collective force. This runs the danger of fostering a politics 'from above' in form, communicative in essence and electoral in scope. As a recent commentary by Arthus Borriello and Anton Jäger stresses, and from a point of view not in principle hostile to left populism, these aspects point to the actual limitations of the 'populist moment' and its linkages to a particular 'post-political' conjuncture:

> Yet the real lesson that has been learned from the 'post-political' era is that a modicum of deliberation over collective ends cannot be kept out of the public sphere forever. Without the re-emergence of mass organization, this can only occur at a discursive level, arbitrated by media: every major event is scrutinized for its ideological character, producing controversies that play out among ever more clearly delineated camps on social media platforms and are then rebounded through each side's preferred media outlets. One with its age, populism thereby revealed itself as a tragically transitory form of politics, tied to a specific electoral cycle and subject to the passing hype of a market society. In the twentieth century, it was hard to speak of a Christian-Democratic or communist 'moment' as parties tied members to them for life and ministers bided their time across decades. In contrast, the left's populist episode took place in a political sphere increasingly oriented on short-term gains and awash with exit options.[64]

Between the hope of finding again a working class always ready for revolutionary action and the left-populist optimism regarding the possibility of discursively constructing a people, an open question remains: that of how to think of a transformative politics that is based on class analysis and dynamics of class struggles (or class over-determined struggles), while also retaining the premise that there is no automatic translation of the social into the political, and therefore that this translation has very specific ideological, organizational and political conditions.

The other open question following from the debates around the current conjuncture has to do with the transformation of the contemporary state. Although we are theoretically still in the aftermath of the Marxist debates of the 1970s, recent research points to a greater apprehension of the complex and pervasive character of the functioning of the modern state, and the many ways that neoliberalism is a strategy inscribed in the very materiality and configuration of the State and not just a political choice. The same goes for the relation between the state and processes of internationalization or even globalization, the kinds of constraints these dynamics impose and also the transformations they induce, exemplified in the contradictory process of European integration.[65] Such research, such as that of Leo Panitch and Sam Gindin, also points to the difficulty of any strategy towards left governance, the realization of the many obstacles it would meet, and an appreciation of the depth of the transformation necessary.

> That is why strategic preparations undertaken well before entering the state on how to avoid replicating the experience with social democracy are so very important. But even with this, the process of transforming the state cannot help but be complex, uncertain, crisis-ridden, with repeated interruptions.[66]

However, in actual practice during the 2010s, such strategic preparation was absent – and this led to significant failures, as attested by the Greek case.

AN IMPOSSIBLE GOVERNMENT?

Does this mean, then, that we simply abandon the question of a potential left government, in the sense that by definition any such attempt is doomed to end up in failure and capitulation? I think that is too easy an answer. The events in countries such as Greece point to a certain historical possibility, singular conjunctures where it is possible to have shifts in electoral representation that can potentially lead to such outcomes. There is a symptom here, a historical 'accident' or 'potentiality', that we need to confront. But how?

The first point is to remember that elections are by definition not democratic. To recall Althusser, parliamentary elections are an ideological apparatus of the state, not simply a democratic process.[67] This has to do with the political and ideological practices they entail and the effect of individualization they inscribe, which reflects a similar effect at the level of relations of capitalist production as a result of the fact that the direct producers do not control the means of production.[68]

Consequently, it is not possible to have an electoral road in the sense of a smooth increase of electoral forces that would bring change. The fear of liberals in the nineteenth century that universal suffrage would lead to the poor outvoting the rich never materialized. The only way that elections can have the effect of a rupture is when there is a crisis of representation and a potential crisis of hegemony, combined with the existence of a political formation that can fill the temporary political void.

This means that unless there is some deeper social and political crisis, and a degree of mobilization of the subaltern classes beyond a 'normal' threshold of discontent, there is no point in discussing the idea of a gradual building of an electoral coalition aiming at political power. Experience shows that an 'electoralist' strategy, the best example perhaps being the Italian Communist Party in the 1970s, usually ends with the opposite result, namely reabsorption into the political system and a gradual transformation into a 'party of the state'. Consequently, we should see the electoral victory more as an aspect of a broader sequence of struggle alongside the social and political crisis that makes it possible, a kind of historical 'accident' that opens up new possibilities (and new dangers) rather than an end in itself.

At the same time, even when there is such an ascendancy to power of a government of the left, the challenges it will face are immense. First of all, it will face the real materiality of the state. In relation to these questions, there is often reference to Poulantzas and his relational conception of the state as the condensation of the material relation of forces, combined with his insistence that the popular classes are always already inside the state.[69] This is often invoked as if it refers to the simple arrival of the left in government changing the relation of forces, helped by the rise of popular movements

However, in Poulantzas things are more complex than that. It is important to stress the material aspect of this relational conception, because 'relational' does not mean non-material or easily adaptable. In contrast we are talking about a materialized relation of forces inscribed in institutions, laws, regulations, the design of cities and buildings, the functioning of the police and the line that courts follow. This becomes clearer when we consider neoliberalism's profound alteration of the materiality of the state and how this was enhanced by globalization and processes such as European integration. As such, there is a particularly contradictory situation where, on the one hand, we have an impressive extension of the functioning of the state and its role in social production and reproduction; and yet, at the same time, what has been described as a strategy of practically abandoning entire segments of society, of creating 'zones of exclusion' and of new forms of unequal access that indeed constantly recreate a demand both for state intervention and for collective self-organizing.[70]

Despite the fact that state power has not diminished in relation to the market, there have been many additional institutional obstacles to any attempt to use the power of the state in its contemporary configuration against the market. One can think here of the difficulties that any rupture with the EU, wave of nationalizations or even an attempt to reverse the dangerous idea of an 'independent' central bank would entail. The contemporary increase in the repressive power of the state has been combined with a very specific institutional arrangement that prohibits any possible use of it for 'despotic inroads' into private property relations. It is in this sense that the question of the institutionally violent character that any process of change would have emerges.

At the same time, the question of physical violence should also be treated as an open one in view of the transformation of repressive apparatuses in a highly militarized and authoritarian direction, including the constant expansion of digital surveillance. It is obvious that this would be a real obstacle to any project of left government, and it cannot be dealt with simply through forms of parliamentary oversight. A strong 'abolitionist' perspective is necessary, but implementing it will not be easy.

This points to the inadequacy of Erik Olin Wright's position that 'large-scale ruptural strategies for constructing a democratic egalitarian socialism, therefore, seem implausible in the world in which we currently live, at least in the developed capitalist economies'.[71] This was the basic premise of his prioritization of strategies of 'interstitial' and 'symbiotic' transformation, which avoid aiming for large scale ruptures. Again, the point is not about the difficulty or the complexity or even indeterminacy of any process of transformation, aspects that are stressed in Wright's work, but rather about the fact that even relatively minor transformations seem to require major ruptures with the institutional articulation of contemporary neoliberalism.

All this points to the necessity of forms of counter-power from below, or even dual power of a *longue durée*, as the means to deal with the by definition institutionally and strategically weak position of any left government. Although not identical, both these notions of counter-power and dual power[72] point to the same challenge, namely that of an antagonistic institutionality from below, a kind of surplus social force to counter the institutional and very material violence inscribed in the configuration of state apparatuses. However, the question is how to permanently mobilize such mass collective participation and politicization. It is one thing to have this kind of collective mobilization and participation during moments of crisis and amidst a sense of abandonment, and another to maintain this when things seem to return to normal. At the same time, unless some of the gains from the exercise of such forms of counter-power from below, or dual power, are transformed into actual institutional arrangements, sanctioned by the power of the state, then they become precarious. Such a perspective of an antagonistic institutionality from below also points to ways of thinking about movements in a strategic manner, as when Hardt and Negri write:

> To construct the common ... the social strike must also become political. It must produce a 'dualism of power,' breaking away from neoliberal governance and developing practices of counterpower. It must create institutions of being and producing together, becoming 'multitudinous enterprises.' The lived passion of all the great multitudinous movements of the end of the twentieth and beginning of the twenty-first centuries, including the occupations and encampments, demonstrates not only what the social strike can mean today but also how it can serve immediately as an instrument to create organization and institution. Even when they have lasted only briefly these movements have produced an institutional desire and have set in motion a constituent machine that will be hard to stop.[73]

Yet still in Hardt and Negri the conceptualization of power remains aporetic: 'to take power, not simply by occupying the existing offices of domination with better leaders, but instead by altering fundamentally the relationships that power designates and thus transforming power itself'.[74]

All of these approaches ultimately must deal with the question of social transformation. However welcome such change would be, a socialist strategy cannot be limited to the idea of reinstating workers' rights, or bringing back the welfare state and guaranteeing free access to public health, education and social insurance. Moreover, in the current conjuncture only a socialist strategy aiming at a broader process of transformation in a non-capitalist direction and changes in relations of power can really accomplish such 'reformist' changes.

In most discussions around left strategy, the urgency of immediate measures usually takes precedence over more profound transformation. However, the ability to project or prefigure alternative social and political configurations is crucial not just in terms of the ability to persuade people about the feasibility of social change, but also in developing the actual resourcefulness of any attempt towards 'left governance'.

That is why it is imperative to think collectively about the extent to which non-capitalist social arrangements and relations can be implemented. This is a question that has been discussed only to a very small degree in most experiences we are discussing. Yet this is where the real power of capital is, namely in the ability to present capitalism as the only possible historical horizon. Surely expanding the free provision of public services, nationalizing part of the infrastructure and enabling and enhancing the development of forms of self-managed and co-operative production are essential aspects of such a strategy, but we need to think beyond this. How can we conceive this confrontation between dominant capitalist relations and non-dominant non-capitalist tendencies? How are we going to really attack the power of capital and the market? How can we experiment with new ways to organize production and distribution in ways that overcome the fetishism of commodity and value? How can we envision a process that is both confrontational as well as experimental and a site of learning?

The urgency of the impending climate catastrophe might be a way to rethink the need for 'exceptional' measures, as is the case with many of the suggestions of the 'Climate Leninism' strategy. But the idea of such a violent change in social property relations cannot be thought in simply the terms of commandeering large parts of industry, but rather must be seen as a more profound change in the entire productive paradigm. After all, one of the most important insights of Andreas Malm's *Fossil Capital* is that the impending climate catastrophe is the outcome of the development of the productive forces being determined by capitalist relations of production, which points to the fact that there can never be a 'technical solution' but instead only a process of social transformation, including the emergence of non-capitalist social relations of production.[75]

The necessity of transformation in social relations points to the open question of new forms of common sense in the Gramscian sense, which could not only enable the necessary ethos of commitment, participation and responsibility that can enhance processes of social change, but also counter the constant disaggregation of the subaltern classes induced by both capitalist organization of production and the functioning of the bourgeois state. This also raises the broader question of creating the conditions for a popular protagonism. In the words of Marta Harnecker: 'Participation, protagonism in all spaces, is what will allow human beings to grow and increase their self-confidence, that is, facilitate human development.'[76]

But this is not an easy process. There is also the important challenge of reconciling the *long durée* of a war of position and political pedagogy, and the 'moment', the short duration, the acceleration inside an acute political crisis. In a certain way, the challenge is of how to prepare for the unexpected. As Daniel Bensaïd insisted, 'the time of strategy is broken [...] full of knots and guts, sudden accelerations and sudden braking, leaps forward and backward, syncopes and counter-times'.[77]

And this needs to be related to another challenge. We already discussed how the question of the ontology of labour resurfaces in contemporary discussions. Yet focusing only on ontology runs the risk of underestimating other aspects of politics. Consequently, the challenge is to pass from ontology to strategy. Because however important is the emphasis on the contemporary ontology of labour in its conflictual and creative potential as a necessary reminder of the ability to envisage new social forms and relations, and of the collective intelligence and ingenuity of the working classes, it does not answer the question of political power. This is the aporia of the first commons, politics second approach of Hardt and Negri. In contrast, we need to think how we move from ontology to strategy and power. And this cannot be an unmediated process. It requires organization as laboratory,[78] as 'factory of strategy'[79] and as prefiguration of alternative social political forms.

This can help deal with another crucial question that sometimes is overlooked when ontology substitutes for strategy, namely the question of social alliances. I believe that only in terms of a potential historical bloc can we think the possibility of forming alliances with a common strategic orientation, overcoming the various forms of fragmentation and disaggregation of the subaltern classes, the contradictory relations between different popular strata, the forms of isolation and individualization.[80] Movements indeed 'perform' such a kind of unifying process and create linkages and common identities not just through common goals but also through common presence, real encounters in struggle. But this is not enough: the political institutions of a modern 'united front' are indispensable in this process. That is why I do not think that all these can be described as a 'non sovereign constituent power'.[81] I still believe that the necessity of institutional violence against the many forms of state arrangements that maintain the reproduction of capital as social relation points indeed to a very strong sense of sovereignty, yet a democratic and popular one, one based on expansive democratization of both the economy and state apparatus and one combined with a conception of politics as constant experimentation.

So far, I have not discussed the question of revolution. It is obvious that the notion of revolution cannot be limited to the narrow sense of insurrection or insurrectionary sequences. Yet neither does it point to a 'smooth' process within the contours of institutional legality. And in this sense, any real change can only be revolutionary in the sense of profound social transformation. But the notion of revolution also invokes that of counter-revolution and, in certain instances, as the Greek case could suggest, the counter-revolutionary reflex is also automatic and most often pre-emptive. So how to prepare for such an eventuality and the kind of intense counterattacks that are to be expected is crucial.

CONCLUSION: LEARNING FROM DEFEAT

What does all this mean for our current political strategizing? It's obvious that we still must treat the experiences discussed not simply as failures or mistakes, but also as learning processes. After all, 'learning from defeat' has been a defining aspect of the entire history of working-class movements.

In the preceding notes I did not try to offer a definite answer on the (im)possibility of a left government. What I tried to do was to suggest that, one way or another, the question of left governance points towards all of the open questions regarding anti-capitalist strategy today. In this sense, the most crucial challenge is not so much to continue an abstract debate on whether a left government is possible, but mainly to deal with the strategic questions outlined above, which is the only way to deal with conjunctures that are by definition singular and original. Such a return to a strategic way of thinking can also put tactical choices into perspective. Here, the crucial element is the extent to which a tactical choice leads to a better relation of forces in favour of the subaltern classes, one that enhances their potential for autonomous initiative, enables them to expand the terrain of their intervention and strengthens their ideological independence. Because without this articulation of strategy and tactics, we end up oscillating between the safety of sectarianism and the abandonment of any strategic ambition in the name of supporting what is the 'lesser evil' in any particular conjuncture.

In such a perspective, revolution is not so much a political design but rather, as Daniel Bensaïd has suggested, a regulatory horizon[82] for radical left political practice. So the question is not whether there is some kind of grand revolutionary design but instead how strategy fits in all aspects of political practice, from organizing to local strikes to electoral campaigns. In this sense, strategy necessitates a constant redrawing of the lines of demarcation with the logics of the state and capital, as an attempt towards a constant political self-pedagogy of the subaltern classes by means of their own involvement, their own initiative, as a constant treating of struggles as experimental sites and learning processes.

NOTES

1   Karl Marx and Friedrich Engels, *Collected Works (MECW)*, vol. 6, London: Lawrence and Wishart, 1976, p. 504.

2   Marx and Engels, *MECW*, vol. 6, p. 504.

3   Karl Marx and Friedrich Engels, *Collected Works (MECW)*, vol. 23, London: Lawrence and Wishart, 1988, p. 175. See Étienne Balibar's reading of this text in: Étienne Balibar, *Cinque études du matérialisme historique*, Paris : Maspero, 1974.

4   Karl Marx and Friedrich Engels, *Collected Works (MECW)*, vol. 22, London: Lawrence and Wishart, 1986, p. 331.

5   Marx and Engels, *MECW*, vol. 22, p. 333.

6   Karl Kautsky, *The Road to Power*, trans. A.M. Simons, 1909, available at: www.marxists.org.

7   Eric Blanc, *Revolutionary Social Democracy. Working-Class Politics Across the Russian Empire (1882-1917)*, Leiden: Brill, 2021.

8   Lars T. Lih, *Lenin Rediscovered: What is to be done? in Context*, Chicago: Haymarket, 2008.

9   Karl Kautsky, 'Revolutionary questions' [1904], in *Witnesses to Permanent Revolution: The Documentary Record*, ed. and trans. by Richard D. Day and Danial Gaido, Leiden: Brill, 2009.

10 Vladimir Illich Lenin, *Collected Works*, vol. 25, Moscow: Progress, 1964, p. 42.

11 Lenin, *Collected Works*, vol. 25, p. 437.

12 Lenin, *Collected Works*, vol. 25, p. 450

13 Lenin, *Collected Works*, vol. 25, p. 464.

14 Lenin, *Collected Works*, vol. 25, p. 491.

15 Lara Douds, *Inside Lenin's Government Ideology. Power and Practice in the Early Soviet State*, London: Bloomsbury, 2018, p. 72.

16 Douds, *Inside Lenin's*, p. 173.

17 Moshe Lewin, *Lenin's last struggle*, trans. A.M. Sheridan Smith, New York: Random House, 1968.

18 Blanc, *Revolutionary Social Democracy*.

19 John Riddel, ed. and trans., *Toward the United Front. Proceedings of the Fourth Congress of the Communist International, 1922*, Chicago: Haymarket, 2012.

20 Hongseng Jiang, *La Commune de Shanghai et la Commune de Paris*, trans. Eric Hazan, Paris: La fabrique, 2014; Alain Badiou, *Pétrograd, Shanghai: Les deux révolutions du XXe siècle*, Paris: La Fabrique, 2018.

21 Roger Martelli, Jean Vigreux and Serge Wolikow, *One Hundred Years of History of the French Communist Party. The Red Party*, London: Palgrave Macmillan, 2022.

22 Colin Barker, ed., *Revolutionary Rehearsals*, London: Bookmarks, 1987; Donald Sassoon, *One Hundred Years of Socialism. The West European Left in the Twentieth Century*, London: I.B. Tauris; Raquel Varela, A People's History of the Portuguese Revolution, London: Pluto Press, 2019.

23 Dan La Botz, *What Went Wrong? The Nicaraguan Revolution. A Marxist Analysis*, Leiden: Brill, 2016.

24 Étienne Balibar, *On the Dictatorship of the Proletariat*, trans. Graham Locke, London: New Left Books, 1977.

25   Louis Althusser, *22ème congrès,* Paris: Maspero, 1977.

26   Louis Althusser et al., *Discutere lo Stato. Posizioni a confronto su una tesi di Louis Althusser,* Bari: De Donato, 1978.

27   Nicos Poulantzas, *State, Power, Socialism,* London: Verso, 2000, p. 258.

28   Stathis Kouvelakis, SYRIZA's Rise and Fall, *New Left Review,* 97, 2016, pp. 45-70.

29   On the notion of the strategic hypothesis, see: Daniel Bensaïd, *La politique comme art stratégique,* Montréal: M. éditeur, 2023.

30   Martha Harnecker, *A World to Build: New Paths Toward Twenty-First Century Socialism,* trans. Fred Fuentes, New York: Verso, 2015.

31   Boaventura De Sousa Santos, 'Participatory Budgeting in Porto Alegre: Towards a Redistributive Democracy', in: Boaventura de Sousa Santos, ed., *Democratizing Democracy. Beyond the Liberal Canon,* London: Verso, 2007.

32   Jeffery R. Webber, *Red October. Left-Indigenous Struggles in Modern Bolivia,* Leiden: Brill, 2011.

33   Álvaro Garcia Linera, *Las tensiones creativas de la revolución. La quinta fase del Proceso de Cambio,* La Paz: Vicepresidencia del Estado Plurinacional, 2011.

34   George Ciccariello-Maher, *We created Chávez. A people's history of the Venezuelan Revolution,* Durham: Duke University Press, 2013; George Ciccariello-Maher, *Building the Commune. Radical Democracy in Venezuela,* London: Verso, 2016.

35   Marta Harnecker, *Rebuilding the Left,* trans. Janet Duckworth, London: Zed Books, 2007; Harnecker, *A World to Build;* Michael A. Lebowitz, *Build It Now: Socialism for the Twenty-first Century,* New York: Monthly Review Press, 2006.

36   Costas Douzinas and Slavoj Žižek, eds, *The Idea of Communism,* London: Verso, 2010; Slavoj Žižek, *The Idea of Communism 2. The New York Conference,* London: Verso, 2013.

37   Marina Sitrin and Dario Azzellini, *They Can't Represent Us! Reinventing Democracy from Greece to Occupy,* London: Verso, 2014.

38   Michael Hardt and Antonio Negri, *Empire,* Cambridge, Mass. and London: Harvard University Press, 2000. Michael Hardt and Antonio Negri, *Multitude: War and Democracy in the Age of Empire,* New York: The Penguin Press, 2004.

39   Michael Hardt and Antonio Negri, *Commonwealth,* Cambridge, Mass.: The Belknap Press of Harvard University Press, 2009.

40   Michael Hardt and Antonio Negri, *Assembly,* Oxford: Oxford University Press, 2017.

41   Daniel Bensaïd, 'On the return of the politico-strategic question', 2006, available at: www.marxists.org.

42   Stathis Kouvelakis, 'The End of Europeanism', in Costas Lapavitsas *et al., Crisis in the Eurozone,* London: Verso, 2012, p. xxi.

43   Richard Seymour, *Against Austerity: How We Can Fix the Crisis They Made,* London: Pluto, 2014, p. 165.

44   Richard Seymour, *Corbyn. The Strange Rebirth of Radical Politics,* London: Verso, 2016.

45   David Broder, 'The State We Need', *Jacobin,* 32, 2019, p. 35.

46   Mark Engler and Paul Engler, 'André Gorz's Non-Reformist Reforms Show How We Can Transform the World Today', *Jacobin,* 2021, available at: www.jacobin.com.

47   André Gorz, *Stratégie ouvrière et néo-capitalisme,* Paris, Seuil, 1964, p. 12

48   Gorz, *Stratégie ouvrière,* p. 13.

49   Íñigo Galván Errejón and Chantal Mouffe, *Podemos: In the Name of the People,* London: Lawrence and Wishart, 2016.

50   Costas Douzinas, *Philosophy and the Resistance in the Crisis. Greece and the Future of Europe*, London: Polity, 2013, p. 217.

51   Costas Douzinas, *SYRIZA in Power. Reflections of an Accidental Politician*, London: Polity, 2017.

52   Christos Laskos and Euclid Tsakalotos, 'From Resistance to Transitional Programme: the Strange Rise of the Radical Left in Greece', in Panagiotis Sotiris, ed., *Crisis, Movement, Strategy: The Greek Experience*, London: Brill, 2018, pp. 238-39.

53   Laskos and Tsakalotos, 'From Resistance…', p. 240.

54   Vivek Chibber, *Confronting Capitalism. How the World Works and How to change it*, London: Verso, 2022, pp. 147-48.

55   Kohei Saito *Marx in the Anthropocene. Towards the Idea of Degrowth Communism*, Cambridge: Cambridge University Press, 2022.

56   Andreas Malm, *Corona, Climate, Chronic Emergency. War Communism in the Twenty-First Century*, London: Verso, 2020, pp. 151-52,

57   Chibber, *Confronting Capitalism*, p. 98.

58   Nicos Poulantzas, *Classes in Contemporary Capitalism*, London: NLB, 1975.

59   Houria Bouteldja, *Beaufs et barbares. Le pari de nous*, Paris: La fabrique, 2023.

60   Hardt and Negri, *Empire*; Hardt and Negri, *Multitude*.

61   John Holloway, *Change the World without Taking Power. The Meaning of Revolution Today*, London: Pluto, 2002.

62   Moishe Postone, *Time, labor, and social domination: A reinterpretation of Marx's critical theory*, Cambridge: Cambridge University Press, 1993.

63   Ernesto Laclau, and Chantal Mouffe, *Hegemony and Socialist Strategy: Towards a Radical Democratic Politics*, Second Edition, London: Verso, 2001; Ernesto Laclau, *On Populist Reason*, London: Verso, 2005; Chantal Mouffe, *For a Left Populism*, London: Verso, 2018.

64   Arthus Borriello and Anton Jäger, *The Populist Moment. The Left after the Great Recession*, London: Verso, 2023, p. 204.

65   Greg Albo, Stephen Maher and Alan Zuege, eds, *State Transformations: Classes, Strategy, Socialism*, Leiden: Brill, 2021.

66   Leo Panitch Leo and Sam Gindin, *The Socialist Challenge Today: SYRIZA, Sanders. Corbyn*, London: Merlin Press, 2018, p. 58.

67   Louis Althusser, *On the Reproduction Of Capitalism: Ideology And Ideological State Apparatuses*, trans. G. M. Goshgarian, London: Verso, 2015.

68   Nicos Poulantzas, *Political Power and Social Classes*, London NLB, 1975.

69   Poulantzas, *State, Power, Socialism*.

70   Emma Dowling, *The Care Crisis. What Caused it and How can we End it?*, London: Verso, 2022.

71   Eric Olin Wright, *Envisioning Real Utopias*, London: Verso, 2010, p. 320.

72   I take the notion of counter-power and antagonistic institutionality from the work of Josep Maria Antentas. See: Josep Maria Antentas, 'Strategic Imagination and Party', 14 June 2017, available at: https://www.historicalmaterialism.org/strategic-imagination-and-party; Josep Maria Antentas, 'Integral strategy, party and the dialectics of dual power and counter-power', presentation at the Historical Materialism Athens Conference, April 2019. I have offered my take on dual power in: Panagiotis Sotiris, 2017, 'Rethinking Dual Power', available at: www.academia.edu/35145688/Rethinking_Dual_Power

73   Hardt and Negri, *Assembly*, p. 245.

74   Hardt and Negri, *Assembly*, p. 71.

75   Andreas Malm, *Fossil Capital*, London: Verso, 2016.

76   Harnecker, *A World to Build*, p. 70.

77   Bensaïd, *La Politique*, p. 156.

78   On this see: Panagiotis Sotiris, 'The Modern Prince as Laboratory of Political Intellectuality', *International Gramsci Journal*, 3(2), 2019, pp. 2-38.

79   Antonio Negri, *Factory of Strategy. 33 Lessons on Lenin*, trans. Arianna Bove, New York: Columbia University Press, 2014.

80   Panagiotis Sotiris, 'Gramsci and the Challenges for the Left. The Historical Bloc as a Strategic Concept', *Science & Society*, 82(1), 2018, pp. 94-119.

81   Hardt and Negri, *Assembly*.

82   Daniel Bensaïd, *Le pari mélancolique*, Paris: Fayard, 1997.

INTERNATIONAL LAW, PALESTINE
AND SOCIALISM

UMUT ÖZSU

David Ben-Gurion proclaimed the establishment of the State of Israel on 14 May 1948, the last day of Britain's mandate over Palestine and roughly a half year before the United Nations General Assembly adopted its much-vaunted Universal Declaration of Human Rights. The Universal Declaration made no mention of colonialism in any form, whether that of direct rule, indirect protectorate-style control or the kind of internationally supervised foreign administration sanctioned by the UN's system of trusteeships, which had itself been taken over from the League of Nations' system of mandates. Nor did it make any reference to national self-determination, a political 'principle' championed by socialist states and anti-colonial movements that would later be transformed into a tenuous and inconsistently applied 'right', particularly in two treaties adopted in 1966 to fortify the Universal Declaration's rather threadbare inventory of bourgeois rights.[1] But if the Universal Declaration, lodestone for the post-war 'human rights revolution', made no mention of colonialism or self-determination, Israel's establishment as an 'independent sovereign state' was tied umbilically to the international organization that was supposed to breathe life into its injunctions. The Israeli declaration of independence found justification for 'the right of the Jewish people to rebuild its National Home' in the 'catastrophe which recently befell the Jewish people', as well as the contributions made by Jews to 'the struggle of the freedom- and peace-loving nations against the forces of Nazi wickedness'. Importantly, and in a departure from most other instruments of its kind, it also made extensive reference to the General Assembly's ill-fated November 1947 resolution recommending that Palestine be partitioned and that two new states – one Arab, another Jewish – should come into being upon the British mandate's expiration.[2] Given the horrors of the Holocaust and the contributions of Jews to the Allied war effort, the declaration appealed 'to the United Nations to assist the Jewish people in the building-up of its State and to receive the State of Israel into the comity of nations'.[3]

This essay takes up the relation between state power and international law that animates not only Ben-Gurion's proclamation but the whole of the 'Palestine question' – more accurately, the 'national question' in historic Palestine[4] – from the standpoint of its victims.[5] I begin with a brief discussion of the International Court of Justice (ICJ). Since its inception, this 'World Court', entrusted by the United Nations with the task of resolving disputes between states, has been asked to preside over several cases relating to Israel and the territories it has occupied. Two cases, one initiated by South Africa and directly concerning Israel's ongoing devastation of Gaza, have attracted a great deal of interest of late, but it is important to appreciate that the ICJ's engagement with events in 'Israel-Palestine' is as old as the State of Israel itself. I then examine some of the ways Israeli lawyers and diplomats have sought to modify existing rules of international law, popularize 'creative' interpretations where modification is not possible, and craft new rules through 'innovative' practices and arguments of various kinds. Such 'legal entrepreneurship', as it has sometimes been called, is integral to the processes whereby international law changes over time, responding to new pressures and adapting to new circumstances. Israeli officials have been at the forefront of many such efforts, particularly in regard to the use of force, the jurisdiction of Israeli courts and the application of international humanitarian law to zones of occupation. I conclude the essay by considering Israel's genocidal onslaught on the Palestinians since the Hamas-led incursion of 7 October 2023 in light of the territory's longer economic and political history. I argue that the brutality of Israel today is in keeping with the brutality of Israel yesterday. Among many other things, I contend, the project of developing a 'greater Israel' out of the deliberate destruction of historic Palestine has always been premised on either selective reliance on international law or outright indifference to it.

A WORLD COURT?

Shortly after its own establishment in 1946, the ICJ found itself confronted with a question of direct relevance to the viability of the newly formed United Nations. In September 1948, only a few months after Ben-Gurion's proclamation, Lehi, an underground Zionist paramilitary organization, gunned down Count Folke Bernadotte, a Norwegian nobleman then working as UN mediator in Palestine, as well as André Serot, a French colonel and UN observer who was accompanying him. Bernadotte had been sent to the post-Ottoman territory – over which Britain's mandate had been terminated at midnight on 14 May 1948, the same day as Ben-Gurion's proclamation –

amid the upsurge in conflict that followed the General Assembly's partition proposal, a solution rejected by Palestinian Arab representatives as well as the UN's Arab member states. In response to his assassination, the General Assembly asked the ICJ to provide an advisory opinion on whether the UN was legally capable of bringing an action against a state that was responsible for harming its representatives. More precisely, the question posed to the ICJ was whether the UN, as an international organization, possessed enough international personality – that is, the rights and duties of a full subject of international law – to institute proceedings against the government of a state in order to secure reparations for injuries to its agents.

The 'Bernadotte affair' was one of the earliest cases to land on the docket of the young ICJ, inheritor of the dubious honorific of 'World Court' from the League of Nations' Permanent Court of International Justice, which had already confirmed Palestine's legal status as a 'state' in a series of cases in the mid-1920s.[6] In the opinion it issued in response to the General Assembly's request, the ICJ stated that the UN was legally possessed of sufficient international personality to institute proceedings against states: 'the Court's opinion is that fifty States, representing the vast majority of the members of the international community, had the power, in conformity with international law, to bring into being an entity possessing objective international personality, and not merely personality recognized by them alone, together with capacity to bring international claims'.[7] Specifically, the court explained that the UN was entitled to seek reparations for damages in cases of injury to itself or its officials, including in situations involving 'the death or disablement of one of its agents engaged upon a distant mission'.[8] The injury could have been caused by the de jure or de facto government of any state, regardless of whether it was a UN member at the time (Israel applied to join the UN shortly after Ben-Gurion's declaration but was not formally admitted until May 1949, one month after the ICJ released its opinion). Tellingly, then, the same case that helped to consolidate the juridical autonomy of the world's foremost international organization was also the first to engage, however indirectly, with the thorny, blood-spattered process through which the 'Palestine Mandate' came to be transformed into the 'State of Israel' and a set of 'Palestinian territories' (initially under Egyptian and Jordanian control). While the ICJ was careful to make no mention of Israel or Bernadotte, its opinion being couched as a general legal answer to a general legal question relating to the UN's powers and functions on the international plane, the case stemmed directly from the Bernadotte assassination. Few cases juxtapose modern international law's proud principles with the ruthless reality of state-making projects as clearly as the 1949 *Reparations* case – a juxtaposition only amplified by the ICJ's studious silence on Israel and Palestine in the opinion itself.

But if the UN came into legal maturity partly through the ICJ's engagement with what has come to be termed 'Israel-Palestine', it was by no means the last occasion on which the international order's nominal apex court would be called upon to do so.[9] In 2004, during the middle of the Second Intifada and amid the carnage doled out by US and 'coalition' forces in Iraq, Afghanistan and other portions of what Washington neoconservatives were then in the habit of calling the 'greater Middle East', the ICJ was again asked to join the fray. In this case, the question concerned the legal implications of the apartheid wall that Israel was in the process of erecting near the 'green line' separating it from the Occupied Palestinian Territory, including in and around East Jerusalem. The resulting opinion was lengthy and wide-ranging, addressing a variety of different facets of Israel's occupation. A large majority of the judges on the court found that the construction of such a wall in occupied territory breached core elements of public international law, including the UN Charter and 1970 Friendly Relations Declaration, the Hague and Geneva conventions and a host of international human rights instruments.[10] In particular, Israel was found to have violated the legal prohibition on acquiring territory by threat or use of force, and also to have suppressed the Palestinian people's right to self-determination, a right the court had previously held to be so fundamental as to generate positive obligations for all other states.[11] That Israel's security wall enveloped some 80 per cent of the settlers it had installed illegally in the Occupied Palestinian Territory was naturally of central importance in this regard.[12] Consequently, the court stated that Israel was obligated to dismantle the wall, repeal the legislative and regulatory acts which authorized it and provide compensation to those who had their homes or properties destroyed as a result. All states were duty-bound not to recognize the illegal situation which had resulted from the wall and to refrain from providing aid or assistance to Israel in maintaining this situation.[13]

Two recent ICJ proceedings involving Israel are especially important in connection with the destruction of Palestinian life and property since 7 October 2023. The first stems from a request from the General Assembly that the ICJ provide its opinion on the legal implications of Israel's ongoing occupation, settlement and annexation of Palestinian territories, including East Jerusalem. Consistent with its own past jurisprudence, including the *Wall* case, the ICJ here confirmed that Israel was legally bound to cease the occupation, making reparations for related damage, and to remove settlers and halt new settlement projects. Again, all other states were legally bound not to recognize as legal the state of affairs generated by the occupation and not to assist Israel in its efforts to maintain it. As is customary, the UN was told that it should take steps to bring the occupation to an end as expeditiously as possible.[14]

The second case concerns the application submitted in December 2023 by South Africa, site of the post-Cold War era's most celebrated case of transitional justice. In its application, South Africa alleges that Israel is actively violating the Genocide Convention.[15] Arguably the most innovative of all post-1945 human rights treaties, the Genocide Convention is also the most contentious of the lot. It defines 'genocide' as the commission of one or more prohibited acts against a particular ethnic, racial, national or religious group – killing or causing serious bodily or mental harm to the group's members, instituting measures to prevent births within the group, forcibly transferring children from it to other groups, or imposing conditions designed to bring about its physical destruction – with the specific intent to destroy that group, whether partly or entirely.[16] Aside from the notorious difficulties of demonstrating genocidal intent legally,[17] many international lawyers (and others) now believe that this definition is dated and limited in a variety of ways, including its omission of cultural genocide (a concept championed by Raphael Lemkin, the Polish-Jewish lawyer who coined and popularized the term 'genocide') and its explicit restriction of population transfer to the forced displacement of children, which excludes both adults and situations involving nominally 'voluntary' movements and evacuations.[18] At the time of writing this essay, the ICJ has yet to rule on South Africa's application, which a number of other states (including Palestine) have joined as intervening parties, but it has already issued several orders that Israel comply with the Genocide Convention. Even if the court ultimately holds Israel responsible for genocide in Gaza, Israeli officials are likely to disregard its judgment. Many other states have done so in the past, perhaps none more notoriously so than the United States when it simply ignored the ICJ's determination that it had illegally intervened in and used force against Nicaragua by training, arming, equipping, financing and supplying the anti-communist Contras in their operations against the Sandinista government.[19]

REMOULDING LAW

Alongside treaties and a motley assortment of other legal instruments, a large part of what is now called 'international law' consists of customary international law, a corpus of legal rules produced from consistent patterns of state practices accompanied by widespread recognition of their legal validity. This has multiple implications for Palestinian and other peoples seeking to rely upon international law's admittedly meagre resources to further national liberation struggles. For one, unlike Security Council resolutions, which are legally binding and concern matters of international peace and security, nearly all General Assembly resolutions are non-binding, at least when considered in isolation and absent evidence that a large number of such resolutions affirm the same point. This often makes it difficult for Palestinian representatives to draw tangible benefits from the enormous body of righteous denunciations and solemn pronouncements that populate the landscape of General Assembly resolutions. For another thing, the relative fluidity of customary international law allows for a significant degree of 'legal entrepreneurship' on the part of states and other actors. By consistently adhering to a specific line and backing this up with a consistent pattern of behaviour, a given state or group of states can modify international legal structures, effectively bringing new rules (and 'norms') into being through their actions (and inactions). Consequently, as Palestinian–American legal scholar George Bisharat observes, 'it is sometimes unclear whether a particular state action that deviates from settled international law is, indeed, simply illegal, or whether it is, instead, the leading edge of a new international legal norm'.[20] Such malleability confers upon much of international law a significant degree of adaptiveness to circumstances, over the long if not always the short term. A group of powerful states subscribing to a particular line, and doing so persistently over time, can sometimes end up triggering a change to international law.

As examples of such 'legal entrepreneurship' in action, Bisharat himself offers three important Israeli precedents: Israel's abduction, relocation and prosecution of Adolf Eichmann in the early 1960s; its attempt to characterize the Palestinian territories it seized during the 1967 war as 'administered' rather than 'occupied'; and its bombing of an unfinished nuclear reactor outside Baghdad in June 1981.[21] Eichmann's apprehension in Argentina and transportation to Israel entailed a host of legal quandaries: his abduction by Israeli agents on Argentinian soil involved a violation of Argentina's sovereignty, a point that Israel conceded; Israel was not itself a state, de facto or de jure, at any point during the Holocaust, when Eichmann committed his crimes; and the Israeli prosecutors and judges relied largely on a 1950 Israeli statute on Nazis and Nazi collaborators which integrated the new, post-1945 concept of 'crimes against humanity'. In effect, the trial was one of the earliest cases in the history of what has since come to be known as 'universal jurisdiction', the idea that some crimes are so heinous that they engage the conscience and interests of humanity as a whole, with the result that all states are permitted – and, in many formulations, expressly mandated

– to seize and try those accused of committing them. Universal jurisdiction has become far more widely accepted since the early 1960s, and Eichmann's trial played a significant role in popularizing it, contributing to the pattern of state practice whereby rules of customary international law (in this case, rules on asserting and exercising jurisdiction over persons, including non-nationals, outside your territory) are modified over time.

Bisharat's second example of Israeli 'legal entrepreneurship' has attracted little support beyond Israel. Israeli officials have tried to justify their policy of establishing settlements throughout the West Bank and other territories conquered during the 1967 war on the grounds that these territories are 'administered' (or 'disputed') rather than 'occupied'.[22] This terminological difference is of great significance, since the Fourth Geneva Convention prohibits settlements in occupied territories, expressly stating that '[t]he Occupying Power shall not deport or transfer parts of its own civilian population into the territory it occupies'.[23] This argument has been rejected by the vast majority of other states, not to mention the vast majority of international lawyers, and runs directly counter to a long series of General Assembly and Security Council resolutions, as well as the ICJ's conclusion in the *Wall* case that Palestinian territories occupied since 1967 are just that, occupied. Notably, though, the United States has repeatedly asserted that new 'facts on the ground' must be incorporated into any final peace agreement, with talk of such an agreement often serving as no more than a fig leaf for continued settlement and territorial expansion. In this case, unlike that of Eichmann-style 'universal jurisdiction', the effort to modify existing international law has failed, even if that does little to stop US presidents from recognizing Israel's annexation of Syria's Golan Heights or moving the US embassy from Tel Aviv to Jerusalem.

Considerably more successful has been Israel's repeated invocation of the right to use military force on a 'pre-emptive' basis, with a view to preventing armed attacks before they materialize. The Israel Defence Forces' June 1981 strike on the *Osirak*, an unfinished nuclear reactor south of Baghdad, which Iran had damaged the year before and which the United States would go on to bomb during the First Gulf War, is a classic example. Predictably, Iraqi officials condemned this operation as a violation of basic international law, falling foul of the UN Charter's prohibition on the threat or use of force. For their part, Israeli officials attempted to justify the strike by appealing to the Charter's permission of force for self-defensive purposes in the event of an armed attack. That no such attack had taken place – indeed, that the reactor itself was not yet in a position to threaten Israel – sapped this argument of its legal plausibility, since the Charter explicitly restricts self-defensive force to instances of actual attack. Notably, even the United States, Israel's long-time benefactor and arms supplier, voted for the Security Council resolution denouncing the strike.[24] Nevertheless, arguments for anticipatory military operations proved catchy over time, particularly after the inauguration of the US-led 'War on Terror', and now circulate as a kind of 'legal commodity' to be purchased by any state interested in striking enemies. It is not hard to see how this argument resonates with broader efforts to loosen post-1945 legal prohibitions on aggression and intervention, particularly after the Kosovo War and Second Gulf War.

To this list may be added a host of other, more recent examples of 'legal entrepreneurship'. These include the cultivation by Israeli state lawyers of arguments about Palestinian groups' alleged use of civilians as 'human shields'. They also include the IDF's practice over the past two decades of 'warning' residents of buildings to leave before they are struck, often by dropping low-yield explosives on their roofs (hence the now colloquial expression 'roof-knocking'). More generally, Israeli lawyers have sought to characterize the IDF's operations in Gaza, the West Bank and the Golan Heights as 'armed conflict short of war', rather than 'armed conflict' as such. The latter would bring IDF operations within the fold of the laws of war, as codified in the Geneva and Hague conventions and expressed in accompanying customary international law. The former would not do so, encouraging practices like targeted assassinations and lending a degree of legitimacy to vindictive policies like the so-called 'Dahiya doctrine', named after a Hezbollah-associated Beirut neighbourhood and designed to bring adversaries to heel by taking disproportionate action and deliberately destroying civilian infrastructure. In some cases, these efforts at 'legal entrepreneurship' have proven successful, contributing to the piecemeal reconstitution of bits and pieces of existing international law. Universal jurisdiction, though still controversial, is now invoked around the world, with prosecutors and courts in a variety of jurisdictions taking on cases against torturers, génocidaires and war criminals. In other cases, though, the success has been no more than partial. The 'Begin Doctrine' – named after Menachem Begin, who authorized the *Osirak* strike – laid the groundwork for the 'Bush Doctrine' two decades later. While a significant pattern of new state practice now points towards growing acceptance of more elastic conceptions of force, the vast majority of states continue to reject the legality of pre-emptive strikes.

CONTINUITY IN DISCONTINUITY

Israel today is a Silicon Valley Sparta, embroiled in *völkisch* eschatology, armed to the hilt with nuclear and other weapons, and grounded above all in the subjugation of an ever-growing number of Helots, whose land it continues to seize and whose labour it continues to exploit. A product of centuries of racism and persecution in Europe, a process that culminated in the systematic, industrial-scale extermination of millions of Jews (alongside many others, particularly communists, disabled persons, Jehovah's Witnesses, LGBTQ persons, Slavs and Roma) by Nazi Germany and its associated states and movements, Israel is now itself carrying out what can only be described as a genocidal war of annihilation against the Palestinian people. The litany of horrors inflicted on Palestinians since 7 October, principally in Gaza but also in the West Bank and elsewhere, is plain for all to see, consisting of some of the most revolting crimes of which humanity is capable: arson, dispossession, expulsion, kidnapping, lynching, murder, pogroms, rape, starvation, torture and much else besides. At the time of writing this essay, more than 40,000 Palestinians, the vast majority civilians and most children and women, are confirmed to have been killed. The real number of total Palestinian deaths will be considerably larger, since thousands of civilians are missing or buried under the rubble of collapsed buildings and infrastructure. One recent study in *The Lancet* has already arrived at a 'conservative' estimate of 186,000 or more deaths from the conflict, both as a direct consequence of IDF attacks and as a result of famine, lack of water and adequate shelter, the destruction of hospitals and other healthcare facilities, inadequate funding for the UN Relief and Works Agency for Palestine Refugees, and the proliferation of reproductive, communicable and non-communicable diseases.[25] Nearly all of Gaza's hospitals have been destroyed or rendered inoperative since Israel's assault commenced, as have nearly all its schools and universities, with healthcare workers and instructional staff often being targeted openly and specifically by Israeli forces.[26] An entire generation of children lies traumatized, malnourished, deprived of education and all too often orphaned amid a whirlwind of executions, bombardments and recurrent displacements. More journalists are recorded to have been killed in Gaza than in any previous conflict.[27] Meanwhile, in a year that went down as the deadliest ever on record for aid workers worldwide, 163 of these 280 deaths were recorded in the Occupied Palestinian Territory, and the 2024 figures for Palestine look set to surpass this total.[28] The tally is seemingly endless, and by any measure one of the most grotesque in recent decades.

That the events of 7 October are pivotal – for Israelis and Palestinians, the wider region, and the world as a whole – is clear enough, however unclear their ultimate consequences may yet be. Still, it is important not to exaggerate the 'rupture' to which 7 October has given rise. While we do not yet know (and may very well never know) the full story of 7 October, particularly as Israeli forces appear to have been responsible for the death of many Israeli citizens,[29] the Hamas-led incursion of several thousand fighters (and also Palestinian civilians) across the Gaza-Israel barrier involved a litany of war crimes, from murdering civilians to kidnapping children. The operation's multi-layered sophistication, military and logistical, distinguished it from others in the past, but few of the acts involved were unprecedented: Hamas and other Palestinian groups have long killed both military personnel and civilians, with abduction being a common tactic for compelling Israeli authorities to release Palestinian prisoners, themselves often adult civilians, teenagers and even children, detained and incarcerated on no substantive grounds. Similarly, Israel's response to 7 October consists mainly of augmented forms of its long-standing practices of counterterrorism and counterinsurgency. As before October, Israel has killed civilians and levelled entire neighbourhoods in the name of destroying Hamas and other Palestinian resistance groups, accusing them of using non-combatants as 'human shields' to deflect criticism against the IDF and Israeli police. And there is also the unceasing, legally formalized land grabs by Israel, in the West Bank and around the city of Jerusalem. Such dispossessions have underwritten the steady expansion of Israeli claims to territory and jurisdiction, with new settlements being constructed and existing ones fortified and enlarged. To the extent that it marks a departure, Israel's response to 7 October stands out less for the kind of military response than for the scale of destruction the IDF has meted out, with much of Gaza having been razed and rendered uninhabitable in an onslaught marked by little regard for Israeli hostages and even less for the distinction between Palestinian civilians and combatants.

Both the continuities and the discontinuities of life within the peculiar juridico-political construct known today as 'Israel-Palestine' become more apparent when the history of the territory's political economy is brought into relief. Prior to the inauguration of the inaptly named 'peace process' in the early 1990s, economic activity in the Occupied Palestinian Territory was marked by a high degree of integration with pre-1967 (or 'green line') Israel. After the 1967 war, calamitous for Arab republicanism, Israel confiscated land and water, restricted access to other natural resources and stymied efforts to establish institutions for development planning in the territories it had seized. Since borders between pre-1967 Israel and these occupied territories were relatively open to labour, large numbers of Palestinians from Gaza and the West Bank worked in Israel. And since they were also relatively open to goods, production and trade in Gaza and the West Bank were oriented largely toward Israel, deepening existing relations of structural dependence. The Clinton administration's post-Cold War 'peace process' altered this arrangement. Israel sealed off the borders of Gaza and the West Bank in early 1993, a few months before the end of the First Intifada and the conclusion of the first Oslo Accord. This exacerbated the Palestinians' persistent 'balkanization' and 'bantustanization', as policy and journalistic discourse has often put it, yielding a pockmarked landscape of territorially disconnected and economically autarchical Palestinian enclaves surrounded by settlements inhabited by hundreds of thousands of religious fanatics and working-class Israelis for whom the occupation has been a 'compensatory mechanism ... from the repercussions of the liquidation of the welfare state'.[30] Since the outbreak of the Second Intifada in 2000, and especially since Israel's 2005 'withdrawal' from Gaza, where poverty, population density and the popular memory of the Nakba have always provided fertile ground for anti-colonial armed struggles, further border closures and increased mobility restrictions have reduced employment opportunities for Palestinians in Israel, which has imported large numbers of workers from abroad, especially from eastern Europe and south and southeast Asia, as a way of attending to labour shortages. Israeli goods continue to dominate Palestinian markets in the West Bank and Gaza, which have been captive to Israel for decades, but bureaucratic hurdles and enhanced security measures complicate the transportation of goods from Gaza and the West Bank to Israel and beyond. The result is that export opportunities for Palestinian enterprises in the occupied territories have been severely limited, and many Palestinians have sought employment in the Palestinian Authority or Hamas-controlled public sectors, including their security services. Failing such employment, many Palestinians have simply fallen victim to the clan politics and social alienation that economic and political insecurity has fostered. In sum, what Sara Roy has aptly termed the 'de-development' of Palestinian life is inseparable from the ongoing imposition of Israel's settler-colonial capitalism in Palestine.[31] Far from 'modernizing' pre-capitalist social formations like those of pre-Zionist Palestine, with its extensive commercial relations, as Shlomo Avineri contended on the basis of a selective misreading of Marx's political commentary in the *New York Daily Tribune*, Israel's occupation only deepened immiseration and stunted development.[32]

Israeli operations in Gaza, the West Bank and beyond after 7 October have only furthered and accelerated this decades-long process of 'de-development'. Increased mobility restrictions on Palestinians have been accompanied by increased efforts on the part of both state and industry to recruit workers from elsewhere. As before 7 October, India has been a particularly large supplier of labour, though recruitment efforts routinely run from eastern Europe to southern Africa, with workers arriving from as far afield as Malawi and Moldova. These workers have typically been employed in low-wage jobs, generally in the construction, agricultural and homecare sectors, and are especially vulnerable to exploitation.[33] Viewed from this perspective, the events of the past year evince not so much a break with the past as a hardening of trends long underway, that is, an intensification of tendencies integral to the material intertwinement of capitalist production and colonial underdevelopment in the southern Levant.[34] Just as Israel's destruction of Gaza has been distinguished not by the abandonment but precisely by the amplification of earlier methods of counterinsurgency and mass displacement, so too has Israel responded to labour shortages by continuing its long-term policy of seeking workers from abroad to replace the reserve army of Palestinian labour it once had at its beck and call.

Israel's engagement with international law since 7 October demonstrates a similar pattern of continuity-in-discontinuity. On the one hand, like the United States, Russia and many other states,[35] Israel retains its long-standing commitment to reshaping existing rules of international law in its own interests (as formulated by its ruling elites). It continues to rely on those rules that conserve its power or shield it from criticism while pressing to revise or simply scrap those that do not. On the other hand, Israel violates international law more overtly and recklessly than at any time in the past. Dedicated above all to the aggressive projection of military and political power in the name of an expansive – and more or less continually expanding – conception of 'national security', its engagement with international law today seems less a species of 'entrepreneurialism' than a form of 'freeloading', with Israeli officials regularly expecting both friends and enemies to abide by the very rules they trample over with enthusiastic glee. Even so, the structural patterns of Israeli state formation dominate its conjunctural tactical responses in both security deployments and law.

Israel today is a continuation of Israel yesterday, its present aggression an outgrowth of a nineteenth-century European vision of national statehood fused with a twentieth-century project in technocracy which had the Jewish Agency relying as early as 1944–45 on US engineers associated with the Tennessee Valley Authority to draw up plans for a Jordan Valley Authority that would lay the material groundwork for the future state.[36] The genocide that Israel inflicts daily upon the Palestinians recalls hauntingly the genocide that authorized its own creation. The ghettoization and murder in Europe that Theodor Herzl and Chaim Weizmann feared is a forerunner to the ghettoization and murder that Benjamin Netanyahu declared just and noble when addressing the US Congress a mere handful of days after the ICJ stated yet again that Israel's occupation of Palestinian territories must end.[37] Undeniable though it is that Israeli society has 'lurched right' over the past decades, and that its government is less inclined than it once was to drape its claims in the garb of international law, the reality is that Israel is a settler-colonial state with property structures rooted in a combination of conquest and land purchase, legitimated through a mixture of the Old Testament, Ottoman land law and the Balfour Declaration. Israel has always drawn upon international law selectively, or simply dismissed it in practice when doing so is to its benefit. After all, the very same 1947 General Assembly resolution that recommended Palestine's partition, and that is also referenced by Ben-Gurion's proclamation of independence, made it clear that any Jewish state would need to exist alongside an Arab state, and one much larger, for that matter, than the present-day Occupied Palestinian Territory.

BEYOND ANALOGIES

In 1977, two Ghanaian scholars of international law published an essay in the *Black Law Journal*, then a fledgling US law review published out of UCLA's law school, analyzing South Africa's apartheid regime.[38] At the time, South Africa was undergoing significant transformations owing to decolonization, the Cold War and growing North-South inequality.[39] Noting that apartheid clearly violated the Universal Declaration, from its general prohibitions on discrimination and arbitrary arrest to its recognition of mobility rights and freedom of expression, the authors argued that the 'international community' had at least 'four methods of redressing the gross violations of human rights that apartheid entails'. The first such method was the use of force by the UN – an unlikely measure despite earlier precedents in Korea and Congo. The second was the imposition of full-scale economic sanctions by the UN, a measure that Britain in particular had traditionally rejected. The third was intensified political and diplomatic pressure by states and other actors, mainly in the form of exclusion from or marginalization in multilateral fora. The fourth and final method involved support for liberation movements, resistance organizations and other opponents of the apartheid regime.[40] 'Not a single one of these methods', they argued, 'may alone suffice to bring about the desired and overdue change'. They thus concluded their essay with the sobering observation that 'in the final analysis, it is the African upon whom much depends. Either he eliminates apartheid or apartheid eliminates him.'[41]

As it happened, the UN never did authorize the use of force against apartheid South Africa. In contrast to Rhodesia, the target of the Security

Council's first mandatory sanctions in 1966, South Africa did not come under mandatory sanctions until late 1977, after the *Black Law Journal* had published the essay, and even then the sanctions were only in regard to arms imports.[42] Nevertheless, when they finally were imposed, the combination of economic coercion, increased geopolitical isolation and internal developments within the Afrikaner community, alongside both covert and overt support for the African National Congress and other groups, proved sufficient to bring apartheid to an end.

As an apartheid state, Israel exemplifies the brutal violence through which most states, especially settler-colonial states, are crafted and consolidated. But the Israel of the early 2020s is not the South Africa of the early 1990s, and the specific characteristics of every such case must be appreciated.[43] In the case of Israel, apartheid South Africa's erstwhile ally and arms supplier, it is not at all easy to see how any of the four methods just listed, or even all of them together, could bring to heel this nuclear-armed fascist state bent on carrying out a messianic project of end-of-days land theft and ethnic cleansing, regardless of the immediate and long-term consequences.

Whatever the future portends, two points seem clear. First, Zionism as a movement must be opposed. It has brought about the genocidal destruction, dispossession and displacement of the Palestinian people – all while offering what Fred Halliday once called 'an incorrect answer to the problem of anti-Semitism in Europe' by forestalling 'the establishment of a common front of Jewish and non-Jewish workers'.[44] Interminable chatter about 'one-state' and 'two-state' configurations of political power belies the social reality of an economically unequal, legally fractured and topographically stratified swath of land between the Mediterranean Sea and the Jordan River home to roughly equal numbers of Jews and Arabs. No progressive development is likely to materialize in this land without the conscious and organized participation of workers, peasants and others in a multifrontal assault on the colonial capitalism that has reshaped historic Palestine and that continues to drive Israeli actions and policies.

Second, Palestinian resistance is by no means simply a matter of military strategy and tactics. Just as 'military resistance has significant political-legal impacts', so too does 'political-legal resistance [have] significant military impacts', making it 'inaccurate to attempt to draw a rigid distinction between them'.[45] Not without irony, some of the very changes to existing law for which Israel has long pressed now figure prominently in efforts to resist its occupation and aggression. Years before prosecutors in The Hague began to move against Netanyahu and Yoav Gallant, his defence minister,[46] the same universal jurisdiction for which Eichmann's trial stands as a key precedent had already begun to pose serious problems for Israeli officials travelling through the United Kingdom and elsewhere.[47] Similarly, arguments about terrorism made by Israeli officials are now regularly leveraged by their Palestinian counterparts, not to mention their opponents in Iran, Lebanon and elsewhere. After all, justifying anticipatory strikes on the grounds that they are necessary to neutralize imminent attacks is no easy business when one is daily carrying out extrajudicial executions, actively supporting settler violence and detonating communication devices abroad by the thousands. Liberation will not be achieved through law – but without legal liberation, no liberation will be complete.

NOTES

1   International Covenant on Economic, Social and Cultural Rights, adopted 16 December 1966, *United Nations Treaty Series*, 993, 1976; International Covenant on Civil and Political Rights, adopted 16 December 1966, *United Nations Treaty Series*, 999, 1976.

2   United Nations, GA Res. 181, 29 November 1947.

3   Declaration of Israel's Independence, 14 May 1948, available at: https://avalon.law. yale.edu/20th_century/israel.asp.

4   See especially: Max Ajl, 'Palestine's Great Flood: Part I', *Agrarian South: Journal of Political Economy*, 13(1), 2024, pp. 62-88; and 'Palestine's Great Flood: Part II', *Agrarian South: Journal of Political Economy*, 13(2), 2024, pp. 187-217.

5   I am here alluding to (but not drawing directly upon) Edward Said, 'Zionism from the Standpoint of Its Victims', in Moustafa Bayoumi and Andrew Rubin, eds, *The Edward Said Reader*, New York: Vintage, 2000.

6   *The Mavrommatis Palestine Concessions (Greece v. United Kingdom)* Judgment, Permanent Court of International Justice Reports Series A, 1924; *The Mavrommatis Jerusalem Concessions (Greece v. United Kingdom)* Judgment, Permanent Court of International Justice Reports Series A, 1925; *Case of the Readaptation of the Mavrommatis Jerusalem Concessions (Jurisdiction) (Greece v. United Kingdom)* Judgment, Permanent Court of International Justice Reports Series A, 1927. For analysis, see: John Quigley, *The Statehood of Palestine: International Law in the Middle East Conflict*, Cambridge: Cambridge University Press, 2010, pp. 59-60.

7   *Reparation for Injuries Suffered in the Service of the United Nations*, Advisory Opinion, International Court of Justice Reports, 1949, p. 185.

8   *Reparation* opinion, p. 181.

9   Since it does not relate to questions of 'Israel-Palestine' per se, I leave aside Israel's 1957 institution of proceedings against Bulgaria for the downing of an *El Al* plane on a scheduled commercial flight. The ICJ declined to hear the case on its merits as Bulgaria had yet to accept its compulsory jurisdiction. See: *Aerial Incident of 27 July 1955 (Israel v. Bulgaria)*, Judgment, International Court of Justice Reports, 1959.

10   *Legal Consequences of the Construction of a Wall in the Occupied Palestinian Territory*, Advisory Opinion, International Court of Justice Reports, 2004, pp. 171-89, 201-3. Thomas Buergenthal, a Jewish-American Holocaust survivor and international law

professor, was the only judge to depart from the court's majority on all basic points. He was joined by Pieter Kooijmans, a conservative Dutch politician and international lawyer, on one point. The Friendly Relations Declaration, adopted by the General Assembly twenty-five years after the UN Charter, is a particularly important articulation of core international legal principles: United Nations, GA Res. 2625 (XXV), 24 October 1970.

11 *Case concerning East Timor (Portugal v. Australia)*, Judgment, International Court of Justice Reports, 1995, p. 102.

12 *Wall* opinion, pp. 183-84.

13 *Wall* opinion, pp. 199-200.

14 *Legal Consequences arising from the Policies and Practices of Israel in the Occupied Palestinian Territory, including East Jerusalem*, Advisory Opinion, International Court of Justice Reports, 2024.

15 *Application of the Convention on the Prevention and Punishment of the Crime of Genocide in the Gaza Strip (South Africa v. Israel)*, Application Instituting Proceedings and Request for the Indication of Provisional Measures, 29 December 2023, available at: www. icj-cij.org/case/192/institution-proceedings.

16 Convention on the Prevention and Punishment of the Crime of Genocide, adopted 9 December 1948, art. 2, *United Nations Treaty Series*, 78, 1951, p. 280. Notably, this definition is reproduced verbatim in: Rome Statute of the International Criminal Court, 17 July 1998, art. 6, *United Nations Treaty Series*, 2187, 1998, p. 93.

17 For discussion in the context of current IDF operations in the Occupied Palestinian Territory, see: Nimer Sultany, 'A Threshold Crossed: On Genocidal Intent and the Duty to Prevent Genocide in Palestine', *Journal of Genocide Research*, 2024, pp. 1-26.

18 On Lemkin's support for the concept of 'cultural genocide', see for example: Raphaël Lemkin, *Axis Rule in Occupied Europe: Laws of Occupation, Analysis of Government, Proposals for Redress*, Washington: Carnegie Endowment for International Peace, 1944, pp. 84-85. Lemkin did not always distinguish sharply between 'cultural' and other forms of genocide. See: A. Dirk Moses, 'Empire, Colony, Genocide: Keywords and the Philosophy of History', in A. Dirk Moses, ed., *Empire, Colony, Genocide: Conquest, Occupation, and Subaltern Resistance in World History*, New York: Berghahn, 2008, pp. 11-17; William A. Schabas, *Genocide in International Law: The Crime of Crimes*, 2nd edition, Cambridge: Cambridge University Press, 2009, pp. 207-21. On the international history of 'population transfer', nearly always compulsory even when couched in 'voluntary' terms, see: Umut Özsu, *Formalizing Displacement: International Law and Population Transfers*, Oxford: Oxford University Press, 2015; Matthew Frank, *Making Minorities History: Population Transfer in Twentieth-Century Europe*, Oxford: Oxford University Press, 2017. The classic study of mass expulsion in the context of Palestine is Nur Masalha, *Expulsion of the Palestinians: The Concept of 'Transfer' in Zionist Political Thought, 1882–1948*, Washington: Institute for Palestine Studies, 1992.

19 *Case concerning Military and Paramilitary Activities in and against Nicaragua (Nicaragua v. United States)*, Judgment, International Court of Justice Reports, 1986.

20 George E. Bisharat, 'Violence's Law: Israel's Campaign to Transform International Legal Norms', *Journal of Palestine Studies*, 42(3), 2013, p. 70.

21 Bisharat, 'Violence's Law', p. 70.

22 On these and other terminological disagreements, see: Ardi Imseis, 'On the Fourth Geneva Convention and the Occupied Palestinian Territory', *Harvard International*

Law Journal, 44(1), 2003, p. 67. For disputes about the wording and interpretation of Security Council Resolution 242, adopted after the 1967 war, see: Rashid Khalidi, *The Hundred Years' War on Palestine: A History of Settler Colonialism and Resistance, 1917–2017*, New York: Metropolitan, 2020, p. 105; Richard Falk, 'Forty Years after 242: A "Canonical" Text in Disrepute?', *Journal of Palestine Studies*, 37(1), 2007, pp. 39-48.

23 This is in addition to prohibiting '[i]ndividual or mass forcible transfers, as well as deportations of protected persons from occupied territory to the territory of the Occupying Power or to that of any other country, occupied or not'. Geneva Convention relative to the Protection of Civilian Persons in Time of War, signed 12 August 1949, art. 49, *United Nations Treaty Series*, 75, 1950, p. 318.

24 United Nations, SC Res. 487, 19 June 1981.

25 Rasha Khatib, Martin McKee and Salim Yusuf, 'Counting the Dead in Gaza: Difficult but Essential', *The Lancet*, 5 July 2024.

26 Ibtisam Mahdi, 'The Decimation of Gaza's Academia Is "Impossible to Quantify"', *+972 Magazine*, 26 July 2024; United Nations Office of the High Commissioner for Human Rights, 'UN Experts Deeply Concerned Over "Scholasticide" in Gaza', Press Release, 18 April 2024, available at: www.ohchr.org.

27 Committee to Protect Journalists, 'Journalist Casualties in the Israel-Gaza War', 16 August 2024, available at: www.cpj.org/2024/08/journalist-casualties-in-the-israel-gaza-conflict.

28 United Nations Office for the Coordination of Humanitarian Affairs, 'World Humanitarian Day: UN Demands Action as Aid Worker Deaths Hit Record High', 19 August 2024, available at: www.unocha.org.

29 See especially: Yaniv Kubovich, 'IDF Ordered Hannibal Directive on October 7 to Prevent Hamas Taking Soldiers Captive', *Haaretz*, 7 July 2024; also Julia Frankel and Alon Bernstein, 'Friendly Fire May Have Killed Their Relatives on Oct. 7. These Israeli Families Want Answers Now', Associated Press, 11 January 2024.

30 Danny Gutwein, 'The Settlements and the Relationship between Privatization and the Occupation', in Marco Allegra, Ariel Handel and Erez Maggor, eds, *Normalizing Occupation: The Politics of Everyday Life in the West Bank Settlements*, Bloomington: Indiana University Press, 2017, p. 26. See also: Danny Gutwein, 'Some Comments on the Class Foundations of the Occupation', *Monthly Review Online*, 16 June 2006, available at: www.mronline.org; Guy Laron, 'Israel's Bonaparte', *Catalyst*, 8(1), 2024. For discussion in the context of a broader intervention on 'Israel/Palestine as a part of a contradictory unity', see: Oded Nir and Joel Wainwright, 'Where Is the Marxist Critique of Israel/Palestine?', *Rethinking Marxism*, 30(3), 2018, p. 338.

31 Sara Roy, *The Gaza Strip: The Political Economy of De-development*, Washington: Institute for Palestine Studies, 1995; Sara Roy, 'De-development Revisited: Palestinian Economy and Society Since Oslo', *Journal of Palestine Studies*, 28(3), 1999, pp. 64-82. Importantly, this also applies to Palestinian citizens of Israel, not only Palestinians in Gaza and the West Bank. See: Raja Khalidi and Mtanes Shihadeh, 'Israel's "Arab Economy": New Politics, Old Policies', in Nadim N. Rouhana and Sahar S. Huneidi, eds, *Israel and Its Palestinian Citizens: Ethnic Privileges in the Jewish State*, Cambridge: Cambridge University Press, 2017.

32   For careful critique of Avineri's musings on the 'Asiatic mode of production', see: Bryan S. Turner, 'Avineri's View of Marx's Theory of Colonialism: Israel', *Science & Society*, 40(4), 1976, pp. 385-409.

33   Rhianna Schmunk, 'After Mass Exodus, Israel's Rush to Replace Foreign Workers Raises Human Rights Concerns', CBC News, 1 December 2023; Sam Sokol, 'Despite War, More Than 12,000 Foreign Workers Have Arrived in Israel, Lawmakers Told', *The Times of Israel*, 20 December 2023; Michelle Buckley and Paula Chakravartty, 'Labor and the Bibi-Modi Bromance', *Boston Review*, 11 April 2024; M. J. Bijulal, 'Keep Indian Migrant Workers Safe in Israel', *Deccan Herald*, 27 April 2024.

34   See also: Mahdi Amel, *Arab Marxism and National Liberation: Selected Writings of Mahdi Amel*, Hicham Safieddine, ed., Leiden: Brill, 2021, pp. 25-28.

35   On the post-Cold War history of 'humanitarian intervention', including the long-fabled notion of a 'responsibility to protect', see: Umut Özsu, 'Humanitarian Intervention Today', in Leo Panitch and Greg Albo, eds, *Socialist Register 2019: A World Turned Upside Down?* London: Merlin Press, 2018. On recent efforts by Russia to leverage such arguments about 'humanitarian intervention' popularized in the wake of NATO's illegal 1999 bombing of Yugoslavia for the purpose of justifying its aggressive interventions in Ukraine, see: Betcy Jose and Christoph H. Stefes, 'Russia as a Norm Entrepreneur: Crimea and Humanitarian Intervention', *Problems of Post-Communism*, 71(2), 2024, pp. 131-44.

36   J. C. Hurewitz, *The Struggle for Palestine*, New York: Schocken, 1976 [1950], p. 206.

37   This was in the above mentioned 2004 opinion *Legal Consequences arising from the Policies and Practices of Israel in the Occupied Palestinian Territory, including East Jerusalem*.

38   J. K. Feimpong and S. Azadon Tiewel, 'Can Apartheid Successfully Defy the International Legal System?', *Black Law Journal*, 5(2), 1977, pp. 287-312.The journal misspelled the surnames of both authors (Frimpong as 'Feimpong', Tiewul as 'Tiewel'); I give the names as printed, here and in the notes below. See also: S. Azadon Tiewul, 'Apartheid: Steps Toward International Legal Control', *Zambia Law Journal*, 6, 1974, pp. 101-27.

39   Among recent appraisals of changes to international law resulting from the post-World War II wave of decolonization, see: Matthew Craven, *The Decolonization of International Law: State Succession and the Law of Treaties*, Oxford: Oxford University Press, 2007; Sundhya Pahuja, *Decolonising International Law: Development, Economic Growth and the Politics of Universality*, Cambridge: Cambridge University Press, 2011; Jochen von Bernstorff and Philipp Dann, eds, *The Battle for International Law: South–North Perspectives on the Decolonization Era*, Oxford: Oxford University Press, 2019; Umut Özsu, *Completing Humanity: The International Law of Decolonization, 1960–82*, Cambridge: Cambridge University Press, 2023.

40   Feimpong and Tiewel, pp. 309-10 (with discussion of the Universal Declaration on pp. 306-8).

41   Feimpong and Tiewel, p. 311.

42   For Rhodesia, see: United Nations, SC Res. 232, 16 December 1966. For South Africa, see: United Nations, SC Res. 418, 4 November 1977.

43   For recent consideration of the apartheid concept's applicability to 'Israel-Palestine', see: John Dugard and John Reynolds, 'Apartheid, International Law, and the Occupied Palestinian Territory', *European Journal of International Law*, 24(3), 2013, pp. 867-913. For the view that the Palestinian Nakba ought to be understood on its

own terms, see: Rabea Eghbariah, 'Toward Nakba as a Legal Concept', *Columbia Law Review*, 124(4), 2024, pp. 887–992.

44   Fred Halliday, 'Origins of Communism in Palestine', *MERIP Reports*, 56, 1977, p. 25.

45   W. T. Mallison Jr. and S. V. Mallison, 'The Juridical Characteristics of the Palestinian Resistance: An Appraisal in International Law', *Journal of Palestine Studies*, 2(2), 1973, p. 70.

46   International Criminal Court Prosecutor Karim A. A. Khan, 'Applications for Arrest Warrants in the Situation in the State of Palestine', 20 May 2024, available at: www.icc-cpi.int.

47   See, for example: Vikram Dodd and Conal Urquhart, 'Israeli Evades Arrest at Heathrow Over Army War Crime Allegations', *The Guardian*, 12 September 2005; Rory McCarthy, 'Israeli Military Cancels UK Visit over Arrest Fears', *The Guardian*, 5 January 2010.

LOSING MOMENTUM: STRATEGIC DILEMMAS FOR SOCIALISTS IN BRITAIN

MICHAEL CALDERBANK
AND HILARY WAINWRIGHT

Judged purely by the metrics of short-term electoral outcomes, Labour's landslide victory in the general election of 4 July 2024 appears to have vindicated Sir Keir Starmer's electoral strategy – at least in terms of seats won, if not in total votes won. Starmer and his circle can claim that by purging his socialist predecessor Jeremy Corbyn and marginalizing, excluding and demoralizing left-wing activists, they have successfully reached out beyond the party membership and demonstrated to a strategically decisive minority of the electorate that Labour has been changed into a moderate party fit for government within the existing economic and political order. Just as Starmer delivered rapid 'change' to rescue the Labour Party from the Corbyn era, they argue, so he successfully presented himself as the agent of 'change' to rescue the nation from Tory rule.

This poses a whole host of questions for the British left: How are we to understand the politics of 'Starmerism'? Does it have goals, policies and strategies beyond those shaped by its overriding priority of obtaining government office? What kind of change does it aim to deliver, and how does that match up with the change sought by different groups of voters? How far is it willing to meet the demands of Labour's more radical – and more powerful – historical sources of support, such as the railway workers' union (the RMT), or students radicalized and organized in response to the injustices of the world, including the human causes and repercussions of climate change? Or does it instead assume that it can isolate or even defeat such organizations? For how long will Starmer be able to sustain his electoral base? If Labour is not seen to have delivered on its promise of change and is instead seen to have failed or betrayed its voters, where will those voters then turn? Is the game finally up for socialists inside the Labour Party and, if so, what are the prospects of the left developing a viable alternative vehicle or strategy? Most notably in this context, what is the character and dynamic of the emergent 'movement' of independents who this year broke through electorally in Westminster and local government, in all their diversity? And, finally, if it isn't accepted that the game is up for socialists in the Labour Party, are there still prospects for developing a significant pole of opposition to Starmer's leadership from within, such that socialists inside and outside of the party can work to turn the policy dial or shift the broader balance of forces to the left?

LOSING MOMENTUM

First, however, some initial reflection might be in order with respect to the speed and extent to which Corbyn's supporters – mainly organized through Momentum, the left-wing campaign group – came to be comprehensively eclipsed following the 2019 election defeat. This is in order not least on account of the initial optimism felt by activists in their focus on the promise of an outward facing strategy to build support within social movements.[1] The 'Forward Momentum' slate which controlled the organization's National Coordinating Group following the 2020 elections (and which was highly critical of the organization's previous, Corbyn-era leadership under Jon Lansman for being too cautious, top-down and undemocratic) set out an ambitious strategy to do just this while also continuing to advance a more radical policy agenda within Labour. Why did this approach fail? Was it that these efforts to turn Momentum from being primarily focused on defensive struggles within the Labour Party to a focus that also took in wider struggles outside of the party were simply exerted too late?

Momentum, formed in the immediate aftermath of Corbyn's victory in the Labour Party leadership campaign, included both largely autonomous local branches as well as a national mailing list that was used mainly to mobilize defensively when Corbyn was under threat from the right. Arguably, the expectation that Momentum could pivot successfully from the tactical internal battles it was obliged to fight as Corbyn's praetorian guard into a pluralistic and outward-looking campaigning force at a grassroots level was always a tough ask. It was still more so given the crushing extent of the 2019 general election defeat and the decisive loss for the left's candidate Rebecca Long-Bailey in the subsequent Labour leadership election, ultimately won by Starmer. To grow and expand in the context of such evident defeats would have been to somehow defy the political laws of gravity by which (according to a favourite adage of Tony Cliff) movements typically 'go up like a rocket and fall like a stick'. Starmer had disingenuously appealed to Labour members (the majority of whom had joined under Corbyn's leadership) on the basis that his leadership would build on the core policy agenda of the Corbyn years (describing the 2017 manifesto as a 'foundational document'), unify the party and bring a level of professionalism and electability to the party's image. Taking him at his word, a minority of members who had previously voted for Corbyn welcomed Starmer's election, even including Momentum's former Chief Executive Laura Parker.

But even those who saw straight through Starmer's temporary leftist façade were nevertheless shocked by the sheer authoritarianism and ruthless factionalism with which his party leadership under him went on to exert an iron grip over the party's internal culture and democratic processes. Such was the climate of hostility towards left activists from the new Labour leadership that many were only too happy to tear up their party membership cards. The wave of support flooding into Labour in support of Corbyn flooded out with similar rapidity, but in diffuse directions or simply by drifting into passive discontent. Whether out of virtue or necessity, Momentum's leadership ultimately came to jettison its more grandiose outward reaching ambitions in order to focus on fighting rear-guard battles and maintaining the left's forces in a defensive retrenchment within the party, despite diminishing forces.[2] In doing so, it saw some small yet significant victories, such as successfully fighting off an attempt to deselect left-wing Liverpool MP Ian Byrne, a leading campaigner against food poverty. However, despite its best efforts, it was ultimately powerless to hold on to control of Labour's National Executive Committee (NEC), and hence control over key structural decisions about the party's future.[3]

LABOUR UNDER LOCKDOWN

What was an incredibly difficult task was made all but impossible when the Covid-19 lockdown of 2020–21 handed the new Labour leadership easy control over online local party meetings and internal elections, the latter of which were now to be conducted through 'Anonyvoter' – an electronic anonymous balloting technology owned by Croydon-based allies of the party's new General Secretary, David Evans, who were apparently awarded the contract in the absence of any competitive tendering process. This system is widely believed to be open to abuse, and even the moderately inclined former BBC and Channel 4 journalist Michael Crick concluded that candidate selections utilizing the technology 'may have involved identity theft and voter manipulation [which] could be part of a much wider campaign that involves senior party figures, a systematic program of data protection offences, and interference in Labour's supposedly democratic procedures'.[4] Access to the membership database Organise – the means by which constituency Labour Party (CLP) officers can communicate with local members – was for a time suspended, owing to an alleged breach of data protection laws.

Procedural control was combined with a massive assault on the democratic rights of CLPs and party members. Crucially, the NEC moved to centralize the longlisting process for the selection of parliamentary candidates, meaning that local members would only have a choice between centrally approved candidates. Elsewhere, Corbyn himself was stripped of the whip for his response to the Equalities and Human Rights Commission report into antisemitism in the Labour Party, even though he was reinstated as a member of the Labour Party in good standing. This then meant that he was not eligible to be chosen as a candidate for the 2024 election by his local CLP. The top-down control of candidate selection also targeted left-wing figures such as Emma Dent-Coad, who sensationally won the Tory-stronghold seat of Kensington in 2017 by a margin of just 20 votes, a constituency never previously held by Labour. After narrowly being defeated in the 2019 general election – by a margin of less than 200 votes – and despite gaining widespread respect for her advocacy on behalf of the victims of the Grenfell Tower tragedy that took place in the constituency, Dent-Coad was barred from even getting on to the candidate shortlist in 2024. As a result of such manoeuvres, of the over 200 Labour MPs elected for the first time in 2024, the number of those sympathetic to the left-wing caucus of the Parliamentary Labour Party, the Socialist Campaign Group (SCG), can be counted on the fingers of one hand.

Activists elected to be officials of local parties were explicitly instructed that no debate about issues such as the suspension of Corbyn's membership of the parliamentary party could be tabled for discussion. Anyone violating this edict would themselves face suspension or expulsion. Perhaps the nadir of this authoritarian culture was an email sent in the name of Labour's General Secretary David Evans on the eve of the first Palestinian solidarity demonstration against Israel's brutal assault on the civilian population of Gaza that began in the autumn of 2023. Labour Party members were told not to join the demonstrations and were explicitly forbidden to take Labour Party banners with them if they did. Nevertheless, as successive demonstrations grew bigger and bigger, it was clear that this embarrassing overreach could not be enforced.

Just as important was the chilling effect of this new authoritarianism on the existing minority of socialist MPs. For example, SCG MPs who had signed a Stop the War Coalition statement critical of NATO's actions in the run up to Putin's invasion of Ukraine were told that they would have the whip withdrawn unless they revoked their signatures. Left MPs continued to fear last-minute deselection right up to the deadline for the nomination of candidates for the 2024 general election. And with good reason: Brighton Kemptown MP Lloyd Russell-Moyle was subject to a last-gasp complaint about past behaviour, the nature of which was not disclosed, and was therefore deemed to be ineligible as a candidate since time didn't allow for any investigation to be completed.

Was this just overzealous message discipline, a requirement to get into power? It appears not, and that the party whips are instead taking this culture of control into government. Just weeks into office, seven rebel MPs (including Corbyn's Shadow Chancellor John McDonnell and Starmer's opponent in the leadership contest Rebecca Long-Bailey) were suspended for voting against the Labour whip in their backing of a Scottish National Party amendment that urged Labour to go further in tackling child poverty by scrapping the notorious two-child limit to Universal Credit welfare benefit payments. This level of authoritarian party management extends well beyond anything attempted under the earlier Labour governments of Tony Blair and Gordon Brown and is already generating a backlash, with well over ten thousand Labour supporters supporting a petition to reinstate the rebel MPs.

Yet Starmer could not have achieved such an iron grip over the internal culture of the party without a notable shift in the mood of the unions on the NEC.[5] Frustration at the Tory victory in 2019 and resentment over the degree of influence held over the party's leadership under Corbyn by Unite, one of the largest unions in the UK (with its staff essentially running his office and former Unite Political Director Jennie Formby becoming Labour's General Secretary) combined to lead the other two largest union affiliates of the party – UNISON (the public sector workers union that includes many in the National Health Service) and GMB (General and Municipal Workers' Union) – to support Starmer in reasserting control and isolating the left. The election of Sharon Graham as Unite's General Secretary in August 2021 further entrenched this process by initiating a clear turn within that union towards a narrow industrial focus and apparent disengagement from attempts to wield political influence more broadly. This is not by any means to denigrate the importance of a focus on building power directly in the workplace, which Graham rightly champions. Yet despite some rhetorical attacks against the new Labour leadership, winning plaudits from Trotskyist groups who had supported her leadership bid, Graham's election initially helped Starmer restore the relative autonomy of the movement's political wing from direct trade union influence. Graham's critics point out that it's possible to walk and chew gum at the same time and that greater autonomy from the Labour Party could be combined with more independent, non-electoral, political campaigning, including a broadening of the scope of collective bargaining to include the purpose of production (e.g., defence diversification and decarbonization).[6]

Crucially, Starmer has used his new majority on the NEC to ram through changes to the rules for the election of future party leaders, scrapping the 'Collins reforms'[7] which created the unforeseen opportunity for Corbyn to make it onto the ballot paper and act as a pole of attraction for thousands of new left-wing members. Starmer initially briefed the press that he would scrap one-member-one-vote as the basis for electing the leader altogether, reverting to the old electoral college model. This would have effectively given the Parliamentary Labour Party a third of the overall vote, massively increasing their power. The unions were incensed that they had not been consulted and, in the end, only a last-minute switch by UNISON delegates on the NEC saved Starmer's blushes, when a watered-down package was passed by just 53 per cent of the conference vote (with a massive majority of CLP delegates against). However, while badly choreographed, the result was enough for Starmer. The new package ensured that to get on the ballot paper for a future leadership contest, a candidate would now need support from at least 20 per cent of the Parliamentary Labour Party, up from 10 per cent. To put that in perspective, the current (post-2024) SCG membership totals no more than 30 of 411 MPs – just 7 per cent. It is hard to envisage anyone from the radical left of the party again being a viable leadership candidate unless these constitutional changes are overturned.

A LOVELESS LANDSLIDE

Will the relative acquiescence of the affiliated trade unions shown toward Starmer be maintained over the medium term? For now, the leadership has largely been given a free hand to say whatever it needs to say to regain office. Insofar as 'Starmerism' has meant anything thus far, it was simply a determination not to lose the election. Starmer was described in the press as adopting a 'Ming vase' strategy, making policy as cautiously as possible so as not to risk any damage to his precious electability. Perhaps for this reason, there has been little evidence of any positive enthusiasm towards the Labour leader or his political vision from the public. A YouGov poll published in the immediate wake of the General Election showed that 56 per cent were either uncertain, very uncertain, or didn't know at all what he stands for.[8] A measly 8 per cent of the electorate (and less than 1-in-4 Labour voters) had a 'very favourable' impression of the new Prime Minister.

Labour's handsome parliamentary representation of 411 MPs gives them a working majority of 167 votes, but this was achieved on a national share of the vote of just 33.8 per cent (an increase of just 1.7 per cent on the 'disaster' of 2019, and well down on the 40 per cent polled under Corbyn in 2017). Labour also benefitted from tactical voting as voters calculated how best to unseat a Tory incumbent, while the split in the right-wing vote between the Conservatives and Nigel Farage's far right populist Reform UK party exacerbated Tory losses. Starmer's victory is far better understood as the outcome of a broad desire to get rid of the Tories, rather than a wave of popular enthusiasm for Labour's offer. Labour's representation in parliamentary seats has also been skewed out of all proportion by the anachronistic 'first past the post' electoral system of single-member constituencies (a system increasingly difficult to justify). We will return to this subject when considering the viability of alternative left electoral strategies. But, for now, let us note that the paradoxical nature of Starmer's 'loveless landslide' (in Corbyn's description) is not necessarily an index of solid support for a particular vision or program.

Understandably, Starmer's electoral strategists concluded that Labour needed to reach beyond its urban heartlands in the big cities and reach out to the small towns and communities in former industrial areas which now feel left behind, including the formerly solidly-Labour so-called 'red wall' constituencies in the North and Midlands. They were aided in this by the transparent failure of the Tories to fulfil their promise to 'level up' these areas with significant regional investment and infrastructure projects. Many Brexit voters – including those in the 'red wall' constituencies, which skewed heavily towards a vote for leave – had also argued that leaving the EU was necessary in order to 'take back control' of Britain's borders and limit the flow of immigration. Starmer, who had won the Labour leadership on policy pledges which included the protection of free movement between the UK and Europe, ensured this option was firmly off the table, refusing to re-open the question of Brexit or membership of the single market/customs union, a debate which had been so divisive in 2019. Yet having neglected to train and skill enough of its own citizens to meet labour shortages in the economy, the Tories continued to preside over large increases in net legal migration, seeking instead to divert voters' attention with new promises to 'stop the boats' bringing in undocumented migrants. Central, here, was the proposal to create a new deterrent by deporting asylum seekers to Rwanda to await the processing of their claims there. This proposal was held up in the courts, which criticized Rwanda's human rights record, and Labour joined the criticism, but less on grounds of principle than on cost and impracticality.

The unexpected intervention of former Brexit Party leader Nigel Farage, who returned during the election campaign to take over leadership of Reform UK, proved ruinous to the chances of Rishi Sunak's Conservatives. The unity of centre-right and populist far-right forces in the 2019 election behind Boris Johnson's pledge to 'Get Brexit Done' was absolutely fundamental to their success. A substantial section of voters who backed the Tories for the first time in 2019 felt by the time of the 2024 election that Brexit had been 'betrayed', in large part due to the government allowing immigration levels to reach record highs. From their perspective, the Tory failure to introduce the Rwanda scheme demonstrated either a criminal failure of nerve or the true face of a political elite unwilling to take the necessary action to give effect to the will of the majority. In response, Starmer adopted a managerial tone, agreeing that the system was failing under the Tories while arguing Labour could deal with immigration more efficiently, including phasing out the use of hotels to house asylum seekers owing to the backlogs in the appeals system.

At times during the campaign, Labour spokespeople appeared to echo the far right, arguing that some migrants should be 'sent back' more quickly. Following the election, recently elected Labour MP for Tamworth Sarah Edwards used her new parliamentary platform to express the supposed concerns of her constituents that they 'wanted their hotel back' from the asylum seekers housed in it. Both Starmer himself and colleagues such as Jon Ashworth (a now former-MP after defeat at the hands of an independent) echoed such rhetoric, with Ashworth even controversially singling out Bangladeshis as a group whose deportation could be expedited – a strange move given the consistent support which Bangladeshi communities have given to Labour over the years. The leadership is in danger of reproducing the tropes of the far right, amplified by powerful vested interests in the mainstream media and increasingly widespread across social media, whereby the issue of immigration is conflated with a supposed threat posed to English culture by a rising Muslim population whose values are 'alien'.

Electoral expediency is not without its own risks. Labour's strategic overtures to the 'red wall' voters risked the comparative neglect of other communities judged to be electorally expendable. The argument that working class voters have 'nowhere else to go' was a familiar Blairite trope. But, especially against the backdrop of renewed arguments about immigration and the politics of Israel/Palestine, Labour's apparent willingness to distance itself from the priorities of South Asian communities in particular seemed to at least flirt with anti-Muslim prejudice. The leadership's response to Israel's assault on Gaza was tone deaf to the concerns of a huge number of party members, particularly Muslims, in relation to Palestine. One anonymous 'Labour source' is said to have briefed the press that local councillors resigning in protest was just 'shaking off the fleas'.[9] Starmer, a former human rights barrister, gave a notorious interview to the LBC presenter Nick Ferrari, in which he argued that Israel was justified in depriving the civilian population in Gaza of power and water. This video was circulated widely and caused understandable fury. Long after the extent of widespread civilian deaths, including women and children, was known, the leadership continued to forestall calls for an immediate ceasefire and the pursuit of peace. Feeling mass pressure from their constituents, even otherwise loyalist MPs broke the whip to support a ceasefire.

In the end, four independent Muslim MPs were elected on a pro-Gaza platform – including in the aforementioned loss for Jon Ashworth of his Leicester South seat – and others narrowly missed out, including Leanne Mohamad in her race against Wes Streeting, now Health Secretary. Critics allege that slates such as The Muslim Vote imply the danger of communalist voting trends, something potentially unwelcome from the vantage point of class politics.[10] Yet the idea that any ethnic or religious community owes permanent loyalty to Labour irrespective of its treatment is surely untenable. There currently appears to be a level of complacency within the party leadership that the present disaffection over Gaza is temporary and conjunctural rather than something more structural, but the assumption that Muslim voters will return to the fold is by no means assured.

While Muslim voters are at the forefront of those who are angry at being taken for granted, they are far from alone. Other large demographics including deprived inner-city communities (in which black people in particular are disproportionately represented), university students and young urban graduates have also had reason to feel overlooked. University tuition fees are now over £9,000 per year, meaning that when including additional accommodation and living costs many students are graduating with an average of around £44,000 of debt.[11] Despite promising to retain Labour's opposition to university tuition fees (which Corbyn had promised to scrap entirely) as a leadership candidate, Starmer swiftly ditched this promise, claiming it to be too costly. In light of widespread resentment toward the party position on Palestine, alongside the decision to scrap the commitment to £26 billion of investment in renewable technologies to combat climate change, voters under 30 are now voting for small parties in increasing numbers.[12] However, research has also shown a consistent correlation between the percentage of younger voters in a constituency and the likelihood of a lower turnout.[13] Amid these trends, the Green Party has made significant inroads into the Labour vote, including defeating Shadow Culture Secretary Thangam Debbonaire in the Bristol Central constituency.

WHAT WILL A LABOUR GOVERNMENT DELIVER?

Electoral success is of course a necessary condition for engaging state power within a parliamentary democracy, but it is very far from being a sufficient condition by itself for achieving durable political success, let alone radical change. Getting elected is one thing. Delivering a positive program of change in government is another order of difficulty altogether. The unions have found themselves conceding ground on broader social and economic policy in order to retain in the party manifesto the commitment to delivering a 'New Deal for Working People'. This relatively bold commitment comprises policies to strengthen employment and trade union rights and was inherited by Deputy Leader Angela Rayner from the Corbyn years, with proposals drawn up under Shadow Ministers Laura Pidcock, and subsequently Andy McDonald, together with leading Employment Rights Barrister John Hendy KC and Professor Keith Ewing of the Institute of Employment Rights.[14] It includes proposals to tackle exploitative zero hours contracts, ban the practice of 'fire and rehire' and scrap recent Tory anti-union legislation. While most of this agenda was retained as policy in the 2024 manifesto, suspicion has already been raised by Starmer's promise to engage in consultation with employers' groups over the implementation of the plans and responsibility for the legislation being passed to the Department for Business and Trade. It is feared that plans to extend sectoral collective bargaining agreements across the economy will be limited to an initial pilot in the social care sector, instead of a wider rollout. More ambitious attempts to repeal anti-union legislation dating from the Thatcher era (and retained by New Labour under the leadership of Tony Blair) are not thought to be on the agenda – maintaining the limits, for example, on the ability of unions to take solidarity action with other groups of workers, to extend collective bargaining to cover questions of purpose of production or to conduct workplace balloting.

Despite concerns about the watering down of these policy commitments, it remains the case that the new government is promising action on restoring employment rights to an extent that would have been unthinkable under the Tories. In its first months in government, public sector pay awards have outstripped inflation, with the junior doctors of the British Medical Association being offered a settlement worth 22 per cent over two years to bring an end to their industrial action. Together with new legislation to bring rail passenger services and track maintenance under public ownership (though, perplexingly, excluding the rolling stock operators, whose shareholders profit from lucrative leasing agreements), the unions can point to genuine gains in the early days of the new leadership. From the perspective of capital too, the fundamental failure of rail privatization and its role in creating Britain's inefficient, expensive and unreliable transportation infrastructure, requires urgent remedial attention. Even among Conservative voters, support for renationalizing rail has been consistently popular.

But while Starmer has wisely avoided any immediate showdown with the unions, will his government manage to reconcile its eagerness to demonstrate tight fiscal rectitude and stability to the financial markets with its commitment to improving public services and working-class living standards? The tension between these objectives has thus far been quickly glossed over, including by union leaderships, but it is nevertheless very real. In a tone reminiscent of a parent berating a naughty child, Chancellor Rachel Reeves has adopted a new mantra: 'if we can't afford it, we can't have it'. Margaret Thatcher's analogy of the national economy with a household budget looms in the background. So far, we've been told we 'can't afford' to scrap the two-child limit to Universal Credit welfare payments, even though the Resolution Foundation has identified that this would help to lift 1.6 million children out of poverty.[15] Likewise, Reeves has moved to scrap winter fuel payments for all but the very poorest pensioners, arguing that we 'can't afford' to provide the benefit on a universal basis. With Labour echoing Tory rhetoric about productivity requiring getting more people out of economic inactivity and into work, sick and disabled people fear further coercive welfare reforms will be in the pipeline. With Reeves already briefing on 'difficult decisions' ahead later this year, it is unlikely that flashpoints with the unions can be averted for long unless self-imposed fiscal restraints are relaxed.

In terms of much needed capital investment in public infrastructure, Labour's flagship policy is the creation of a National Wealth Fund worth £7.3 billion, effectively opening up lucrative new revenue streams to private finance while the state agrees to nationalize the risk. This has been described by economist Daniela Gabor as a plan to 'get Blackrock to rebuild Britain'[16] and by Grace Blakeley as 'PFI 2.0',[17] a reference to the widely reviled Private Finance Initiative pursued by the Blair/Brown governments, which locked the taxpayer into expensive long-term repayment agreements in return for often cheaply and poorly constructed facilities such as schools and hospitals. The National Audit Office concluded that, over the lifetime of these new projects, the cost will be headed towards £200 billion, around 40 per cent more than if they had been fully publicly funded.[18] Whereas Corbyn's Shadow Chancellor John McDonnell had proposed ripping up existing PFI contracts, Reeves appears determined to double-down on them. Similarly, Labour's plan to address the acute lack of genuinely affordable housing is simply to let the private sector build, build and build some more – but without empowering local councils to build social housing to ensure that rents are kept down. Starmer's focus has instead been on deregulating the planning system, allowing protected 'green-belt' land to be built on, and allowing objections from local communities to be more easily ignored.

Looking to foreign policy, Starmer has made no secret of his desire to return to a full-blooded Atlanticism (in the face of threats from China and Russia in particular), with an unequivocal commitment to NATO, together with an effort to rebuild relationships with European nations to tackle barriers to trade that have emerged in the wake of Brexit. Foreign Secretary David Lammy has called Labour's approach 'progressive realism', evoking the spirit of Ernest Bevin and Robin Cook. As a backbench MP in 2013, Lammy put his name to an Early Day Motion tabled by Corbyn calling on the government to scrap plans to replace the UK's Trident nuclear weapons.[19] In his current praise for Bevin, he is applauding a figure who wanted Britain to have the atom bomb 'with a bloody union jack on it'. Quite a journey in just over a decade! The invocation of Cook, on the other hand, is clearly meant to indicate that any moves towards an 'ethical foreign policy' must be firmly within the limited parameters set by global realpolitik. Labour is committed to £3 billion per year of aid to Ukraine and is seeking the admission of Ukraine to NATO after a military victory over Putin. Meanwhile, any recognition of Palestinian statehood is to be deferred.

It is not entirely clear what kind of Labour government we will get over the next five years. It is entirely possible that we are offered the continuation of austerity-lite and a continued drive towards marketization in public services, albeit under a thin progressive veneer. But despite Starmer's landslide victory, as MPs start to weigh up their chances of re-election, might an instinct for self-preservation kick in and result in a recalibration toward an attenuated form of social democracy, albeit within neoliberal constraints? Andy Beckett, whose book *The Searchers* chronicles the political careers of Tony Benn, Ken Livingstone, Corbyn, McDonnell and Diane Abbott,[20] draws the stark conclusion that while such a recalibration is the best that can be hoped for by socialists staying in the Labour Party, it is still the least worst option, preferable to the alternative – which is effectively marching out into wilderness of electoral oblivion.[21]

WHAT IS TO BE DONE, REDUX?

Is Beckett's pessimism justified? Is he right to argue that, for now at least, there is no realistic alternative for socialists in Britain but to pursue a strategic orientation toward work in the Labour Party, even if the scope for any gains to be had from such engagement is negligible? The obstacles to developing an alternative party should certainly not be underestimated. We need only recall the litany of failed recent attempts to launch such an alternative formation – Militant Labour and the Scottish Socialist Party, the Socialist Labour Party, the Socialist Alliance, RESPECT, and the Trade Union and Socialist Coalition (TUSC), to name only the most prominent – to be reminded of the challenge. But there is now no shortage of voices on the left arguing that what has happened to Labour under Starmer has taken us into decisively new territory.[22] Victories for independents and Greens, while modest in comparison with Labour's yield in seats, provide a platform that left-of-Labour parties haven't had before. Corbyn, meanwhile, was able to see off the Labour Party machine and defend his own constituency of Islington North by mobilizing a vibrant grassroots campaign. To receive nearly half of the votes cast as an independent candidate is a notable achievement.

Perhaps while still elated from his victory, Corbyn published an article for *The Guardian* heralding his win as 'the start of a new politics', arguing that

> public discontent with a broken political system will only grow as the government fails to make the real change that people expect ... That energy needs somewhere to go. It needs to be channelled. It needs to be mobilized. That's why our campaign will organize with those who have been inspired by our victory to build community power in every corner of the country. Once our grassroots model has been replicated elsewhere, this can be the genesis of a new movement capable of challenging the stale two-party system ... I have no doubt that this movement will eventually run in elections. However, to create a new, centralized party, based around the personality of one person, is to put the cart before the horse. Remember that only once strength is built from below can we challenge those at the top.
>
> Look at where other independents challenged the main parties most effectively. They built on community power to stand up for themselves and against those who had ignored their demands for peace and humanity. It's that sort of power that needs to be built everywhere.[23]

The vision is attractive and certainly it is hard to envisage a credible alternative party emerging without these kinds of community organizing initiatives. It reads like a local scale version of the rather more panoramic strategic vision James Schneider offered in *Our Bloc*.[24] But presenting a strategy in outline is one thing. Delivering it in concrete terms quite another.

In moving so quickly from 'once our grassroots model has been replicated elsewhere', Corbyn elides the question of whether the model is so easily replicable. Corbyn had represented his constituency in Parliament for over forty years; four decades worth of contacts, casework records and community links, on top of which he had extensive national media exposure as Leader of the Official Opposition. His campaign was also a lightning rod for disaffection with Starmer nationwide, drawing in activists from across London and beyond.

By comparison, other independent candidates associated with Corbyn fared less well. Pamela Fitzpatrick, Director of Corbyn's Peace and Justice Project received 9.1 per cent as an independent in Harrow West, while Andrew Feinstein polled 18.9 per cent contesting Starmer's seat of Holborn and St Pancras. These are far from discreditable figures for left-of-Labour candidates historically speaking, but some way from giving any real scares to Starmer's party under the present electoral system. Even on his own Islington patch, Labour's relatively comfortable byelection defeat of a Corbyn-backed independent council candidate just weeks after the General Election highlights the difficulties of sustaining and consolidating independent support more broadly.[25] Calls for proportional representation are now being voiced right across the political spectrum, and the Labour conference has officially adopted policy in favour of it, but with Starmer now steadfastly opposed (yet another U-turn) no immediate movement can be anticipated.

As we have seen, the independents with decisive cut through were Muslim candidates in areas with large Muslim communities in the constituency, at a time when community opinion was justifiably inflamed over Labour's position in relation to Gaza. This is certainly not to assume that many of the political currents driving Corbyn's support in his highly diverse constituency were not also in play in places like Blackburn or Dewsbury. But the rhetoric of independently representing the interests of a local community does not necessarily imply – and might even militate against – an appeal based on class politics. Corbyn's record speaks for itself, but it remains to be seen how far other independent MPs will prioritize union struggles or campaigns on other progressive issues beyond the most non-contentious issues. Similarly, whether the Green Party is capable of responding to Labour's lurch to the right by deepening and developing its own trade union links will also prove instructive for the possibilities of any political realignment.

Events subsequent to the general election have already begun to pose these questions in new and more pressing ways. The unexpected success of the Nouveau Front Populaire in the French Assembly Elections was widely welcomed as evidence that a pluralistic coalition of left forces could provide a credible alternative both to the failed centrism of Macron and the divisive far right populism of Le Pen and her Rassemblement National (RN). This led *The Guardian* columnist Owen Jones to make a direct call for the tactic to be replicated in the UK.[26] While the five seats won by the British equivalent of RN, Reform UK, is meagre in comparison with the representation held by its French counterpart, of the 98 seats in which Reform UK candidates were second place, 89 of them were held by Labour. This indicates Labour's main local challenger in dozens of places across the country is now the far right. The danger is that MPs desperate to hold onto their jobs try to meet this threat by accommodating it. In some ways, the 2024 election results merely scratch the surface of the discontent. The race riots and attacks which erupted in Britain in August 2024 are an early warning of the threat from the far right should Labour fail to deliver on people's expectations of change. If trade union leaders were not already conscious of the stakes involved in Labour's performance in office, they should be now.

Conversely, if the Labour leadership fails to break decisively from Islamophobia and divisive rhetoric on immigration, the trends away from Labour in the big cities are likely to be compounded. Already the Stand Up to Racism counterprotests drew Labour, Green and non-aligned left activists together with an immediate practical purpose. Not least with the seven Labour MPs who defied the whip and voted for urgent action to tackle child poverty now obliged to sit in parliament as 'independents', the Labour whips may have inadvertently sown the seeds of a new informal cross-party caucus which may yet take on a more concrete form, even if only a future electoral non-aggression pact. The forces which came together to form the Corbynite left may have fragmented and dispersed as a result of recent defeats. But that defeat might be much less absolute and definitive than Starmer's circle believes.

CORBYN AS CATALYST?

One of the less explored consequences of the movement of radical socialist activists enlivened by Corbyn's brief period as would-be and then as actual Labour leader, was the way that it inspired many activists to raise their game from their own civic base outside parliament. We are thinking here of trade unionists who expanded their campaigning demands to take on the needs of working-class communities beyond the workplace, for example on food security or housing,[27] or addressing through collective bargaining and consciousness raising campaigns major national political issues such as climate change and a transition to a low carbon economy[28] and the possibility of democratic forms of public ownership.[29] The qualitative and quantitative expansion of an alternative media infrastructure during the Corbyn years is another example of a strengthening of extra-parliamentary politics, albeit one that has probably been weakened but not entirely dissipated since the 2019 defeat. Similarly, political education has been back on the agenda both during and in the aftermath of the Corbyn years.[30]

One reason for this game-raising effect was that the ethos driving the radical leadership of these years was not one that aimed to focus attention on the power of a potential Corbyn government and thus draw energy away from the present struggles, toward a promised future – there was much less of the rhetoric of 'elect us and we can sort it'. Instead, the speeches of Corbyn, McDonnell and the majority of the team encouraged activists to build *their own* grassroots power and to exert *their own* agency, in cooperation with others, to achieve the transformation they desired. For these radical left politicians, the role of Labour in parliament included supporting and encouraging extra-parliamentary sources of transformative power. This was not a fully worked out or coherent strategy: it was more of the foundations of a distinct theory of transformative change. The point here is that it was in the nature of the movement that Corbyn's campaign to be Labour leader and then to be Prime Minister did not focus on the delegation of power to him and his parliamentary comrades in the conventional manner of Labour's parliamentary and 'parliamentarist' left.[31] Some of its constituent parts therefore, especially those with a pre-existing collective, socially or culturally rooted character, have not disappeared along with Corbyn's prospects of becoming Prime Minister, because they had in fact developed their own distinct momentum, albeit not as a coordinated or coherent movement.

We do not want to exaggerate the strength of these disparate transformative initiatives which emerged under Corbyn, but they provide an important point of contrast between his political project and that of Starmer. They are not on different ends of the spectrum of Labourism, understood as the project of representing organized labour within the British parliamentary system. Although, we would suggest that Starmer is within the classical tradition of Labourism in a way that Blair was not. Whereas Blair showed a contempt for organized labour (except when it suited him in order to get their support) and promoted individual aspiration, positively welcoming the private market economy, Starmer adopts a weakly Labourist stance by which he at least claims to aim to meet working class needs, but very firmly within the existing economic, financial and political order. In this understanding of representing the working class, the working class is understood as the subordinate class, despite its apparent representatives being in government. This is a consistent feature of Labourism, shared by Michael Foot and the old Tribune Group, as well as Harold Wilson, James Callaghan and other pre-Blair Labour leaders. Corbyn's project, by contrast, represented an understanding of the working class as an agent of social, economic and political transformation. Yet Corbyn himself did not theorize his project in this or indeed in any way at all. It was the product more of positive practical responses to transformative working-class initiatives – a radical tradition revived by Corbyn's great mentor, Tony Benn, in response to the 'work-in' of engineering workers at the Upper Clyde Shipbuilders and proposals for alternative products and workers control throughout the engineering and shipbuilding industries.[32]

The legacy of this transformative tradition in workplaces and localities across the country, now evident in creative radical initiatives such as those in solidarity with Gaza,[33] provides significant, potentially material bases for new alliances on the left, especially with the Green and independent left in Parliament. With a realistic but creative approach to possible new alliances, and a rejection of the parliamentarist socialism of the past, the British left might finally find a way to move beyond the fragments as the limitations of Starmer's project are exposed.

NOTES

1   See: James Schneider interviewed by Hilary Wainwright, 'Finding a Way Forward. Lessons from the Corbyn Project in the UK', in Greg Albo, Leo Panitch and Colin Leys, eds, *Socialist Register 2022: New Polarizations, Old Contradictions. The Crisis of Centrism*, London: Merlin Press, pp. 299-326.

2   Momentum continues to exist as an organization but very much in the mode of defensive retrenchment at present, with a dramatically reduced membership and little reach or authority in the left outside the ranks of those who have chosen to stay in the Labour Party. It has a small staff and continues to do important work in terms of training and supporting activists and candidates, and broadcasting support for positions taken by Socialist Campaign Group rebels against Starmer on social media. Meanwhile, Corbyn launched his own new formation – the Peace and Justice Project. This effort has not sought to contest elections and doesn't have a clear membership or democratic structure but hosts interesting discussions with international left forces.

3   Although Corbyn swept the board in the Constituency section of the NEC elections (taking all 7 out of 7 places for CLP representatives), he only narrowly controlled a majority on the NEC overall, making his control over the party far less comfortable than his dominant vote in the two leadership contests would suggest. While he could rely on Unite (under the leadership of Len McCluskey) and other smaller left unions and the broadly sympathetic leaderships of the party in Scotland and Wales, other

representatives included those from the PLP, sections representing youth/students, women and black members, and affiliated socialist societies (such as the Co-Op, the Socialist Health Association, the Labour Party Irish Society and more). The 'Democracy Review' launched under Corbyn, despite the best intentions of Katy Clark who oversaw the project, delivered very little in the terms of throughgoing democratization, partly out of deference to the unions who feared the dilution of their influence. Thus, the shift described in the attitudes of big affiliates such as the GMB and UNISON was sufficient to tilt the balance in Starmer's direction. They then used this narrow majority to consolidate their position, for instance by changing the electoral system for CLP representatives to the Single Transferable Vote (guaranteeing that the 'moderate' slate would gain representation), a move disingenuously sold as a 'inclusive' and 'unifying' rather than nakedly factional move. A blatant coup was carried out to dislodge Richard Leonard, the leftist leader of the party in Scotland. As thousands of left activists were purged or resigned from the party in disgust at the treatment of Corbyn and his supporters, the left on the NEC became ever more isolated.

4   Michael Crick, 'Did Labour Rig its Selection Votes?', *Unherd*, 29 November 2023, available at: www.unherd.com.

5   While the majority of trade unions in Britain have not historically been affiliated to any political party, the Labour party in Britain is, at least in part, the creation of those trade unions, which – together with socialist organizations – formed the Labour Representation Committee in 1900, leading to the election of the first Labour MPs. The three biggest unions (UNISON, Unite and GMB) continue to be affiliated, along with a number of smaller unions, and provide substantial (although proportionately declining) financial resources. Critically, their foundational status is reflected in the constitutional structures of the party, with affiliates representing 50 per cent of the electoral college at the party's Conference, the National Policy Forum and at the Clause V meetings which approve general election manifestos. They are also formally represented on the NEC.

6   With Labour now in office, Graham has seemed more comfortable in re-engaging at the political level from an oppositional perspective, leading the charge against the cuts to the Winter Fuel Payment which saw Starmer embarrassed by losing a vote at the 2024 Annual Conference.

7   The reforms to the party's rules introduced under the leadership of Ed Miliband, following a Special Conference called to endorse the recommendations of a review undertaken by Lord Ray Collins in 2014. The best account of how this ultimately enabled Corbyn's victory is: Alex Nunns, *The Candidate: Jeremy Corbyn's Improbable Path to Power*, London: OR Books, 2016.

8   Matthew Smith, 'Keir Starmer: What Do Britons Think of the Incoming Prime Minister', *YouGov*, July 2024, available at: www.yougov.co.uk.

9   Kiran Stacey, Aletha Adu and Ben Quinn, 'Labour Deeply Divided Over Starmer's Line on Israel-Hamas war', *The Guardian*, 20 October 2023

10   See: www.themuslimvote.co.uk. Other than Corbyn, the 'pro-Gaza' independents all voted against Labour's plan to levy Value Added Tax (VAT) on the fees charged by independent schools, historically seen as a source of social and educational privilege and a generator of inequality. This would appear to have been motivated by a concern to protect private Muslim faith schools from the tax.

11   Data from the National Union of Students, available at:
     www.nus.org.uk/highest-outstanding-student-debt-data.

12   Stuart Fox, 'Young People Led Surge for Smaller Parties but No Reform
     "Youthquake", Says UK Election Survey', *The Conversation*, 12 July 2024, available at:
     www.theconversation.com.

13   Parth Patel and Viktor Valgarðsson, 'Half of Us: Turnout Patterns at the 2024 General
     Election', Institute for Public Policy Research, July 2024, available at: www.ippr.org.

14   Pidcock lost her seat in the 2019 general election, was briefly elected as a member
     of the NEC before resigning that position in protest, and subsequently resigned her
     membership of the party. McDonald resigned from his position in Starmer's Shadow
     Cabinet at the 2021 Annual Conference, in protest at being told that Labour would
     not commit to raising the minimum wage to at least £15 per hour.

15   Figures from the Resolution Foundation, 'Almost Two-In-Five Large Families Are
     Now Affected by the Two-Child Limit – and the Majority Are Set To Fall Into
     Poverty When the Policy Is Fully Rolled Out', *Resolution Foundation*, 11 July 2024,
     available at: www.resolutionfoundation.org.

16   Daniela Gabor, 'Labour Is Putting Its Plans for Britain in the Hands of Private
     Finance. It Could End Badly', *The Guardian*, 2 July 2024.

17   Grace Blakeley, 'Building the Klarna Country', *Tribune Magazine,* 21 August 2024,
     available at: www.tribunemag.co.uk.

18   Rajeev Syal, 'Taxpayers To Foot £200bn Bill for PFI Contracts – Audit Office',
     The Guardian, 18 January 2018.

19   House of Commons Early Day Motion 150 (2013-14 session), available at: https://
     edm.parliament.uk/early-day-motion/45628/trident-replacement.

20   Andy Beckett, *The Searchers: Five Rebels, Their Dream of a Different Britain and Many
     Enemies*, London: Penguin, 2024.

21   Andy Beckett, 'Starmer Won by Shifting to the Right. But the Labour Left Doesn't
     Need To Spend These Years in the Wilderness', *The Guardian*, 6 July 2024.

22   Not only commentators like Owen Jones but also former Labour MPs including
     Laura Pidcock, Laura Smith, Emma Dent-Coad and Thelma Walker.

23   Jeremy Corbyn, 'People-Power Led To My Re-election. It Is the Start of a New
     Politics', *The Guardian*, 12 July 2024.

24   James Schneider, *Our Bloc: How We Win*, London: Verso, 2022.

25   See: 'Hillrise By-election Result', available at:
     www.islington.media/news/hillrise-by-election.

26   Owen Jones, 'The Left in France Has Beaten Back the Far Right. This Is How We
     Do the Same in the UK', *The Guardian*, 9 July 2024.

27   See, for example: The Right to Food campaign (www.ianbyrne.org/righttofood); the
     Food and Work Network, (www.fawn.org.uk); and renters' union Acorn
     (www.acorntheunion.org.uk).

28   For details of trade union initiatives for low carbon alternatives, see: Hilary
     Wainwright, 'Beating the Climate Clock', *Transnational Institute*, 21 February 2024,
     available at: www.tni.org.

29   Local examples include Norwich RMT's campaign on democratic public ownership.

30   The World Transformed is the exemplary case, but that has also spawned several local
     initiatives. The Lipman-Miliband Trust, whose mission is to fund socialist education,

has seen a significant rise in the demand for its resources and has initiated a network of organizations involved in radical education.

31 Ralph Miliband, *Parliamentary Socialism*, London: Merlin Press, 1972 [1964].

32 Benn, remarkably for a front bench politician, intervened to support the worker-led occupation of the Upper Clyde Shipyards in 1971 in protest at the planned closure of the site and resultant threat of widespread unemployment. See: John Foster and Charles Woolfson, *The Politics of the Upper Clyde Shipbuilders' Work-In: Class Alliances and the Right to Work*, Lawrence & Wishart Ltd, 1986

33 See, for example: 'Workers, Trade Unionists Mobilise to Block Arms Supply Sites in the UK', *MEMO*, 1 May 2024, available at: www.middleeastmonitor.com.

BARCELONA EN COMÚ: OPENINGS, CLOSURES AND A BITTERSWEET LEGACY

GREIG CHARNOCK, JOSE MANSILLA AND RAMON RIBERA-FUMAZ

In *Socialist Register 2018: Rethinking Democracy*, two of the present authors drew readers' attention to the unfolding political landscape within Barcelona – Spain's second city and capital of the autonomous community of Catalonia.[1] In the space of just a few years, we had witnessed the 'sudden' and 'remarkable' rise to power of the citizens' platform Barcelona en Comú (Barcelona in Common, or BeC). We devoted much of our discussion to outlining the radical intent and potential of the new city leadership that had campaigned in the 2015 municipal elections with the promise to 'win back Barcelona' for the 'common good'. We were not alone in our excitement. Some fellow leftist commentators hailed the city's new government as a 'beacon of resistance' against far-right forces, while others suggested that the new mayor, Ada Colau, could well be 'the world's most radical mayor'.[2]

Critical urban researchers have since put Barcelona at the vanguard of a 'new municipalist' network or complex of 'fearless cities' that had emerged to 'contest neoliberal conditions … in response to neoliberal austerity emanating in the urban heartlands of the global financial crisis'.[3] They have pointed to how BeC and other new municipalist governments might expand their citizens' capacity to engage in democratic self-management, even pointing to their predisposition to radicalism given their wish to pursue 'structural transformation from the root, rather than incremental reforms in accommodation with hegemony'.[4] Writing in 2018, and with our sense of optimism buoyed by the wave of victories by similar citizen's platforms across Spain in the 2015 elections, we similarly pondered as to whether BeC's ascendance would come 'to represent what Leo Panitch and Sam Gindin … posit[ed] as a constructive first step toward taking power at the sub-national scale in order to effect meaningful political and social change'.[5]

The occasion of the 2025 *Socialist Register* is an apt moment in which to take stock of BeC's record in office. As of 2023, Colau is no longer city mayor and BeC is now just one member of an ideologically inchoate ruling coalition formed principally on the premise of keeping the elected representatives of right-wing parties in opposition. It does appear that last year's elections in Spain marked the end of the new municipal experiments across the country that so excited many on the left after 2015. Is that it then? Is the experiment over?

As Laura Roth, Bertie Russell and Matthew Thompson rightly underline, it is always naïve to suppose that radical municipalist experiments will ever, in practice, be likely to realize their full potential as drivers of deep-rooted institutional and policy change at the local state level.[6] Rather, they need to be seen as what they are: instantiations of struggle against the prevailing order, as well as platforms through which a diverse – and therefore fragile and possibly transient – association of political and social movements can project a more positive, but still speculative, vision of possible urban society. As such, they will always be imperfect, limited and constrained by a plethora of systemic and conjunctural contexts and contingencies, perhaps even self-contradictory and therefore likely to leave a bittersweet legacy at best.

Yet, across Europe the far right continues its disconcerting trajectory at the ballot box while traditional centrist parties cling to neoliberal dogma, rejecting any prospect of redistribution and therefore perpetuating the very crisis of representation that feeds reactionary support for authoritarianism and fascism.[7] In this context, even the bittersweet legacies of imperfect experiments can lend sustenance to ongoing efforts on the left to realize a better, more inclusive, socialist future. With this in mind, we look back on BeC's eight years at the helm of Barcelona's city government – identifying the platform as both a product of, and a corrective to, deep-rooted crisis in Spain in general and Catalonia specifically, even if its chances of fully realizing its vision of the 'common good' were only ever slim.

A BROKEN SYSTEM

It is impossible to understand the context in which Colau and BeC assumed leadership of the municipal government of Barcelona without taking into account three intertwined crises: the fallout from the 2007–2008 global financial crisis and the imposition of austerity policies in Spain from 2011 onwards; the subsequent fragmentation of the Spanish party system that had emerged from the post-dictatorship Constitution of 1978; and, in more localized terms, the exhaustion and delegitimization of the once acclaimed

'Barcelona model' of urban governance and transformation. All three crises created the fertile terrain – if not the necessity – for new forces and forms of activism and protest to take root from 2011, epitomized by the 15-M Movement (the Indignados) against austerity, creating in turn the localized networks of political activism that would coalesce in the form of BeC a few years later.

There is, of course, an already voluminous literature on the global crisis in general, a crisis which went on to hit Spain especially badly.[8] The emergency stimulus plan for the national economy implemented by the nominally 'socialist' government of the Partido Socialista Obrero Español (PSOE) in response failed to provide any kind of protection from the decimation of jobs, the threat of foreclosures for hundreds of thousands of homeowners or the driving of the Spanish banking system to the precipice of complete collapse. The plan failed. The 2011 general election saw the centre right Partido Popular (PP) form a government that quickly turned to the so-called Troika (the International Monetary Fund, European Central Bank and European Commission) for further emergency assistance. Of course, the ensuing $100 billion rescue package came with strict conditionalities attached to it that required the Spanish state to adopt similarly austere policies of 'fiscal consolidation' and 'structural adjustment' to those that were being imposed upon other crisis-stricken populations within the Eurozone. The immediate effects of the crisis and these austerity cuts were devastating in terms of record high unemployment, mass housing evictions, depleted public services and elevated levels of poverty across Spain. Although experts would conclude that the Spanish economy had formally recovered from the crisis by 2014, studies of the longer-term impact upon the material and affective wellbeing of the population continued to emerge, causing shock and dismay in the decade that followed.[9]

Amid this period of crisis and austerity, much to the surprise of many commentators, tens of thousands of citizens across Spain took to the streets in May 2011 to protest, many under the slogan 'Real Democracy NOW!'. This demand signalled that the rage of the so-called indignados was not merely the product of short-term grievances about the mishandling of this specific crisis but was instead directed at a deeper rot within the Spanish political system and among the political class that had presided over Spain's governance since the end of the Franco dictatorship.[10] They were protesting the settlement reached with the 1978 Constitution that consolidated the essentially conservative two-party system, which time and again revealed itself to be well oiled by egregious practices of clientelism, bribery and corruption – not least during the post-2007 crisis.[11] Activists within the movement therefore looked to develop new practices and technologies of democratic governance that could potentially function in spite of conventional representative politics. In this context there emerged examples such as the Barcelona-based network that would develop the Decidim ('we decide') open-source online platform for citizens' input into strategic city planning and budgeting – a platform adopted by BeC and other progressive councils across Spain and Europe after 2016.[12] Unfortunately, however, the movement comprising the indignados and technopolitical activists of the left had a counterpart in the form of an increasingly emboldened reactionary right across Spain. The warning signs had been there since the murderous 2004 Madrid train bombings by Islamic extremists, when the incumbent PP government made attempts to attribute responsibility for the attack to Basque regional separatists. Despite the reactionary right's efforts, the PSOE would win that year's election and govern until 2011.

Yet, from 2004 onwards ultra-conservative and far-right sentiment among some quarters of the Spanish population began to gain traction, as revealed in subsequent anti-PSOE campaigns by right-wing groups on such issues as same-sex marriage and immigration. Meanwhile, in Catalonia, popular discontent with crisis, austerity and the post-1978 settlement translated into an upswell in support for independence from Spain after 2011 – a development that further ignited nationalist fervour among segments of the national population drawn to the reactionary right and its commitment to protecting the integrity of the Kingdom of Spain. The brewing discontent coming from all sides against austerity, the post-1978 political order and the Catalan independence question came to a head in the 2015 national elections, marking the end of the hitherto stable two-party system.[13] An increasing number of voters turned away from the PSOE and PP and supported new and disruptive entrants – initially, Podemos on the left and Ciudadanos of the conservative right.[14] By 2019, the far-right party Vox would win more than 10 percent of the national vote, further fragmenting an already weakened party system.[15] This fissuring in established systems of representation was also reflected in Spain's local elections of 2015 and 2019 – elections which twice carried BeC to office in Barcelona.

MEANWHILE, IN BARCELONA

While crisis and chaos ensued across Spain after 2007, Barcelona experienced its own share of political upheaval. The 2011 municipal elections put an end to over thirty years of government led by the regional branch of the PSOE, the Partit Socialista de Catalunya (PSC), in what was seen by many commentators as a popular plebiscite on the future of the 'Barcelona Model' of urban governance. For onlooking city authorities across the world in the 1990s, the Barcelona Model represented the epitome of determined municipal leadership that encapsulated the virtues of public-private, 'third way' strategic urban interventions. By adapting urban policy to the wider landscape of globalization, inter-urban competition and new-European left understandings of market-friendly growth, Barcelona's leaders were revered for an urbanism that supposedly put 'the citizen' front and centre of its post-industrial renewal.[16] But by 2011 this model was seen as being in need of reinvention amidst the collapse of the local economy and the corresponding reputational damage suffered by the PSC. For some critics, the Barcelona Model had represented an archetypally neoliberal, entrepreneurial project oriented towards the promotion of real estate development and the crass commercialization of the city – fuelling crisis dynamics and processes of gentrification.[17] Despite these criticisms, the 2011 election empowered a new city government, led this time by Xavier Trias of the Catalan nationalist party Convergència i Unió (CiU), to embark upon what would prove to be an even more pro-market and shamelessly entrepreneurial strategy aimed at promoting the 'Barcelona Brand' internationally, luring inflows of investment and tourism from abroad.[18]

From the get-go, the CiU dedicated itself to dismantling some of the already quite lax regulations of urban management introduced by the previous governments. These included the planning limitations pertaining to Ciutat Vella, Barcelona's central historic old town, and the prevailing restrictions (*els Plans d'Usos*) limiting the opening hours of establishments linked to the tourism sector, such as convenience stores and souvenir shops, which served a means of limiting disruption to local residents. In another move, some nine thousand new licenses were granted by the CiU government to allow rental apartments to be reallocated for short-stay tourism – in a city already suffering from inadequate housing supply. The CiU also approved a new terraces ordinance (*la ordenança municipal de terrasses*), making it easier for traders such as butchers and bakeries to set out store-front terraces if they could prove they had delicatessen services – a move that quickly amplified the encroachment on public sidewalks and squares by private businesses aiming to draw tourist business in already overcrowded hot spots within the city. Elsewhere in the sphere of urban planning, it relaxed the regulations on the kinds of companies that could operate in the city's main business district, creating the permissive conditions for the proliferation of hotels and short-term foreign student accommodation in the erstwhile largely residential district of San Martí, further compounding longer-standing and now mutually reinforcing problems of gentrification and 'touristification'.[19]

Meanwhile, the government pressed on with austerity cuts to public services as well as raising local taxes and selling off municipal assets at fire sale prices.[20] Dissent within the city persisted as squatters' movements, alternative civic and food distribution centres, and popular athenaeums proliferated throughout Barcelona's distressed neighbourhoods, while critics accused the Trias government of fomenting tensions between the police, activists and residents.[21]

CONJUNTURAL OPENINGS AND CLOSURES

By 2014, the Barcelona Model-cum-Brand appeared to epitomize what the critical geographer Jamie Peck has termed the 'late entrepreneurial' conjuncture in urban governance. Here, 'urban growth machines themselves do not appear to be anything like the locus of decisive strategic action they once were', having shifted 'quite decisively' to a next-stage form of 'austerity urbanism … marked by the effective exhaustion and practical stagnation of the staple (if not banal) repertoire of entrepreneurial-city interventions, culminating in a tangle of crisis-assisted movements in the direction of post-democratic, technocratic, and financialized modes of urban governance'.[22] With the classic entrepreneurial Barcelona Model of the 1990s and 2000s having been closely implicated with the crisis due to its reliance on real estate development and speculation, the Trias government's response was to double-down on a policy mix of austerity and the commercialization of the city, its public spaces and its neighbourhoods. Popular dissent in Barcelona therefore not only reflected the more general sense of indignation across Spain against austerity, joblessness, the housing crisis and the illegitimacy of the political class, it was also directed against the grotesque effects of late entrepreneurial governance upon citizens' everyday lives. A tipping point came in August 2014, when, in what became known as 'the explosion' (*l'esclat de la Barceloneta*), hundreds of beleaguered locals from the central-seafront La Barceloneta neighbourhood mobilized to protest the antisocial impact of low-cost, short-stay tourism after three inebriated Italian youths paraded naked through the streets and into convenience stores in the middle of the day.[23] While it would be an overstretch to say this protest changed everything, it certainly signalled to many that Barcelona was in need of radical change.

The networks of progressive activism that had been consolidated during the national protests of 2011 continued to flourish during the Trias years. In the context outlined above, various social, political, cultural, environmental and urban movements or 'waves' (*las mareas*) converged in dialogue with one another, resulting in the formation of the radical citizens' platform Guanyem

Barcelona in 2014, later renamed BeC. In its foundational manifesto, BeC announced that 'the economic powers have launched an offensive against the rights and social achievements of the majority of the population ... the time has come to take back the institutions and put them at the service of the majority and of the common good'.[24] In the momentous 2015 municipal elections, BeC won 11 from a total of 41 council seats up for election and over 70 thousand more popular votes than Trias and CiU. Ada Colau was elected city mayor with the support of the other sitting parties of the Left: PSC, Esquerra Republicana de Catalunya (ERC – the social-democratic pro-independence party) and la Candidatura de Unidad Popular (an anti-capitalist, pro-independence party). BeC's moment had come.

This moment nevertheless placed constraints on the next four years of office, since, firstly, BeC learned the hard way that just as the sudden fracturing of a party system can present opportunities for new entrants, it can also limit the potential for them to govern with autonomy if they attain office. In May 2016, BeC found itself in need of coalition partners within the city council to command a legislative majority. With relations between BeC and the pro-independence parties of the Left complicated by the latter's strategizing to secure a secessionist coalition including the CiU within the regional parliament, the Generalitat de Catalunya, BeC had little option but to ally itself with the PSC within the city council.[25] As explained below, this fragile coalition would last less than two years. Even so, it would again need to be renewed on pragmatic grounds after the 2019 municipal elections when BeC ceded ground to ERC. After that election, Colau's reinstatement as mayor depended upon a bloc vote comprising councillors of the right-wing PP and Ciudadanos who effectively used her and BeC to scupper the installation of the pro-independence Ernest Maragall of the ERC as mayor. Looking back at these conjunctures, the potential for BeC to secure stable, long-term governing capacity – so-called regime incumbency – in the context of a fractured society and political system was always going to be stymied, as it was for several of the other new municipalist governments that assumed power in Spain in 2015.[26]

The composition of BeC itself also meant that its leadership had to strike a careful and precarious balance between internal cohesion, on the one hand, and strategy in the service of its radical agenda going forward. Many activists and politicians within BeC were not new to politics. Some had served in previous city councils in coalition with PSC, while others had years of experience of urban social movement activism and protesting the city council and the Barcelona Model. These came together with a diversity of only recently politicized groups emerging out of the 15-M protests, ranging from housing activists (like Colau herself) to coders and hackers obsessed with technology and the democratic promise of open-source internet platforms. Activists from avowedly anti-capitalist movements such as Procés Constituent found themselves within a broad BeC association containing members of Podemos – a party that had openly declared itself to be 'neither left nor right'.[27] The list of councillors chosen as candidates in the municipal elections of 2015 reflected this heterogeneity, as did the 11 candidates elected to office. A crucial constituent partner in all of this was the Iniciativa per Catalunya Verds (ICV) – a descendent of the historical Catalan party of communists (Partit Socialista Unificat de Catalunya). The ICV had, since the revolts across Central and Eastern Europe in 1989 against the Soviet bloc, drifted toward eco-socialism and away from orthodox Marxist-Leninist politics. Members of the ICV were crucial to the founding, organization and programmatic development of BeC. In return, ICV representatives were granted positions three and five on the BeC proportional representation list during the 2015 primaries. But they had also spent the preceding three decades in PSC-led governing coalitions, becoming tainted in the eyes of some commentators and voters by association with the entrepreneurial urbanism of the 1990s and 2000s – precisely the model other constituent elements within the BeC movement were so intent upon transforming.

The heterogenous and precarious internal composition of BeC therefore also explains a second characteristic of its tenure in office – namely its uneasy partnership with PSC. The alliance had its practical benefits, considering that BeC was to oversee a large city bureaucratic apparatus with one of the largest municipal budgets in the country. But the entrenched political differences between the PSC and various other constituent groups within BeC proved difficult to manage – not least because of the PSC's chequered history of urban entrepreneurial governance and its complicity in the forms of real estate development and speculation that proved so damaging when the global financial crisis hit Spain. To this was added the dissonance between BeC's ambivalent stance on the 2017 Catalan independence referendum, on the one hand, and the PSC's firm alignment with the right-wing PP national government's insistence upon the illegality of the vote. This episode put an end to the first BeC-PSC alliance, as we alluded to above. A second governing coalition between the two parties after the 2019 elections also ended with predictable acrimony in 2023. PSC councillors had voted against some of the more radical proposals tabled by BeC during this second term, while pursuing its own characteristically entrepreneurial agenda in those council departments in which its own members held the brief. Eventually, four months before the 2023 local elections, PSC's Jaume Collboni resigned his position as deputy mayor to begin his own campaign for the top office in earnest, promising to overturn many of the policies enacted by the BeC-led council.[28]

Other constraints on BeC's ability to pursue a radical agenda proved to be even further beyond its leadership's control – importantly, those attributable to the multi-scalar institutional design of the Spanish national state. While a range of policy areas – including fiscal policy, funding and housing governance – fall within the remit of the national government based in Madrid, the regional governments of the autonomous communities such as Catalonia can legislate in other areas including welfare services. Meanwhile, the regions are themselves composed of provinces which attend to such matters as the promotion of territorial economic development and cultural policy, but which are, in turn, comprised of municipal or city councils with their own autonomy over such policy areas as local urban planning. This multi-scalar framework of potentially incongruous policymaking powers and agendas was always going to make progress toward the resolution of Barcelona's housing crisis – the keystone of BeC's radical agenda and Colau's own personal motive for entering politics – arduous to say the least.[29] A BeC-led city council was never going to enjoy the policy space enjoyed by Berlin city officials, for instance, in their recent pursuit of a policy to expropriate corporate housing landlords.[30] This is for two main reasons: first because of the relatively low degree of policy autonomy and resources afforded to a city council under the Spanish constitution, compared to those of a city-state such as Berlin; and, second, because of the greater number of smaller private landlords in operation in Barcelona compared to a city like Berlin, whose 2023 court ruling to deal with misappropriated housing was targeted at large corporate landlords with more than 3,000 properties. Moreover, in some areas, such as tourism, policy agendas at different levels of government have even directly contradicted themselves – with Barcelona city council looking to stem the inflow of short-stay arrivals to the city and the Generalitat promoting the exact opposite outcome.

Meanwhile, BeC found itself mired in a contentious political battle over Catalan independence waged within and between the regional and national scales of government, despite the question of secession being of lesser importance to addressing a crisis of social reproduction for many of its constitutive members. The stakes of the conflict rose in 2017 after an illegal referendum went ahead in Catalonia, to be then followed by the incarceration or entry into exile of its principal organizers. Yet the BeC leadership's own apparent ambivalence on the issue undermined one of its own bases for support among leftists with sympathy for the independence cause.[31] The final external constraint on BeC's capacity to mobilize support for a radical agenda within and beyond a second term came with the global coronavirus pandemic. Any remaining energy among even BeC's most loyal supporters was sapped by the sudden imposition of a national state of emergency in March 2020, followed by a ban on all non-essential activity that confined the city's population to its homes for extended periods. The referendum and the pandemic resulted in palpable fatigue among the political left in Barcelona, and a loss of momentum in electoral terms. This, together with the straightforward result of pursuing divisive policies such as the superblocks (*les superilles*), diminished Colau's chances of retaining office while boosting electoral support for the right. Championed by many as a world-leading innovation in 'tactical urbanism', the superblocks are car-free zones created at the intersections of streets across Barcelona since 2016. They have, however, proven unpopular with car owning local residents as well as local businesses that have blamed them for a decline in footfall, while critics on the left have questioned their role as drivers of 'green gentrification' in working-class neighbourhoods.

Ultimately, while BeC only suffered a marginal loss of support in the popular vote in the 2023 elections, losing just one seat, CiU, PP and Vox all picked up more council seats than in 2019. In June 2023, Collboni was appointed the new mayor of Barcelona after the PSC formed a coalition as majority partner with BeC and the PP – the rationale for the unlikely alliance being to prevent the reinstatement of Trias as mayor eight years after his ousting.

A BITTERSWEET LEGACY ...

If we are to view new municipalist platforms and governments in terms of imperfect, inevitably constrained vehicles for struggle toward the advancement of radical urban transformation, then we ought to recall what progress BeC did achieve while in office these last eight years – however bittersweet the experience. There are indeed substantive and, one would hope, enduring advancements of note. First, under BeC the city council approved the pioneering and holistic Special Tourist Accommodation Plan, which restricted short stay rentals and placed controls on 'sharing' platforms such as Airbnb, as well as identifying areas of the city in which numbers of rental units for this purpose would be downsized.[32] As testament to BeC's determination to dislodge the city's development from its late entrepreneurial trajectory, the policy was introduced in 2017, much earlier than the now-acclaimed and perhaps better-known legislation to regulate internet platform-mediated tourist accommodation in New York City, for instance.[33] This policy intersected in important ways with a further advancement made by BeC – namely, an integrated attack on the housing crisis in Barcelona. This took the form of a battery of measures including regulations to prevent landlords from withholding vacant housing from the market in anticipation of rising future rents, an increase in the supply of social and affordable housing, the compulsory purchase of units susceptible to falling into the hands of investment funds, the creation of an anti-evictions unit, and a new observatory dedicated to monitoring the state of housing provision and quality.[34]Although the housing crisis has not been completely resolved, these measures have proven effective in ameliorating its depth– and the results of Barcelona's handling of the crisis compares favourably with other, less interventionist cities across Spain since the mid-2010s. Third, under BeC's auspices, the city council significantly increased the budget for social services at a time of continued austerity across the rest of Spain. In all these cases, BeC managed to either secure the support and consent of the more conservative elements of Barcelona's middle class and their political representatives, or else it was able to mobilize sufficient support among urban social and working-class movements to be able to counter any effective opposition.

Barcelona's new municipal government of 2015–2023 therefore did indeed make a positive difference. BeC has perhaps had its moment, but the struggle to win back the city for the common good continues. Many of the urban social, feminist, ecological and working-class movements that came together to fight the 2015 election remain politically active. Back in 2015, Jaume Asens – one of the founders of BeC – remarked that the platform would need to keep 'one foot in the institutions and one hundred feet in the streets'.[35] Currently, however, there is something of a rift between BeC and the city's social movements. Many of BeCs original leaders and principal organizers have left public policy or even activism altogether, and others have moved on to different issues or localities. Meanwhile, those that remain face the hard task of restoring the trust lost among some former supporters who feel let down by BeC's apparent transformation from a movement of movements into a formal party organization.[36] Still, the situation in Barcelona is better than in other Spanish cities in which new municipalist governments came to office in 2015, such as Zaragoza, Cadiz or Madrid. In Madrid, for instance, there presently appears to be much less of a basis for an effective political alliance between the actors than constituted the BeC-inspired Ahora Madrid electoral platform and the leaderships of the capital city's main political parties of the left, such as Podemos and Más Madrid. In Barcelona, at least, BeC continues to function as the city's main effective opposition party of the left within the city council. Given the right conjuncture and the political will to seize the opportunity, maybe we will see a radical municipal government again in Barcelona. Let us hope it is sooner rather than later.

NOTES

1   Greig Charnock and Ramon Ribera-Fumaz, 'Barcelona en Comú: Urban Democracy and the Common Good', in Leo Panitch and Greg Albo, eds, *Socialist Register 2018: Rethinking Democracy*, London: Merlin Press, 2017, pp. 188-201.

2   Raffaele Bazurli and Pablo Castaño Tierno, 'Barcelona, a Beacon by the Sea', *Jacobin*, 7 September 2018, available at: www.jacobin.com; Dan Hancock, 'Is This the World's Most Radical Mayor?, *The Guardian*, 26 May 2016.

3   Matthew Thompson, 'What's so new about New Municipalism?, *Progress in Human Geography*, 45(2), 2021, p. 320.

4   Iolanda Bianchi, 'The democratising capacity of new municipalism: beyond direct democracy in public-common partnerships', *Policy & Politics*, published online ahead of print, 2024; Laura Roth, Bertie Russell and Matthew Thompson, 'Politicising proximity: Radical municipalism as a strategy in crisis', *Urban Studies*, 60(1), 2023, pp. 2009-35.

5   Charnock and Ribera-Fumaz, 'Barcelona en Comú', p. 190.

6   Roth, Russell and Thompson, 'Politicizing proximity', p. 2017.

7   Ingar Solty, 'Market Polarization Means Political Polarization: Liberal Democracy's Eroding Centre', in Greg Albo, Leo Panitch and Colin Leys, eds, *Socialist Register 2022: New Polarizations, Old Contradictions. The Crisis of Centrism*, London: Merlin Press, 2021, pp. 53-71.

8   Greig Charnock, Thomas Purcell and Ramon Ribera-Fumaz, *The Limits to Capital in Spain: Crisis and Revolt in the European South*, Basingstoke: Palgrave Macmillan, 2014.

9   See, for example: Samuel Bentolila et al, 'Lost in recessions: youth employment and earnings in Spain', *SERIEs* 13, 2022, pp. 11-49; Hadas Weiss, 'Elusive adulthood and surplus lifetime in Spain', *Critique of Anthropology*, 41(2), 2021, pp. 149-64.

10 Greig Charnock, Thomas Purcell and Ramon Ribera-Fumaz, '*Indígnate!* The 2011 popular protests and limits to democracy in Spain', *Capital & Class*, 36(1), 2012, pp. 3-11.

11 See: Javier Moreno Zacarés, 'The Iron Triangle of Urban Entrepreneurialism: The Political Economy of Urban Corruption in Spain', *Antipode*, 52(5), 2020, pp. 1351-72.

12 Paolo Cardullo, Ramon Ribera-Fumaz and Paco González Gil, 'The Decidim "soft infrastructure": democratic platforms and technological autonomy in Barcelona', *Computational Culture*, 9, 2023, available at: www.computationalculture.net.

13 Thomas Jeffrey Miley, 'Austerity politics and constitutional crisis in Spain', *European Politics and Society*, 18(2), 2017, pp. 263-83.

14 Lluis Orriols and Guillermo Cordero, 'The Breakdown of the Spanish Two-Party System: The Upsurge of Podemos and Ciudadanos in the 2015 General Election', *South European Society and Politics*, 21(4), 2016, pp. 469-92; Guillem Vidal and Irene Sánchez-Vítores, 'Spain – Out with the Old: The Restructuring of Spanish Politics',

in Swen Hutter and Hanspeter Kriesi, eds, *European Party Politics in Times of Crisis*, Cambridge: Cambridge University Press, 2019, pp. 75-94.

15   Stuart J. Turnbull-Dugarte, Jose Rama and Andres Santana, 'The Baskerville's dog suddenly started barking: voting for VOX in the 2019 Spanish general elections', *Political Research Exchange*, 2(1), 2020.

16   Spurred on by the city's hosting of the 1992 Olympic Games, Barcelona's regeneration from the late 1980s was widely celebrated as having produced an exemplary urban form. This culminated in the accolade of being the first city, rather than practitioner, ever to be awarded the prestigious Gold Medal of the Royal Institute of British Architects in 1999.

17   Manuel Delgado, *La ciudad mentirosa. Fraude y miseria del Modelo Barcelona*, Barcelona: La Catarata, 2007; Greig Charnock, Thomas Purcell and Ramon Ribera-Fumaz, 'City of Rents: The Limits to the Barcelona Model of Urban Competitiveness', *International Journal of Urban and Regional Research*, 38(1), 2014, pp. 198-217.

18   Jose Mansilla, *Los años de la discordia. Del modelo a la marca Barcelona*, Barcelona: Apostroph, 2023.

19   Jose A. Mansilla and Claudio Milano, 'Becoming centre: tourism placemaking and space production in two neighborhoods in Barcelona', *Tourism Geographies*, 24(4-5), 2022, pp. 599-620; Agustín Cocola-Gant, 'Place-based displacement: Touristification and neighborhood change', *Geoforum*, 138, 2023.

20   Jonathan S. Davies and Ismael Blanco, 'Austerity urbanism: Patterns of neo-liberalisation and resistance in six cities of Spain and the UK', *Environment and Planning A*, 49(7), 2017, p. 1523.

21   Stefania Gozzer, 'Cuarto noche de disturbios en Barcelona por el desalojo de Can Vies', *El País*, 30 May 2014.

22   Jamie Peck, 'Transatlantic city, part I: Conjunctural urbanism', *Urban Studies*, 54(1), 2017, p. 21; Jamie Peck, 'Transatlantic city, part 2: Late entrepreneurialism', *Urban Studies*, 54(2), 2017, p. 330.

23   See: Melissa Garcia Lamarca, 'La Barceloneta's Struggle Against (Environmental) Gentrification', *Green Inequalities* blog, 23 November 2017, available at: www.bcnuej.org.

24   Guanyem Barcelona, 'Manifesto: Let's Win Back Barcelona', 2014.

25   Clara Blanchar, 'La entrada en el Gobierno del PSC da aire a Colau', *El País*, 10 May 2016.

26   Adrian Bua and Jonathan S. Davies, 'Understanding the crisis of New Municipalism in Spain: The struggle for urban regime power in A Coruña and Santiago de Compostela', *Urban Studies*, 60(11), 2022, pp. 2054-72.

27   Francisco Medina, '"Ni de izquierda ni de derechas", una proclama de Pablo Iglesias que trae incómodos ecos', *El Plural*, 21 October 2014.

28   Toni Sust, 'Collboni comunicó por WhatsApp a Colau que abondona el gobierno de Barcelona', *el Periódico*, 23 January 2023.

29   Charnock and Ribera-Fumaz, 'Barcelona en Comú', pp. 191-94.

30   Peter Matthews, '"We're closer than ever" What next for Berlin's housing referendum?', *The Berliner*, 8 September 2023, available at: www.the-berliner.com.

31   Colau famously described her own position on the independence question as '*equidistante*'.

32 Barcelona.cat, 'Pla Especial Urbanísticd'AllojamentsTuristics', Barcelona: Ajuntament de Barcelona, 2017.

33 Amanda Hoover, 'The End of Airbnb in New York', *Wired*, 5 September 2023, available at: www.wired.com.

34 Ajuntament de Barcelona i Barcelona Regional, *Habitatge Barcelona: Barcelona 2015-2023*, Barcelona: Ajuntament de Barcelona.

35 InfoZazpi Irratia, 'Jaume Asens (Barcelona en Comú): Tendremos un pie en las instituciones y cien en las calles', *InfoZazpi Irratia*, 21 May 2015, available at: http://info.info7.eus/.

36 Jordi Mir, '10 años de Barcelona en Comú', *El País*, 25 June 2024, available at: https://elpais.com.

EUROPEAN INTEGRATION
AND STRATEGY FOR THE LEFT:
PORTUGAL AS A CAUTIONARY TALE

CATARINA PRÍNCIPE

Capitalism has not escaped the state but rather [...] the state has, as always, been a fundamental constitutive element in the very process of extension of capitalism in our time. Leo Panitch[1]

The outcome of the Global Financial Crisis of 2007-8 revealed and accentuated a pattern that was until that moment only debated in academic or restricted political circles: the European Union was not a project of or for the peoples of Europe, but a neoliberal project of and for the European elites. The way in which this became evident was the treatment given by the international institutions such as the European Commission, the European Central Bank, and the International Monetary Fund to the peripheral countries such as Portugal and Greece: heavily indebted, these countries were forced into repayment by engaging in draconian austerity measures that led to skyrocketing unemployment, poverty, and emigration.

The response to this implementation of the "shock doctrine", imposed by parties of both centre left and centre right – and even by technocratic governments such as in Italy – was primarily felt on the streets: the big occupations of Syntagma square in Athens and in Puerta del Sol in Madrid or the massive demonstrations in Portugal were centrally about austerity and employment and regarded with some degree of condescension by the respective governments. But when a left-wing party won the elections on an anti-austerity and EU-critical program in 2015 in Greece, the condescension disappeared: especially for the peripheral European countries, the possibility of negotiating labour and welfare reforms was impossible within the confines of the EU, in general, and the eurozone, in particular. But so was leaving the eurozone project altogether: the threats of profound impoverishment, sanctions, and blockades from the side of the European elites showed that these countries are locked in a situation of dependence on the European core.

This moment sparked vibrant debates in political as well as in academic circles. Within left-leaning political circles, the debate circled around whether to leave the eurozone and even the EU or to reform them. The two main tendencies were based on fundamentally different understandings of the EU project: for the remain and reform line, the European Union retains an original progressive and anti-nationalist character that can be preserved if its institutions are reformed in a sort of federalist way; for defenders of leaving, the eurozone and the European Union are designed to be undemocratic and, therefore, there is no possibility or capacity to transform them.

In academic circles, the debate was centred around the origins of the Eurozone crisis. This was not so much about the 'nature' of the EU, but mainly about what went wrong after the Global Financial Crisis (or as an outcome of it). In this sense, most contributions start by identifying the crisis as a crisis of the Eurozone. For most of the (self-described) post-Keynesians who dominated the academic space (with very few exceptions), it is not the architecture of the European Union that is wrong but the architecture of the single currency – and therefore they start their analysis in the 1990s.

The fundamental problem that must be addressed is what is it about the European Union project that makes it so hard for states – namely peripheral ones – to *both* thrive and leave? Is there something essentially biased in the design of the European project that enforces undemocratic decision-making and unequal economic stature? And, if so, how did this come about? Addressing these questions is critical for considering the central strategic dilemmas for the left in this interregnum. Can the left navigate the European conundrum without losing sight of its limitations and, if so, how? What is it about the EU that makes it so difficult for the left to develop a coherent strategy? Are there spaces of manoeuvre for the left in central or peripheral countries?

The EU holds a double nature, meaning that it is both a transnational project that aims at competing for surplus value in neo-imperial forms with the US and China and a space where national capitals compete for internal market shares. This double nature leads to uneven and combined dynamics that create core-periphery imbalances. This means that the left, if it is to develop a coherent strategy on how to deal with European integration, must tackle different levels and levers simultaneously to capture the full scope of political and economic state transformation: the tensions between classes in the determination of a specific state form, together with the tensions within capitalist classes themselves, in addition to the tensions involved in the constitution of a transnational European space *through* the creation of uneven and combined economic profiles. What I call this *double dynamic* of European integration demands a *double strategic dynamic* for the left.

The Portuguese left is an excellent illustration of what is entailed by this task. Or, better said, it is a cautionary tale. The strategic decisions of the Portuguese left towards austerity and the European Union, and how they concretely played out in the realm of national politics, are a very useful case study of what it means for the left to deal with a progressively hollowed-out state in the European periphery. As the experience of Portugal demonstrates, neither level can be looked at separately: an autonomous, left-wing project is impossible to be implemented nationally without breaking the shackles of the European diktats and, therefore, reclaiming a state form that rebuilds the state-society nexus.

THE POLITICAL ECONOMY OF EUROPEAN INTEGRATION: A BRIEF OVERVIEW[2]

The European Union as a project is not written in stone but has evolved through time in response to specific economic and political moments in contemporary history. The postwar moment asked for a particular set of institutional structures that were translated into, firstly, the European Coal and Steel Community and later, through the Treaty of Rome in 1957, into the European Economic Community. This process of international integration is generally justified as an attempt to prevent further wars between European states – and it can be so read if we are to understand economic integration as a path of interdependence between national states and capitalist economies that, due to the logic of integration, changes modes of competitiveness. However, the process of European integration is more than a political project towards capitalist peace. It is an attempt to reorganize the dynamic of capital accumulation.

The post-war Keynesian moment can be broadly described by high growth rates and rising wages. The social contract between labour and capital implied a mixed economy where private property was not at risk within its boundaries, but the state was a central actor in guaranteeing high employment rates and a functional welfare system through a degree of economic planning and public ownership.

However, the dynamic of international economic integration and the growing presence of American capital throughout the world would, in the context of increasing inflationary pressures, challenge the competitiveness of European nation-states and economies. The solution was to abolish customs tariffs between European states so as to hinder the search for non-European goods.

But the postwar Keynesian moment would not last long and its crisis would slowly develop at the national level. The notion of eternal growth and social compromise between capital and labour was already unravelling in the late sixties. We must, then, consider the Keynesian years as a specific political and economic temporality relatively favourable to labour (rising real wages) that squeezed profit margins over time. The attempt to protect and reassert profit margins meant larger social conflict, feeding inflationary policies. Thus, the economic crises of the seventies and eighties must be seen as continuation of already-existing tensions – and not solely as a cause for what was to come next.

The next steps in deepening integration were the approval of the European Monetary System in 1979 and the Single European Act in 1985, which paved the way for a further process of liberalization and subjecting former state monopolies to competition. Their successes reflected the ongoing changes within nation-states at a time of profound public sector reforms that were not possible within the former post-war consensus. The Maastricht Treaty in 1992, beyond establishing European citizenship (in the sense of free movement of people), fully adopted the European Single Market and paved the way for the Economic and Monetary Union (EMU), including the introduction of the euro as a central device to promote price stability and fixed exchange rates. The expectation was that to achieve currency stability, competitiveness would be augmented through private-sector adjustments and not through possible devaluations of national currencies. These steps changed the previous capital-labour nexus in favour of capital, which profoundly altered state functions. This took place through the creation of what Christopher Bickerton calls the 'member-state' – a state institutional form that *self-imposes external constraints* to break with the previous state-society nexus of social-democratic legitimation in order to try to accelerate the rate of capital accumulation.[3]

Nonetheless, the nation-states that entered the process of European integration and, therefore, of member-statehood, were not equal in terms of economic specialization, productive capacities, technological development or even longevity of their democracies and state structures. This diversity was even more strongly felt with the expansion of European membership to states in the southern and eastern peripheries. Integration has produced divergent paths for different countries that, despite the shared form of member statehood, have become locked into different possibilities of economic development and political capability.

What these dynamics have led to is a matter of debate: from theoretical proposals that focus on the creation of a transnational capitalist class through the growing transnationalization of capital,[4] to contributions that frame the relations between national and supranational structures as dynamic and multidirectional,[5] to a focus on the preponderance of Germany (and, to a lesser degree, France) in the decision-making processes of integration,[6] to the analysis of core-periphery dynamics within the EU through the entrenchment of the semi-peripheries.[7] Clearly, institutional harmonization is far from given in the process of European integration. Rather, 'uneven development ... is the hallmark of geographical space' within the EU, 'locking states such as Greece and Portugal into a subordinate position within Global Value Chains'.[8] In this regard, it is necessary to analyze the overarching tendencies with the necessary caution to understand differences within them.

EUROPEAN INTEGRATION AS STATE TRANSFORMATION

European integration is a process of state transformation and not something that occurs beyond or despite the state. The transformations in a growing globalized economy opened the political space for a specific dynamic of regional integration in the form of the EEC/EU to try to accommodate the necessities of capital accumulation within a particular historical context. Moreover, because the state's configuration is always an ongoing crystallisation of a given relation of forces between capital and labour, the state has to assure the protection of private property through legal contracts, guarantee an available workforce and legitimate the capitalist system. As a result, diverse class and social compromises have shaped different states in different historical moments. Because of this, integration is not something that happens beyond or despite the state; rather 'integration refers to the geographical spread of state functions in response to the exigencies of capital accumulation and the realization of surplus-value, on the one hand, and their associated legitimation problems, on the other'.[9]

However, the creation of new layers of state power through deterritorialization and reterritorialization as means to overcome obstacles embedded in nation-states by the configuration of previous class relations did not prompt the creation of a European statehood. The process of regulation promoted strategies within states that gradually excluded labour from decision making and public governance, thereby minimizing the possibilities for democratic engagement nation-states still (partially) retain. Thus, as Christopher Bickerton has suggested, 'the development of coordinated macro-economic policymaking at the European level, which today encompasses most aspects of economic policy including micro-economic supply-side reforms, has been driven by the transformation of the state in Europe'.[10]

Bickerton's central argument is that 'European integration corresponds to the shift from one state form – the *nation-state* – to another, the *member state*'.[11] The social contract between labour and capital of the postwar era gave rise to a specific kind of state, the *national corporatist state*, which was characterized by 'the defence of private ownership as a condition for continued investment by business in production and the focus on full employment as the key commitment of governments of all political stripes'.[12] Together with this commitment arose a strong welfare regime that provided unemployment benefits, pensions, housing and health care. This not only changed the paradigm of nation-states – which had formerly competed for territory as their main source of wealth creation and accumulation, and had as their sole functions the guarantee of peace and order – but also crystallized a specific relation of forces between labour and capital that promoted a form of state that not only aimed to achieve peace by economic and political integration and interdependence, but also to guarantee its citizens' wellbeing. It also meant the beginning of the 'end of ideology',[13] since the class compromise valorized centrist politics that, over time, could not be substantively differentiated from one another, as well as an erosion of 'the extremes' that could threaten this political balance. In time, labour became progressively entrenched in this dynamic, and its organization grew weaker. However, many of the state's functions remained mainly national – characteristic of the first phase of European integration.

The economic crisis of the seventies and eighties, together with the shift in the balance of forces between capital and labour in favour of capital and the political and social unrest that this tension created, gave rise to the second phase of European integration, which is defined by a different state form: the *member state*. Member statehood is marked by a break in the state-society nexus, as the dismantlement of the Keynesian framework has meant that national executives can no longer even pretend to represent national communities, but rather exercise power and build legitimation through participation in supranational structures. To become more resilient to political turmoil, governments bind themselves to a growing body of rules created by governments themselves, but at the EU level.

In sum, 'the aim is to liberate national governments from the stranglehold of organized labour'.[14] States are becoming 'hard but hollow' entities, in the words of Vincent della Sala. They are becoming harder as 'state structures … are less permeable to penetration and demands from civil society'. Meanwhile, 'a "hollowed out" state becomes a less likely target for societal interests as state authority is displaced'.[15] Or, as Perry Anderson put it, 'economically speaking, the Union remains, with its dense web of directives, and often dubious prebends, far from a perfect Hayekian order. But in its political distance from the populations over which it presides, it approaches the ideal he projected.'[16] The shifts from the national to the EU level are in fact not about the incapacity of nation-states to control internationalized capital, but the reverse: 'the upward shift has been impelled by capital's insufficient ability to control nation states from the national level. Thus, paradoxically, the European level of governance facilitates the formation of neoliberal national policies and class relations.'[17]

Nevertheless, this dynamic is paradoxical, because on the one hand states enjoy more autonomy concerning their societies, while on the other hand, they lose the historical, cultural, and political features that traditionally defined and located their action. As Bickerton notes, 'the paradox of member statehood is thus the way in which political power is exercised by national governments but in ways that appear external to and far removed from the national societies over whom these governments rule'.[18] For him, this is the origin of the democratic representation crisis lived in the European Union today.

In this sense, European integration did not bypass states, since it is centrally about their transformation; nor did it rescue states in a traditional form, since their democratic basis is being increasingly shattered.[19] And if the process of European integration is a *de facto* process of state transformation, it then allows for the questioning of whether all states – in their relative position towards one another – transformed with the same scope.

UNEVEN AND COMBINED

In a 1974 article entitled *Internationalisation of Capitalist Relations and the Nation-State,* Nicos Poulantzas debated with Ernest Mandel about the level and degree of the presence of American capital in Europe, and what that would mean both for the redesign of the capitalist class and for left strategies concerning this new moment of imperialism.[20] Contrary to Mandel's expectation that the growing presence of American capital would create – due to the pressure of competition – a European capital (to which a transnational capitalist class would correspond), prompting the establishment of a European historical bloc, Poulantzas argued that this imperialist stage no longer related to merely a dynamic of competition between centre and periphery, but consisted of a process of interpenetration and interdependence of capitals of both core and periphery.[21]

Critically, Poulantzas argued that the capitalist mode of production does not simply dominate social formations externally, but forces the reproduction of dominant logics within them.[22] Consequently, the internationalization of capitalist relations internationalizes the state – and this *internationalization occurs through internalization*.

However, he did not believe that this will bring about supranational state forms, since the reproduction of capital in its contemporary imperialist form still requires states to organize the mode of production.[23] Thus as Costas Lapavitsas has observed, 'EU member states are also capitalist states, and class relations are fundamental to their make-up as well as to their interactions. ... Class relations mark the interactions of each member state with the union but also among member states, determining the interests that are to be defended and promoted.'

Although Poulantzas was specifically writing about what the presence of American capital would produce through a world-scale imperialist dynamic (and particularly in relation to European states), I would argue that similar tendencies can be seen in core-periphery dynamics within the European realm itself. For peripheral countries such as Portugal, Spain and Greece, becoming an EU member led to partial deindustrialization and economic dependence on the core countries. Joining the eurozone further consolidated the weakness of the productive sectors of these countries by undermining their competitiveness.[24] The re-regulation of the financial sector in Germany, while limited, was achieved by German financial business becoming very closely involved with highly financialized and de-industrialized economies in the periphery through investment and the provision of credit.

The main difficulty of addressing the problems of the European Union is that it is at one and the same time a transnational project aiming at competing in the world market with the US over the extraction of surplus value from the 'third world' (even if some have shown that this process accentuated the perpetration of American capital and American dependency in Europe) and lately, with China; it thus prompts a dynamic that constitutes a proto-form of a transnational capitalist class without its correspondent socio-political bloc, (as in the example of the European RoundTable for Industry); and simultaneously, it is a space where national economies compete with one another for market shares and adjust their economic specialization to the demands of the most economically and politically powerful countries, establishing a German ordo-liberal order upon all member states.[25] It is thus important to point out that different states have very different capacities in negotiating the conditions for their accension.[26] Moreover, economic specialization as a central means for integration implies that different countries occupy different positions within the EU's hierarchy – which in turn means that their capacity to assert their interests in the body of European legislation differs widely.[27] Furthermore, the importance of the public sector or the welfare state diverges across the particular histories of different member states. For the southern periphery, European integration was the result of the end of long-lasting authoritarian regimes, where the popular understanding of the role of the state in both the economy and public provision was different from many of their counterparts in Europe. It could even be said that these states 'skipped' the first phase of European integration and went directly into the second, but with a specific historical reference to what state functions were supposed to be.

More contemporary examples of this differentiation are the memoranda that Greece and Portugal were subjected to as a response to the financial crisis of 2007–8. I believe it is fair to say that, for both countries, the state was the main adjustment variable of these austerity programs. And this meant dismantling former state capacities to a degree that the core countries have not experienced. The EU is, in this sense, a disciplinary tool that progressively promotes integration through disintegration – in wage differentials, public spending, fiscal laws and economic specialization.[28] This, in turn, profoundly changes state capacities and creates ever more dependent states.

Moreover, states are not impervious entities, but embedded processes of syntheses in constant mutation that reflect different strategies of accumulation and hegemonic projects, led by different fractions of the ruling class and social blocs. Although state power is structured according to the interests of the dominant class, there can be divergent hegemonic projects that reveal frictions between the different fractions of the bourgeoisie in their projects of capital accumulation, and that need the support of the middle and the popular classes.

The processes of state-building are, then, syntheses that emerge from conflicts and dissonances, not only *within* the state but directly between different social actors, mediated by the nature of the state-capital relation that defines a determined pattern of development or economic growth. And it is this internal dynamic that is missing from the member statehood concept.[29] European integration meant that there were winners and losers or, at least, a profound recomposition of different national bourgeoisies in order to adapt themselves to a globalized economy. And these shifts do not only mean a specific type of uneven and combined development within the EU, but different capacities to resist the process of state transformation that European integration entails.

To tackle all these subtleties, we need a concept that I will call the *double dynamic* of European integration. This means that we must tackle different levels simultaneously if we are to capture the full scope of political and economic state transformation: the tensions between classes in the determination of a specific state form, together with the tensions within the capitalist class itself, as well as the tension of a project of European integration that entails the constitution of a transnational space *through* the creation of uneven and combined economic profiles.

As Leo Panitch argued, 'the international constitutionalisation of neo-liberalism has taken place through the agency of states, and there is no prospect whatsoever of getting to a *somewhere else*, inspired by a vision of an egalitarian, democratic and cooperative world beyond global competitiveness, that does not entail a fundamental struggle with domestic as well as global capitalists over the transformation of the state'.[30] In this sense, if the left is to be capable of developing coherent strategies concerning the European Union it needs to tackle not only the strategic difficulties that a *double dynamic* imposes, but also the different starting points that different national contexts entail.

HOLLOWED STATES, HOLLOWED STRATEGIES

The left's relation to the process of European integration has been as controversial as it has been voluble. Not only did the deepening of integration happen in a moment when labour was growing increasingly entrenched, but the building of some of today's most important left wing experiences in the EU started in the end of the 1990s and beginning of the 2000s, when the obvious agenda was a social democratic one, centred on reclaiming a state that had been hollowed out by reviving the classic agenda now abandoned by the classic social democratic parties – and amidst the boom of globalization – which meant an understanding of the rescaling of power centres and an interlinked agenda based on the centrality of building transnational networks.

At the time of writing, faith in left-wing political parties across the European Union is steadily declining. The 2021 German elections delivered a disastrous result for the left party Die Linke; the Spanish Unidas Podemos was dealt an immense blow during the last electoral cycle; the left in Italy does not play a significant role; and the Portuguese solution – a parliamentary agreement since 2016 between the social liberal Socialist Party, the Left Bloc, and the Communist Party – dissolved, prompting snap elections that delivered appalling results for both left-wing formations. The recent reconfiguration of the left in France is still an ongoing process, and the Syriza's experience in Greece is widely known.

The dynamics of European integration and state transformation made possible through consensus at the political centre allowed for traditional social democratic demands to be orphaned for several decades. For the political left, this meant that a traditional progressive agenda was in need of political actors to push it forward given that the centre of gravity had moved to the right. At the end of the 1990s and beginning of the 2000s, the recomposition of the left meant occupying that space, but bringing together new agendas put forward by social movements. And this was no small thing: it meant constructing a political synthesis between more reformist agendas (of electoral politics) with more transformative agendas (of labour and social movement politics). The state, then, became a central territory for the actuation of left wing parties, ending a decades-long estrangement from popular, mass politics.

One of the ways in which this process succeeded was by developing a party form with looser ideological commitments, meaning parties that were composed of groups from different ideological traditions that were capable of finding commonalities for the tangible, present moment. But this move created tension, as growing moves toward electoralism meant steadily abandoning the labour and movement orientation which had been central to their identity. This prompted an increasing proximity to the centre-left: either supporting (as was the case in Portugal), entering, or even substituting for governments of the neoliberalized centre-left (such as was the case in Greece with PASOK, but seen elsewhere with its European counterparts). This was the outcome of an electorally oriented politics that substituted for the assembling of actual mass parties with a strong base of support and that could develop counter-hegemonic narratives. (It is important to recall that most of these parties subsist through state funding that grows accordingly to institutional representation). As a result, the left's political programs grew more and more focused on demands on states that are 'hard but hollow', with 'hollow democracies'.[31]

Meanwhile, the ideological moderation of the communist and post-communist party family, with most being 'softly' Eurosceptic (as abandoning the eurozone and the EU is a marginal position even after consecutive crises), together with the ideological 'looseness' of the new radical left parties in Europe,[32] meant that most radical left parties tended to focus on medium-term programmatic demands that fell short of an outspoken anticapitalism or even radical social democracy, both utopian within EU strictures. Moreover, unlike social democratic parties in the early-to-mid-twentieth century, radical left parties today have relatively small memberships. Most are small or midsize parties with memberships of a few thousand.

Another central point of tension is European integration. Although the radical left strongly opposed neoliberal processes of European integration, there are significant divisions within and between parties about whether member states should try to exit the EU or attempt to transform it from within. Breaking with the European Union, the 'iron cage' as Magnus Ryner calls it, is a proposal which is very difficult to articulate for all member states given the degree of institutional transformation that integration has brought and the fact that it remains a very powerful ideological tool.[33] The critique of the EU is especially difficult in some countries due to fears of economic collapse. Therefore, most left-wing formations in the EU have unstable positions concerning the EU *together with* a growing focus on electoral policies that dismiss the strategic orientation of social and labour movement building. These two orientations are, in my opinion, concurrent: breaking with the EU is a very unpopular demand that tendentially will not be put forward by electorally oriented and small membership parties.

Moreover, the uneven and combined nature of the EU means that left-wing formations will have different spaces of manoeuvre concerning their actions and programs. Paradoxically, it has been in the most dependent peripheral countries, such as Greece and Portugal, that the harshest critique of European integration has been made by left-wing parties, especially during the Global Financial Crisis. However, the failure of the Greek experience and the disciplinary actions taken by the Troika (European Commission, European Central Bank and International Monetary Fund) have again shut down this space of critique. The left in the core countries, such as Germany, has yet to develop a coherent stance on European integration, something that could produce openings for the breaking with this dynamic.

Portugal is an interesting example of this dilemma. And the strategic decisions of the Portuguese left show both the problem of parties that are disputing a hollowed-out state, as well as the difficulty of finding a coherent and popular stance concerning European integration.

PORTUGAL: THE MYTH, THE LESSONS, AND THE ARDUOUS WAY FORWARD

Austerity and its consequences for Portugal

Over the past fifteen years, Portugal has experienced austerity as a state of exception.[34] Initially implemented through minor adjustment programs following the 2007–2008 financial crisis under a minority Socialist Party (PS) government, austerity measures included bank bailouts, wage cuts and reduced social services. These measures intensified from 2011 to 2014 under a right-wing coalition government that enforced a Memorandum of Understanding with the Troika, resulting in one of the swiftest and most severe neoliberal transformations in Portugal's history.

Austerity can be understood as a state of exception in that it was implemented in an 'exceptional' political moment that justified the enactment of extreme measures with minimal social resistance, bolstered by the pervasive TINA (There Is No Alternative) narrative that constrained the left's ability to propose viable alternatives. This state of exception legitimized the imposition of severe labour devaluation, social spending cuts and widespread impoverishment. This era saw widespread impoverishment of workers and pensioners, increased taxes, privatization of public services and assets and the erosion of labour laws, notably including the near disappearance of collective bargaining.

In addition, austerity has influenced social and interpersonal dynamics, fostering more conservative and reactionary policies that undermined progressive initiatives related to education, sexuality, women's rights, racism and LGBT rights. The societal fabric was altered, with increased reliance on private structures such as families, leading to heightened violence against women and minorities and a more protectionist societal outlook, including in economic behaviours. Such can be witnessed in the level of economic adaptations in the realm of the household, as well as the obvious difficulty of leaving violent relationships due to economic incapacity and lack of state support. Fear-induced spending cuts further hindered economic recovery, demonstrating the multi-layered impact of austerity. Addressing austerity and its fallout requires a nuanced approach encompassing various levels of analysis and transformation. Despite severe neoliberal policies, Portugal did not witness a sustained resistance movement. Although mass mobilizations, like the significant anti-austerity protests on September 15, 2012, and March 2, 2013, occurred, they failed to translate into a continuous resistance capable of altering class dynamics in Portugal. One key reason was the 'rootlessness' of the social movements, which lacked workplace or community-based organizational structures, making sustained, locally grounded resistance difficult.

The labour movement's diminishing influence also contributed to this weakness. With rising precarious employment, trade unions, particularly the CGTP, saw declining membership and struggled to organize workplace disputes. The CGTP, closely aligned with the Portuguese Communist Party (PCP), maintained a bureaucratic and insular stance, limiting collaboration with newer activist groups, many associated with the Left Bloc or autonomist organizations. This organizational disconnect forced movements to operate outside traditional labour structures, focusing on precarious workers but highlighting the underlying organizational frailty rather than strength.

Trade unions did organize several strikes during the austerity period, but tensions remained between unions and mass mobilizations, as unions failed to integrate new protest dynamics into their organizational strategies.

For effective resistance, union membership would have had to transcend employment status, and a coordinated effort between movements and unions would have been essential to build a consolidated anti-austerity, anticapitalist front.

Nor was the radical left, including parties like the Left Bloc and the PCP, immune to the political challenges of the austerity era. Following significant mobilizations and the snap election in June 2011, the Left Bloc's electoral support declined from 9.8 per cent in 2009 to 5.2 per cent in 2011, while the PCP maintained steady support. Several factors contributed to this decline. The entrenched TINA narrative limited perceived alternatives to austerity, constraining the left's appeal. Additionally, unlike Syriza in Greece, Portugal's SP remained a viable alternative despite its involvement in austerity measures, affecting the Left Bloc's electoral prospects.

A critical strategic challenge for the Left Bloc was navigating the 'dual strategy' dilemma. This involved balancing institutional credibility to attract disillusioned centre-left voters with maintaining a distinct, anti-establishment stance to appeal to those disenchanted with traditional politics. This dual strategy created tensions, as the Left Bloc needed to simultaneously advocate for systemic reforms and fundamental transformations, often leading to fluctuating electoral results.

The interplay of rootless movements, organizational weaknesses and the strategic duality of the Left Bloc underpins the challenges faced by the radical left. In a context of significant but transient mobilizations, achieving sustained political change remains complex, highlighting the need for robust, coordinated and adaptable organizational strategies to counter neoliberal austerity effectively.

The 2015 Portuguese Election: Outcomes, Implications, and Political Realignments

On October 4, 2015, Portugal held a national election, which resulted in a surprising victory for the right-wing coalition, Portugal Ahead (PaF). Having governed for the previous four years under a regime of harsh austerity measures, PaF's success was seen by some mainstream commentators as an endorsement of these policies. However, this interpretation overlooked a significant decrease in the right-wing's total vote share and a notable increase for the radical left, particularly the Left Bloc, which achieved its best electoral result ever. This unexpected outcome raised new questions about the left's potential to contend for state power and called for a revaluation of the shifting dynamics in Portuguese politics.

The right-wing coalition, composed of the Social Democratic Party and the Popular Party, did not secure an absolute majority, receiving only 36.9 per cent of the vote. This result puzzled many, given the unpopularity of the government and its policies. To understand PaF's electoral performance, it is crucial to consider several factors beneath the surface.

One significant factor was the European Central Bank's Public Sector Purchase Program, introduced shortly before the election. This program lowered interest rates, enabling Portugal to meet Troika-imposed criteria without needing a second bailout. This manoeuvre highlighted the political nature of European institutional actions aimed at preventing a left-wing resurgence. Additional factors included a perceived decrease in unemployment, misleadingly reported to the public, and the right-wing coalition's strategic, non-confrontational campaign. Moreover, the anti-austerity movement struggled to effectively counter mainstream narratives about the necessity of shared sacrifice and the distribution of austerity's benefits. The PS failed to present a robust opposition, which contributed to the perception of a lack of viable alternatives. The PS political program was vague and barely distinguishable from that of the right, and its campaign was marred by errors and inconsistencies. This incompetence played a crucial role in the subsequent political developments.

Despite the right-wing victory, they did not retain control of the parliament, since they did not achieve the minimum number of MPs to guarantee an outright majority. The Left Bloc and the Portuguese PCP made significant gains, winning 10.2 per cent and 8.2 per cent of the vote, respectively. The Left Bloc's achievement, garnering over half a million votes, was particularly notable. This result marked a historic moment in Portuguese politics, with nearly 20 per cent of the new assembly composed of representatives explicitly opposed to both austerity and capitalism. The election results underscored the deepening polarization within the Portuguese electorate.

The Left Bloc's activities and electoral program was shaped around the central issue of austerity. Its focus included unemployment, job insecurity and the dismantling of public services through budget cuts, school and hospital closures, and the destabilization of social security. Migration also emerged as a critical issue, with Portugal experiencing unprecedented emigration levels, further complicating the socioeconomic landscape. The Left Bloc also emphasized the issue of national debt, recognizing that austerity measures exacerbated rather than alleviated the debt problem. The debt served as a pretext for implementing a neoliberal agenda aimed at dismantling the social state, weakening trade unions and commodifying public goods. Addressing the illegitimacy of the debt became a central political demand for the Left, as debt restructuring and interest rate renegotiation were deemed essential for economic recovery.

A pivotal issue during the campaign was Portugal's future in the EU. The Left Bloc's position on these matters had been underdeveloped, initially mirroring Syriza's stance in Greece. However, Syriza's failure to challenge European elites pushed the Left Bloc to clarify its position. During the campaign, the Left Bloc faced attacks labeling them as irresponsible, using Syriza's experience as evidence. Nonetheless, the party successfully shifted this narrative, attributing Greece's troubles to European officials rather than Syriza. This enabled the Left Bloc to strengthen its critique of the EU and the euro, with a willingness to exit the eurozone if necessary to end austerity and restore sovereignty. This position, unfortunately, would not last long.

In the lead-up to the election, the Left Bloc had taken a firm stance against the PS, rejecting any coalition with the 'socialists' who were seen as proponents of 'soft austerity.' The PS had initially dismissed the possibility of a left-wing government. However, in the final debate rounds, Left Bloc spokesperson Catarina Martins challenged PS leader António Costa to consider a left-wing government, contingent on abandoning certain liberal policies. The election results, which yielded no absolute majority, necessitated coalition negotiations. The Left Bloc's impressive performance and proactive stance in offering baseline terms for an agreement with the PS pushed them to the forefront of these discussions. The PS, unable to negotiate with right-wing parties without exacerbating the political crisis, had to consider the Left Bloc's conditions: unfreezing pensions, halting further reductions in the Single Social Tax and ending labour market liberalization.

The negotiations sparked a prolonged political crisis, with President Aníbal Cavaco Silva attempting to maintain the right-wing in power. However, his efforts failed, and the Left Bloc could not retreat from its initial overtures. After extensive discussions, an agreement was reached between the PS, the Left Bloc and PCP, forming the basis for the 2016 state budget. On November 26, 2015, a PS government with parliamentary support from the left took office, marking a significant shift in Portuguese politics. This election and the subsequent political realignments highlighted the complexities and evolving dynamics within Portuguese politics, emphasizing the critical role of left-wing parties in shaping the country's future amidst austerity and economic challenges.

The negotiations following the 2015 election were intricate, characterized by tense moments and primarily conducted behind closed doors. Both left-wing parties, the Left Bloc and the Communist-Green coalition (CDU), negotiated separately with the Socialist Party, a decision that granted the PS access to all information while the left remained fragmented, unable to present unified proposals.

Internal discussions within the Left Bloc were fraught between differing tactical views. On one hand, there was a need to not push the PS too far, as a failed agreement could result in the right-wing returning to power, for which the blame could be placed on the Left Bloc. On the other hand, it was argued that the PS needed an agreement with the left to survive politically and avoid the fate of other European social democratic parties, which were experiencing significant declines (often referred to as 'Pasokification'). This presented an opportunity to press for bolder proposals, not just to halt impoverishment but to reverse austerity measures in the medium term, including placing public debt renegotiation at the forefront. Ultimately, the more cautious approach prevailed, shaping the Left Bloc's position during negotiations.

After over a month of negotiations, the Left Bloc and CDU reached terms with the PS. They agreed to provide parliamentary support by approving the budget and other laws while retaining autonomy to propose independent policies. This arrangement allowed the parties to distance themselves from the government, maintaining that while it might not address fundamental issues, it aimed to mitigate the most damaging austerity measures. The left retained the freedom to oppose certain governmental measures in parliament, avoiding the discipline typically required in a formal coalition. Despite the right-wing's attempt to belittle the new government by dubbing it the 'contraption' (*Geringonça*), the term gained widespread usage, even among critical supporters of the coalition.

The agreement, initially set for one year, became a baseline for ongoing discussions about state budget measures. It would end up lasting almost 7 years, in the end leading to the most difficult political scenario that the country had experienced in decades. As would soon become clear, the *geringonça* coalition, often hailed as a model of left-wing pluralism, was in reality a pragmatic response to the specific socioeconomic context of post-crisis Portugal rather than a replicable template for progressive governance. Despite some progressive social policies, the coalition's achievements were ultimately circumscribed by broader structural constraints.

The Elections of 2019

The 2019 national elections provided a critical juncture to assess the political landscape following the four-year tenure of the *geringonça* coalition. The elections underscored the complexity and constraints of the *geringonça* coalition as a model for left-wing governance. While the coalition achieved some notable social policy successes, its inability to effect significant structural reforms highlighted the limitations imposed by broader economic and political constraints. The election results ultimately reflected both a consolidation of PS dominance and a fragmentation of the political landscape, with significant implications for the viability of future coalitional arrangements and the potential for progressive policy initiatives.

The election outcomes were multifaceted, reflecting significant shifts and continuities within Portuguese politics. The PS, under the leadership of António Costa, consolidated its position as the dominant political force, securing 36.7 per cent of the vote – a notable increase from its 32.4 per cent share in 2015. This translated into an additional twenty parliamentary seats, bringing the PS total to 106 MPs, just ten shy of an outright majority. Costa's campaign emphasized stability and continuity, suggesting a potential renewal of the *geringonça* arrangement. The Left Bloc experienced a slight reduction in its vote share, from 10.2 per cent to 9.7 per cent, though it retained its 19 parliamentary seats. In contrast, the PCP-led CDU coalition saw a more significant decline, with its vote share dropping from 8.3 per cent to 6.5 per cent, resulting in the loss of five MPs. Meanwhile, the centre-right Social Democratic Party (PSD) suffered a substantial electoral setback, with its vote share falling from 36.9 per cent (in coalition with the CDS) to 27.9 per cent when running independently. This loss translated into a reduction of 25 parliamentary seats, underscoring the right-wing's weakened political position.

The election was also marked by the parliamentary entry of new parties, reflecting evolving political dynamics. The liberal environmentalist party PAN increased its representation from 1.4 to 3.3 per cent, securing four seats. Additionally, three new parties each gained one seat: Liberal Initiative, the far-right populist Chega and the social-democratic Livre. This diversification of the parliamentary landscape underscores increasing political fragmentation. The results highlighted other underlying political tensions, exemplified by the simultaneous rise of renewed racist tendencies and antiracist movements. Voter engagement declined, with abstention rates increasing to 45.5 per cent, up from 43 per cent in the previous election cycle, indicating a growing disenchantment with the political process. Costa's advocacy for continuing the *geringonça* with a stronger PS presence, and potentially including PAN and Livre, reflected a strategy to maintain political stability. However, the diminished electoral strength of the Left Bloc and CDU suggested reduced leverage for these parties in negotiating future coalitional arrangements.

The coalition implemented several progressive measures, including increases to the minimum wage and pensions, restoration of public sector wages, and reversal of some privatizations. However, these initiatives fell short of achieving substantial structural reforms. The persistence of income inequality, high levels of indirect taxation and underfunded public services remain significant challenges. The coalition's policy achievements were facilitated by favorable economic conditions, such as low oil prices and a tourism boom, rather than by a fundamental restructuring of the Portuguese economy. The European Central Bank's Quantitative Easing program also provided temporary fiscal breathing space. Nonetheless, the underlying debt burden remains a significant constraint on sovereign fiscal policy, with public debt only marginally reduced from 130.6 per cent of GDP in 2014 to 121.5 per cent by 2018. Critical issues such as labour market precarity, public sector underinvestment, and the rigidity of the Troika-imposed labour laws remained largely unaddressed. The Troika's influence persisted, reflecting the limits of the *geringonça* in enacting comprehensive anti-austerity measures within the existing European economic governance framework.

The 2019 electoral campaign largely avoided substantive debates on the financial system, the EU, the euro or public debt, indicating a depoliticization of these critical issues. Anticipating a fragmented parliament necessitating coalition-building, political parties refrained from delineating firm stances or red lines for potential governmental agreements. The Left Bloc and the PCP failed to reshape the public discourse or expand their electoral support base. Both parties witnessed a decline in their vote percentages and absolute voter numbers, with the PCP also losing parliamentary seats. This diminished political capital undermines their bargaining power in negotiating any prospective coalition agreements, rendering them even less influential than in the 2015 *geringonça* configuration.

Historically, the PS has been a principal agent of neoliberal policies within Portuguese democracy, excluding the period of the Memorandum from 2011 to 2015 under the PSD's centre-right governance. The *geringonça* arrangement did not signify a fundamental transformation in the PS's ideological orientation. Instead, it represented a strategic manoeuvre to rejuvenate the party and avert a fate like that of Greece's PASOK, which collapsed after years of austerity measures. In the 2015 elections, the PS did not secure a decisive victory against the ruling right-wing coalition despite the latter's imposition of severe austerity. The 2019 election results, marked by a clear strengthening of the PS, underscore a significantly altered political context compared to 2015. This shift further constrained the left's capacity to advocate for and implement the structural changes it was unable to secure during the previous geringonça. Given the bolstered position of the PS, the left's weakened electoral mandate implied that any renewed coalition would likely leave the left in a more precarious and marginalized state than before.

The electoral campaign's avoidance of core economic and political issues, combined with the left's diminished influence, illustrates the complexities and limitations of the *geringonça* model. The historical neoliberal inclinations of the PS and its strategic adjustments to preserve its relevance within the shifting political landscape reveal the inherent challenges in achieving substantial structural reforms. The 2019 elections highlighted the intricate interplay between political strategy, electoral outcomes and the feasibility of progressive governance within the constraints of contemporary European politics.

The Snap Elections of 2022 and 2024: an Uncertain Future for the Left

The 2022 elections marked the consolidation of the Chega party in Portuguese politics and the definite end of the myth that Portugal was immune to far-right politics. Simultaneously, it was also the year that the PS was able to achieve an absolute majority for the second time in Portugal's democratic history.

The unwillingness of the PS to negotiate the state budget with the left – and its unwillingness to deviate from European budget rules and invest in public services – prompted them to call elections in late 2021 after the PCP and the Left-Bloc announced that they were voting against the budget. The centre-left party, however, was able to achieve an absolute majority and garner most of the left-of-centre votes because of the electorate's fear of a right-wing government with Chega's support. This meant a significant decrease in the votes for the radical left: from almost 16 per cent of the vote in 2019, the left's vote in 2022 was reduced by half (8.7 per cent); from 31 seats in 2019, the left was diminished to 11 MPs in these elections.

Although António Costa's party was successful in positioning itself as the antidote to Chega's ascent while refusing to tackle the chronic underfunding of Portuguese public services, this didn't stop the quick rightward shift in Portuguese politics. The success of the PS in these elections was mainly due to the fragmentation of the Portuguese right but it did not stop the far-right party's rise: Chega's vote rose from 68,000 to 400,000 in the 2022 elections. And that enabled the party to dominate the political debate and media narratives since then. In 2024, the year commemorating the fiftieth anniversary of the Portuguese revolution, the populist far-right emerged as the dominant force in the snap elections held on March 10. Chega, a party led by André Ventura and influenced by figures such as Matteo Salvini, Marine Le Pen, and Santiago Abascal of Vox (who participated in the campaign), garnered over one million votes, positioning itself as the third largest political force in Portugal.

The election came just two years after the PS achieved an absolute majority with the backing of left-wing parties, namely the Left Bloc and the PCP. The resignation of Prime Minister António Costa amidst a corruption scandal – yet to be fully investigated – further tarnished the party's image. This scandal, alongside the challenges of the post-austerity period, the Covid-19 pandemic, the Ukraine war, inflation crises and various internal government issues rendered the PS unable to withstand additional controversy. Consequently, on November 7, 2023, the government fell, prompting the call for snap elections.

Pedro Nuno Santos, newly elected Secretary General of the PS and long associated with the party's left wing, faced a formidable challenge in leading the party. Meanwhile, the centre-right, represented by the Democratic Alliance (AD) coalition – comprising the PSD, the People's Party (CDS-PP) and the Monarchist People's Party (PPM) – seized an opportunity to present itself as a viable alternative to the PS. However, the election results reflected a narrow margin: the AD received 28.9 per cent of the vote, securing 80 seats, while the PS obtained 28 per cent with 78 seats. Chega emerged in third place with 18.1 per cent of the vote and 50 seats, followed by the Liberal Initiative (IL) with 4.9 per cent, retaining its eight seats. The Left Bloc obtained 4.4 per cent and maintained its five seats, the PCP coalition 3.2 per cent and four seats (a loss of two), Livre 3.2 per cent and four seats and PAN with 1.9 per cent and one seat.

The elections preserved the same parties in the Assembly as in 2022, but with the significant shift of the right gaining a clear majority. AD, IL and Chega collectively garnered over 50 per cent of the vote, securing 135 seats – surpassing the 116 needed for an absolute majority. Luís Montenegro, leader of the AD, consistently stated during the campaign that he would not form a government coalition with Chega, leading to a potential political crisis or necessitating a reversal of his pre-election stance. Similarly, Pedro Nuno Santos of the PS ruled out participating in a central bloc government with the AD, complicating the formation of a stable government. An AD minority government assumed power on April 2, with challenging negotiations anticipated post-summer, likely focusing on the state budget.

An intriguing aspect of these elections was the low abstention rate, under 34 per cent, which expanded the electoral base and led to a more dispersed vote distribution. For instance, while the Left Bloc's percentage remained steady compared to 2022, it received approximately 34,000 additional votes. The low abstention rate contributed to Chega's growth, as the party's combination of anticorruption rhetoric and neoliberal economic agenda attracted disillusioned voters. The far-right's dominance of antisystem discourse also appealed to many young voters. Furthermore, AD's and

Montenegro's campaign stance against any coalition with Chega has made the party a receptacle for protest votes, contrasting with the PSD's approach in 2022 that led to tactical voting for the PS to prevent Chega's rise, resulting in a PS absolute majority. Chega also achieved a significant milestone by winning two of the four seats allocated to the diaspora community – a novel occurrence, as no party outside the centre-left or centre-right had previously elected MPs abroad. This reflected the fact that the emigration issue, which has been central to Portuguese political discourse over the past decade, was leveraged by the far-right to garner support from the migrant vote.

Since 2015, the Left Bloc and PCP's support for the PS government has diminished their electoral influence, culminating in the 2022 elections when their withdrawal of support led to early elections and electoral punishment for both parties of the left. The March 10 elections reaffirmed this trend, despite the Left Bloc securing more votes than in 2022. The left remains caught between asserting its stance and compromising with the PS to mitigate the far-right's ascendance. Nevertheless, the Left Bloc and PCP campaigns succeeded in highlighting critical issues such as labour rights, healthcare, public education and housing, but these were overshadowed by their willingness to negotiate with the PS. This underscored the extent to which the left must undergo a strategic reassessment to address its decline, emphasizing grassroots organization to counteract the far-right's appeal driven by fear and dissatisfaction.

The subsequent European elections reaffirmed this the trend seen in the 2024 national contest. The Left Bloc changed (again) its position concerning the euro, declaring the party a critical supporter of the common currency. Even the far-right Chega is pro-EU, showing this is a central but very difficult issue to navigate in the country. Only the PCP has maintained its principled EU-critical position.

STRATEGIC CONCLUSIONS

Portugal is, in this sense, a clear illustration of a hollowed-out state that pushed hollowed-out strategies upon the left. It shows both the medium-term inefficacy of subsuming a political program and practice to the centre, as well as the impossibilities of applying left-wing programs within European constraints. But the solution for the European left's conundrum is not an easy one, and I do not pretend to hold all the answers. However, I propose three ideas for future debates.

First, contesting the European Union cannot be done solely by targeting its undemocratic constitutional procedures; it needs to be done at the level of states and translated into concrete proposals: restructuring public debt, building a public banking sector, reforming labour laws, nationalizing strategic sectors of the economy, rebuilding green productive sectors are all measures that can seem attainable (even if difficult) and that put into question the limits of the EU.

I call this *politicizing the rupture*: 'exiting' is not, in itself, a left-wing program. In order to transform a possible clash with European institutions into a collective, mass and popular program, the left needs to fill the void left by slogans such as 'Brexit' or 'Grexit'. Building a genuine 'Lexit' means grappling with the concrete transformations that the member-state process has imposed upon forms of sovereignty. Regaining these forms politicizes the necessary rupture, leaving no space open for other forms of Euro criticism, such as those of the new populist far-right. This is only possible through collective, concrete, political action and organizing. By collectively building an understanding of the boundaries of the EU, the left might be able to implement measures that allow for the end of austerity and the regaining of forms of democratic control over the state itself. In sum, to try to rebuild the state-society nexus.

Second, we need to understand that sovereignty is not an end in itself. If the contemporary demand for democracy and popular sovereignty is a result of a break in the former state-society nexus, the solution can only be found in a transformation and repoliticization of the economic realm: in the words of Panagiotis Sotiris, 'in this sense, reclaiming popular sovereignty is also a class strategy'.[35] Proposals that mainly target the state must be accompanied by experiences of self-organization and self-management. This also means that rebuilding a strong labour movement, capable of contesting the processes of precarization, capitalist automation and atomization, must be a central priority. It is concrete experiences of organization that rebuild political subjects capable of shifting the balance of forces between capital and labour. In sum, we need a transformation in the organization of ownership linked to alternative forms of organizing production outside the realm of capital.[36]

Third, it is important to remember that the European Union does not promote unity among the oppressed, but only between those who organize that oppression. The European Round Table of Industrialists can insert their demands into the function and decision-making processes of the EU in a much more far-reaching way than any organization on the side of labour – this is the structural selectivity of the European Union that, nonetheless, exists without any form of statehood, as we have seen.[37] In this sense there is no European *demos* since, as Costas Lapavitsas writes, no class or other social divisions in Europe take a homogeneous 'European' form, for there are no occupational, organizational, habitual, cultural, and historical norms able to create such an overarching social integration. Actual class divisions in Europe always take a national form, as do the party politics that correspond to these divisions.[38]

As a result, the left will experience uneven and sometimes contradictory developments in any progressive movement.[39] The positions articulated within each relation of forces – and the different limits and constraints of each experience – will determine how we can manoeuvre and coordinate strategy more broadly. If, for the periphery, it is more difficult to openly criticize and propose breaks with the EU, the left in core countries has a larger space for manoeuvre. This is not to say that the supranational level must stay untouched or unconsidered. The experiences of the Plan B summits are an interesting example, especially in terms of conceptualizing the contemporary constraints and impositions of the EU and drawing out forms of collective coordination that need to be translated into concrete proposals at the national level. However, they fell short after the blowback that most left parties experienced after 2015 at the national level. We need to *bring internationalism back home* and understand that progressive shifts in one place will create domino effects in others. For this, the left needs coordination without the idealism that all change will happen everywhere at once.

To the *double dynamic* of European integration, must then correspond a *double strategic dynamic* that knowingly combines the organization of class struggle at the national level with a coordinated critique at the European level. The proposals to transform the European Union from within lack the understanding of its undemocratic nature and how the dynamic of integration changed states themselves. On the other hand, a simplistic or purely national approach to rupture does not provide the necessary answers – neither for the questions of interdependence nor on the degree of institutional transformation and adaptation that integration has meant – and may lead to results that are less than progressive.

In sum, we need organizations that enable experiences of self-management, political parties and movements that dispute the state at the national level, and movements at the supranational level that emerge from the encounters of these political subjects. The problem of European integration is, at its core, a matter of the role and form of the state – the two questions cannot be looked upon separately.

ACKNOWLEDGEMENTS

I am deeply indebted to my advisor João Rodrigues, not only for his invaluable insights, which have been central to deepening my thinking, but also for reviewing this article. I would also like to thank my friend Filipe Teles, who has helped me with the structuring and the writing of this article. But most of all, I want to thank Leo Panitch. I met Leo in 2014, on the outskirts of New York, and after a somewhat heated panel discussion. After my critical intervention, he came up to me and said: 'I want to have lunch with you'. And we had quite a few lunches whenever we met in the same part of the world over the next few years. I think my critical intervention in 2014 was instinctive and not really theorised. Leo was central in helping me to find the theory to support my instinct – and that is, in many ways, one of the most important tasks for a leftist. His writings and our debates helped to focus my intellectual interests – this article would never have been possible without him. We often disagreed, but we always debated with respect for disagreement and honour for commonalities. I believe that this is precisely the kind of relationship that defines a comrade.

NOTES

1   Leo Panitch, 'Globalisation and the State', in Ralph Miliband and Leo Panitch, eds, *Socialist Register 1994: Between Globalism and Nationalism*, London: Merlin Press, 1994, p. 87.

2   This section aims at providing a very brief overview of key moments and reasonings of the European integration process and not an extensive analysis of them. For further and comprehensive reading, see: Perry Anderson, *The New Old World*, London: Verso Books, 2011; Christopher J. Bickerton, *European Integration: From Nation States to Member States*, Oxford: Oxford University Press, 2012; John Gillingham, *European Integration, 1950–2003: Superstate or New Market Economy?*, New York: Cambridge University Press, 2003; Andrew Moravcsik, *The Choice for Europe*, New York: Routledge, 1999.

3   Bickerton, *European Integration*.

4   Bastiaan van Apeldoorn, 'The European Capitalist Class and the Crisis of its Hegemonic Project', in Leo Panitch, Greg Albo and Vivek Chibber, eds, *Socialist Register 2014: Registering Class,* 2014, pp. 186-206; Kees van der Pijl, *Transnational Classes and International Relations*, London: Routledge, 1998.

5   Magnus Ryner, 'Europe's Ordoliberal Iron Cage: Critical Political Economy, the Euro Area Crisis and Its Management', *Journal of European Public Policy*, 22(2), 2015, pp. 275-94.

6   Costas Lapavitsas, *Crisis in the Eurozone*, London: Verso Books, 2012; Susan Watkins, 'The Political State of the Union', *New Left Review*, 90, Nov/Dec 2014, pp. 5-25.

7   João Rodrigues and José Reis 'The Asymmetries of European Integration and the Crisis of Capitalism in Portugal', *Competition & Change*, 16(3), 2012, pp. 188-205.

8   Andreas Bieler, Jamie Jordan and Adam David Morton, 'EU Aggregate Demand as a Way out of Crisis? Engaging the Post-Keynesian Critique', *JCMS: Journal of Common Market Studies*, 57(4), 2019, p. 814.

9   Peter Cocks, 'Towards a Marxist Theory of European Integration,' *International Organization*, 34(1), 1980, p.15.

10   Bickerton, *European Integration*, p. 148.

11 Bickerton, *European Integration*, p. 12; 'The concept of member state expresses a fundamental change in the political structure of the state, with horizontal ties between national executives taking precedence over vertical ties between governments and their own societies.' (Bickerton, *European Integration*, pp. vi-vii).

12 Bickerton, *European Integration*, p. 107.

13 'Looking at national corporatism as a form of state, two features stand out. One is the emphasis on consensus and compromise. Central to the political systems of corporatist Western European State was the avoidance of conflict. Any disagreements were the subject of negotiation at the elite level rather than a basis for public mobilization in the streets. What made this consensus and compromise possible was the absence of ideological conflict. … Another key feature is the power of administrative actors relative to that of national political representatives. With the attenuation of political conflict, choices appeared as technical rather than as political, making them seem resolvable by bureaucratic actors.' (Bickerton, *European Integration*, p. 88).

14 Bickerton, *European Integration*, p. 108.

15 Valerio Della Sala, 'Hollowing out and hardening the state: European integration and the Italian economy', *West European Politics*, 20(1), 1997, p. 14.

16 Anderson, *The New Old World*, p. 541.

17 Jamie Gough, 'Changing scale as changing class relations: variety and contradiction in the politics of scale,' *Political Geography* 23(2), 2004, p. 199.

18 Bickerton, *European Integration*, p. 4.

19 This is a reference to Alan Milward's work *The European Rescue of the Nation-State*, London & New York: Routledge, 2000.

20 Nicos Poulantzas, 'Internationalisation of Capitalist Relations and the Nation-State', *Economy and Society*, 3(2), 1974, pp. 145-79; Ernest Mandel, 'International Capitalism and "Supra-Nationality"', in Ralph Miliband and John Savile, eds, *The Socialist Register* 1967, London: Merlin Press, 1967, pp. 27-41. For an interesting overview of the debate, see: Tristan Auvray and Cédric Durand, 'A European Capitalism? Revisiting the Mandel–Poulantzas Debate', in Jean-Numa Ducange and Razmig Keucheyan, eds, *The End of the Democratic State: Nicos Poulantzas, a Marxism for the 21st Century*, 2018, pp. 145-65.

21 Poulantzas, 'Internationalisation of Capitalist Relations', pp. 160-61

22 Poulantzas, 'Internationalisation of Capitalist Relations', p. 146

23 Poulantzas, 'Internationalisation of Capitalist Relations', p. 172

24 Joachim Becker and Johannes Jäger, 'Integration in Crisis: A Regulationist Perspective on the Interaction of European Varieties of Capitalism', *Competition & Change*, 16(3), 2012, pp. 169-187; João Rodrigues, Ana C. Santod and Nuno Teles, 'Semi-peripheral Financialisation: the Case of Portugal', *Review of International Political Economy*, 23(3), 2016, pp. 480-510; 'In part due to the disappearance of several national mechanisms to promote development and sustainable catch-up, from industrial to exchange rate policies, the Euro consolidated a division between the core 'Northern' countries, led by (for example) Germany and the Netherlands, which registered important surpluses in their current accounts and therefore capital outflows, and the peripheral 'Southern' countries, registering, given the balanced relations of the Eurozone with the rest of the world, deficits in their current accounts and inflows of financial capital. Actually, the financial surpluses of the European periphery may well be responsible for its current account deficits, another manifestation of the price paid by less developed

countries for their reliance on international markets to finance investment and/or consumption activities. These were generally biased towards non-industrial activities, as the multiplication of bubbles followed by financial crises attests.' (Rodrigues and Reis, 'The Asymmetries of European Integration', p. 191).

25   Ryner, 'Europe's Ordoliberal Iron Cage'; Watkins, 'The Political State of the Union'; 'In the course of the Eurozone crisis it became clear that sovereignty has not drained away from individual member states to remotely the same degree. The EU is not simply a political body – 'intergovernmentalist' or 'neo-functional' – that generates mutual benefits and is jointly supported by all member states. Power and domination run through its transnational institutions, as has been nakedly manifested in the past decade. The ascendancy of neoliberal ideology since Maastricht has coincided with the hegemonic ascendancy of Germany in the institutions of the EU, matched by a growing divergence among member states. German hegemony is conditional on the transnational nature of the EU, and three factors are paramount in this respect.' (Lapavitsas, *Crisis in the Eurozone*, p. 30).

26   Christopher Preston, *Enlargement and Integration in the European Union*, London: Routledge, 1997.

27   Preston, *Enlargement and Integration in the European Union*.

28   Felix Syrovatka, Etienne Schneider and Thomas Sablowski, 'Ten Years of Crisis: European Economic Integration Between Silent Revolution and Breakup', Berlin: Rosa Luxemburg Stiftung, December 2018.

29   Nicos Poulantzas, *A Crise das Ditaduras: Portugal, Grécia, Espanha*, Rio de Janeiro: Paz e Terra, 1976.

30   Panitch, 'Globalisation and the State', p. 87.

31   Peter Mair, 'Ruling the Void: The Hollowing of Western Democracy', *New Left Review*, 42, 2006, pp. 25-51.

32   March, L, *Radical Left Parties in Europe*. New York: Routledge, 2011.

33   Ryner, 'Europe's Ordoliberal Iron Cage'.

34   This section is a combination, actualization and maturation of previous work published in different outlets: Xavier Lafrance & Catarina Príncipe, 'Building "Parties of a New Type": A Comparative Analysis of New Radical Left Parties in Western Europe,' in Paul Christopher Gray, ed., *From the Streets to the State: Changing the World By Taking Power*, New York: SUNY Press, 2018; Catarina Príncipe, 'Anti-Austerity and the Politics of Toleration in Portugal A way for the Radical Left to develop a transformative project?', Berlin: Rosa Luxemburg Stiftung, 2017; Catarina Príncipe, 'The Portuguese Myth', *Jacobin*, 9 June 2018; Catarina Príncipe, 'What the Left Should Do in Portugal', *Jacobin*, 7 October 2019; Catarina Príncipe, 'How Portugal's Right Won the Election', *Jacobin*, 30 March 2024; Catarina Príncipe & Bhaskar Sunkara, eds., *Europe in Revolt*, Chicago: Haymarket Books, 2016.

35   Panagiotis Sotiris, 'The Strategic Question Revisited: Ten Theses', *The Bullet*, 23 May 2019, available at www.socialistproject.ca.

36   Sotiris, 2019

37   Cédric Durand and Razmig Keucheyan, 'Financial Hegemony and the Unachieved European State', *Competition & Change*, 19(2), 2015, pp. 129-44.

38   Lapavitsas, *Crisis in the Eurozone*, p. 147

39   Catarina Príncipe, "The Deferred Portugese Revolution," in Principe & Sunkara, eds., 2016.

THE AUTUMN OF THE PATRIARCHS:
A NEW CONJUNCTURE IN PAKISTAN

AYYAZ MALLICK

The general elections held in Pakistan on 8 February 2024 signalled a decisive shift in the country's political terrain. Candidates backed by Imran Khan's effectively banned Pakistan Tehreek-e-Insaf (PTI, Pakistan Movement for Justice) were on course for a large plurality, if not a majority, in the new parliament before being cut down to size.

PTI candidates had been suppressed during the election campaign through military-judicial manipulations, including being deprived of a unified party symbol and platform. Khan himself had been incarcerated in targeted cases ranging from the plausible to the ridiculous. In a particularly egregious instance of the latter, Khan and his (most recent) wife were sentenced on spurious theological grounds of contracting their marriage without enough of a gap between divorces.

On polling day, mobile and internet services were shut down to suppress voter turnout. Intelligence officers intervened in favour of parties currently backed by the military. A series of has-beens on their way to resounding defeats, including the former prime minister Nawaz Sharif in a Lahore constituency and the Muttahida Qaumi Movement (MQM, United Nationalities' Movement) in Karachi, were parachuted into parliament through manipulation of the vote count. Military manipulations in peripheralized Balochistan and former 'tribal areas' were even more blatant, with popular nationalist and antiwar candidates handed defeats by barely known competitors.

A hung parliament emerged, with PTI-backed independents in a plurality but without a party platform. After dithering over taking power, established dynastic parties of the centre and centre-right, the Bhuttos' Pakistan People's Party (PPP) and Sharifs' Pakistan Muslim-League Nawaz (PML-N) respectively, came together – with military cajolement – to form a 'compromise' coalition government aiming for economic 'reforms'.[1] The new executive is a mélange of Sharif relatives, loyalists, elite brokers and the usual technocrats that have cycled through domestic and international finance.[2]

The machinations of 2024 are in line with tendencies that matured during 2017–18, culminating in the previous, also military-manipulated, elections that brought Imran Khan to power.[3] The 2018 elections themselves took place in the context of increasing conflict within the ruling bloc. At the same time, the flux in the polity's imperial moorings, such as the drying up of War on Terror (WoT) aid and uncertainties regarding Chinese investment, was beginning to have pertinent effects, including in the fiscal capacities of the state. Khan's government between 2018–2022, alongside his personality, served to temporarily absorb social discontent and perpetuate a moribund ruling bloc. However, this last semblance of popular coordination for the military-centred ruling bloc fell out with the latter in 2022. Consequently, the recent elections saw military machinations reach qualitatively new heights – this time to keep Khan out of power.

On election night, much consternation and humour ensued on internet platforms when the vote count stopped updating. One Urdu columnist caustically declared, 'you are not alone; the Election Commission is also waiting for results [i.e. from the military]'. If the 2018 elections served as dress rehearsal, in 2024 any sartorial pretensions were discarded completely. The emperor is now, well and truly, naked.

The most prominent shift registered by the recent elections is that of an electorate increasingly inclined to voting along party lines instead of for influential candidates who act as intermediaries with the state to deliver limited public services.[4] This shift is an index of wider social, economic and ideological changes. In combination with the multi-level crisis facing the ruling bloc, these shifts have served to structure the political terrain in the short- and medium-term around Khan and the military.

The last time Pakistan faced a multi-level crisis of such depth was between the late 1960s and early 1970s. This period saw the complete delegitimization of the powerful army after a civil war resulted in the independence of East Pakistan/Bangladesh, with the ending of this neocolonial relationship exacerbating a deep economic crisis.[5] The chaos within the ruling bloc was conditioned by the concomitant upsurge of labour, students and ethno-national movements. This interregnum initially saw the ascension of Zulfiqar Ali Bhutto, first as president then as prime minister, on a left-nationalist program. Bhutto attempted an ambiguous project of limited concessions for subaltern and radical groups, even while these groups were coerced and purged from his party in favour of big landlords. In the midst of the 1960s–70s global capitalist stagnation, Bhutto's developmentalist program floundered, while the attack on labour and the left made him reliant on a social base of extant elites. His execution by military-judicial forces in 1979 and the subsequent institutionalization of the US-backed General Zia dictatorship in the 1980s served to organize mainstream politics along Bhutto/anti-Bhutto lines for the next three to four decades.

Today, a similar multi-level crisis confronts the Pakistani ruling bloc, but with a distinct confluence of domestic and international forces. With the long decline of the left and the deepening of neoliberal commodification, it is the figure of Imran Khan that has become a nucleus for multiple alienations. The coming together of diverse processes lends itself to the Khan-centric but unstable character of the conjuncture and the ambiguous potentials of his right-populism. Without Khan, the new parliament and government have little legitimacy. The interregnum is unsustainable.

The sartorial unravelling of Pakistan's security establishment, the unstable see-saw between Khan, the military and established parties, is conditioned by the long-durée, organic crisis of the ruling bloc. Crisis, as Antonio Gramsci reminds us, is not a punctual event but a process. It is an immanent tendency built into the order of capital, always present and threatening to burst through, even while it is immunized by countertendencies.[6] At particular moments, there is a 'quantitative intensification of certain phenomena, neither new nor original', while other elements which 'operated simultaneously with the first, sterilising them, have now become inoperative or have completely dissipated'. Due to these conjunctural sutures coming undone, 'events that go under the specific name of crisis … burst onto the scene'.

Related to this processual understanding of crisis, Gramsci differentiates between the 'organic' and the 'conjunctural' as terrains of distinct-but-interrelated temporalities.[7] The organic terrain is characterized by 'relatively permanent' phenomena whose 'subject is wider social groupings'. Conjunctural processes are more day-to-day and 'immediate', but are at the same time integrally related to organic phenomena. In fact, the 'terrain of the conjunctural' is where 'political forces which are struggling to conserve and defend the existing structure … [and] forces of the opposition organize'. The conjuncture is thus the terrain on which different temporalities (long-, medium-, and short-term) come together and varied social forces organize to perpetuate or upend the organic terrain. The delineation of organic and conjunctural phenomena is a key task for strategy: an overestimation of one or another harbours the danger of mechanical determination and economism or, conversely, 'excess ideologism' and voluntarism.

Gramsci's conception of 'passive revolution' is also related to this understanding of permanent crises and organic–conjunctural phenomena. Passive revolutions are modes of instituting 'molecular changes' within the whole complex of state-civil society (the 'integral state') which serve to preserve reigning ruling blocs while offering limited concessions due to popular pressures from below. It is therefore a political strategy that mediates between the organic and conjunctural so as to preserve the organic terrain. As the characteristic pacifying form of late bourgeois modernity, passive revolution is thus the pre-eminent modality of regressive mediation between organic and conjunctural terrains.[8]

This Gramscian conceptual constellation – of permanent (organic) crisis, organic–conjunctural terrains and passive revolution – is key for understanding Pakistan today. The punctual manoeuvrings of the recent elections are integrally related to the long-durée trends and organic crisis of Pakistan's ruling bloc. Indeed, the elections represent a decisive conjunctural shift: a conjuncture here forming a 'condensation' of contradictions that are 'moving according to very different tempos', leading to a 'change [in] the nature of the terrain itself on which struggles of different kinds are taking place … [with] pertinent effects on these struggles. Their effect is to constitute a new balance of political forces.'[9] It is these shifts, the articulation of organic and conjunctural terrains, and their telescoping (for now) through the persona of Khan, that this essay will discuss.

In the dissolution of an old confluence of sterilizing forces and the open emergence of the ruling bloc's organic crisis, the left in Pakistan is faced with both new dangers and new opportunities. To fully understand the openings and closures of this new conjuncture, we will delineate the character of the organic crisis and the passive revolutionary manoeuvres through which the ruling bloc has anaemically perpetuated itself over the last half a century. The organic crisis of the Pakistani ruling bloc is that of a congenital deficit, i.e., an inability to forge a sustainable hegemonic project, with its necessary but insufficient socioeconomic core, leading to a crippling dependency on (sub-)imperial patrons and coercion for coherence. This permanent crisis, and the concomitant search for imperial salvation, has been a feature of the ruling caste for at least half a century. As passive revolutionary and imperial salves have fallen through over the last decade and half, the organic crisis has now emerged into the open, though signs of its latency have been ever-present.

This then is the chronicle of a death foretold: a walk into disaster with eyes wide open, (almost) inevitable in its outcome, and unbearable in its lucidity for all those involved.

PASSIVE REVOLUTIONS, LIMITED INCORPORATION

To understand the unravelling of the Pakistani ruling bloc, a brief recap of its history, especially post-1970s, is required. Since the last multi-level crisis in the 1960s–70s, Pakistan has undergone two phases of 'passive revolution' which, in response to popular upsurges, served to preserve the reigning ruling bloc through coercion, 'molecular' changes and limited incorporation.[10]

The post-1970s mechanisms of limited absorption and militarized coercion had lineages in the travails of partition and formal decolonization in 1947. While subaltern groups had struggled to give pro-worker and pro-peasant inflections to the Pakistan Movement,[11] the landlord-proto-capitalist combine that dominated the new country quickly acquiesced to a centralized bureaucratic oligarchy taking over as ruling caste. Both the fiscal-security concerns of the new ruling bloc (vis-a-vis neighbouring India and the Kashmir dispute) and their unwillingness to concede national-federal and social-class concessions precluded the forging of broad social-organizational bases for the new state.[12] Social incapacity and limited hegemony thus led to reliance on military-bureaucratic centralization along with imperial patronage for coherence.

The resulting confluence of US-sponsored military dictatorship and limited developmentalism through the 1950s–60s generated massive social and geographical inequalities, and faced an intense challenge from labour, peasant, students and (sub-)national upsurges in the late-60s and early-70s. The fall of General Ayub Khan's dictatorship in 1969 and the independence of Bangladesh in 1971 were indexes of the multi-level crisis of the ruling bloc. In response, a passive revolutionary program of concerted coercion and *trasformismo* was instituted with regards to emergent (and insurgent) middle class and subaltern groups.[13]

The post-1970s passive revolutions worked through multiple spheres – political, ideological and economic – to secure a renewed military-centred ruling bloc. Passive revolutionary mechanisms were conditioned by the Pakistani ruling bloc's general incapacity and its inability to forge an expansive hegemonic project through socioeconomic concessions to subordinate groups, leading to crisis-prone modes of maintaining hegemony and dependency on coercive and compensatory mechanisms.

The military-centric form of coercive hegemony was integrally shaped by the ruling bloc's specific historical insertion into the world-system as a regional gendarmerie of US imperialism. These passive revolutions saw a renewed insertion into the US imperium's regional wars, which served to shore up the military-centred ruling bloc in the economic sphere through aid, grants and easy access to international loans. US aid arrived first for the anti-Soviet Afghan jihad in the 1980s (almost $5 billion) and then for the anti-jihad WoT in the twenty-first century (almost $30 billion). During the WoT period from 2001 to the early 2010s, aid and concessional grants to Pakistan from Western sources reached upwards of $4 billion per year, while the Paris Club rescheduled $12 billion of foreign debt.[14]

This period also saw an upsurge of labour export to Gulf and Western countries. In the initial upsurge of emigration, almost $20 billion was remitted into Pakistan between 1977 and 1987.[15] Today, over ten million Pakistanis are based abroad, remitting upwards of $20 billion annually. Stop-start privatization and economic liberalization from the 1990s onwards, and then a temporary upsurge of Chinese Belt and Road Initiative (BRI) investment in the mid-2010s, fed into this economic dependency. Privatization led to massive job losses: between the first IMF structural adjustment facility signed in 1988 and 2005, close to 160 state enterprises were privatized, out of which 130 collapsed.[16] Moreover, foreign investment whether from Chinese or other sources, remained overwhelmingly concentrated in the tertiary sector (such as infrastructure, finance and services), with the little investment that did come into manufacturing concentrated in consumer goods. Foreign investment thus did little to generate sustainable industrial development or backward-forward linkages between different sectors of the economy.[17]

In the ideological sphere, there was assertion of a militarized form of religious nationalism. This reactionary nationalism was given a fillip by US and Saudi-sponsored jihad in Afghanistan and then by the religious turn taken in the 1990s by resistance against Indian occupation of Kashmir. The Pakistani military became the node around which discourses of Islam, patriotism and national security were fused.[18] The popularization of this ideological complex had disastrous effects for subaltern groups. From the reversal of limited land reforms to the oppression of women and religious minorities, all were justified through regressive interpretations of Islam. Indeed, resort to right-wing groups and discourse became a staple for all sections of the ruling bloc, whether in suppressing opposition from outside or in settling fratricidal conflicts. Ideological hypertrophy and militaristic-theological dissimulation thus served as compensation for the lack of a coherent hegemonic project and leavened the ground for insurgencies from even further to the right.

In the political sphere, minimally absorptive modes of patronage politics were instituted, especially in central parts of Pakistan.[19] These worked through intermediaries forging direct links to the state for limited public service delivery. The power of big landed and capitalist elites persisted through economic diversification, even while during the 1980s there was an infusion of new political elites from petty bourgeois backgrounds spanning the formal-informal, urban-rural and agro-service sector domains as part of the *trasformismo* mechanisms of passive revolution.[20] In Punjab, Pakistan's biggest province, between 1985 and 2008 approximately two-thirds of legislators came from just 400 families.[21] Organized politics thus became dominated by 'party apparatuses built on an edifice of dynastic families and their networks rather than political party machines organized around ideology, ethnicity, class and/or programmatic platforms'.

A structurally limited ruling bloc would thus come to rely on war-mediated insertion into the imperial world-system. As the coercive institution providing coherence to a low-absorption social structure, the Pakistani military retained an arbitrator role in the polity. The military's role as the 'articulating principle' of a fractious ruling bloc was enhanced by being the main beneficiary of imperial patronage.[22] Bouts of martial rule through the 1980s and 2000s, along with facilitation by the International Financial Institutions (IFIs), also saw the military turn 'into a sovereign capitalist power that ... utilizes its authoritarianism for economic, territorial, and political purposes'.[23] Today, the Pakistani military is a multibillion dollar conglomerate spanning virtually all economic sectors, with a concentration in infrastructure, logistics and real estate. It is the country's largest institutional landowner, controlling approximately 12 per cent of state land, while being involved in myriad and proliferating housing schemes up and down the country.

Increasing worker remittances and economic liberalization (accelerated in the 2000s) also generalized cultures of conspicuous consumption. The emergence of professional middle class fractions went hand-in-hand with the deepening penetration of the commodity form. These emergent middle-class fractions, estimated to be between 40 and 60 million out of a total population of 200 million in 2010, were concentrated in core, urban(izing) areas and formed a growing constituency often exceeding the incorporatory mechanisms of vertical patronage politics.[24] Among these social groups, sociologically and ideologically close to the military, commodity fetishism merged with marketized conceptions of 'corruption' and the prevalent religious common sense.[25]

Political elites shaped this commodified culture through a kind of 'infrastructure populism' – the glitz of high-profile 'mega-projects' (motorways, shopping malls, gated communities and luxury apartments) serving to signal Pakistan's 'arrival' on the world-stage of neoliberal modernity and as weak ideological compensation for limited hegemony.[26] The flip-side of this infrastructure populism was a veritable gravy train of contractors, musclemen, bureaucrats, politicians and military officials making billions out of massive dispossession of indigenous and peri-urban groups for real estate and financial speculation.[27] Pakistanis are now the third largest foreign investors in the real estate sector in Dubai (after the British and Indians), with close to $12.5 billion invested in the emirate's property market.[28] Meanwhile for the subordinate classes, limited cash transfer programs were instituted with the restoration of formal democracy in 2008 (such as the Benazir Income Support Program under the PPP and PML-N, and the Ehsaas social protection program under PTI). These served as thin amelioration in line with the IFIs 'social turn', even while stealth privatization of public services under the 'Washington Consensus' continued.[29]

In peripheralized regions such as Balochistan and former 'tribal' areas, the balance between coercion and patronage tended towards the former. Here, the brutalization engendered by imperial wars and militarized exploitation of resources led to uneven processes of incorporation accompanied by intense resistance (both armed and non-violent). Extant elites in peripheral areas were either wiped out by religious fundamentalists receiving a fillip due to the neoimperial WoT or selectively absorbed into the military-linked war economy. Among working class and lower middle class youth, regimes of militarization and ritualized, corporeal humiliation in the name of 'security' and 'development' generated resistance movements which overflowed the pacificatory pressures of the state and elders.[30] Historical struggles against such uneven development and oppression also led to constitutional reforms in 2010. These provided limited power devolution and greater fiscal space to the provinces, while also tying middle class fractions from marginalized nations to the ruling bloc.[31]

Thus, uneven mechanisms of absorption and coercion working through multiple spheres and spaces came to characterize Pakistan's post-1970s passive revolutions. Stop-start mechanisms of procedural democracy and constitutional change increased the ambit of both formal political participation and the importance of mechanisms of vertical patronage. The deepening of commodity cultures merged with the prevailing religio-patriotic common sense. New middle-class fractions emerged with increasing economic liberalization and urbanization. The structurally limited ruling bloc came to rely on war-mediated insertion into the world-system.

Imperial dependence, patriotism, praetorianism and patrimonialism – these formed the economic, political and ideological nodes of the Pakistani ruling bloc post-1970s.

ORGANIC CRISIS

In the late-2000s and from the mid-2010s especially, the passive revolutionary sutures of the ruling bloc started giving way. In the ideological sphere, the WoT and the off-and-on conflict between the Pakistani military and formerly-allied Islamist groups brought the complex of Islam and praetorian patriotism under stress. The millenarian violence of fundamentalist militants, along with repeated military operations and US drone strikes in the peripheral regions, left over 60,000 dead and millions displaced. The military's acquiescence to imperial adventures led to widespread criticism from a war-weary and brutalized public, especially in the peripheries. Relatedly, the generals' rapacious economic expansionism gave the lie to pretensions of Islamic piety and national interest.

At the political level, procedural democracy, federal devolution and the politics of patronage had contradictory effects. On one hand, patronage mechanisms offered limited forms of inclusion, access and service delivery for subordinate groups with regards to a narrow ruling bloc.[32] On the other, urbanizing middle classes were increasingly unmoored from traditional vote-banks and clientelist networks.[33] Thus, the expansion of expectations and claims over the state started to exceed the bounds of patrimonialism itself.

Indeed, among upper middle-classes and elites, such limited expansion of franchise and devolution was registered in fearful terms as a loss of centrality. The plebian democratization characteristic of deepening commodification and procedural democracy activated centralizing, even reactionary responses among the military and historically pro-state middle and upper classes. This upper and middle class-centred reaction had parallels in the upper-caste response to the post-Mandal upsurge of subaltern castes in India and its feeding into the Hindutva project of the RSS-BJP.[34]

In the economic sphere, the imperial salve of the Pakistani ruling bloc wore off. US aid for the WoT decreased sharply in the 2010s – from a high of more than $4 billion in 2011, today foreign aid inflows are about $1 billion annually. However, fortuitous global circumstances temporarily served as renewed media of dependency. Easy liquidity from international banks in the aftermath of the 2008 recession, a fall in international oil prices in the 2010s and a temporary upsurge in Chinese BRI capital served to shore up foreign inflows. Between 2012 and 2024, Pakistan's external debt increased from about $40 billion to over $100 billion.[35] As the WoT concessions receded, external debt servicing quintupled from $3 billion in 2011 to over $16 billion in 2022 (and will increase to $25 billion annually for the next three to five years). While China is now the largest single bilateral creditor to Pakistan, disproportionately large amounts in debt servicing are paid to private, commercial, mostly Western banks: in 2021, these owned 23 per cent of Pakistan's debt stock while receiving close to 60 per cent of debt servicing. Where through the 1990s and 2000s, almost 60 per cent of state expenditure was on a combination of debt servicing and defence, today almost all state revenue is spent on these two accounts, while everything else – from civil servants' salaries to anaemic social expenditure – is financed through further debt.

With falling Western aid in the mid-2010s, the ruling bloc enthusiastically looked towards Chinese BRI investment as a 'game-changer'. However, the expected magnitude of Chinese investment did not materialize and indeed fell sharply post-2018 due to a combination of bureaucratic lethargy, intra-elite conflicts over BRI spoils and resistance from sections of domestic capital.[36] Indeed, as mentioned earlier, Chinese and other investments intensified the import- and consumption-dependent nature of Pakistani political economy and served to sharpen the limited incorporatory modes of ruling bloc hegemony. Together with the recent rise in international commodity prices and an onerous increase in debt servicing, these falling foreign inflows have heralded a deep-rooted economic crisis. Ideological stresses and failing political coherence are thus exacerbated by the lack of imperial economic support to paper over long-term, structural cracks. Modes of dependency that provided the material basis for previous passive revolutions are no longer operative. The very ground beneath the ruling bloc's feet has given way.

KHAN AS NUCLEUS

It is this long-term organic crisis which conditioned the rise of Imran Khan's right-populist movement through the 2010s and lends the current moment its ambiguous quality.[37] Khan's rise is part of a global crisis of neoliberalism, whereby centrist-technocratic forms of bourgeois hegemony are increasingly in conflict with contradictory, populist forms of the same.[38]

On one hand, in conditions of narrowing economic space, Khan and the PTI emerged as vehicles for the centralizing aspirations of upper-middle classes and elites (including those from the civil-military bureaucracy) in response to post-1970s plebian democratization. The emergent middle classes were also prime purveyors of deepening commodity cultures and market-centric discourses of moral corruption.[39] The technocratic, corruption-centric understanding of Pakistan's political economy promoted by Khan and his middle-class supporters fits neatly into marketized conceptions of 'good governance' peddled by IFIs, whereby 'making the system work is merely a matter of honest administration, stability, law and order, and an adequate infrastructure'.[40] Additionally, deeper penetration of the commodity form in the social formation laid the grounds for myriad fetishisms. With the reduction of (human) subjects to objects, thereby turning society into a reified thing beyond human intervention, the other polarity took on a concrete possibility of its own, i.e., of 'great men' who can stand above history and society itself.[41] In this context of deepening commodification and failing social-ideological cement, Khan's philanthropic and cricketing achievements, private media-fuelled celebrity, and self-fashioning as a playboy-turned-pious Muslim served to turn his personality into an anchor for a reformulated Islamic nationalism.

On the other hand, the narrow political modus operandi and fraying economic basis of the ruling bloc created vast reservoirs of discontent among subordinate classes and especially the youth (two-thirds of Pakistan's population today is under thirty years of age). With the elite unwilling to tax itself – Pakistan has one of the lowest tax-to-GDP ratios in the region – and indeed awarding itself $18 billion dollars of state subsidies annually, expenditure on defence and debt servicing takes up almost all the anaemic public revenue generated.[42] Consequently, the amount spent by the Pakistani state on debt interest payments alone is double that of total investment and quadruple the amount spent on health.[43] Over 2022–23, unemployment increased by two million and as many as 18 million fell below the poverty line. An extraordinary recent report by the Pakistan Institute of Development Economics put the unemployment rate among young graduates as high as 33 per cent, with a full 23 per cent taking on 'unpaid jobs'.[44] On top of this socioeconomic constriction, political parties working through locally entrenched dynasties and brokers offering limited incorporation through patronage networks is no longer practicable or acceptable.

The deepening penetration of digital technologies served to cement the mediatized celebrity of Khan and helped supporters outflank prevailing modes of political mediation and manipulation in the recent elections. For example, the PTI's TikTok base is 75 times larger than its main rival, the PML-N, and generates a hundred times more engagement.[45] Such hyperactive social media platforms were extensively deployed to mobilize voters during Khan's rise and then in the wake of his arrest and disqualification.

Thus, the upper and middle classes found in Khan a vehicle for countering perceptions of decline in conditions of plebian democratization. For the subordinate classes, Khan was the outlet for frustrations engendered by the economic and political conceit of the extant ruling bloc. In conditions of deepening commodification and digital atomization, Khan's media-fuelled celebrity thus formed a fetishistic nucleus for the coming together of multiple currents of discontent.

Khan's stint in power (2018–2022) was characterized by the dominance of military-linked elites and the upper middle classes. The alliance with the military and the pro-state inclinations of his core middle class base served to absorb and dissipate popular discontent through Khan's charismatic figure. Soon after coming to power, and as with previous governments, Khan had to sign a $6 billion IMF program to tackle an inherited balance of payments crisis. This led to an immediate drop in the GDP of 0.4 per cent, the first instance of negative growth in seven decades, and a three-fold increase of inflation to 10 per cent that subsequently proved to be only the beginning of a stratospheric rise.[46] As in previous governments, a series of finance ministers and public finance managers were imported from the IFIs, while the state bank itself was 'autonomized' under IMF diktat, following its patently ideological obsession with controlling the money supply as a means to tame inflation.

The period of economic contraction in the initial years of Khan's rule in the wake of the 2018–19 IMF program was eased somewhat by the fortuitous arrival of the Covid-19 pandemic in 2020–21. Governments all over the world bucked neoliberal dogma to institute expansionary fiscal policies, while foreign debt payments were temporarily suspended for peripheral countries. This provided the government with valuable fiscal space and an economic relief program of Rs. 430 billion (approximately $2.8 billion) was instituted.

However, here too the elite character and indeed the continuity of the Khan interregnum with previous governments was evident. The Covid relief package included a massive amnesty scheme for property developers to the tune of Rs. 186 billion in the hopes of 'trickle down' to workers in the booming construction sector. Of the Rs. 200 billion allocated for direct disbursement to day labourers, only Rs. 15 billion was actually distributed, while government ministers proudly boasted on Twitter of a 69 per cent rise in corporate profits.[47] Other forms of real-estate chicanery were also instituted. One particularly egregious case involved Pakistan's biggest property tycoon, Malik Riaz, a man with deep pockets and links to all sections of the civil-military elite. In 2019, Riaz was facilitated in repatriating almost $245 million from the UK in lieu of a $3 billion fine imposed by the Pakistani Supreme Court for illegal land dealings domestically.[48] In a tragicomic perversion, personally helping Riaz in this blatant corruption was Shahzad Akbar, Khan's Special Assistant on Accountability.

Targeted welfare programs instituted by the Khan government were an expansion of previous governmental schemes. However, these programs were not only situated in a wider environment of increasing austerity but also facilitated neoliberalism through stealth. For example, the Khan government introduced a scheme providing universal, set-amount health insurance, which became a way of incentivizing private healthcare and gutting the already emaciated public system. In Punjab alone, four years of the scheme has seen the amount of C-sections increase forty-fold, with 80 per cent taking place in private hospitals, while 70 per cent of all public sector patients were shifted to private facilities for unnecessarily expensive procedures.[49] Instead of upgrading and investing in public healthcare, the PTI's seemingly universal health program incentivized its further destruction through a massive transfer of public wealth into private hands.

Indeed, this kind of stealth privatization was in line with what previous governments instituted in other sectors, such as the previous PML-N government's restructuring of education through IFI-promoted public-private partnerships.[50] Limited welfarism here served as a means for deeper integration of citizens into the market economy. In this, as in most respects, PTI worked as a typical right-populist party: rhetoric of rupture and reform, but deep continuities in terms of class power and accumulation – and a direct product of the conceit and incapacity of the mainstream liberal-conservative parties preceding them.

Thus, the elite- and middle class-centred coalition that formed Khan's core base was unable to forge wider social bases in power. Indeed, in the absence of a wider transformative program of productive investment, delinking from the restrictive diktat of global neoliberalism and democratization of the state, fiery rhetoric and an increasing penetration of the military into all spheres of governance came to serve as compensatory mechanisms. In accelerating a trend instituted by previous governments, military officials took up increasing roles in the public and private sector – as ambassadors, as heads of the oversight body for the China Pakistan Economic Corridor, as whips keeping Khan's restive parliamentary allies in line and even as HR managers (read: musclemen) hired by factory owners to discipline workers.[51]

The fraying bases of imperial patronage and limited hegemonic capacity also conditioned Khan's nativist bluster at home and geopolitical posturing abroad. Domestically, Khan regularly held audiences with media personnel, social media influencers and the like, proclaiming both Bollywood and 'Western values' to be the root of Pakistan's various social ills, including highly publicized cases of the rape and murder of women. This took place even while the deepening political and economic crisis translated into popular discontent and multiple divisions within the ruling coalition. Divisions in the coalition and bureaucratic logjams were especially evident in the crucially important Punjab province, which is home to the majority of

Pakistan's population and serves as the military's main recruitment ground.

On the international front, relationships with the US continued their downward trajectory as the American withdrawal from Afghanistan approached, while Chinese links weakened due to the aforementioned investment blockages. In the context of fraying imperial linkages, the Khan government attempted to take up the leadership mantle of the so-called 'Muslim world'. Prominent stances against Islamophobia in global forums struck a popular chord at home. The Khan government attempted to forge links with emergent Muslim powers such as Turkey, even while attempting to maintain historical dependencies on contending sub-imperial powers such as Saudi Arabia. In a particularly telling case in 2019, the plug was pulled at the last minute on a much-publicized strategic alliance between Pakistan, Turkey and Malaysia after the Saudis conveyed their utmost displeasure.

As Samir Amin has reminded us, imperialist globalization stands on two legs: geopolitical and economic.[52] The resort merely to geopolitical rhetoric is therefore of limited use in the absence of an alternative socioeconomic program. The grotesque dance over the hot coals of (sub-)imperialism offers little without the consolidation of popular bases at home. In Khan's case, ideological overdrive and narrow cultural nationalism served as compensation for the lack of an integral hegemonic project. It was a means of dissimulation rather than organization of the masses for a serious assault on the entrenched structures of power in Pakistan.

The fault lines which conditioned Khan's rise thus also became his undoing in government. The fraying imperial and fiscal bases of the state, along with the growth of popular discontent among restive allies, opposition and within the ranks of the officer corps itself, led to Khan's eventual falling out with the military leadership in late 2021. The opposition, given a nod and a push by the praetorian guard, moved in to remove Khan from power through parliamentary-judicial manoeuvrings in March–April 2022. But instead of calling for fresh elections, they instead came to rely even more closely on the military for another round of IMF-mandated austerity, thus betraying their own lack of trust in the people.

Khan's rupture with the military leadership and subsequent ouster thus radicalized the quasi-martial law situation that marked his ascension and time in power. This was the case even while the deepening economic crisis and political suppression expanded his support base, including among the military's rank-and-file and officer corps.[53] The historical incapacity of the ruling caste and its constant resort to right-wing dissimulation to suppress opposition now faces its long-overdue comeuppance in the figure of Khan and a radicalized Pakistani nationalism. Indeed, the ideological coordinates of Islam and patriotism have become disassociated from the military and are now articulated around Khan.

Today, the militarized ruling bloc has neither a popular face to provide it legitimacy, nor concerted imperial patronage to initiate a new passive revolution. In the absence of imperial economic salve, the coordinates of the political terrain have become scrambled. Passive revolutions aborted, we have entered the territory of chaos.

A BANKRUPT ANCIEN RÉGIME

It is thus in the overlap of Pakistan's social history and economic structure that we can understand the current crisis of the ruling bloc and the new, Khan-centred conjuncture. The coalition currently in power, a who's who of Pakistan's *ancien régime*, is the most unpopular government since the last open military government ended in 2007–8. Bereft of ideas and social capacity, their estrangement from the people is total and thus too their reliance on the praetorian guard. Their most recent budget, a prelude to yet another IMF program of $7 billion, has onerously increased taxes on middle and working classes, while granting key exemptions to their own ever-narrowing social base of civil servants, military men and trading sectors.[54] This even while Pakistan's foreign debt servicing requirements have doubled to $25 billion annually and the country's elites continue to award themselves a yearly $18 billion in state subsidies – debt and its repayment of course ultimately being a class relation too.[55] A renewed round of austerity and dispossession thus beckons. Attempts to roll back limited federal devolution are also being attempted so as to increase fiscal space for the ruling bloc and attract foreign investment without restrictions or qualification.[56] The ruling bloc promises of reform and renewal will thus come to naught.

The best bet for the elites is another imperial war in the region, turning on the taps of US largesse. This is unlikely in the short-term due to US imperialism's preoccupation with China and Russia-Ukraine. However, with Israel's colonial depravities in Palestine escalating the risk of regional confrontation, other local gendarmeries of US imperialism such as the Pakistani military might yet receive their calling.

More prosaically, the ruling bloc is desperately searching to renew its imperial dependency in investment-focused terms. A Special Investment Facilitation Council (SIFC), led by the army chief, has been functioning as a shadow government for over a year.[57] Its aim of attracting close to $60 billion of investment over the next five years, mainly from Gulf countries, is yet more wishful thinking. However, there are regular reports of Saudi interest, especially in acquiring agricultural land and mineral resources in

Pakistan. Parts of the ruling bloc also hope to (re)attract Chinese investment, especially in relocating light industry and low-value added manufacturing as Chinese industry moves to products higher up in the global value-chain.[58]

Even if such foreign investment materializes, the social coalitions and capacity for export-oriented growth are simply not present. A colonial bureaucratic structure and a capitalist class entrenched in unproductive sectors do not bode well even for 'normal' neoliberal integration. Breaking this stasis will require a program of coercive reorientation not just with regards to subordinate classes but also among sections of the elite. There is no organized social force besides the military that can carry out such a program, yet it is doubtful that even they have such capacity. Indeed, there are (sporadic) noises from within both the big bourgeoisie and parts of the intelligentsia in support of a greater role for the military and even the possibility of a direct takeover.[59]

The ruling bloc's congenital incapacity is compounded by its crippling lack of imagination. There is much talk among legislators and intellectuals linked to the ruling bloc and IMF about a new 'Charter of Economy' for Pakistan – heralding turbo-charged, as opposed to stop-start, liberalization. There are even suggestions of working toward restructuring of the crippling foreign debt.[60] However, there is no recognition of the international situation or the unequal world-system into which these ideologists are advocating for Pakistan's 'better' integration. An unbridled focus on exports has already led to socially deleterious changes in cropping patterns and, most recently, resulted in record levels of inflation in food items.[61] For every dollar of foreign investment, Pakistan loses almost three dollars through profit transfer and repatriation by multinational corporations.[62] Moreover, in light of global capitalist stagnation and increasing economic protectionism even in core countries,[63] the advocacy of 'export-oriented growth' and an 'East Asian path' for economic development is wishful thinking.

The discourse around debt is even more limited. Between 1988 and 2022, Pakistan took on almost $203 billion in foreign debt (in current dollar terms) from private, multilateral and bilateral lenders. Over this same period, Pakistan also paid back almost $153 billion in debt servicing. However, due to the unequal structure of international trade and compounding terms of foreign debt, the country still owes close to $130 billion. The debt, as Fidel Castro once put it, is simply unpayable.[64] It needs to be cancelled.

However, among ideologists of the bourgeoisie there is no cognizance of the impossibility of a peripheral, elite-dominated country like Pakistan following the 'East Asian path' in the current confluence of domestic and international forces.[65] Nor is there the imagination for thinking through a program of delinking and internally-focused development.[66] Such a program would require the democratization of land and other productive factors (in both urban and rural areas), labour-absorbing forms of industrial and agricultural development, and public direction of finance and investment. It would also have to prepare for a managed default on foreign debt.

MOVEMENT WITHOUT HEGEMONY

The popular opposition likewise possesses neither the social coalition nor imagination to resolve the organic crisis. Khan has retained his core upper- and middle-class base even while expanding this into the popular classes. However, it is in their modes of organization that the effectiveness (or lack thereof) of the PTI may be discerned.

Subordinate classes are not organized in any institutionalized manner within the PTI. Their engagement is mediated through the reified sphere of social media, whose cult of immediacy is distinctly unsuited for the kind of program Pakistan's multi-level crises require. The ephemeral engagement fostered by virtual platforms lends itself well to one-off actions such as voting and protest, and the internet offers powerful weapons for mobilization. But it is also the case that the ruling classes have real weapons at their disposal. A sustained attack on entrenched nodes of power thus requires building institutions and movements around alternative and coherent social-economic programs. Neither the modes of PTI's (non-)organization, its personality-centred politics, nor its previous stint in power inspire confidence in this regard.

Conversely, extant elites and middle classes are organized within PTI's party structure itself. For example, party candidates in the recent elections consisted mostly of professional middle class members (such as lawyers and doctors) along with local business and landed elites.[67] The PTI's current chairman (in Khan's absence) is a lawyer. The party's most-recent general secretary was Omar Ayub Khan, grandson of Pakistan's first military dictator and inheritor of an industrial and insurance conglomerate. Its chief minister for Khyber Pakhtunkhwa province Ali Amin Gandapur is the son of a former army major who served as a minister in General Musharraf's military dictatorship. Significantly, PTI-backed independents in parliament merged with a right-wing religious party (the Sunni Unity Council) to try and secure indirectly elected seats for women and minorities.

The most organized elements within the PTI are thus an alliance of newly emergent middle classes and remnants of the *ancien régime* previously linked to the military. That sections of the elite are sticking with the party despite its falling out with the military leadership is indicative of the Khan-centred structuring of the new political terrain. In the persona of Khan, fratricidal bleeding within the *ancien régime* has fused with the mass frustrations and crisis of absorption from below.

In Gramscian terms, the PTI has foregone the war of position in civil society and moved directly to a war of manoeuvre in political society. That is, it has attempted to take on the state and ruling bloc without organizing subaltern groups. This is a recipe for aborted hegemony and chaos.

CHAOS, PARADOX AND OPENINGS

The confluence of crises today, therefore, is profound and explosive: narrow bases of accumulation; the ruling caste's congenital inability to sacrifice short-term gain for long-term stability; fraying bases of absorption and consent; a growing mass of the disaffected and alienated; the constant resort to right-wing dissimulations as (non-)solutions to social contradictions; and, finally, the drying up of imperial salve to paper over structural cracks.

Indeed, for large sections of the popular masses, especially those in core areas and those who had invested their hopes in Khan and his alliance with the military, the turning of the praetorian dagger towards its erstwhile allies has come, to speak with the Manifesto, as that douse of cold water, whereby 'man [sic] is at last compelled to face with sober senses his real conditions of life'.[68] Large sections of the young and the alienated are now forging a critique of the militarized ruling bloc in the crucible of practical experience. Concomitantly, there is a desperate search for opportunities to emigrate to increasingly hostile Gulf or Euro-American destinations. Close to a million Pakistanis left the country through official channels in 2023. Those of more limited means try their luck against the cruelties of Fortress Europe, where almost three hundred people recently lost their lives to the treacherous Mediterranean waters.[69] Pakistan's youth have moved from insurgency to despondency. As one young comrade put it recently, '*zameen hum per tang ho chuki hai*' – 'the land has shrunk upon us'.

It is this literal and metaphorical shrinking of the land that results in myriad intense but distinct struggles in both central and peripheral Pakistan today. For now, this conjuncture of discontent and chaos is structured mostly around Khan. However, considering the PTI's lack of social capacity and program, this will not remain the case for long. Thus, even if Khan finds a way back into power, the ruling bloc's organic crisis – of fraying hegemonic capacity, imperial dependence and limited incorporation – will remain operative in the absence of a deep-rooted program of socioeconomic reorientation, redistribution and anti-imperial delinking.

The unstable character of the conjuncture and the nodes of its social-ideological articulation present some key axes of reflection and practice for the left. First is the renewed round of dispossession that is going to be visited upon Pakistan's oppressed peripheries. In the highly brutalized Balochistan province, a long-running, armed nationalist movement centred around disaffected youth has moved to a stage of forging deep bases in civil society through female political workers of the Baloch Yakjehti Committee (BYC, Baloch Solidarity Committee).[70] BYC women have led organizing and popular marches throughout Balochistan and even to Pakistan's federal capital demanding accountability for the thousands of Baloch disappeared by the Pakistani state in its quest for monopoly over the province's natural resources. In a related vein, militarized dispossession and 'anti-terrorism' operations have created a large base of battered, war-weary populations in the Afghan-border regions that has manifested itself in the ebb and flow of the antiwar and civil rights Pashtun Tahaffuz Movement (PTM, Pashtun Protection Movement) since 2018.[71] In Pakistani-administered Kashmir and the adjacent Gilgit-Baltistan region, long-standing demands for territorial autonomy are inflected with anger over tourism-mediated land grabs, decreasing subsidies for basic commodities and a lack of control over natural resources (such as waterways and hydropower). In the past year, this anger has led to intense mass movements organized through local, often neighbourhood-level, peoples' committees.[72]

In all these cases, subordinate classes and youth have demonstrated active disaffection with the reigning class of state-appointed political elders that have historically acted as agents of pacification in the peripheries. Indeed, in the SIFC's manoeuvrings to offer Pakistan's mineral and agricultural resources to foreign patrons along with recent moves towards yet more 'anti-terror' military operations,[73] a new round of militarized dispossession and humiliation beckons. The intensity of Pakistan's national oppressions and uneven development will thus ineluctably continue to produce movements of (sub-)national autonomy and self-determination. The overflowing of these demands from extant vehicles of mediation, and their centering by disaffected youth and subordinate classes, offer avenues of intervention and organizing for the left.

Relatedly, and this is the second key axis of reflection and practice, the intensity of uneven development – Pakistani society and polity's *multinational* character and the concomitant dissonances of land, labour, language and history – has also conditioned an unevenness of the time and space of political insurgency. Finding social and organizational points of mediation, where peripheral and partisan universals can come together in convergent points of struggle, has always been a key struggle for the left. This is a delicate dialectic, one which cannot ignore the terrain of the particular and its moment of immediacy, and indeed must deepen it substantively. Yet it is also one which – even where the departure points are (separate) partisan universals – is condemned to isolation, involution and, ultimately, failure if it fails to undergo a 'mutual transformation in convergent points of struggle or processes of organizational condensation',[74] a relational socio-spatial imbrication of partisan universal(s), the sublation of immediacies into a concrete universality. In short, if it fails to achieve that cherished crowning point of the dialectic, i.e., the function of mediation and, therefore in Pakistan's case, of a genuinely plural, multi-national hegemony.

Two contemporary realities point towards possible and progressive resolutions of this articulatory puzzle. First, as mentioned above, are emerging expressions of Pakistan's (sub-)national questions beyond extant, elite-mediated nodes of containment. In building popular bases and a Fanonist 'national consciousness' which is 'not nationalism' but 'national, revolutionary, and social' at the same time, such struggles have the potential of escaping self-enclosed involution, while forging a concrete universality: a non-reductive practice of mediating particulars through convergent points of struggle.[75] The second reality is that of Pakistan's emergent urban question and its telescoping of reformulated and respatialized (sub-)national questions. For the dispossession and militarization visited upon peripheries are linked concretely – through spatially-extended networks of displacement, loss and labour – to the ruling bloc's land-hungry rapaciousness and socio-spatial inequality in core urban areas.[76] The postcolonial state and capital's incessant drive towards simultaneous convergence and differentiation has thus positioned the urban question in Pakistan as one which concentrates all the contradictions of polity and society – from land inequality, lack of political-economic absorptive capacity and the hierarchized and multi-national character of its working classes, to the ritualized and corporeal humiliation of neoimperial/postcolonial militarization.

That the urban question is laying the grounds for new resolutions of national question(s) is indicated by emergent struggles themselves. In this regard, the urban and spatially extended articulations of the PTM over the last half a decade have offered key avenues of deepening and extension.[77] The PTM's mass mobilization against 'anti-terror' operations and militarized dispossession have linked core and peripheral regions, while forging both non-elite articulations of the ethnic Pashtun national question and potential nodes of solidarity with other oppressed social groups in urban Pakistan and beyond.

In the current conjuncture, the coalescing of a radicalized Pakistani nationalism around Imran Khan gives further indication of this evolving terrain of 'the national'. Reactionary and right-wing though Khan's politics are, his populism addresses real, lived and historical experiences of Pakistan's popular classes. Khan's anti-Western and anti-corruption rhetoric latches onto nodes of anti-elite and anti-imperial common sense, while serving to personalize and thus neutralize these potentially transformative moments of popular consciousness. Relatedly, the linkages made by the PTI between Khan's persona and *haqeeqi azaadi* (true independence) point to the unfinished business that Frantz Fanon once termed 'false decolonization'. Again, by drawing upon deep-seated popular understandings of imperial influence on the Pakistani ruling bloc, but then reducing these to Khan's personality itself, the PTI's populism serves to domesticate such potentially transformable nodes of common sense. Indeed, the very fact that a radicalized Pakistani nationalism has coalesced around Khan and has gained support in almost all corners of the country, illustrates the shifting socio-spatial bases of the national question(s).

What Khan's popularity demonstrates is the need for a genuine program of national sovereignty which can work through Pakistan's deeply uneven and multi-national society. As indicated earlier, tendencies of convergence-differentiation working through spatially extended networks of capital, labour, militarization and displacement have served to concentrate Pakistan's myriad contradictions in its urban(izing) areas. Here, we have the burgeoning of a concentrated and precarious but still multi-national/multi-ethnic working-class and, indeed, a largely downwardly mobile middle-class. It is in these popular sectors that, alongside the continuing currency of ethnic-national questions, a reformulated *Pakistani* national question is also finding fertile ground.

It is in this realm that an energetic and creative left can forge genuine bases, provided that we overcome some of our own historical hangovers. Historically, the militarized and theological dissimulation associated with mainstream Pakistani nationalism has served to suppress all stirrings of subaltern assertion, especially in the ethnicized peripheries.[78] Given this sordid political and cultural history, the left has understandably shied away from Pakistani nationalism, oscillating between the valorization and even tailing of (often elite-centred) ethnic-national articulations or, conversely, mechanical formulas whereby 'class' is denuded of all its historical, geographical and experiential joints, i.e., without the understanding of how class is produced *through* difference (especially around ethnicity and gender). However, due to the shifting condensations of class, space and difference discussed above, these formulas are now under pressure from both sides. On one hand, the continuing vitality of regional-ethnic national questions has begun to escape elite-centred nodes of containment. On the other hand, the shifting social character of core Pakistani areas, cannot but give the lie to both reductionist understandings of class and Pakistani nationalism.

As pointed out by a long tradition of revolutionaries, the socio-spatial changes wrought by (post)colonial capitalism and the real weight of unevenness, association and struggles engendered therein position 'the nation' in postcolonial contexts not as a 'derivative discourse' but as an ineluctable ground of material-discursive appropriation.[79] For the late Aijaz Ahmad, the imbrication of Hindutva fascism in India in exactly such historical-spatial rhythms pointed to the 'objective necessity for the definition of a national project, in the form of an identity and its future projection'.[80] In engagement with Ahmad, concretely linked as this need for a 'powerful ideological cement' is to the objective coordinates of capitalist economy and spatiality, the left in Pakistan can neither *abandon* 'the terrain of nationalism itself', nor can it occupy that terrain '*empty handed*, without a political project for the re-making of the nation and its existing structures of power'.[81]

In our case, the weight of uneven development, the *multiple* historically formed communities of language, feeling and nation, complicates this terrain of the Pakistani nation. Thus, the left can neither abandon the terrain of the Pakistani nation nor do without articulating this as a *pluri*-national project. The shifting socio-spatial articulations of ethnic-national questions and the popularity of Khan's personalized nationalism indicate the real substrate on which a progressive pluri-national consciousness may find fertile ground. Relatedly, the organic crisis of the ruling bloc and the overflowing of popular articulations of 'the national' from its extant military-centred coordinates, are indicative of the flux in this eminently appropriable terrain. In this sense, the limited incorporatory mechanisms of the ruling bloc, its historical lack of a coherent project of ideological-material hegemony, along with the social-structural weaknesses of even right-populist articulations (such as the PTI's), make the terrain of 'the national' potentially open to alternative, more emancipatory articulations.

This is not to minimize the dangers the left faces. The chaos within and outside the ruling bloc, its historical patronage of all kinds of reactionary formations, its institutionalization of masculinized cultures of cruelty in everyday life, and the vast reservoirs of lumpenization and alienation all serve to make corporeal and deathly violence a palpable possibility within everyday politics in Pakistan – both in core areas and especially in the peripheries. Even with such ever-present dangers, however, the new conjuncture of chaos and attendant socio-spatial shifts provides grounds for a re-appropriation of the terrain of 'the national' for the left.

Of course, such a reformulated Pakistani national-popular will or, in Fanonian terms a *pluri*-national consciousness, cannot confine itself merely to discursively cutting-edge formulations. Here, questions of strategy are crucial and the subject of active debate. The conceptual coordinates of a reformulated (pluri-)national consciousness, with its necessary but insufficient core of national sovereignty and anti-imperial economic delinking, have been discussed above. Additionally, vexing questions of the scale and scope of organizing required confront the left. Through the preceding passive revolutions, everyday politics in large parts of Pakistan came to be structured around localized patronage networks and issues of access to the police, courts, markets and limited public service delivery. Indeed, such a limited sphere of contention was systematically institutionalized by the militarized ruling bloc, such that major questions around the economy and foreign policy remained divorced from popular aspirations and everyday contestation.[82]

It is also within this delimited terrain of the everyday that a left re-emerging from the tribulations of US-backed dictatorship and the 'End of History' has attempted to organize over the last two decades. Thus, against the locally instituted networks of patronage which serve to disorganize horizontal, subaltern organizing, sections of the left attempted to embed themselves in issues of everyday life and local politics on the strength of peoples' organizing, as opposed to through access to influential patrons in civil and political society. Meanwhile, the resurgence of patriarchal oppression, youth alienation, the eminence of climate catastrophe, and the proliferation of private and virtual media led many sectors of the left to attempt to intervene in the reified sphere of images and cultural-discursive contention.

The Khan phenomenon and recent elections point to another important shift characteristic of the current conjuncture, i.e., the overflowing of everyday politics from established coordinates of patronage and localized containment toward a growing constituency's tendency to act according to national (and anti-imperial) imperatives. That this shift is related to the open emergence of the ruling bloc's organic crisis and the social, spatial and technological shifts elucidated above goes without saying. The questions that these signs in the street, this shifting terrain of politics and subjectivity, throw up for the left are thus of the depth and scale of its organizing. Do we continue with and double down on a deep(er) organizing method of forming localized zones of subaltern autonomy and assertion, such as at the neighbourhood and village levels, in a wager that a few key breaks in the homeostasis of patronage politics will catalyze popular cleavages in other parts of the country? Or do we concentrate on (pluri-)national-level organizing, campaigns and movements, including in the increasingly influential virtual sphere?

To be sure, a strategy of forging a national-popular will (i.e., of hegemony) is concretely different from one of (right or left) populism. Populism's top-down articulation of 'the people' – unindexed by class, region or gender – into a hierarchical and ultimately demobilizing subservience to singular leaders serves more as a strategy of the right than of the left. A national-popular hegemony or a pluri-national consciousness, however, is based on an active construction of 'the people' through 'political mobilization and democratic experiments' which account for 'the differentiated and uneven relations among dominated groups by, for example, combining moments of autonomy with moments of alliance'.[83] In this respect, while the social-spatial conditions for shaping a national project are clearly emergent in today's Pakistan, the scalar and geographical questions of organizing and strategy, and the delicate dialectic between building localized networks of subaltern assertion beyond the 'politics of common sense' and that of articulating a (pluri-)national project need to be carefully worked through. This is a debate that is just beginning on the left and will be definitive for how we deal with the decisive shifts in polity and society represented by the recent elections specifically and by the trends of the last decade more generally.[84]

What is beyond doubt, however, is that we have moved to a new conjuncture of chaos, marked by the open emergence of an organic crisis. Here is a ruling bloc with no living ideals, its sources of succour and sustenance now dried up, surviving for a time by the weight of sheer inertia.

From its core to the peripheries, the autumn of Pakistan's patriarchs has arrived. We are faced, therefore, with a series of tragicomic paradoxes: narcissistic celebrities elevated, by dint of circumstance and stubbornness, to the status of heroes. Spent forces of the *ancien régime* posing as heralds of renewal in government. Cowardice camouflaged as compromise. Chaos in the cover of a stalemate. It is an interregnum that will not last long.

NOTES

1   Editorial, 'What next for PTI?', *DAWN*, 23 February 2024.

2   Dawn.com, 'All you need to know about the new faces in PM Shehbaz's 19-member cabinet', *DAWN*, 12 March 2024; Kamal Munir and Natalya Naqvi, 'Privatization in the Land of Believers: The political economy of privatization in Pakistan', *Modern Asian Studies*, 51(6), 2017, pp. 1695-1726.

3   Ayyaz Mallick, 'Elections in Pakistan: A Populist Moment?', *The Bullet*, 16 September 2018, available at: www.socialistproject.ca.

4   Mariam Mufti, Sahar Shafqat and Niloufer Siddiqui, eds, *Pakistan's Political Parties: Surviving between Dictatorship and Democracy*, Washington, DC: Georgetown University Press, 2020.

5   Hamza Alavi, 'Bangladesh and the Crises of Pakistan', in Ralph Miliband and John Saville, eds, *Socialist Register 1971*, London: Merlin Press, 1971; Aijaz Ahmad, 'Democracy and Dictatorship', in Hassan Gardezi and Jamil Rashid, eds, *Pakistan, The Roots of Dictatorship*, London: Zed Books, 1983, pp. 94-147.

6   Antonio Gramsci, *Further Selections from the Prison Notebooks*, Derek Boothman, trans., London: Lawrence & Wishart, 1995, Q7§15, p. 220.

7   Antonio Gramsci, *Selections from the Prison Notebooks*, Quintin Hoare and Geoffrey Nowell Smith, eds. and trans., NY: International Publishers, 1971, Q13§17, pp. 177-80.

8   Peter Thomas, 'Modernity as "passive revolution": Gramsci and the Fundamental Concepts of Historical Materialism', *Journal of the Canadian Historical Association/Revue de la Société historique du Canada*, 17(2), 2006, pp. 61-78; Peter Thomas, 'Gramsci's Revolutions: Passive and Permanent', *Modern Intellectual History*, 17(1), 2020, pp. 117-46.

9   Stuart Hall, 'The Great Moving Right Show' [1979], in Stuart Hall, *The Hard Road to Renewal*, New York: Verso, 1988, p. 56.

10   Ayyaz Mallick, 'Beyond "Domination without Hegemony": passive revolution(s) in Pakistan', *Studies in Political Economy*, 98(3), 2017, pp. 239-62.

11   Kasim Tirmizey, 'Labour Geography of the National Question in Times of Decolonisation: Sharecropper Politics in Western Punjab, c. 1945–1953', *Antipode*, 55(1), 2023, pp. 286-306; Taj Ul-Islam Hashmi, *Pakistan as a Peasant Utopia: The Communalization of Class Politics in East Bengal, 1920-1947*, New York: Routledge, 2019.

12   Ayesha Jalal, *The State of Martial Rule: The Origins of Pakistan's Political Economy of Defence*, Cambridge: Cambridge University Press, 1990.

13   Aasim Sajjad Akhtar, *The Politics of Common Sense: State, Society and Culture in Pakistan*, Cambridge: Cambridge University Press, 2017.

14   Ayyaz Mallick, Tayyab Safdar and Bilal Ayaz Butt, 'History, Structure, and Conjuncture: Imperialism and the Polity in Pakistan', forthcoming; Ateeb Ahmed, 'The rise of military capital in Pakistan: Military neoliberalism, authoritarianism and urbanization', *Geoforum*, 146, 2023, p. 5.

15   S. Akbar Zaidi, *Issues in Pakistan's Economy*, Oxford: Oxford University Press, 2005, p. 503.

16   Aasim Sajjad Akhtar, 'Privatization at Gunpoint', *Monthly Review*, 57(5), 2005, pp. 26-33.

17   Muhammad Tayyab Safdar, 'Domestic Actors and the Limits of Chinese Infrastructure Power: Evidence from Pakistan', *Journal of Contemporary Asia*, 54(2), 2022, pp. 317–341; Mallick, Safdar, and Butt, 'History, Structure, and Conjuncture'.

18   Maria Rashid, *Dying to Serve: Militarism, Affect, and the Politics of Sacrifice in the Pakistan Army*, Stanford, CA: Stanford University Press, 2020.

19   Akhtar, *Politics of Common Sense*; Asha Amirali, 'A Case of Rampaging Elephants: The Politics of the Middle Classes in Small-Town Pakistan', *Journal of Contemporary Asia*, 54(2), 2022, pp. 299-316.

20   Jan Breman, 'Land Flight in Sindh', *Economic and Political Weekly*, 48(9), 2013, pp. 35-39.

21   Ali Cheema, Hassan Javid, and Muhammad Farooq Naseer, 'Dynastic Politics in Punjab: Facts, Myths and their Implications', Institute of Development and Economic Alternatives, Working Paper No. 01-13, 2014, p. 1-2.

22   Mushtaq H. Khan, 'Aid and Governance in Vulnerable States: Bangladesh and Pakistan since 1971', *The ANNALS of the American Academy of Political and Social Science*, 656(1), 2014, pp. 59-78.

23   Ayesha Siddiqa, *Military Inc.: Inside Pakistan's Military Economy*, Second Edition, London: Pluto Press, 2017; Ahmed, 'The rise of military capital', pp. 3, 6.

24   Durr-e-Nayab, 'Estimating the Middle Class in Pakistan', Working Papers & Research Reports, Islamabad: Pakistan Institute of Development Economics, 2011.

25   Ammara Maqsood, '"Buying Modern": Muslim subjectivity, the West and patterns of Islamic consumption in Lahore, Pakistan', *Cultural Studies*, 28(1), 2013, pp. 84-107.

26   Ayyaz Mallick, 'Urban space and (the limits of) middle class hegemony in Pakistan', *Urban Geography*, 39(7), 2018, pp. 1113–20.

27   Nausheen H. Anwar, 'Receding Rurality, Booming Periphery: Value Struggles in Karachi's Agrarian-Urban Frontier', *Economic and Political Weekly*, 53(12), 2018, pp. 46-54.

28   Annette Alstadsæter et al., 'Who Owns Offshore Real Estate? Evidence from Dubai', EU Tax Observatory Working Paper No. 1, 2022; Atika Rehman and Naziha Syed Ali, 'Dubai Unlocked: Pakistanis' $12.5bn property empire', *DAWN*, 15 May 2024.

29   Pablo Idahosa and Bob Shenton, 'The layers of social capital', *African Studies*, 65(1), 2006, pp. 63-78; Sher Ali Khan, 'Why Punjab is outsourcing its public schools', *Herald*, 2 October 2017.

30   Hafeez Jamali, 'A Tempest in My Harbor Gwadar, Balochistan', in Madiha R. Tahir, Qalandar Bux Memon and Vijay Prashad, eds, *Dispatches from Pakistan*, Minneapolis: University of Minnesota Press, 2014, pp. 168-84; Ayyaz Mallick, 'From Partisan Universal to Concrete Universal? The Pashtun Tahaffuz Movement in Pakistan', *Antipode*, 52(6), 2020, pp. 1774–93.

31   Julien Levesque, 'Beyond Success or Failure: Sindhi Nationalism and the Social Construction of the "Idea of Sindh"', *Journal of Sindhi Studies*, 1(1), 2021, pp. 1-33.

32   Shandana Khan Mohmand, *Crafty Oligarchs, Savvy Voters: Democracy under Inequality in Rural Pakistan*, Cambridge University Press, 2019.

33   Asad Rehman, *Politics of Socio-Spatial Transformation in Pakistan: Leaders and Constituents in Punjab*, Abingdon: Routledge, 2023.

34   Christophe Jaffrelot, *India's Silent Revolution: The Rise of the Lower Castes in North India*, London: Hurst & Co., 2003.

35   Mallick, Safdar and Butt, 'History, Structure, and Conjuncture'.

36   Safdar, 'Domestic Actors and the Limits of Chinese Infrastructure Power'.

37   Umair Javed, 'Continuity and Change in Naya Pakistan', *Catalyst*, 2(4), 2019, pp. 81-104.

38   Gillian Hart, 'Modalities of Conjunctural Analysis: "Seeing the Present Differently" through Global Lenses', *Antipode*, 56(1), 2024, pp. 135-64.

39   Ali Usman Qasmi, 'Making Sense of Naya Pakistan I-IV', *The Friday Times*, September–October 2018.

40 William Graf, 'The State in the Third World', in Leo Panitch, ed., *Socialist Register 1995: Why Not Capitalism?*, London: Merlin Press, pp. 140-62.

41 Richard Westerman, 'Populism and the Logic of Commodity Fetishism: Lukács's Theory of Reification and Authoritarian Leaders', in Gregory R. Smulewicz-Zucker, ed., *Confronting Reification: Revitalizing Georg Lukács's Thought in Late Capitalism*, Leiden: Brill, 2020, pp. 289-321.

42 UNDP, *Pakistan National Human Development Report 2020*, United Nations Development Programme, Pakistan, 2021.

43 UNCTAD, *A World of Debt: Debt at a Glance*. United Nations Conference on Trade and Development, 2023, available at: https://unctad.org/publication/world-of-debt/dashboard

44 Hafiz A. Pasha, 'Big rise in poverty, unemployment', *Business Recorder*, 4 February 2023; Tanzeel Hassan, 'Why are more Pakistanis taking their own lives?', *Dawn. com*, 12 May 2019; Nadeem Ul Haque and Durr-e-Nayab, 'Pakistan, Opportunity to Excel: Now and the Future', PIDE Monograph Series, Pakistan Institute of Development Economics, 2022.

45 Abdul Moiz Malik, 'TikTok: The new frontier for political info-wars', *DAWN*, 22 May 2023.

46 Ammar Ali Jan, 'The IMF Is Using the Debt Crisis to Hollow Out Pakistan's Sovereignty', *Jacobin*, 4 April 2021.

47 Khurram Husain, 'The party ends', *DAWN*, 18 February 2021; Khurram Husain, 'The great Covid dole', *DAWN*, 4 March 2021.

48 Naziha Syed Ali, 'Malik Riaz & the art of the deal', *DAWN*, 17 April 2021; Naziha Syed Ali, 'Bahria Town & others: Greed unbound', *DAWN*, 12 September 2019.

49 Asif Chaudhry, '"Misuse" of health card scheme: 80 per cent of C-section procedures conducted at private hospitals in Punjab', *DAWN*, 6 March 2024; Asif Chaudhry, 'Sehat card "corruption": Punjab Institute of Cardiology head removed for "shifting heart patients to private hospitals"', *DAWN*, 16 June 2024.

50 Khan, 'Why Punjab is outsourcing its public schools'.

51 Our Correspondent, 'Asim Bajwa wins kudos for advancing CPEC', *Express Tribune*, 6 August 2021; Fawad Hasan, 'Labour in Karachi's Fast Fashion Industry', *Jamhoor*, 1 March 2022.

52 Samir Amin, 'Contemporary Imperialism', *Monthly Review*, 67(3), 2015, pp. 23-36.

53 Baqir Sajjad Syed, 'Ministry of Defence disowns "unrecognized" veterans' bodies', *DAWN*, 3 September 2022; Kamran Yousaf, 'Army axes high-ranking officers over May 9 chaos', *Express Tribune*, 26 June 2023.

54 Umair Javed, 'Death and taxes', *DAWN*, 8 July 2024.

55 Murtaza Syed, 'Between debt and the deep blue sea', *The News*, 8 February 2023; UNCTAD, *A World of Debt*.

56 Iftikhar A. Khan, 'Law on foreign investment passed amid barbs from government benches', *DAWN*, 13 December 2022; Ashfaq Laghari, 'A High-Stakes Showdown Unfolds over Water Distribution', *Lok Sujaag*, 25 March 2024.

57 Khurram Husain, 'Orphaned disputes', *DAWN*, 18 January 2024.

58 Nasir Jamal, 'Attracting China's relocating industries', *DAWN*, 11 March 2024; Shahbaz Rana, 'Pakistan sweetens terms to lure Saudi investment', *Express Tribune*, 20 April 2024.

59   Kazim Alam, '"Hybrid model" keeps politicians on right track, says Arif Habib',
      DAWN, 6 August 2023; Yousuf Nazar, 'Is Pakistan Headed For A Military
      Takeover?', *Express Tribune*, 6 June 2024.

60   Staff Report, 'Charter of Economy is needed to revive the economy: Miftah Ismail',
      Pakistan Today, 28 May 2022; Nadir Cheema, 'The case for sovereign default',
      DAWN, 2 February 2023; Mubarak Khan, 'PM Shehbaz to unveil new economic
      plan on August 14 to drive liberalisation', *DAWN*, 11 August 2024.

61   Zofeen T. Ebrahim, 'Pakistan is abandoning cotton for water guzzling sugarcane',
      DAWN, 10 April 2020; Muhammad Arfan, 'Reviving Punjab's Dying Rivers', *The
      Friday Times*, 13 March 2024; Mubarak Zeb Khan, 'Unbridled food exports force
      domestic consumers to pay record prices for essential items', *DAWN*, 3 July 2024.

62   Mallick, Safdar, and Butt, 'History, Structure, and Conjuncture'.

63   Ilias Alami, Adam D. Dixon, and Emma Mawdsley, 'State Capitalism and the New
      Global D/development Regime', *Antipode*, 53(5), 2021, pp. 1294-318.

64   Fidel Castro, 'The debt is unpayable' [1985], CADTM.org, 29 November 2016.

65   For example, see congruent debates in the context of post-apartheid South Africa:
      Gillian Hart, 'The agrarian question and industrial dispersal in South Africa: Agro☒
      industrial linkages through Asian lenses', The *Journal of Peasant Studies*, 23(2–3),
      1996, pp. 245-77; Giovanni Arrighi, Nicole Aschoff and Ben Scully, 'Accumulation
      by dispossession and its limits: The Southern Africa paradigm revisited', *Studies in
      Comparative International Development*, 45, 2010, pp. 410-38.

66   Samir Amin, 'The Sovereign Popular Project; The Alternative to Liberal
      Globalization', *Journal of Labor and Society*, 20(1), 2017, pp. 7-22.

67   Umair Javed, 'Ruptures in 2024', *DAWN*, 19 February 2024.

68   Karl Marx and Friedrich and Engels, 'Manifesto of the Communist Party' [1848],
      p. 16, available at: www.marxists.org.

69   Alia Chughtai and Abid Hussain, '"If I die, I die": Pakistan's death-trap route to
      Europe', *Al Jazeera*, 9 December 2023.

70   BMR Team, 'Birth of a Movement: Transformation of Bramsh Solidarity
      Committees', *Balochistan Marxist Review*, 8 October 2020.

71   Mallick, 'From Partisan Universal to Concrete Universal'.

72   Qaiser Khan, 'Azad Kashmir's Now Or Never Movement', *The Friday Times*,
      12 May 2024.

73   Anwar Iqbal, 'Pakistan asks US for small arms to achieve "Istehkam"', *DAWN*,
      29 June 2024.

74   Stefan Kipfer and Gillian Hart, 'Translating Gramsci in the Current Conjuncture',
      in Michael Ekers et al., eds, *Gramsci: Space, Nature, Politics*, West Sussex: Wiley-
      Blackwell, 2013, p. 338.

75   Frantz Fanon, *The Wretched of the Earth* [1967], London: Penguin Books, 2001, pp.
      117-9; Mallick, 'From Partisan Universal to Concrete Universal'.

76   Sanaa Alimia, *Refugee Cities: How Afghans Changed Urban Pakistan*, University of
      Pennsylvania Press, 2022.

77   Mallick, 'From Partisan Universal to Concrete Universal'.

78   Saadia Toor, *The State of Islam: Culture and Cold War Politics in Pakistan*, London:
      Pluto Press, 2011.

79   Vladimir Ilich Lenin, 'A Caricature of Marxism and Imperialist Economism' [1916],
      in *Lenin Collected Works, Volume 23,* Moscow: Progress Publishers, 1964, pp. 28-76;

Manu Goswami, *Producing India: From Colonial Economy to National Space*, Chicago, IL: University of Chicago Press, 2004; Gillian Hart, 'The Provocations of Neoliberalism: Contesting the Nation and Liberation after Apartheid', *Antipode*, 40(4), 2008, pp. 678-705; Sam Moyo and Paris Yeros, eds, *Reclaiming the Nation: The Return of the National Question in Africa, Asia and Latin America*, London: Pluto Press, 2011.

80   Aijaz Ahmad, 'Culture, Community, Nation: On the Ruins of Ayodhya', *Social Scientist*, 21(7-8), 1993, p. 31.

81   Ahmad, 'Culture, Community, Nation', p. 34, emphasis added.

82   Akhtar, *Politics of Common Sense*.

83   Stefan Kipfer, 'Populism', in Kelly Fristh, ed., *Keywords for Radicals: The Contested Vocabulary of Late Capitalist Struggle*, Chico, CA: AK Press, 2016, p. 317.

84   For example, see: Aasim Sajjad Akhtar, *The Struggle for Hegemony in Pakistan: Fear, Desire and Revolutionary Horizons*, London: Pluto Press, 2022.

LATE FASCISM AND THE TURKISH STATE: QUESTIONS OF STRATEGY

ŞEBNEM OĞUZ

The question of left strategy turns on the particular form taken by the capitalist state in a certain historical conjuncture and social formation, as well as the political perspectives of the actors involved. This holds true for the left in Turkey. As the Turkish state has undergone a contradictory process of fascistization over the twenty-two-year reign of the political Islamist AKP (Adalet ve Kalkınma Partisi – Justice and Development Party), the left has been compelled to adapt its strategy accordingly. With the increasing authoritarianism of the regime after the Gezi Park resistance in 2013 – another instance of the 'struggle of the squares' – there has been a prevailing strategy across various factions of the left that prioritizes forming alliances to collectively challenge the AKP regime, with some taking the form of electoral coalitions. In this essay, I explore the left's strategy against this new form of regime in Turkey and seek lessons that may inform strategy against late fascism in other contexts.

Left strategies must adapt to different settings such as the constraints of a certain capitalist state form, the shifts between different social forms of the capitalist state and the transition from capitalism to socialism. When discussing the relationship between state form and left strategy in these contexts, three distinct historical conjunctures hold particular significance. First is the revolutionary situation in Russia before October 1917, where two powers co-existed: the soviets comprising workers and peasants directly engaged in decision-making, and the Provisional Government which emerged following the February Revolution. In this conjuncture, Lenin advocated for the soviets to seize and dismantle the existing state apparatus, thereby resolving the 'dual power' dynamic through the creation of a 'workers' state'.

The second conjuncture is the rise of classical fascism in Europe during the interwar period, where the critical question centered on determining the composition of the alliances against fascism. The united front strategy sought an alliance of all working-class and socialist organizations, whereas the popular front strategy aimed for a broader coalition involving various political parties and societal factions opposed to fascism but not necessarily to capitalism. The popular front strategy, for example, stalled the advancement of fascism in some countries for a time, such as in France during the 1930s. These strategies were centered on how to stop fascism from coming to power, rather than how to overthrow fascism in power. Once fascism did come to power, the terrain of struggle depended on how that power was constituted and consolidated in a given country. In the cases of Germany and Italy, elections were suspended and the state apparatuses gained the support of broad sections of society through mass mobilization. This differed from the military dictatorships in Greece, Portugal and Spain which, while also suspending elections, failed to establish themselves within the masses. In these contexts, social struggles from outside the state persisted and hastened the collapse of these regimes by deepening intra-state contradictions.[1]

The third conjuncture is the emergence of what Nicos Poulantzas called 'authoritarian statism', marked by the decline of the political sphere and the strengthening of the executive in the face of the deepening contradictions of capitalism since the early 1970s.[2] Poulantzas argued that it is not possible to transform this new state form through a 'dual power' strategy, because the state in this context is not a fortress to be conquered by outside forces and replaced by a new contending source of power. Instead, he proposed a strategy of 'democratic socialism', advocating for the importance of social movements gaining power through direct democracy while also trying to transform intra-state relations and apparatuses through representative democracy and a series of political ruptures.

This formula guided parties like Greece's Syriza to power, and other parties attempting new strategies of rupture with existing capitalist states; and it was also a meaningful option in Turkey prior to the June 2015 elections. However, since these elections the conjuncture in Turkey has foreclosed the possibility of any such left strategies, yet in a way that displays different characteristics from both authoritarian statism and classical fascism. In the case of Turkey, elections have not been suspended, but there is an evident transformation within state apparatuses towards a form that can be termed 'late fascism'.[3] Unlike classical fascism, which abolished liberal state forms and elections to mobilize war-like violence against revolutionary organizations, late fascism does not require the suspension of elections given the absence of a communist threat.[4] Instead, continuity with parliamentary politics serves a strategic function for the right-wing populist parties that emerged after the

2008 crisis. These parties depict an alienated elite as the architects of the established order in opposition to an uncorrupted populace. By claiming to represent the genuine will of the people, they create an internal enemy, polarizing society and consolidating their support. Frequent elections and an active parliamentary scene keep this internal enemy alive as an interlocutor that the leaders of these parties need in order to reproduce themselves. Unlike classical fascism, which destroys the enemy through physical violence, late fascism neutralizes its enemy through, in the first instance, symbolic violence, and through judicial and coercive state apparatuses. Consequently, late fascism as a state form is intricately linked to populism as a political modality for right-wing leaders.

In this distinct state form, the dominant central state apparatuses extend beyond the bounds of neoliberal authoritarian statism, adopting certain characteristics of fascism while retaining parliamentary institutions. When discussing strategy against this emerging state form, it is important to first understand its specificities without falling into historical analogies. In this essay, I will discuss the Turkish case as a contribution to this effort. It is divided into four parts. The first discusses the nature of late fascism and its manifestation in Turkey; the second explores late fascism as an emerging state form in the Turkish context; the third outlines the Turkish left's strategy so far against this state form; and the final part examines the question of strategy in the landscape emerging from the 2024 local elections.

UNDERSTANDING LATE FASCISM AND
ITS MANIFESTATION IN TURKEY

In his last interview, Leo Panitch made the following statement:

> I've been saying for some years now that those who speak of capitalism in the twenty-first century and do not speak of fascism should remain silent. It seems to be the case that the longer capitalism continues to exist, and the longer that socialists are unable to replace it with something humane, democratic, and egalitarian, that the likelihood is that fascism will gain more and more ground in a capitalist framework in the twenty-first century.[5]

So how should we conceive this process of 'fascism gaining ground in a capitalist framework in the twenty-first century'? There is now a burgeoning Marxist debate on this question, from which I extract two key insights. First, fascism is a unique response to capitalist crisis. While classical fascism was a response to the 1929 crisis, late fascism reflects the challenges posed by the 2008 crisis. The specific form fascism takes today compared to that of its classical iteration stems precisely from the historical differences between these two crises. According to William Robinson, classical fascism was based on the alliance of reactionary political powers with their own national capitals in search of markets. Late fascism, however, is based on the alliance of reactionary political forces with transnational capital and, for Robinson, the rise of a 'global police state'. In this conjuncture, nation states constantly try to create new opportunities for accumulation by contracting the production of conflict and war to transnational capital.[6] Unlike classical fascism, the wars of this period do not revolve around mutual conflicts between states that cease once markets are divided. Instead, states resort to unlimited violence in cooperation with non-state actors (such as mercenaries, proxy groups, mafia-type crime syndicates and paramilitary forces).

Robinson's attempt to differentiate late fascism from classical fascism by highlighting the new role of the internationalization of capital is insightful. However, his assertion regarding late fascism's foundation on the 'alliance of reactionary political powers with transnational capital' and the emergence of a 'global police state' is contentious. This standpoint overlooks how late fascism offers new avenues for accumulation not only for transnational capital, but for various capital fractions internalized in national states. Hence, there is also a need to address how authoritarian states undergo transformation while navigating conflicts between different capital fractions. Furthermore, the concept of a 'global police state' risks oversimplifying the essence of the state itself. From the perspective of this essay (and the influence of Poulantzas), late fascism addresses the valorization crisis of capital in an advanced stage of internationalization. In this context, nation-states manage international accumulation, internalizing the contradictions of imperialism into class conflicts within each social formation. This results in the creation of new accumulation spheres, with imperialism and warfare becoming internal affairs of authoritarian states, as specific capital fractions align with distinct state policies. These dynamics manifest in the coercive and ideological apparatuses of states, taking distinct forms based on their articulation with imperialism. The shift of authoritarian states towards a late fascist form is, therefore, contingent and influenced by how the contradictions of the internationalization of capital are addressed. In Turkey, the convergence of the effects of the 2008 economic crisis and the internal political crisis of 2013 granted the state greater autonomy from the previously prevailing power bloc. This facilitated a transition, with the emergence of a new power bloc characterized by different hegemonic capital fractions and imperial realignments. The organization and practices of state apparatuses consequently began a transformation towards late fascism.

In the Turkish context, the recent efforts of the state to adopt a sub-imperial role in the Middle East, particularly in northern Syria, is reflected in its coercive apparatuses by the rise of a new military-intelligence complex collaborating with internationalized fascist gangs, proxy groups and paramilitary forces. Here, the creation of new spheres for capital accumulation functions as a mechanism of resource transfer to the burgeoning and internationalizing pro-AKP capital groups that constitute the emerging power bloc. The defence industry, for example, engages in commercial activities with the military-industrial complexes of various imperialist countries, including the US and Israel, while broadening the base of capital accumulation from large companies at the top to pro-AKP subcontractors and small and medium enterprises in the sector.[7] However, this process is not reflected in the ideological apparatuses as anti-immigrant racism, differentiating the Turkish case from its far-right counterparts in Europe, with the AKP employing a rhetoric of hospitality toward Syrians. This rhetoric is deployed as part of the state's strategic use of refugee containment as a bargaining tool with the European Union. Through this formal policy conflict, the AKP seeks to ensure Europe's silence regarding its authoritarian steps toward establishing a political Islamist regime. These dynamics underscore the intricate connection between the Turkish state's particular form of late fascism, its pattern of articulation with imperialism, and its own historical context of racial capitalism.[8]

This brings us to the second point. Late fascism takes different forms in each country where it emerges. In Aijaz Ahmad's words, 'each country gets the fascism it deserves'.[9] As he puts it: 'Strategically speaking, we need to pay less attention to what a fascism might share with the fascism of another country and more to the innovations it has made in accordance with the peculiar history and politics of the country where it takes organized form … Fascism succeeds only in certain conjunctures and when it takes root in certain deep structures.'[10]

For this reason, it is necessary to look at the history of the social structures, ideological currents and the institutions in which fascism gains a foothold, which pivotally emerge in every country during the process of nation-state formation.[11] In Turkey, three key historical moments highlight the roots of late fascism. The first is the marginalization of groups such as Kurds, Alevis, Armenians and Greeks in favour of the dominant Turkish-Sunni identity during the formation of the Kemalist regime in the 1920s. Among the marginalized groups, the Kurds hold a unique status as a national group characterized by linguistic and regional distinctiveness within the framework of 'internal colonization'. Alberto Toscano's emphasis on the 'longue durée' of racial capitalism, or internal colonialism, as an historical foundation for late fascism is helpful for grasping this aspect.[12] Toscano argues that fascism is implemented differently based on race, gender and sexuality within the same country and time period. To elucidate this differentiated experience of domination, Toscano draws upon Ernst Fraenkel's concept of the 'dual state', originally employed to describe Nazi Germany – wherein the 'normative state' operates within legal norms, while the 'prerogative state' makes arbitrary decisions. Building on this, Toscano introduces the concept of the 'racial dual state',[13] highlighting the fact that 'political orders widely deemed liberal-democratic can harbour institutions that operate as regimes of domination and terror for significant sectors of their population'.[14] This conceptualization is necessary for understanding the differential application of law concerning Kurds as the enduring feature of the fascist regime in Turkey.

The second moment is the formation of the covert operations unit known as 'counter-guerrilla' within the state, operating along the lines of the Turkish arm of Operation Gladio, a clandestine anti-communist initiative backed by NATO and the US after World War II. The 'counter-guerrilla' initially operated within the Turkish Armed Forces and persisted under various guises and names. It collaborated with the Grey Wolves, the ultranationalist paramilitary youth organization of the MHP (Milliyetçi Hareket Partisi – Nationalist Action Party) in actions against the socialist movement in the 1970s. The legacy of the counter-guerrilla structure has endured in various forms in the post-Cold War era, notably being deployed in the Kurdish conflict since the 1990s. This longstanding tradition of employing counter-insurgency tactics lends to late fascism in Turkey particular suppressive features, exemplified by the crushing of movements like the Gezi Park protests in 2013 and the ongoing Kurdish conflict. This sets the Turkish context apart from other examples of late fascism, as it does not solely focus on preventing social uprisings; instead, it actively engages in the suppression of social movements.

The third moment is the coup d'état of 12 September 1980, which broke the organized power of the workers and the left and made a 'Turkish-Islamic synthesis' the official ideology of the state. The late fascism shaped by the AKP incorporates all three of these historical moments and gives them a new form. It rejects a peaceful solution to the Kurdish question; maintains the structure of the counter-insurgency operations in different forms; deepens anti-labour economic policies; and it increases the prominence of Islamism in the 'Turkish-Islamic synthesis' without stepping back from the

'Turkish' element. In other words, it articulates conflicts from the nation-state building process with contemporary capitalism in a unique way. It also involves a shift from the power bloc rooted in Western-oriented big capitalists established during the early Kemalist regime to a new bloc composed of emerging Islamic and pro-AKP capitalists, internationally connected to capital groups from countries such as Russia, Qatar, Venezuela and Azerbaijan. This shift has not entailed a transfer of resources from pro-Western capital to Islamic capital that would compromise profits. Instead, the former has maintained or even boosted profits through its established connections with global capital, as well as political compliance with the regime. Meanwhile, the growth of Islamic capital has been facilitated through both the military expansion mechanism sustaining market demand and facilitating new supply chain networks and the use of extra-economic coercion in the accumulation process. The latter entails elements such as the commodification of nature and public services through methods like urgent expropriation; the use of black market operations in the creation of illicit financial resources; leveraging public tenders and the political control of the Central Bank for wealth transfer to pro-AKP capitalists; state seizures of hundreds of companies on the grounds of their alleged links with terrorist organizations; and the establishment of the Turkey Wealth Fund, under the direct control of Recep Tayyip Erdoğan, with fiscal functions that parallel the central government budget. Undoubtedly, the major overall policy that satisfies both the established and emerging sections of capital has been the increased pressure on labour in general.

This transition to a new power bloc in Turkey was made possible through radical restructuring of the state apparatuses over the last decade. In the US and Brazil cases, Trump and Bolsonaro came to power with hard right forces part of the electoral bloc, but the political regime did not take a fascist form. At this juncture, the emergence of far-right populist leaders, parties, movements and ideologies is a widespread political reaction to the enduring contradictions and polarizations of this phase of capitalism. In contrast, in Turkey late fascism not only exists as an ideology and political party/movement, but also as an emerging state form, with fascist practices entrenching themselves within the state apparatuses in ways that bear comparison to countries where the hard right has also gained power such as India and Hungary. These developments bear witness to Ahmad's contention that 'fascism succeeds only in certain conjunctures and when it takes root in certain deep structures'.

In order to understand late fascism as a state form, it is crucial to revisit Poulantzas' state theory, with theoretical and historical revision necessary at two key junctures. First, as with its classical iteration, the emergence of late fascism as a state form unfolds as a contradictory process. However, caution should be exercised in drawing historical analogies. Late fascism, as a process, does not neatly fit into Poulantzas' theory of the stages leading to the establishment of a 'fully fascist' state.[15] While pivotal moments may have marked the development of classical fascism in Germany and Italy, these cannot be transposed onto late fascism. Furthermore, the concept of a 'point of no return' in Poulantzas' theory poses challenges from both an epistemological and a historical standpoint. In any transition between capitalist state forms, reverting to a previous state form in its entirety is highly improbable if not impossible. Change can unfold in various directions, underscoring the importance of viewing fascism as a contradictory process and a terrain of struggle among diverse actors rather than a linear and predetermined transformation with an anticipated endpoint.

Second, Poulantzas criticizes the Comintern theses that proposed parliamentary democracy and fascism as only differing in degree, arguing that while parliamentary democracy may carry the seeds of fascism, the growth of fascism is not simply a linear process resulting from the germination from a few seeds.[16] He distinguishes between ordinary and exceptional forms of the capitalist state and argues that exceptional state forms, such as fascism, emerge after a political crisis and require a radical transformation in the relationships between ideological and coercive apparatuses for the reorganization of hegemony. But at the same time, he distances himself from approaches that analyze the relationship between bourgeois democracy and fascism using the normal/pathological distinction.[17] There is a tension that remains between this argument and Poulantzas' use of the term 'exceptional state', as this term implies that fascism is a deviation from the norm. This tension requires a thorough theoretical reassessment, both in terms of terminology and conceptualization, before applying the ordinary/exceptional state form dichotomy to late fascism. It is essential to revise the portrayal of fascist regime components as passive 'seeds' within parliamentary democracy waiting to germinate during a crisis. Instead, these components are actively utilized towards certain sections of society, as seen in phenomena such as the racial dual state. There is, then, both continuity and rupture between parliamentary democratic and fascist state forms. In the context of Turkey, where fascist state components have been systematically deployed against Kurds for an extended period, late fascism is characterized by the expansion of these components to a broader section of society.

LATE FASCISM IN TURKEY

The AKP government was authoritarian from the moment it came to power in 2002, under the leadership of Erdoğan, not only in terms of its policies of deepening the neoliberal authoritarian state form institutionalized since the 1980s, but also in its attempts to redesign the state apparatuses in line with its political Islamist project. As a late-forming political actor entering into the Turkish state apparatus, the AKP needed an ally to pursue this project. It formed an alliance with the Islamic sect known as Gülen movement,[18] already rooted within the coercive apparatuses, especially in the police and judiciary. Following the political crisis induced by Gezi resistance and the breakdown of the alliance between AKP and the Gülenists in 2013, the regime then began to move from the authoritarian statism characteristic of neoliberalism towards late fascism. In this new state form, the strengthening of the central executive continued but the way it functioned changed in two crucial aspects. First, in contrast to the neoliberal authoritarian state form where technocrats pursue economic policies relatively independently of the political party in power, the economic apparatuses of the state became deeply politicized in order to be used for wealth transfer to the emergent power bloc centred on Islamist capital. Second, the executive not only dominated the legislative and judiciary but also all coercive and ideological apparatuses, deeply transforming each of them along political Islamist lines.

The Gezi resistance marked a pivotal moment in the process of regime change, as the fascist state practices previously confined to Kurdish regions began to spread westward. This expansion raised consciousness of the Kurdish movement among the broader left in Turkey. As a result, many segments of the Turkish left supported the pro-Kurdish HDP (Halkların Demokratik Partisi – People's Democracy Party) in the 2015 elections.[19] HDP received 13 per cent of votes and won 80 seats in parliament in the 7 June 2015 elections, through a democratic socialist strategy that combined direct democracy induced by the Gezi resistance with party politics based on a broad coalition of Kurds, socialists, feminists, ecologists and other democratic forces. Paradoxically, this victory paved the way for the deepening of late fascism, as HDP denied Erdoğan the absolute majority to change the Constitution towards a presidential system and sparked a violent reaction in the emerging power bloc. Erdoğan pushed the AKP to reject any coalition, in order to bring about a new election with the hope of achieving a majority. In order to do this, he ended the peace process between the state and PKK (Partiya Karkerên Kurdistanê – Kurdistan Workers' Party) which had been initiated in 2013, presented the HDP as a supporter of 'terrorism'. He escalated the politics of violence not only against the PKK but also Kurdish civilians and the HDP, while exploiting the Suruç and Ankara massacres to create an atmosphere of fear and instability.[20] In this context, the AKP emerged as victor in the November 2015 elections.

Another crucial turning point in the movement toward late fascism took place on 15 July 2016. On this date, a faction within the military, associated with the Gülenists, initiated a coup attempt, which was ultimately unsuccessful. In the aftermath, the government declared a state of emergency and governed the country with decrees having the force of law for two years. With these decrees and the transition to a presidential system in 2018, elements of late fascism deepened in Turkey as a whole. The executive assumed the function of the judiciary and dismissed hundreds of thousands of people from their jobs in the public sector on the grounds of alleged links with either the Gülenist movement or the outlawed PKK. This not only resulted in the alignment of the lower echelons of the state bureaucracy with the AKP, but also created a new mechanism of resource transfer to the newly emerging capital bloc through extra-economic coercion mechanisms such as the seizure of Gülen-linked companies.

The process gained new dimensions with the AKP's formation of the 'People's Alliance' (Cumhur İttifakı) with the ultra-nationalist MHP in 2018. This was not a solely electoral alliance. The AKP needed a new ally within the state apparatuses after its alliance with the Gülenists had been broken. The MHP was the best choice, as both a nationalist party inclined to Islamism and as an actor deeply rooted in the coercive apparatuses since the 1970s. This also meant enhanced formal and informal coalitions with ultranationalist gangs and mafia leaders. Throughout this process, the ideological and coercive apparatuses of the state, as well as the nature of intra-state conflicts, went through a radical transformation.

Changes within the ideological and coercive apparatuses

In the late fascistization of the Turkish state, the critical transformation in the ideological apparatuses was the prominence of the Diyanet (Directorate of Religious Affairs), through a tremendous increase in its budget and personnel as well as the expansion of its functions. The Diyanet cooperated with the Ministry of Family, Labour and Social Policies to promote conservative family values. Universities and the wider education system were also radically transformed. In 2016, thousands of academics were dismissed from their posts on the grounds that they were 'affiliated with terrorist organisations'. Meanwhile, the media lost its relative autonomy through arrests of opposition journalists, closure of opposition media outlets and confiscation of their assets.

The most important transformation in the making of Turkish late fascism, however, was the prominence of the coercive apparatuses in the internal hierarchy of the state, the transformation of the judiciary being the most critical. The major mechanism for intimidating the 'enemy' operated through the legal mechanisms of the judiciary, instead of physical elimination. A typical example of this is the AKP government's intervention in the electoral process through decisions made by the Supreme Election Board, instead of through violence, thus generating consent by the formal legality of the measures taken. The principal method employed to elevate the judiciary as the primary instrument of the 'prerogative state' has involved the addition of the charge of 'association with terrorism' to various laws resulting from the decrees after the 15 July coup attempt. The decrees were thereby made permanent and available to be deployed for arbitrary purposes. For example, under a provision added to the Municipality Law via decree, in the event that a mayor, deputy mayor or council member is suspended or arrested on charges of 'terrorism' or 'aiding and abetting terrorist organisations', the entire administration of the municipality in question had to be transferred to centrally-appointed trustees. The Municipality Law thus formed the basis for the replacement of elected mayors by trustees in Kurdish regions known as the 'trustee regime'. Elsewhere, the judiciary has been used as an instrument of revenge in cases such as the Gezi and Kobani trials,[21] with judges in these cases acting according to the will of Erdoğan instead of following the law, inventing judicial covers to ensure the continued detention of defendants.

Regarding other coercive apparatuses, the military completely lost its autonomy vis-à-vis the executive after the 15 July coup attempt, as force commands were transferred from the General Staff to the Ministry of National Defence under the control of the AKP. Furthermore, the status of the Milli İstihbarat Teşkilatı (MİT – National Intelligence Organisation) within the hierarchy of the state increased, resulting in its complete politicization, with its functions diversified so as to conduct operations 'in matters related to foreign security, counterterrorism and national security'. After the 15 July coup attempt, the MİT was directly subordinated to the president. Its increased prominence in foreign operations has been marked by the use of armed and unarmed drones linked to the MİT, especially in the Middle East. The powers of the national and local police were also increased after the 15 July coup attempt, and their special operations division became a fully politicized and Islamized apparatus acting directly under the president in order to protect the AKP government.

Finally, the state's relationship with paramilitary forces deepened, especially after the end of the peace process in 2015.[22] Paramilitary organisations both increased in number and diversified in terms of their form. Private military companies carrying out unofficial operations of the state or jihadist gangs recruited from various countries are examples of this diversification. In this process, paramilitarism evolved from something denied to something in the open, with the state embracing the existence of paramilitary groups used in operations in Kurdish provinces in 2015–2016.[23] The AKP government also allied with paramilitary groups in its wars in the Middle East, composed of both Turkmen from Syria as well as radical nationalists and Islamists from Turkey itself. After the initiation of the alliance between Erdoğan and the MHP in 2018, the reappearance of the pro-MHP paramilitary forces also formed part of the coercive alliances.

The radical changes within the state's ideological and coercive apparatuses did not proceed without contradictions: on the contrary, new contradictions emerged, multiplied and diversified within the state at every turn. These contradictions have manifested in two distinct forms. The first form arises from the tensions between Kemalist bureaucrats, representing the old power bloc, and pro-AKP bureaucrats associated with the new power bloc. The first group is rarely influential in the top-level bureaucracy, and the contradictions between this group and the emerging power bloc are political. The second and more decisive form of intra-state contradictions is within the emerging power bloc, which is more related to the distribution of wealth obtained through extra-economic coercion. In order to better understand the organizational form these new contradictions take, it should be stressed that intra-state contradictions take on a different character in fascism.

In liberal-democratic or authoritarian state forms, Poulantzas observes that 'power is organized mainly through the specialization of the apparatuses; this is one of the reasons for the "separation" of powers in a "representative" state'.[24] Thus, class contradictions manifest themselves in the form of contradictions among apparatuses. But in the fascist state form, the principle of the separation of powers is abolished, so contradictions arise across each apparatus rather than contradictions among the apparatuses. The ruling party 'never fully fuses with the state', and thus tries to establish its own sovereignty by penetrating each apparatus. In this process, a section of state personnel within each state apparatus becomes directly subordinate to the ruling party, with a consequence of creating parallel networks of power within each apparatus. Conflicts within the state materialize in the form of 'behind-the-scenes wars between teams' formed in each apparatus.[25]

Since the AKP initially came to power, it used this mechanism of politicizing state administration to transfer resources to the Islamic capitalists forming its own base. As this process progressed, disputes over the distribution of these resources within Islamic capital began. Following the 17 December 2013 anti-corruption operations initiated by Gülenists against the AKP, it was the Gülenists themselves that were eliminated from their position in the state system. The internal war within the Islamic capital bloc, however, continued through the state apparatus involving other religious sects. With the formation of the AKP-MHP alliance in 2018, new actors joined the 'turf war'. But with the deepening economic crisis in this period and the transfer of three metropolitan municipalities to the centre-left CHP (Cumhuriyet Halk Partisi – Republican People's Party) in the 2019 local elections, the financial resources inside the state that fed these networks decreased. As these resources started to be transferred to a narrower group of capitalists and bureaucrats through their loyalty to Erdoğan, the war of distribution within the power bloc escalated with conflicts between cliques intensifying and becoming increasingly public.

The new intra-state contradictions did not lead to the dissolution or even a fracturing of the regime as often predicted. Rather the conflicts provided the environment for the deepening of late fascism. As a state form, fascism is based on the arbitrariness and uncertainty brought about by the struggle between different power centres inside the state. The uncertainty created expands the political terrain and room of manoeuvre for the executive leadership at the apex of the state. The existence of multiple power centres and conflicts within the Turkish state had the effect, paradoxically, of increasing Erdoğan's ability to tactically play various cliques against each other and to reorganize the basis of the AKP's hegemony. The AKP government continues to exploit this room for manoeuvre, and the internal contradictions, and actively deploys the ideological and coercive apparatuses of the state to its own advantage every day. Under these conditions, it is clear that the left cannot rely on strategies specific to either liberal-democratic or authoritarian state forms. Indeed, this is what now needs to be explored. The left in Turkey has been unable to develop organizational forms and political strategies that address the emerging late fascist state form effectively.

LEFT STRATEGIES AND THE NEW REGIME

In Turkey, the strategies of different factions of the left vary depending on how they define the political regime. Broadly speaking, the left in Turkey can be categorized into three main factions: the center-left, aligned with the CHP; various sections of socialist left organized in small parties and groupings; and the HDP (now incorporated within the Dem Parti), acting as the umbrella organization for the Kurdish freedom movement alongside five Turkish socialist parties. The CHP identifies the sources of 'regime autocratization' as stemming from an extreme concentration of presidential powers alongside the diminishing role of parliament and the erosion of the rule of law. That is why, in the lead up to the 2023 elections, the CHP and its allies proposed a shift towards a 'strengthened parliamentary regime' to replace the presidential government system. Their strategic approach is centered on instituting reforms within the existing state structure. Within sections of the socialist left, a significant faction perceives the character of the regime to be one of 'neoliberal authoritarianism'. Their strategic focus revolves around anti-neoliberalism or anti-capitalism, without addressing a specific anti-fascist political intervention. Another faction perceives the state apparatus as a product of Turkey's historical fascism and does not consider late fascism as a distinct phenomenon of this conjuncture of capitalism. Consequently, they advocate for a revolutionary strategy that overlooks the unique characteristics and challenges posed by late fascism in the Turkish political scene. By contrast, the Dem Parti and its socialist components define the AKP regime as in a process of fascistization and use terms such as 'institutionalization of fascism' (a transformation of the whole state apparatus along fascist lines) and 'socialization of fascism' (with society steadily embracing fascism). Accordingly, Dem Parti prioritizes a strategy of 'pushing back fascistization'.

Before going into the details of each strategy, it should be noted that the establishment of the new regime in Turkey was not solely implemented through the actions of the AKP. The new conjuncture emerged also via the responses of the opposition and the interplay between strategies and counter-strategies. After the Gezi resistance, for example, the AKP government imposed bans on demonstrations, to make sure that different sections of society could not come together for a common political goal. This situation narrowed down the options for opposition forces, particularly from the left, and increased the importance of electoralism in political calculations. It is in this context that the strategies of each camp of the Turkish left must be analyzed.

CHP's contradictory role in the consolidation of the regime

As the major opposition party against the AKP, the CHP's strategies have shaped the evolution of the regime at critical turning points. Until 2010, CHP's strategy centered on acting as the 'guardian of the secular republic' against AKP's Islamism. In 2007, the CHP formed a coalition with the military, judiciary and bureaucracy against the AKP presidential candidate Abdullah Gül. Despite this, the AKP increased its votes in the parliamentary elections that year and Gül was elected President. As the opposition from within the state led by the CHP intensified, the AKP retaliated by fomenting an intra-state struggle through the purge of Kemalists from the military, judiciary and police, in collaboration with the Gülenists. After 2010, under the leadership of Kemal Kılıçdaroğlu, the CHP shifted its strategy towards societal opposition rather than intra-state struggle, with the goal of undermining the AKP through broader alliances. However, the CHP pursued this strategy by forming connections with right-wing parties rather than by aligning with the left.

The crucial moment in terms of the CHP's contribution to the fascistization of the regime came in April 2016, when Kılıçdaroğlu supported a bill amending the constitution to remove immunity from prosecution for MPs. This constitutional change made possible the later arrest and imprisonment of CHP MP Enis Berberoğlu and HDP co-chairs Selahattin Demirtaş and Figen Yüksekdağ.[26] Kılıçdaroğlu also specifically rejected street protests like those in Gezi Park, countering that everything should progress through elections. Even in the face of electoral fraud in the 2017 constitutional referendum on the transition to a presidential system, he did not call for the people to take to the streets, instead continuing to pursue an election-focused strategy based on alliances, as if the regime they faced were a liberal democratic one. Against the MHP-AKP based 'People's Alliance', the CHP formed the 'Nation's Alliance' (Millet İttifakı) with five right-wing parties before the 2023 elections. The CHP's consistent preference for aligning with right-leaning allies has resulted in the emergence of a nationalist right-wing opposition bloc that closely mirrors the ruling coalition, differing only in minor ways.

After the electoral defeat of the opposition in the 2023 general elections, a new period started in the CHP under the leadership of Özgür Özel. They contested the 2024 local elections independently, and this strategy proved successful as it enabled them to articulate stronger positions on secularism and the problems faced by the increasingly impoverished working class under the new economic policies managed by Mehmet Şimşek, the Minister of Treasury and Finance after 2023 elections. The success of this strategy formed part of the basis for the success of the CHP in the 31 March 2024 local elections, where they won not only in the three major urban centres but also in cities known as strongholds of the AKP.

The strategy of the socialist left after the Gezi resistance

The suppression of the Gezi resistance in 2013 marked the turning point for the transformation of the state form toward late fascism. However, the socialist left struggled to formulate an effective strategy against this transformation. Many socialists continued to grapple with the dichotomy between strategies of street activism and electoral politics. Post-Gezi, a significant portion of the socialist left opted to channel the momentum generated by the resistance into parliamentary politics through support for the HDP in the 2015 elections, pursuing a democratic socialist strategy. Even the Halkevleri (People's Houses) community organizations, despite historically prioritizing street movements over the ballot box, supported the HDP in these elections, before later returning to their anti-electoral stance.

Some factions of the socialist left who distanced themselves from the Kurdish movement formed the BHH (Birleşik Haziran Hareketi – United June Movement) in 2014.[27] This coalition comprised socialist parties, social democrats, unionists, Gezi activists and left-wing NGOs. They advocated for grassroots assemblies and neighborhood forums as the true embodiment of the Gezi resistance. However, by abstaining from electoral processes, the BHH lost momentum and became an insular forum. Their lack of agreement on how to engage with the 2018 elections led to their dissolution.

Before the 2018 elections, the Sol Parti (Left Party) had insisted on maintaining the BHH's independent stance, whereas the TİP (Türkiye İşçi Partisi – Turkish Workers Party) decided to field its prominent members as HDP candidates. Two TİP candidates were elected to parliament and, along with two others who defected from the CHP and HDP, formed the TİP parliamentary group. Later, the Sol Parti shifted its position on electoral participation. In the 2023 elections, it formed the Socialist Power Union with the TKP (Türkiye Komünist Partisi – Communist Party of Turkey) and three other socialist groups, distancing themselves from alliances with the HDP.

HDP and the Labour and Freedom Alliance

In contrast to the CHP's election-based strategy and the BHH's non-electoral strategy, the HDP had a strong emphasis on combining grassroots movements with electoral politics since its foundation in 2012.[28] The HDP's roots go back to the establishment of two organizations allied with the Kurdish movement: DTK (Demokratik Toplum Kongresi – Democratic Society Congress), founded in the Kurdish provinces in 2007 as a broad platform for NGOs; and the HDK (Halkların Demokratik Kongresi – Peoples' Democratic Congress), founded in Ankara in 2011 as a horizontal, participatory platform operating through local assemblies, unifying the struggles of thirty-five organizations including socialist parties, feminists, LGBTQ and environmental movements, trade unions and representatives of various religious minorities. In 2012, the HDK set up the HDP as an electoral project to be activated solely during election campaigns and subject to decisions by the HDK. However, the HDP quickly gained prominence, overshadowing the HDK. Following its success in the 2015 elections with 13 per cent of the vote, the HDP became a target for attacks from the government and nationalist circles, resulting in the arrest of its co-chairs as well as some of its MPs, central executive board members and provincial co-chairs. Additionally, the parliamentary status of 15 MPs was revoked and numerous municipality co-mayors were arrested or removed, and replaced by trustees after local elections in both 2014 and 2019. Subsequently, a lawsuit was filed in 2021 with the aim of closing down the HDP (a legal battle that remains unfinished).

Despite this repression, the HDP has contributed to the struggle against late fascism in quite novel ways. The culture of self-criticism and openness to renewed strategies is a crucial gain for the left. The institution of 'co-presidency' at each level of governance has meant a tremendous increase in women's participation in politics across Turkey. Ideologically, the presence of the Kurdish movement within the party makes it an organization which always draws a distinction between the Turkish state and AKP, aiming not just to defeat the AKP but to transform the Turkish state as a whole. The strategy of the HDP, popularly known as the 'Third Way', is also vital. Rejecting the neoliberalism and nationalism of both the AKP-MHP and CHP, the HDP offers an alternative combining anti-capitalist economic policies with a radical democratic project proposing a resolution to the Kurdish issue through peaceful methods. In that sense, it aims to radically democratize the state rather than older notions of 'encircling' or 'smashing the state'. As part of this strategy, the HDP attempted to become a key actor in the last three elections.

The HDP electoral strategy since 2015 has been based on 'pushing back the fascistization process'. Toward this objective, in the 2019 local elections the HDP focused on reclaiming municipalities in Kurdish regions where trustees had been appointed, as well as aiming to defeat the AKP-MHP alliance in the west. As part of this strategy, the HDP leadership called on its supporters to vote for the party most likely to defeat the People's Alliance in the western provinces, which effectively meant supporting the CHP. The outcome saw the AKP lose control of major cities such as Ankara, Istanbul, Izmir and Antalya to the CHP, marking the first time in 15 years that the AKP lost in Ankara and Istanbul.

In 2022, the HDP formed the Labour and Freedom Alliance, together with five socialist parties.[29] While initially intended as a unified platform for broader struggles beyond electoral politics, the Alliance evolved into a negotiation hub for the 2023 elections. Subsequently, the HDP, which ran in the 2023 general elections under the banner of the Yeşil Sol Parti (Green Left Party), prepared a joint list to contest these elections, combining candidates from the HDP's five socialist component parties,[30] alongside others from Kurdish political parties and three Turkish socialist parties from the Labour and Freedom Alliance. However, it could not convince the TİP to join a common list, which led them to field candidates separately in 41 provinces. This resulted in a decrease in the overall number of Alliance seats won. The TİP received 1.76 per cent of the vote, with which it declared itself content as they saw it as an indication of a 'socialist mass party' proving its worth in Turkey for the first time in many years. The Green Left Party got 8.8 per cent, which it deemed a failure as this was 2.88 per cent lower than in the previous elections. Alongside this, their decision to support Kılıçdaroğlu, the CHP leader and the candidate of Nation's Alliance in the presidential elections, led to two problems. First, Erdoğan exploited the Green Left Party's endorsement of Kılıçdaroğlu to discredit him as a supporter of the PKK and thereby influence nationalist voters. Second, Kılıçdaroğlu's alliance with the secular ultranationalist Zafer Partisi (Victory Party) in the presidential run-off disappointed Green Left Party supporters, leading to criticism of the party's backing him without tangible gains.

After the elections, the Green Left Party relaunched itself as the Dem Parti, initiating a process of self-criticism and organizing public meetings as part of this process of transformation. While maintaining a focus on pushing back the AKP, it emphasized the 'Third Way' strategy more prominently. During the 2024 local elections, it refrained from openly endorsing the CHP in western cities, thwarting Erdoğan's attempts to label the CHP as terrorist-linked and alleviating the Kurdish community's frustrations with constantly being redirected to a different political party. The Dem Parti introduced an 'urban consensus model' for candidate selection in western cities, aiming to support candidates regardless of party affiliation based on specific principles. Due to this method, Ahmet Özer, DEM Parti's preferred CHP candidate was elected as mayor of Esenyurt, a district in Istanbul with a significant Kurdish population. Additionally, it developed a creative strategy to ensure that Istanbul did not fall to the AKP. It nominated its own candidates in Istanbul, while avoiding direct competition with the CHP, to secure Kurdish community support. In Kurdish regions, Dem Parti nominated candidates through an innovative primary election process. This approach successfully re-engaged the local populace with the party, allowing it to take back previously held municipalities. Consequently, the AKP did not emerge as the leading party in the local elections. As a result, the CHP not only became the leading party, but a political setting resembling 'dual power' emerged in many cities, with the state's coercive apparatus in the hands of the AKP while the municipalities are in the hands of the CHP in the west and the Dem Parti in Kurdish provinces.

THE QUESTION OF STRATEGY
AFTER THE 2024 LOCAL ELECTIONS

After the elections, the first reaction of Erdoğan was to put the mechanisms of the 'racial dual state' into action. Just two days after the election, the Dem Parti's elected mayor in Van, who secured 55 per cent of the vote, was replaced by the AKP's candidate, who had only received 27 per cent. The substitution was based on a court decision initially allowing him to stand for election but then reversing it just two days before the vote. This led to widespread protests across the city, met with a violent response from the police and criticism from most of the opposition parties. As a result, the Provincial Electoral Board was compelled to reverse its decision and reinstate the Dem Parti's candidate as mayor.

In the meantime, CHP leader Özel launched what he termed a 'normalization' process, emphasizing the importance of dialogue. He sought a meeting with Erdoğan to discuss the future of Turkey, which took place on 2 May at the AKP headquarters. Following the meeting, Erdoğan stated that politics has entered a 'period of softening'. Özel rejected the term 'softening', insisting that the process was one of 'normalization'. Özel portrayed the CHP as the main opposition domestically but as a 'Turkish party' abroad, positioning his party as a potential part of the ruling bloc. His attendance in the celebrations to commemorate the 50th anniversary of the Cyprus invasion underscored the CHP's continued support for Erdoğan's military actions. For Erdoğan, this development added another group to the list of factions that he could manoeuvre against each other in order to reorganize the AKP's hegemony.

Özel's strategy ultimately contributed to the regime's legitimacy but yielded no significant concessions, such as his request for the release of political prisoners from the Gezi trial. The Kobani trial verdict on 16 May imposed severe additional sentences on several already-imprisoned politicians, including HDP co-chairs Selahattin Demirtaş and Figen Yüksekdağ, furthering the ongoing criminalization of both the Gezi and Kobani resistances. On 3 June, a trustee was appointed to Hakkari municipality. The elected Co-Mayor from Dem Parti was arrested and replaced by the pro-AKP Governor of Hakkari.

On 1 October, the opening day of parliament, Erdoğan set forth a discourse emphasizing the urgent need to strengthen the 'internal front' to shield Turkey from the potential regional fallout of Israel's escalating aggressions. MHP leader Bahçeli followed this discourse with gestures of peace toward Dem Party deputies, and on October 22, he proposed allowing Abdullah Öcalan, the PKK's imprisoned leader, to call for the PKK's disbandment in parliament in exchange for his release. This maneuver is far from a genuine peace overture; rather, it signals the Turkish state's strategic recalibration of its engagement with Kurdish constituencies amid an expanding regional conflict now involving Lebanon, Iran, and Syria alongside Israel's sustained assault on Gaza. By leveraging this regional context to reinforce its sub-imperial stance, the ruling bloc aims to consolidate power at home while inviting socio-political opposition to align with an 'internal front', thus aiming to neutralize them within the current regime. On October 30, in a striking example of this strategy, Ahmet Özer, the CHP mayor of Istanbul's Esenyurt district – elected with support from the Dem Parti through the urban consensus model – was arrested on terrorism-related charges, with a pro-AKP trustee promptly appointed in his place. This marks a significant escalation, as it is the first instance of a trustee replacing a municipal leader in western Turkey.

At this juncture, it is crucial for formations like the Labour and Freedom Alliance to expand their efforts to mobilize the masses for genuine struggles centered on bread and peace. Should such a strategy gain momentum, the role of 'game changer' could be undertaken not by Özel, Bahçeli or Erdoğan, but by the people themselves, and the real conditions for dismantling the regime, which is impossible to 'soften', could come into being. In order to do this, the Dem Parti and its allies need to revive the Third Way strategy and organize the broad masses around this strategy, starting from the grassroots level.

CLOSURES OF LATE FASCISM: OPENINGS FOR THE LEFT?

In this essay, I have emphasized the importance of shaping the strategy of the left in alignment with the specific political regime in any given state. It is imperative to explicitly name and describe the prevailing political regime to effectively form a strategic approach that accounts for the political closures that exist and new openings of struggle for the left that have emerged. The emerging state form in Turkey, I have argued, has the characteristics of late fascism. Unlike neoliberal authoritarian statism, this state form incorporates elements of fascism while maintaining elections and parliamentary institutions. To effectively counter late fascism, we must understand the differences between late fascism, neoliberal authoritarian statism and classical fascism, while also recognizing any continuities between them. Late fascism, for example, witnesses the strengthening of the executive but also a shift in its operational dynamics. The economic apparatuses of the state become deeply politicized, serving as a mechanism for wealth transfer to the emerging power bloc. The central executive of the state not only comes to dominate the legislative and judiciary, but all coercive and ideological apparatuses.

When compared to classical fascism, late fascism exhibits two primary continuities. First, law no longer regulates, and arbitrariness reigns. The state does not even lay down rules for functioning. It has no system for predicting its own transformations.[31] Second, as the principle of separation of powers is abolished, contradictions arise within each state apparatus rather than exclusively between government departments and agencies. The creation of parallel power networks within the bureaucracy offers the leader a terrain of manoeuvre for reorganizing hegemony.

But there are three key differences between late fascism and classical fascism. One significant distinction is the approach to elections. Elections are not suspended, but instead are utilized even more frequently for the ideological legitimation of the regime and the naming of its internal enemies. In the context of Turkey, there have been six elections since the Gezi resistance of 2013, the pivotal point marking the shift towards late fascism. In late fascism, elections allow a reconfiguring of hegemony while also diverting the left's energy away from long-term organizing and building connections with the masses. The most threatening and effective strategy against the regime is sacrificed to concentrate primarily on short-term electoral battles. The late fascist state undermines the potential for substantial opposition to the regime itself. In fact, elections have become the most ineffective way for the left to confront the regime, given the weakened power of parliament and the ability of late fascist states to control election outcomes through coercive and ideological mechanisms. Despite this, the left in Turkey has directed the majority of its resources and energies towards electoral strategies due to the constraints on other means of opposition.

Second, in the development of classical fascism, the suspension of elections marked a pivotal moment in consolidating a fully fascist state. In late fascism, however, there is no such turning point. This does not imply that fascism is absent from power; rather, in today's Turkey, we are confronted with a form of late fascism that is deeply entrenched yet continues to evolve through its contradictions. The key question, therefore, is not how to stop a fascist movement from coming to power, but how to dismantle a fascist regime in power. Thus, the united front/people's front debate – originally focused on preventing fascism from coming to power – must be revisited in light of this new context.

A third demarcation between late fascism and classical fascism lies in the form the mobilization of the masses takes in the context of the polarization tactics of right-wing populist leaders. Unlike classical fascism, the focus of the populist leader is not on mobilizing society as a whole but rather on consolidating support from their own political base by constantly vilifying other sections of society as 'enemies of the nation'.

Considering these three specificities of late fascism, the most pressing challenge for socialist strategy in Turkey is engaging with the labouring masses who currently support the regime and working to reduce this support. While many small-scale labour protests continue to emerge, these movements, which often begin with economic demands, tend to become politicized as they confront the state's coercive apparatuses. It is crucial that these acts of resistance be turned into permanent, organized structures capable of opposing the regime. Given the transformed role of elections and the limited scope for street protests, socialists should focus on long-term organizing within the labouring masses to reconnect politics with the people's needs, in a move from a 'war of manoeuvre' to a 'war of position'. This involves sustained organization in working-class neighbourhoods, living and working within these communities, rather than focusing on symbolic protests for internal consolidation within the socialist movement.

Finally, late fascism is not solely a product of the crisis of neoliberalism but is also influenced by the state's specific relationship with imperialism and its own history of the racial and national divisions that emerged with capitalism. Consequently, an effective left strategy against late fascism must intertwine anti-capitalist, anti-imperialist and anti-fascist principles in a creative manner. At this point, it is essential to deepen the connections between anti-capitalist and anti-fascist struggles both theoretically and practically. Theoretical discussions should not only highlight how war budgets impoverish workers but also underscore how neoliberal policies further disempower the working class politically, perpetuating conditions conducive to fascism. Likewise, it must be stressed that the imposition of trustees in Kurdish municipalities not only increases political pressure on Kurds but also funnels resources to pro-government capital in these areas. This exemplifies yet another form of extra-economic coercion utilized to reinforce the emerging power bloc. In practice, the interconnections between these movements can only be strengthened through the expansion of the coalition between socialists and the Dem Parti, further integrating with the working classes and broader sections of society.

The political landscape post–2024 local election presents an opportunity in this regard. The regime's oppressive measures have sparked increased societal responses. Worker and farmer activism, along with ecological, women's, peace and other resistance movements, are gaining momentum across Turkey. The challenge lies in leveraging these struggles to break the fascist practices of state apparatuses. At this point, it is crucial to link these struggles to a broader international anti-capitalist peace movement. Demonstrating the interconnectedness of global capitalist crises with widespread wars in the Middle East and Europe may direct the reactions of the masses, faced with increasing impoverishment, towards their own national states rather than other oppressed groups. We are currently in a time where it is most evident that standing against war and fascism is only possible by being anti-capitalist.

NOTES

1   Nicos Poulantzas, *Crisis of Dictatorships: Portugal, Spain, Greece,* London: NLB, 1976.

2   Nicos Poulantzas, *State, Power, Socialism,* London: NLB, 1978.

3   I find Alberto Toscano's term 'late fascism' to be most appropriate when discussing contemporary manifestations of fascism, as it suggests the sustained presence of fascism across various time periods. In Toscano's words, 'like "late capitalism" or "late Marxism", it gestures toward the fact that fascism, like other political phenomena, varies according to its socioeconomic context'. See: Alberto Toscano, *Late Fascism: Race, Capitalism and the Politics of Crisis,* London: Verso, 2023, p. 16.

4   Aijaz Ahmad uses the term 'post-democratic' to refer to the state form in this conjuncture. But as he points out, this term presumes a prior democratic structure, which is not the case for countries like Turkey. See: Aijaz Ahmad, 'Extreme Capitalism and "The National Question"', in Leo Panitch and Greg Albo, eds, *A World Turned Upside Down: The Socialist Register 2019,* London: Merlin Press, 2019, p. 33.

5   Ana Garcia et al., 'The Growing Contradictions Within the Empire: An Interview with Leo Panitch', *Studies in Political Economy,* 102(1), 2021, p. 5.

6   William I. Robinson, 'Global Capitalist Crisis and Twenty-First Century Fascism: Beyond the Trump Hype', *Science and Society,* 83(2), 2019, pp. 481–509.

7   For details, see: İsmet Akça and Barış Özden, *A Political-Economic Map of the Turkish Defense Industry,* Report prepared for the Heinrich Böll Stiftung, 2021.

8   This interplay also reveals the hypocrisy of the Turkish state in relation to Palestinians, Syrians and Kurds. While condemning Israel's violence against Palestine, it does not sever its commercial agreements with Israel, while it also denies its own violence against Kurds in northern Syria. Also, while using a rhetoric of embrace toward Syrian refugees, it simultaneously allows racist opposition parties and paramilitaries to escalate anti-immigrant racism on the streets.

9   Here Aijaz Ahmad plays on Clara Zetkin's famous statement that fascism is our just reward for not having made the revolution. See: Vijay Prashad and Aijaz Ahmad, *Nothing Human is Alien to Me: Aijaz Ahmad in Conversation with Vijay Prashad,* New Delhi: Leftword, 2020, p. 187.

10   Prashad and Ahmad, *Nothing Human is Alien to Me,* pp. 188-9.

11   Prashad and Ahmad, *Nothing Human is Alien to Me*, p. 189.

12   Toscano, *Late Fascism*, pp. 135-6.

13   Toscano, *Late Fascism*, p. 135.

14   Toscano, *Late Fascism*, p. 135.

15   These stages are: the period from the start of the process to the point of 'no return'; the period from the point of no return until fascism comes into power; the first period of fascism in power; and the period of fascist stabilization. Nicos Poulantzas, *Fascism and Dictatorship*, London: Verso, 2018[1970], pp. 82-3.

16   Poulantzas, *Fascism*, p. 76. The understanding of fascism that dominated the Comintern, established in 1919, from the 1920s until the 7th Congress in 1935, viewed fascism as an organic process that gradually developed from within bourgeois democracy without the need for a specific upheaval. This understanding would only change at the 7th Congress, when Dimitrov stated that the accession to power of fascism is not an ordinary succession of one bourgeois government by another, but a change in the state form. This realization enabled the Comintern to revise its previous ultra-leftist stance, which had classified social democrats as 'social fascists' in 1928 and adopt the popular front strategy.

17   'Fascism is a form of State and of regime at the extreme "limit" of the capitalist State. By "extreme limit", I do not in the least mean a *"pathological"* form of the bourgeois political system (i.e. a form somehow alien to "parliamentary democracy"); but a form due to a quite particular conjuncture of the class struggle.' Poulantzas, *Fascism*, p. 75.

18   Led by the US-based preacher Fettullah Gülen, this movement emerged in the 1970s as a religious and educational network. Over time, it developed an extensive global presence through schools, businesses and media outlets, while embedding itself within the Turkish state starting in the 1980s.

19   The HDP was formed in 2012 but ran in the 2023 general elections under the banner of the Yeşil Sol Parti (Green Left Party) to mitigate the risk of potential closure. Following the elections, the party rebranded as Dem Parti.

20   The Suruç massacre took place on 20 July 2015, where 32 young Turkish socialists expressing their solidarity with the people of Kobani were killed in an ISIS attack. This was followed by the Ankara massacre on 10 October of the same year, where over 100 people were killed by ISIS at a peace rally organized by labour organizations.

21   The Kobani trial is a legal proceeding targeting numerous pro-Kurdish politicians for their alleged role in the protests of fall 2014, which took place in various Kurdish cities in Turkey against the siege by ISIS on the city of Kobani in Rojava.

22   Ayhan Işık, 'Pro-state paramilitary violence', pp. 231-49.

23   Ayhan Işık, *Paramilitarism in Turkey: From Denial to Overtness*, interview by Bekir Avcı, *Express*, 20 October 2021, available at: www.birartibir.org/from-denial-to-overtness.

24   Poulantzas, *Fascism*, p. 302.

25   Poulantzas, *Fascism*, pp. 302-3.

26   Berberoğlu was re-elected as MP and released from prison, but Demirtaş and Yuksekdağ are still in prison.

27   For detailed analyses of UJM, see: Mehmet Fatih Çömlekçi and Serhat Güney, 'In Search of Free Spaces to Breathe: Turkey's United June Movement, Social Uprising, and Spatial Maintainability', *Antipode*, 55(6), 2023, pp. 1641-61; Eren Karaca and Özgür Balkılıç, 'The Legacy of the Gezi Resistance and Its Effects on Turkey's Socialist Movements of the Past Decade', in Ozan Siso, Ufuk Gürbüzdal and Eren

Karaca, eds, *Gezi at Ten: Domination, Opposition and Political Organization*, Leiden: Brill, 2024.

28   For detailed analyses of HDP, see: Rosa Burç, 'Kurdish Transformative Politics in Turkey', *Journal of Ethnographic Theory*, 12(1), pp. 17-26, 2022; Erdem Yörük, 'The Radical Democracy of the People's Democratic Party: Transforming the Turkish State', in Paul Christopher Gray, ed., *From the Streets to the State: Changing the World by Taking Power*, Albany, NY: Suny Press, 2018; Muzaffer Kaya, 'The Potentials and Challenges of Left Populism in Turkey: The Case of the Peoples' Democratic Party (HDP)', *British Journal of Middle Eastern Studies*, 46(5), 2019, pp. 797-812.

29   TİP, EMEP (Emek Partisi – Labour Party), EHP (Emekçi Hareket Partisi – Labourist Movement Party), TÖP (Toplumsal Özgürlük Partisi – Social Freedom Party) and SMF (Sosyalist Meclisler Federasyonu – Federation of Socialist Assemblies SMF)

30   ESP (Ezilenlerin Sosyalist Partisi – Socialist Party of the Oppressed), SODAP (Sosyalist Dayanışma Platformu – Socialist Solidarity Platform), SYKP (Sosyalist Yeniden Kuruluş Partisi – Socialist Renewal Party), Devrimci Parti (Revolutionary Party) and YSP (Yeşiller ve Sol Gelecek Partisi – Green and Left Future Party).

31   Poulantzas, *Fascism*, p. 297.

THE PARADOX OF LATIN AMERICAN POPULISM: A VIEW FROM BOLIVIA

JEFFERY R. WEBBER

Populism has been the main idiom through which reformism has found expression in the Latin American context since at least the 1930s.[1] Now, due to the well-known malleability of the concept of populism in contemporary journalism and academia it becomes immediately necessary to negatively dispense with *what is not meant by populism* for my purposes before moving on to its positive contours.[2] The first caveat is that my entire discussion proceeds within the domain of debates over populism in the Latin American context specifically, setting aside the radically distinct historical development of the theoretical category and historical phenomenon in North America and Europe. The second is that I ignore entirely the veritable tidal wave of journalistic commentary on the rise of the global far-right that makes use of the category of populism, including that subset of the genre dealing explicitly with the far-right in Latin America. For my purposes here, populism is considered as a type of reformism and thus I am interested only in what is often referred to as 'left-populism'. The third caveat is to insist that while discourse is important to understanding populism, it is fundamentally misguided to reduce populism to a transhistorical, formalistic, discursive strategy. In this regard, the reverence with which Ernesto Laclau's theorizations of populism have been treated in recent decades has been a significant obstacle to meaningful comprehension of the phenomenon.[3] The fourth is that populism is not best understood as fundamentally a question of political style, one in which personalistic leadership is forged through a particular rapport with 'the people'.[4] Neither a definition rooted in discursive strategy, nor one based on political style, is capable of differentiating between the straightforwardly disparate politics of, say, Hugo Chávez and Alberto Fujimori, or Evo Morales and Carlos Menem, or Carlos Salinas and Rafael Correa. Neither are these approaches sufficiently attentive to the conditioning role played by the world market – and associated subordinate patterns of capital accumulation in Latin American economies – in shaping the rise and demise of populist cycles in the region over the last century or so.

With those caveats in place, it is possible to offer, in cursory form, the positive contours of a framework for understanding Latin American populism. The most fruitful points of departure are two distinct and contending, but also inadvertently overlapping, currents within an earlier season of debate over the regional phenomenon – that is, those seminal contributions from the 1960s and 1970s emerging, on the one hand, from modernization theory, and, on the other, from Marxism and dependency theory.[5] From their different vantage points, each current in this debate was attempting to explain the rise, consolidation and exhaustion of the classical phase of Latin American populism, beginning in the 1930s and definitively being eclipsed by the 1970s. In the 1930s and 1940s, a number of socioeconomic and political factors had congealed in a series of countries that enabled the rise of populism, even if populism was not the only possible outcome to the situation. The paradigmatic cases were Argentina (Juan Perón), Brazil (Getúlio Vargas) and Mexico (Lázaro Cárdena), but also, if in distinct ways, Bolivia (Víctor Paz Estenssoro) and Ecuador (José María Velasco Ibarra).

The modernization literature suffered from a caricatured stylization of 'the masses' as simply available for manipulation through demagoguery, a teleological evolutionism premised on a standardized schema of societal development from 'tradition' to 'modernity', and a lack of interest in the political economy of capitalism. With this in mind, we can still find persuasive Adrián Piva's observation that the fundamental analytical problem we face in understanding the populist governments and regimes that emerged in early twenty-first century South America as part of the 'pink tide', on the back of accelerated neoliberal transformations in class structures in the 1980s and 1990s and a subsequent wave of rebellions against neoliberalism in the late-1990s and early-2000s, are proximate to those tackled by perhaps the most influential modernization theorist of classical Peronism, Gino Germani. That is, the problem of the relationship between levels of social mobilization that, in a situation of crisis, exceed the integrating capacities of existing political institutions.[6] Indeed, 'the nucleus of the populist phenomenon in Latin America', according to Piva, 'is the political incorporation of socially mobilized and politically excluded groups, in contexts of accelerated transformations and hegemonic crisis'.[7]

Marxist and dependency theorizations of classical populism of the 1960s and 1970s dealt with the same concrete developments as modernization theory but with a more encompassing theoretical lens. Here, the problem of the mode of capital accumulation was central. The obvious twin problems most common to Marxist and dependency theories of Latin American populism in this period were determinism and functionalism.[8] As Aníbal Viguera points out, 'the political aspects of the phenomenon appear ... to be more or less "necessary" correlates of the stage of economic growth in the period roughly between 1930 and 1960'.[9] The underlying thesis of the dominant thread in this literature, according to Juan Grigera, 'follows a functionalist logic', whereby, 'populism exists to fulfill the requirements of a specific mode of accumulation, ISI [import substitution industrialization]'.[10] These are undeniable shortcomings. And yet, the aspiration on the part of dependency and Marxism to develop an enveloping framework is exemplary. Within a single, totalizing frame, they sought to encompass Latin America's dependent incorporation into the world market, the specific mode of accumulation (ISI), the form of political incorporation (populism) and the configuration of class alliance/conciliation, as well as the form of state, all of which were treated as interrelated moments of capitalist totality. None of this *necessarily* requires functionalism or determinism, even if many actually existing dependency theorizations fell into that trap. As Grigera points out, the dominant discursive and stylistic approaches to populism in the literature today represent an '(over)reaction to the deterministic approaches' of the 1960s and 1970s, and as a result the important question of 'the relationship between existing populisms in Latin America and modes of capital accumulation' has been neglected, masking the explanatory role played by 'enabling conditions' in both the rise and demise of populism.[11]

Drawing inspiration from the puzzle first posed by Germani and the best of Latin American Marxism and dependency, the following five elements are understood for my purposes here to be constitutive of populism and are designed to encompass, in a dynamic manner, both the processes and outcomes of populism, across its many modalities – movements, parties, regimes and state forms.

1. *Crisis of hegemony.* Populist possibility arises out of a crisis of hegemony in the existing sociopolitical order. The definitive feature of the crisis is a level of social mobilization of politically excluded labouring classes that exceeds the integration and containment capacities of the existing political institutions. At the same time, the social mobilization is insufficiently powerful and coherent to provide the basis for a revolutionary transformation of society on its own terms. This level of social mobilization – from the vantage point of order, an *excess*, from that of revolution, a *shortfall* – is itself the product of recently accelerated

transformations in class structures of the society in question, followed by intense economic contraction or veritable depression. An *impasse* is reached, and populism is one possible exit.[12]

2. *State as arbitrator of class struggle.* In the wake of a crisis of hegemony, populism fundamentally involves the institutionalization of excess mobilization via the recomposition 'of the state as mediator capable of arbitration of social conflict',[13] and in so doing establishes conditions for the renewal of expanded capital accumulation, albeit on terms that involve concessions to the labouring classes. Given Latin America's subordinate incorporation into the international division of labour, an expansionary phase in the world market is a conditioning factor for this possibility.[14]

3. *Asymmetrical multi-class coalition.* The capital-labour contradiction is displaced and assumes myriad forms.[15] In the amorphous ideological appeals of populism, class conflict and the zero–sum nature of capitalist development are minimized, just as classically reformist themes of integration and a fairer distribution of an expanding economic pie are elevated. Concessions are sought from the capitalist class, but on terms that will not threaten its reproduction.[16] Class antagonisms internal to the populist coalition are displaced through ideological reframing in which the category of 'the people' and/or 'the nation' are pitted against a power bloc consisting of 'the oligarchy' and/or imperialism and/or the 'anti-nation'.[17] The working class and/or peasantry participates in the coalition not out of irrationalism, manipulation or anomie, but because of the extent to which populism *actually* incorporates and responds to selective elements of the socioeconomic and political demands raised by the 'excess' of social mobilization during the preceding crisis of hegemony.[18] 'The specific nature of the crisis, the social groups in question and their mobilization capacity', as Grigera points out, 'will give shape to the populist regime'.[19] The relative capacity of populism to selectively respond to popular demands is conditional upon the rate of capitalist expansion, just as reformism generally is more plausible in periods of capitalist dynamism compared to periods of downturn.[20]

4. *Mobilizes broad popular support, on the basis of top–down, controlled inclusion.*[21] The labouring classes are mobilized but only within the strict parameters that allow for the reproducibility of the asymmetrical multiclass coalition and the stability of the state as class arbitrator – i.e., the juridical sanctity of private property and the profitability of capitalist investors must ultimately be protected against any renewal of mobilizational 'excess'. The populist regime separates, coopts and

rewards 'cooperative' elements of the trade unions, peasant associations and social movements with the material and political resources of the state, while selectively coopting, subverting and repressing 'radical' and/or autonomous elements.[22] In the terms of Torcuato di Tella, populism is 'a political movement which enjoys the support of the urban working class and/or peasantry but which does not result from the autonomous organizational power of either of these two sectors'.[23] Here we witness the molecular processes of passive revolution, where capacities for self-organization and self-activity from below – comparatively high during the preceding crisis of hegemony – are gradually undermined, such that autonomous organizing is disarticulated and demobilized while the mobilization that persists is channeled and contained within the remit of the populist regime.[24]

5. *Contains a self-undermining paradox.* Like reformism generally, populism exhibits a characteristic paradox. The militant mobilization of the labouring classes is the condition of possibility for the rise of populism out of the crisis of hegemony, but once the leading layers of the multiclass populist coalition assume the mantle of state administration they will, in pursuing their own immediate social interests, undermine the autonomous mobilizational capacities of the labouring classes. Once the conditioning factor of an expanding capitalist dynamism is retracted through economic contraction or crisis and the accompanying diminishment of state revenue pinches, populist leaders will more aggressively signal 'viability' to capital through the administration of austerity measures. But in so doing they are unlikely to win the allegiance of capital which, under conditions of contraction, will fight against reformism and reformist politicians more aggressively than ever. At the same time, because labouring-class support for populism can never properly be explained by the irrationalism, manipulability or anomie of the lower orders, once the *actual* selective socioeconomic and political rewards of populism recede, so too will labouring-class ideological allegiance and political support. Populism, in this context, like reformism generally, will dissolve the basis for its own existence.[25]

Far from an arbitrary list to which others might add or subtract different factors on a whim, each element included in the category populism above is articulated with the others according to a master logic, coming together in a 'coherent totality organized around an axis or frame'.[26] That axis, to repeat the Piva quotation again, 'is the political incorporation of socially mobilized and politically excluded groups, in contexts of accelerated transformation and hegemonic crisis'.[27]

ANTINOMIES OF BOLIVIAN POPULISM

In light of the theoretical framework above, the following section offers a stylized periodization of the phases of recent populist experience in the case of Bolivia – crisis of neoliberal hegemony; selective incorporation of movements and demands; consolidation, controlled inclusion and selective repression; and slow-motion crisis, coup and internal rupture. Although the Bolivian case is the exclusive focus of our attention in this essay, one could easily orient an analysis of other pink tide populist experiments – in Argentina, Ecuador or Venezuela, among others – using the theoretical premises advanced here. Properly understanding the rise, consolidation and crisis of pink-tide populism in the region promises to be a decisive factor in comprehending the 'destituent moment' that has followed, characterized as it is by pervasive negative rejection of the political elite, inconformity, electoral volatility, the ascendance of 'outsiders', a crisis of representation, short-sighted political horizons, citizen discontent, and the absence of a sustained and coherent political and ideological north star (on the right or the left).[28] More than polarization and attendant contests for hegemony, it is rather fragmentation, fluidity and the absence of hegemony that appears to be the order of the day throughout much of the region. The distinctive, cross-ideological characteristic of those in office throughout Latin America is precisely their ephemeral legitimacy, fleeting power and fragile social composition.

Crisis of Neoliberal Hegemony, 1999–2005

Radical neoliberal economic restructuring in Bolivia was carried out between 1985 and 2000, amounting to the harshest orthodox stabilization program in Latin America since Augusto Pinochet's counter-revolution in neighbouring Chile.[29] Between 1989 and 1996, average annual growth in Bolivia was just 4 per cent, reaching a high of 5.27 per cent in 1991, a low of 1.65 per cent in 1992, and a new peak of 5.03 per cent in 1998.[30] However, contradictions in neoliberal capitalism at the global, regional and national levels struck Bolivia hard in 1999. GDP growth plummeted to 0.43 per cent that year, rose only to 2.28 per cent in 2000 and declined again to 1.51 per cent, which measured out to roughly zero per cent growth in GDP per capita. Overall poverty rates in the country soared to 65 per cent of the population, and income inequality increased. All of this transpired in the poorest country in South America, and one of the most unequal countries in the most unequal region of the world.[31] Popular discontent with the social consequences of neoliberalism began to grow discernably in the late 1990s and early 2000s. Over 90 per cent of the Bolivian population reported that they thought the income distribution in the country was 'unfair' or 'very unfair'.[32] The number of strikes and slowdowns across the country was more than double that of the early 1990s.[33]

The Cochabamba 'Water War' of 2000 against the privatization of water in that city, Aymara indigenous roadblocks and mobilizations of the western *altiplano* (high plateau) against the privatization of access to water in the region, and proletarian anti-tax revolt in La Paz and El Alto in February 2003, constituted the opening acts of what developed into a five-year cycle of left-indigenous revolt in Bolivia.[34] The cycle culminated in the two 'Gas Wars' of October 2003 and May–June 2005, led by informal indigenous workers in the city of El Alto, allied with layers of the indigenous peasantry, the organized labour movement of the formal working class and (at least in 2003) sections of the middle class. The mass rebellions shook the country to its foundations, cutting short the presidential terms of Gonzalo Sánchez de Lozada (2003) and Carlos Mesa (2005). The key demands were the nationalization of the natural gas industry and a Constituent Assembly to reestablish state-society relations.[35]

Here, then, we find a paradigmatic case of social mobilization of politically excluded groups in excess of the capacities of the existing institutional frameworks of the state to incorporate them, in a context of accelerated transformation and hegemonic crisis.

Selective Incorporation of Movements and Demands, 2006-2009

Unexpected in its scale, the triumph of the Movimiento al Socialismo (Movement Toward Socialism, MAS) in the December 2005 elections enabled Evo Morales to take direct possession of the presidency, obviating any need for inter-party bargaining or a second round of votes in Congress to determine the presidency.[36] The MAS, together with the allied Movimiento Sin Miedo (Movement Without Fear, MSM), won a majority in the lower house of Congress (Chamber of Deputies), but only a minority in the upper house (Chamber of Senators). This became a pivotal point of disputation and negotiation between the ruling party and the opposition, and led Morales to frequently deploy executive decrees as a way of getting around stalemates in Congress.[37] Support for the MAS in the national elections was scarce in the *media luna* (half moon) departments of the lowlands – Pando, Beni, Santa Cruz and Tarija – whereas in the highlands and valleys – La Paz, Oruro, Potosí, Cochabamba and Sucre – turnout for Morales was impressive. In the simultaneous prefectural elections at the department level, much of this regional dynamic was reproduced, although with further ground lost by the MAS to the opposition, attenuating more sharply Morales' dominance in the domain of the presidency. In addition to the departments of the *media luna*, the opposition took the prefectures (later renamed governorships) in La Paz and Cochabamba, two strongholds of the MAS at the national level.[38] With widespread legitimacy in their departments, and fiercely opposed to the new indigenous president, the regional elite of prefects – Manfred Reyes Villa in Cochabamba and José Luis Paredes in La Paz, but especially Rubén Costas in Santa Cruz, Leopoldo Fernández in Pando, Ernesto Suárez in Beni, and Mario Cossío in Tarija – took advantage of their institutional strength to foment political instability in the country and undermine Morales' national governance in the coming years.[39]

The composition of Morales' first cabinet was designed to signal resolute commitment to the popular left-indigenous social bases responsible for bringing Morales to office as the country's first indigenous president since the founding of the republic in 1825. Of the 16 ministers selected, there was unprecedented representation of the rural and urban indigenous popular classes. According to the calculus of sociologist Fran Espinoza, 10 of the 16 posts were taken up by individuals whose trajectories were marked by activism in the 'social sectors' of Bolivian society, with the remaining six filled by 'technocrats', broadly defined.[40] The reticence of life-long bureaucrats to take orders from some of the new ministers of popular ethnic and class descent, combined with the inexperience and lack of education of many such ministers given the historical inequalities of access to education and public sector portfolios, meant that their time in office was often short-lived, and rotations of cabinet makeup were frequent and thoroughgoing: 'in the government's first three years, the minister of hydrocarbons was substituted annually and the state oil and gas company Yacimientos Petrolíferos Fiscales Bolivianos (YPFB), raced through five presidents. The price has been highly uneven ministry performance.'[41]

In late January 2006, festooned in traditional indigenous regalia, Morales broke protocol by inaugurating his accession to the presidency, not before Congress, but on the symbolic grounds of Tiahuanacu, in the department of La Paz, in a ceremony brimming with elaborate cultural and political rites and symbols.[42] On Monday, 1 May 2006, amidst celebrations and marches commemorating the day of the working class internationally, the Bolivian government appeared to nationalize the country's hydrocarbons sector. Of any policy introduced by Morales since he came to office, this was undoubtedly the most significant.[43] Morales' nationalization decree of 2006 allowed the government to reclaim state control of Bolivia's hydrocarbons above and below ground, set the stage for the renegotiation of contracts, favourably alter the royalty and tax scheme, and thus facilitate the priming of state revenue, and associated social programs, during a period of high international prices. At the same time, progress toward the wider strategic goals of rebuilding YPFB, industrializing gas, diversifying the economy, reclaiming control from multinational domination in the sector was minimal, and longstanding contradictions of labour, ecology and indigenous rights quickly resurfaced.[44]

Soon after assuming office, on 4 March 2006 the MAS government also introduced a law convening a Constituent Assembly in response to a central demand arising from the 2000–2005 left-indigenous cycle of revolt.[45] An important social movement alliance called the Unity Pact was formed to coordinate the orientation of organized movements toward the assembly. Representatives of the Unity Pact within the Constituent Assembly were allied with MAS representatives, but often took independent positions to the left of the party's leadership. The Unity Pact was composed of an array of lowland and highland indigenous-peasant and labour organizations. These organizations sought to take advantage of the assembly process to refound Bolivian state-society relations on new grounds, understanding as they did that the Morales government owed its existence to the movements' extraordinary effervescence between 2000 and 2005.[46]

The autonomist right of the lowlands, meanwhile, was attempting to subvert the functioning of the Constituent Assembly through both formal opposition from inside its institutional structures and extra-parliamentary mass destabilization directed at undermining the central government. In August 2008, the government was strengthened after a recall referendum organized by the opposition to oust the government led instead to the ratification of the president and vice president with an impressive 67 per cent of the national vote. The opposition prefects of the departments of La Paz and Cochabamba were also revoked and replaced with government supporters. As expected, the referendum also saw the ratification of oppositional prefects in Santa Cruz, Tarija, Beni and Pando.[47] After losing ground in the electoral domain, the autonomist right of the lowlands opted for extra-parliamentary destabilization in the form of a 'civic coup' at the departmental level, with militant and mass right-wing mobilizations from 9–16 September 2008. The Civic Committee of Santa Cruz coordinated the actions from on high, while their violent shock troops in the Unión Juvenil Cruceñista (Union of Cruceño Youth, UJC) carried out the necessary thug violence in the street.[48] However, events in Porvenir, in the department of Pando, took a turn that eventually ground the opposition's momentum to a halt. Dozens of peasant and student supporters of the government were murdered by right-wing oppositionists linked to the Pando prefect Leopoldo Fernández.

In response the Morales government took over Pando militarily, and peasant and indigenous organizations loyal to the party began to organize a massive march, threatening to surround Santa Cruz. Organized indigenous youth from the shantytown of Plan 3000 in Santa Cruz also engaged in increasingly successful street battles with UJC hooligans. The fundamental outcome of this dynamic was ultimately a concerted spike in support for the government and the near disappearance of an organized oppositional bloc, with decisive consequences for the rhythm of politics in Bolivia thereafter.[49]

The Constituent Assembly had agreed on the text for the new constitution back in December 2007. However, in the context of persistent political instability in the country, a modified and moderated version of the text was only ratified by the Bolivian Congress in late October 2008. In an influential essay published at the beginning of Morales' second term in 2010, vice president Álvaro García Linera theorized these moments as the 'point of bifurcation' in Bolivia's extended state crisis, ultimately leading to the 'historical-moral and cultural-political defeat of the old dominant classes and the consolidation of a new integral state power bloc in the Gramscian sense'.[50] While García Linera exaggerated the scale of defeat of the old dominant classes, he was right to point out that the setback for the right-wing opposition lad the basis for the consolidation of MAS rule.[51]

With respect to our theoretical schema of populism developed above, the period of selective incorporation and movements and demands under MAS rule confirms a number of important features: the restoration of the Bolivian state as arbitrator of social conflict, thus setting the conditions for expanded capitalist accumulation alongside selective benefits for the labouring classes; the government's confrontation with sections of the Bolivian capitalist class produced and reproduced the ideological axis of 'the people' (associated with the MAS) and the oligarchic-anti-nation (associated with the autonomist bourgeoisie of the eastern lowlands), strengthening the government's capacity to survive the most volatile initial stage of populist regime formation; and there was an *actual* economic and political response by the state to popular demands (nationalization of gas, convening of a constituent assembly and popular representation in cabinet), within a framework unthreatening to the viability of capital accumulation because of the commodity-driven expansionary character of the period.

Consolidation, Controlled Inclusion, Selective Repression, 2010–2014

According to García Linera, by 2010 MAS hegemony had been achieved, after which tensions and contradictions of the 'process of change' became creative, internal forces operating within the national-popular bloc supporting the government.[52] What is certainly clear is that while the relationship between the agro-industrial elite of the lowlands and the Morales regime was one of antagonism between 2006 and 2009, from 2010 relations between the two were altered dramatically. After the political defeat of the autonomist movement of the lowlands, the agro-industrial elite changed tactics and opted for a close working relationship with the Morales government.[53] The new agro-capital-state-alliance corresponded with a rupture in the relationship between the government and lowland indigenous organizations.[54] By mid-2011, the emergent division within the national-popular bloc escalated when Morales gave a green light to a decades-old plan to build a highway connecting Villa Tunari (in the department of Cochabamba), north to San Ignacio de Moxos (in the department of Beni) through Isiboro-Sécure Indigenous Territory and National Park (TIPNIS).[55] The TIPNIS highway conflict set off marches by those lowland indigenous groups asserting their right to self-government and prior consultation before any development project in their territories was planned and executed. The government in turn sponsored counter demonstrations and sent in police to repress the marches. By this stage, the relative autonomy from the government that the Unity Pact had enjoyed was seriously eroded. The Unity Pact split over TIPNIS, with the predominant lowland indigenous organizations leaving the social movement alliance, and with those social movement organizations remaining within it becoming increasingly inseparable from the MAS itself.[56] This tendency was compounded by the expulsion or desertion from the party of a series of high-profile left-wing intellectuals and activists who had supported the government between 2006 and 2010 – Lino Villca, Román Loayza, Féliz Patzi, Alejandro Almaraz, Alex Contreras, Raúl Prada, Gustavo Guzmán and Pablo Solón.[57]

With respect to the organized labour movement, the period from 2006 to 2009 witnessed Morales make powerful pro-labour statements and involve in select policy developments, especially those around pensions, the Central Obrera Boliviana (Bolivian Workers' Central, COB), the main trade union federation in the country. The COB was also a key player within the Unity Pact, mobilizing to influence the course of the Constituent Assembly and defend the government against autonomist right-wing destabilization. Between 2010 and 2014, however, the MAS proposed a new labour code that would set new limits on the right to strike, drive up working hours for public health sector workers and remove fuel subsidies, affecting both organized and unorganized workers alike. The result was a dynamic of heightened but largely sectional disputes between organized labour and the state – particularly involving public school teachers, manufacturing unions and salaried miners at different intervals – as well as the massive, nationwide mobilizations against the proposed cut to fuel subsidies, known as the *gasolinazo*, that were largely organized by the COB. The Morales government responded by selectively backtracking on proposed anti-labour reforms when faced with sufficient mobilization, as in the case of the government's withdrawal of its proposed cut to fuel subsidies following the *gasolinazo*. The MAS was effective in containing the COB leadership in this way. Although the COB had even considered the creation of an independent working-class party following the anti-labour momentum beginning in 2010, at its November 2013 general assembly, the COB's leadership 'dropped the initiative, endorsing the MAS in the upcoming elections in October 2014 and return[ed] to its role in supporting the government by helping to suppress popular demands'.[58]

The inherent class contradictions within the model of development pursued by the MAS since 2006 were partially concealed for many years by the conditioning factor of an extraordinary commodities boom, driven above all by China's rapid growth, which absorbed increasing levels of Bolivia's extractive exports. In 2005, Bolivia's per capita GDP was lower than what it had been in 1980, whereas by 2018, real (inflation-adjusted) GDP per capita was 50 per cent higher than in 2005.[59] Average expansion of the country's GDP under Morales between 2006 and 2014 was 5.1 per cent, with a low of 3.4 per cent in 2009 following the onset of the global crisis, and peaks of 6.2 and 6.8 per cent in 2008 and 2013 respectively.[60] Growth was highly dependent on primary commodity exports.[61] Natural gas exports to Brazil and Argentina, for example, accounted for 54.7 per cent of total exports in 2013, while mining exports were 25.4 per cent of the total. Just over 80 per cent of total exports that year were of primary materials (if primary materials are understood to include mining minerals, hydrocarbons and agricultural products).[62] Public investment as a percentage of GDP in Bolivia was the highest in Latin America over this period.[63] In real terms, social spending from 2005 to 2017 grew by 80 per cent, even as social spending as a percentage of GDP actually decreased between 2005 and 2013.[64] Much of this social spending was used to lubricate three cash transfer programs incentivizing children's school attendance, medical care for pregnancies and early motherhood and pension supplements. By 2018, 52 per cent of the population received a direct cash transfer from the government of one sort or another.[65] The combination of public spending, increased employment, rising real wages, remittances from abroad and direct government cash transfers explain a reduction in the poverty rate from 66.6 per cent of the population in 2005 to 33.7 per cent in 2014, and a drop in the extreme poverty rate from 36.9 per cent of the population to 14.9 per cent over the same period.[66]

Natural gas exports were essential to the generation of substantial current account surpluses and the accumulation of Bolivia's foreign reserves during this period, with gas exports reaching a peak value of $5.9 billion in 2014, at the same time as foreign reserves peaked at $15 billion.[67] After running current account deficits for the entirety of the 1990s, the situation turned around beginning in 2003, and the upturn continued during the first two administrations of the MAS. Between 2006 and 2014, Bolivia experienced an average current account surplus of 6.6 per cent of GDP.[68] High gas prices, increases in royalties and taxes in the hydrocarbons sector and the subsequent sustained surplus in the current account underpinned macroeconomic stability and the capacity to carry out high levels of public investment, including relatively significant absolute increases in social spending.[69]

With regard to our theoretical schema, the period of MAS rule from 2010 to 2014 is indicative of the following features: an asymmetrical multi-class coalition, rooted in the consolidation of a novel agro-capital-state alliance, even as the livelihoods of the labouring classes continued to improve; top-down, controlled-inclusion, involving selective concessions to moderate popular movements, repression and isolation of radical dissidents and generalized divide and conquer strategy aimed at the subordinated incorporation of the organized and unorganized lower orders (witness the Unity Pact split in TIPNIS, the departure of a number of prominent left intellectuals and activists from the party, and the mix of sectional dispute, selective concessions and ultimate controlled inclusion of the organized labour movement, especially its peak organization, the COB); the conditioning factor of capitalist expansion in the context of a commodity boom; and the *actual* selective socioeconomic and political rewards to the labouring classes for their participation in reformist populism during a period of robust economic growth.

Slow-Motion Crisis, Coup and Internal Ruptures, 2014-2024

Over the next decade the MAS's populism became much more difficult to reproduce, and to the extent that it has been reproduced it has only been in an emaciated, internally fractured version of its former self. Lower gas prices and a consistent fall in the volume of gas exports since 2014 have been fundamental in driving this trajectory.[70] While GDP growth averaged 5.1 per cent between 2006 and 2014, the average from 2015 to 2023 was only 2.7 per cent.[71] An average current account surplus of 6.6 per cent of GDP between 2006 and 2014, meanwhile, fell to an average deficit of 2.6 per cent of GDP between 2015 and 2023, a deficit largely financed by drawing down foreign reserves.[72] Net foreign reserves plummeted from $15 billion in 2014 to $3.8 billion in 2022.[73] External debt in foreign currency more than doubled between 2013 ($5.6 billion) and 2022 ($12.7 billion).[74] The Bolivian government averaged a budget surplus of 0.7 per cent of GDP between 2006 and 2013, whereas it averaged a 3.85 per cent deficit between 2014 and 2017.[75] Bolivia became an energy importer, with imports of domestically subsidized fuels, such as gasoline and diesel, increasing from a value of $1.2 billion in 2013 to $ 4.3 billion in 2022.[76] Recall that poverty dropped dramatically between 2005 and 2014, from 66.6 to 33.7 per cent of the population. After this sharp initial reduction, improvements in poverty have been comparatively cosmetic, stagnating not only because of changed conditioning factors, but because of the limits to reducing poverty further without fundamentally transforming social property relations in the country. The poverty rate inched upwards to 35.1 per cent in 2016, remaining basically steady at 34.9 per cent in 2017, before dropping to 31 per cent in 2019, climbing to 32.3 in 2020 during the pandemic and after a right-wing coup d'état temporarily ousted the MAS government, and descending to 29 per cent in 2021, when a new MAS government assumed office.[77]

At the outset of the last decade of populist decline, Morales had already become Bolivia's longest serving president and was constitutionally unable to seek re-election.[78] Yet in 2016 he attempted to override these limits through a series of legal and political manipulations. In February of that year, he held a referendum on whether to amend the constitution to allow him to campaign for a fourth term. When 51 per cent of the electorate voted 'No', he ignored the results and ran for the presidency anyway, on the basis of a dubious legal verdict from the country's highest electoral tribunal. This fiasco became a call to arms among middle-class rebels and regional civic committees bent on ousting the MAS.

Bolivia's electoral system requires the leading presidential candidate to secure more than 50 per cent of the vote, or more than 40 per cent of the vote plus a margin of 10 per cent over the second-place candidate, to avoid a run-off. On the evening of the general election, in late October 2019, the 'quick count' tally showed Morales with 45 per cent, compared to 38 per cent for the centre-right runner-up Carlos Mesa. Then, after an unexplained delay of 22 hours, the updated count indicated Morales enjoying a lead over Mesa in excess of 10 points, obviating the need for a second round. The late shift in votes to Morales' advantage was plausible given the demographics of the regions where ballots were counted later in the process, but the delay between the two tallies created the impression of foul play.[79] Though it could not provide any evidence, the entire opposition cried fraud – as did the Organization of American States. Violent protests against Morales erupted across the country, and the far right of the eastern lowlands, backed by the military and police, launched a soft-coup that forced his resignation. The coup was petit-bourgeois and mestizo in composition, with some plebeian layers drawn into the *antimasista* hysteria. Its rallying cry was one of pure negation: 'Fuera Evo'. No positive, alternative agenda was ever advanced by its leaders. Yet there was never any doubt about whose interests they were serving: those of agro-industrial, financial and hydrocarbon capital.

The coup-plotters succeeded in installing Jeanine Áñez, an ultra-conservative Catholic senator from Beni whose party had won only 4 per cent in the previous election. With Morales and his inner-circle exiled to Mexico and Argentina, the obvious task for Áñez was to dismantle the statist elements of the MAS era – such as the quasi nationalization of hydrocarbons – and reverse collective indigenous rights. With the popular classes caught in a momentary stupor, and left-wing forces weakened by years of clientelist integration into the state under Morales, Áñez had the tools for oligarchic restoration at her disposal. Yet her regime was undermined from the start by its own ideological and practical excesses: above all, state repression – 36 assassinated, 80 injured, hundreds detained and exiled – and bureaucratic ineptitude in the face of the Covid-19 pandemic. In Latin America, only Peru had a higher per capita excess mortality rate in 2020 than Bolivia.[80] Áñez had no plan to assemble a viable support base or manage the country's economic instability. Instead, its stand-out features were brutal state violence, brazen corruption, administrative incompetence and a colossal decline in living standards, as the growth rate plummeted in 2020 and more than 3 million Bolivians became unable to meet their basic nutritional needs. The government also unleashed a new, virulent wave of anti-indigenous racism in civil society, with the dog whistles of state officials providing a soundtrack.[81]

As such, Áñez rapidly concentrated workers and peasants into a powerful opposition force, while at the same time losing the loyalty of the petit-bourgeois layers that had originally supported the coup. Amid the ongoing economic and health crises, significant parts of the new middle-class – forged during the expansionary period under Morales – were horrified to find themselves returned to proletarian or lumpen status. At the same time, social movements and unions, which were initially slow to respond to the coup, managed to rally their forces, erecting street barricades and disrupting supply chains. By the time the general election of December 2020 rolled around, the *golpistas*, having failed to prevent the MAS from running, had split into three rival presidential campaigns. Carlos Mesa's centre-right Citizen Community led the pack, followed in the distance by the right-wing extremist Luis Fernando Camacho, followed by Áñez, who saw the writing on the wall and eventually withdrew from the race.[82]

The 2020 Bolivian general election marked the return of the MAS to government.[83] Since then, the administration of Luis 'Lucho' Arce Catacora has tried to fortify itself against another antidemocratic campaign of destabilization by projecting an image of unity and strength. Yet during Arce's tenure, the internal components of the MAS have grown increasingly discordant – with each factional dispute amplified by a hostile media. The respective supporters of President Arce, Vice-President David Choquehuanca, and former president Evo Morales had each been vying for power, attempting to outmanoeuvre their factional opponents ahead of the 2025 elections. Over time, the three-way contest reduced to a polarization between Arce and Morales, with Choquehuanca backing the former.[84] Although the MAS technically controls a majority of seats in both houses of congress, the internal division within the party mean that Arce enjoys no guaranteed congressional support and, in fact, usually guarantees hostility, from both the right-wing and *evista* oppositions. Meanwhile, centrifugal tendencies on the right have become even more pronounced, with different currents blaming one another for return of the MAS. The result is an ongoing process of fragmentation across Bolivia's two major political blocs, neither of which can articulate a coherent ideological project. The country's historic fault-lines – separating the cities from the countryside; indigenous masses from non-indigenous elites; the south and the east from the north and the west; the media, universities and middle classes from peasant confederations and workers' unions; agro-industrial, hydrocarbon and financial capitalists from a burgeoning informal proletariat – no longer find self-evident political articulation in two antipodal camps, as they did in the high-populist period. Beneath the superficial split between *masistas* and anti-*masistas* lies a more complex patchwork of rivalries and power centres.

All those who had participated in the disaster of the Áñez administration were duly punished by the electorate. Arce returned the MAS to office with a decisive 55 per cent of the vote, while Mesa obtained a paltry 29 per cent. Nostalgia for the bonanza years during the first stretch of Morales' rule was a fire easily stoked. Arce could point to his relatively orthodox reign as MAS finance minister during an era of high commodity prices, dynamic capitalist accumulation, historic profits in extractive sectors and modest improvements in the livelihood of the urban working class and peasantry. Morales was still abroad during the 2020 ballot, yet he had personally selected Arce as the candidate after David Choquehuanca had been put forward by the grassroots, including the coalition of social movements known as the Unity Pact. Unlike Choquehuanca, Arce was non-indigenous, had never shown any leadership ambitions and had no social base of his own, so his ability to fill Morales' shoes was questionable. Yet the election results made clear that *masismo* could not be reduced to *evismo*. His victory showed that it was possible to win without the party's historic *caudillo*, while demonstrating the enduring popularity of the MAS's populist model.

Now, three years into Arce's tenure, how can we characterize his record? The president fulfilled his first policy commitments immediately upon taking office, including cash transfers of $140 per month to roughly a third of the population, a symbolic tax on large domestic fortunes and investigations into the repression of the Áñez regime. Yet, on the whole, his administration is a workaday technocracy, lacking any of the transformative aspirations that the early Morales period kindled among the poor and dispossessed. As sociologist Vladimir Mendoza Manjón has noted, the prevailing view within Arce's cabinet is that the era of transformation has come to an end.[85] Instead, the current period demands a defensive, administrative posture: at best, the consolidation of previous gains amid more challenging material conditions. The aim is to prioritize political stability and slowly reactivate the economy.

But conditioning factors are not congenial for either political stability or renewal of capital accumulation. The structural dynamics of a slow-building economic crisis were set in motion as early as 2015. Today, the crisis is proceeding at full steam, in lockstep with the political, ideological and institutional degeneration of the populism project. The next general election will take place in October 2025. Morales, who continues as president of the party apparatus of the MAS, has long-since declared his intention to run as the MAS candidate and it is only a matter of time, according to most analysts, before Arce openly declares his intention to do the same. A formal split in the MAS appears inevitable in the near future, with the only question being whether it will be the *arcistas* or *evistas* who manage to assert control of the original party apparatus in the lead-up to 2025, and who will be left to hastily build a new party formation of some kind.[86]

The natural gas sector has continued to spiral downwards. Daily gas production in Bolivia has plunged from 60 million cubic metres daily in 2015, to only 38 million in 2023. State revenue generated from gas exports now amounts to roughly $2.4 billion annually, whereas imports of fuels such as gasoline and diesel are roughly $3.2 billion, explaining the novelty of Bolivia's current position as net importer of energy. This is the major factor behind the current account deficit climbing to more than $500 million in 2023. According to the neoliberal opposition, the fall in gas production is traceable to the taxation and royalty reforms in the hydrocarbons sector carried out under Morales which supposedly led multinational companies to extract as much as they could as quickly as possible from known deposits, in the absence of sufficiently profitable incentives for investment in new exploration. Given the multibillion dollar profits accrued by multinationals during the boom period, this is an implausible explanation for the absence of sufficient exploratory investment. Instead, intense capital flight was driven by declining gas prices beginning in 2015, the political uncertainty generated by the 2019 coup and the extreme Áñez administration, the pandemic and the eventual return of the MAS to office in a much more volatile regional and global economic period. A growing number of geological specialists in the country claim that the reason for declining gas production and failure to discover significant new deposits is straightforward – the available supply is simply running dry.[87]

Whether or not the geologists are correct, natural gas will be unreliable as a revenue stream in the near to medium future at least, as Argentina, one of Bolivia's major export destinations, has recently ramped up domestic production of its own to meet almost the entirety of its gas needs, with the expectation that it will soon start exporting surplus to Chile, Brazil and perhaps even Bolivia. While lithium mining promises to be a major focus of development strategy in Bolivia in coming decades – Bolivia is home to one of the largest reserves of the metal, and lithium is a key component in many of the technologies central to the various 'green capitalist transitions' envisioned around the globe – it is unlikely to generate any revenue for several years, given the high-cost and high-tech nature of the kind of extraction required for Bolivia's contaminated deposits, and growing local movements in opposition to its mining. Meanwhile, public deficits are rising, the debt burden is mounting, new lines of credit are becoming more difficult and expensive to obtain, foreign reserves are disappearing, the cost of living is rising sharply and dollars are becoming scarce.[88]

A recent assessment by the Economist Intelligence Unit contends that 'soybean exports will also help to compensate for the decline in natural gas exports, but neither soybeans nor lithium will generate enough income to resolve Bolivia's macroeconomic imbalances, leaving the authorities with no option but to devalue the currency and adjust fiscal policy to prevent future crises'.[89] While Arce has thus far resisted currency devaluation, a black market in dollars has opened up, with a 30 per cent differential compared with the official exchange rate.[90] Arce's ability to associate himself with the boom times functioned well as a campaign strategy in 2020 against the backdrop of the calamitous Áñez regime. But his ability to project the staid and steady image of competent economic manager has quickly faded in the light of diminishing performance. In May 2024, Arce's approval rating hit

18 per cent, among the lowest of the region's presidents. His only saving grace thus far has been that the approval ratings of the opposition leaders are even more dismal.[91]

On 26 June 2024, the political symptoms of the crisis became darker and more bizarre at once, when General Juan José Zúñiga, leader of Bolivia's Armed Forces, mounted a quixotic, highly mediatized coup attempt, which was routed almost as soon as it had begun. Arce had just given Zúñiga a few days notice that his term as head of the Armed Forces was coming to an end due to the general's intemperate threats against Morales in a recent television appearance. Zúñiga's televised message to the former president was that he would be imprisoned if he continued to pursue the 2025 presidency. However fierce Arce's rivalry with Morales, this was an unsanctioned step too far on the part of the general. For reasons that remain unclear, Arce failed to make Zúñiga's termination immediate, allowing him time to mobilize some troops under his direct command and organize a cavalry of armed vehicles that theatrically stormed the Plaza Murillo and proceeded to ram the front doors of the Palacio Quemado (Burnt Palace, the official presidential residence), in which Arce was meeting with members of his cabinet. Arce, Choquehuanca and half the cabinet then engaged in a surreally broadcasted, non-violent faceoff at the doors of the palace. It quickly became evident that, unlike the coup that installed Áñez in 2019, Zúñiga could count on no public support from any of the political parties across the ideological spectrum, nor did he enjoy popular appeal in society, nor a base of any depth in the Armed Forces.

The coup fizzled almost immediately, Zúñiga was arrested, and now faces up to twenty years in prison. The details of the coup attempt beyond these broad outlines remain largely unknown, but the right-wing opposition quickly declared that the whole episode had been merely a show, designed to provide cover for an *autogolpe*, or self-coup. According to this view, Arce orchestrated the entire spectacle himself in order to strengthen his position vis-à-vis Morales against the backdrop of internecine civil warfare in the MAS. Zúñiga helped launched this version of events when he claimed the whole thing had been Arce's idea during one interview with the press, as he was being led to prison by the police. He had offered a different explanation earlier in the day and he developed a third version of events later that evening. For his part, Morales denounced the military mobilization on the day of the coup, but later adopted a position very close to the right-wing opposition's narrative. Here is a social media post from Morales two days after the spectacle: 'I don't now what kind of coup this would be. It started with happy cabinet ministers walking through the Plaza Murillo, touching tanks. A coup d'état with zero wounded, zero disappeared, zero deaths', he joked.[92] While much about the events in June remain murky, the self-coup thesis does not have much to offer by way of evidence or explanatory power. As the journalist Fernando Molina has pointed out, what was in this for Zúñiga, who now faces the potential of two decades in prison? And if Arce had intended to carry out an *autogolpe* – in the tradition of Boris Yeltsin or, closer to home, Alberto Fujimori – why was there no closure of Congress or rule by emergency decree, but instead the immediate arrest and imprisonment of the dissident general? How did the chaos fomented by the coup strengthen Arce's ability to project an image of stable governance in anticipation of the 2025 elections?[93]

A final crisis symptom worth noting has to do with Arce's manipulation of the judiciary. In Bolivia, the highest magistrates of the judiciary are selected through popular election. At the moment, the Constitutional Court, the highest judicial body, is stacked with supporters of Arce. According to a ruling by this institution in December 2023, the judges will stay in their posts until their replacements are sworn in, despite their elected terms officially coming to a close at the end of 2023. Meanwhile, Arce has consistently postponed judicial elections which now look likely to occur only alongside the 2025 general election. The president has engaged in such unconstitutional maneuvers seemingly in order to secure judicial support for his executive decrees that frequently bypass congress, defend himself against any possible impeachment attempts and potentially circumvent Morales' run for the presidency in 2025.[94]

With regard to our theoretical framework for understanding populism, the last decade of Bolivian politics has fundamentally revealed the self-undermining paradox of populism. Although Morales' original ascent to the presidency would be unimaginable without the left-indigenous cycle of revolt between 2000 and 2005, once in office MAS populism gradually, but thoroughly, undermined social movement and trade union capacities for autonomy, self-organization and mobilization outside the remit of top-down, controlled inclusion. In so doing, it helped to ensure that the popular movement response to the 2019 coup that installed Áñez in power was relatively weak and ineffectual at the crucial juncture. Furthermore, once the conditioning factor of expanding capitalist dynamism, driven by high commodity prices, was undermined by the delayed reverberation into Bolivia of the global crisis of 2008, populist state managers in Bolivia no longer had the same room to maneuver. In attempting to signal 'viability' to capital they both undermined part of the ideological and political appeal of reformist populism among labouring classes, while at the same time failing to command the loyalty of capital – unsurprising insofar as capital, all other things being equal, is least likely to accept reformist measures under conditions of economic contraction or crisis. One successful anti-populist coup (2019), another failed attempt (2024), and fierce and mounting internal divisions within the MAS, are all morbid symptoms of populism's self-undermining paradox.

CONCLUSION

This essay has tried to demonstrate, first, that populism has been the predominant method of reformist politics in the Latin American context since at least the 1930s. Second, it has sought to reorient recent discussion of Latin American populism through a revisionist reworking of some of the animating theoretical premises of both modernization and dependency and Marxist approaches to the classical populist question in the region developed in the 1960s and 1970s. These premises, properly adapted, are superior to the pervasive treatment of populism as pre-eminently a discursive or stylistic political phenomenon. Articulated by a framing axis holding together each of the elements, it has sought to organize our understanding of populism – as both process and result, and across its movement, party, regime and state modalities – around five constitutive features: crisis of hegemony; state as arbitrator of class struggle; asymmetrical multi-class coalition; mobilization of broad popular support, on the basis of top-down, controlled inclusion; and containing a self-undermining paradox.

The Bolivian case has been used as an exemplar of populism's rise, consolidation and crisis in the context of the twenty-first century regional pink tide. Between 2000 and 2005 the country experienced a crisis of neoliberal hegemony, in which the social mobilization of politically excluded groups exceeded the incorporative capacities of the existing institutional framework of the state, in an overarching context of accelerated transformations. Between 2006 and 2009, Bolivian populism under the MAS involved the selective inclusion of popular movements and demands, indicating the reassertion of the state as arbitrator of class conflict and facilitator of conditions for the expanded renewal of capital accumulation, with selective benefits to the labouring classes. This period also saw government conflict with sections of the Bolivian class, reinforcing the ideological axis of 'the people' versus the 'oligarchic-anti-nation'. This phase, finally, demonstrated that it was not the demagogic manipulation of the masses by Morales' charismatic authority that accounts for the reproduction of populism in this period, but rather the actual economic and political response of the populist government to selective popular demands – 'nationalization' of gas, constituent assembly and a more representative cabinet, being among the most important.

Between 2010 and 2014, the country witnessed populism's consolidation, controlled inclusion of moderate popular forces, and selective repression and isolation of radical dissidents among the labouring classes. The agro-capital-state alliance forged in this period revealed the asymmetrical class coalition of the populist experiment, while state-social movement dynamics in the TIPNIS and the organized labour movement were indicative of selective concession/repression tendencies within an overarching framework of divide and rule, followed with subordinated incorporation. This is also apparent in the exit from the party of a number of leading left intellectuals and activists. Especially important in the 2010–2014 period were the conditioning factors of capitalist expansion in the context of a commodity boom and the extent to which ongoing popular support for populist reformism was built on foundations of actual selective socioeconomic and political rewards to the lower orders of society. Finally, the last decade in Bolivian politics, from 2014 to 2024, was characterized by the gradual unfolding of a socioeconomic crisis under changed conditioning factors, one successful and failed anti-populist coup d'état and corrosive internal ruptures within the MAS in the lead up to October 2025 elections. This essay has attempted to demonstrate how these are confirming symptoms of the self-undermining paradox of populism, as disarticulated popular movements were unable to respond to the 2019 coup d'état, and as the MAS government reveals the limits of sustaining a multi-class populist alliance under conditions of economic contraction and crisis.

NOTES

1   I presented a trial run of some of these arguments at Marxism 2024, in Melbourne, organized by Socialist Alternative. I benefited from the formal discussions during the two sessions I was involved in, as well as informal conversations throughout the conference. Thanks to the organizers for the invitation, and especially to Sarah Garnham and Robert Narai. Thanks to Greg Albo and Chris Little for their editorial suggestions.

2   One commentary notes how the label has been used recently to describe such wildly disparate historical figures as Atatürk, Mao, Perón and Thatcher, not to mention contemporary politicians ranging from Trump, to Sanders, through Corbyn. See: Tony Wood, 'Some Theses on "Populism"', *E-Flux Journal*, 76, 2016, available at: www.e-flux.com.

3   Ernesto Laclau, *Politics and Ideology in Marxist Theory: Capitalism, Fascism, Populism*, London: Verso, 2012; Ernesto Laclau, *On Populist Reason*, London: Verso, 2007. In the former text, first published in 1977, discursive ideology remains tied in some respects to a class order, whereas the break with Marxism is definitively on display in the latter book. For powerful criticism, see: Aníbal Viguera, '"Populismo" y

"Neopopulismo" En América Latina', *Revista Mexicana de Sociología*, 55(3), 1993, pp. 49-66; Omar Acha, 'From Marxist to Post-Marxist Populism: Ernesto Laclau's Trajectory within the National Left and Beyond', *Historical Materialism*, 28(1), 2020, pp. 183-214.

4   Political style is central to the argument made by Alan Knight, for example. Alan Knight, 'Populism and Neo-Populism in Latin America, Especially Mexico', *Journal of Latin American Studies*, 30(2), 1998, pp. 223-48. While Kenneth M. Roberts is more attentive to political economy, the plasticity of his model is excessive, in no small part due to the stress he places on political style. Kenneth M. Roberts, 'Neoliberalism and the Transformation of Populism in Latin America: The Peruvian Case', *World Politics*, 48(1), 1995, pp. 82-116.

5   For representative contributions to the modernization stream, see: Gino Germani, *Política y Sociedad en una Época de Transición,* Buenos Aires: Paidós, n.d.; Torcuato S. Di Tella, 'Populismo y Reforma en América Latina', *Desarrollo Económico*, 4(16), 1965, pp. 391-425; Steve Stein, *Populism in Peru: The Emergence of the Masses and the Politics of Social Control*, Madison: University of Wisconsin Press, 1980. For influential interventions to the Marxism and dependency stream, see: Octavio Ianni, *La Formación del Estado Populista en América Latina*, Mexico City: Serie Popular Era, 1984; Guillermo O'Donnell, *Modernization and Bureaucratic-Authoritarianism*, Berkeley: University of California Press, 1973; Fernando Henrique Cardoso and Enzo Faletto, *Dependency and Development in Latin America*, Marjory Mattingly Urquidi, trans., Berkeley: University of California Press, 1979; Francisco Weffort, 'El Populismo en la Política Brasileña', in *Brasil Hoy*, ed., Various Authors, Mexico City: Siglo Veintiuno Editores, 1968; Carlos Vilas, 'El Populismo Latinoamericano: Un Enfoque Estructural', *Desarrollo Económico*, 111, 1988, pp. 323-52; Alain Touraine, *América Latina: Política y Sociedad*, Madrid: Espasa-Calpe, 1989. For a useful recent survey of the classic debates and their relationship to the present, see: Maristella Svampa, *Debates Latinoamericanos: Indianismo, Desarrollo, Dependencia y Populismo*, Buenos Aires: Edhasa, 2016.

6   Adrián Piva, '¿Cuánto Hay de Nuevo y Cuánto de Populismo En El Neopopulismo?: Kirchnerismo y Peronismo En La Argentina Post 2001', *Trabajo y Sociedad*, 21, 2013, pp. 135-57; Germani, *Política y Sociedad en una Época de Transición.*

7   Piva, '¿Cuánto Hay de Nuevo?', p. 141.

8   It should be noted that among the most influential contributors to the dependency school, Cardoso and Faletto succumbed the least to these two common methodological deficiencies. Within the general approach they lay out regarding ISI in *Dependency and Development in Latin America*, for example, they stress that '*history determined* how these contradictory factors of industrialization combined' (emphasis added), in particular cases, 'and how they then devised models of development', which presupposes the bounded agency of social classes and the possibility of diverse trajectories within an overarching unity. Cardoso and Faletto, *Dependency and Development*, p. 131.

9   Viguera, '"Populismo" y "Neopopulismo"', p. 55.

10   Juan Grigera, 'Populism in Latin America: Old and New Populisms in Argentina and Brazil', *International Political Science Review / Revue Internationale de Science Politique*, 38(4), 2017, pp. 443-44.

11   Grigera, 'Populism in Latin America', pp. 441-42.

12   For a treatment of populism that develops the concept of 'impasse', see: Agustín Cueva, *El Proceso de Dominación Política En Ecuador*, Mexico City: Editorial Diógenes, 1974.

13   Grigera, 'Populism in Latin America', p. 447.

14   Cardoso and Faletto's 'conditioning factors' are more or less synonymous with Grigera's 'enabling conditions'. Cardoso and Faletto, *Dependency and Development in Latin America*, p. 13.

15   Piva, '¿Cuánto Hay de Nuevo?', p. 151.

16   Philip Oxhorn, 'The Social Foundations of Latin America's Recurrent Populism: Problems of Popular Sector Class Formation and Collective Action', *Journal of Historical Sociology*, 11(2), 1998, p. 226.

17   Piva, '¿Cuánto Hay de Nuevo?', p. 141.

18   Oxhorn, 'Social Foundations', p. 223.

19   Grigera, 'Populism in Latin America', p. 447.

20   Robert Brenner, 'The Paradox of Social Democracy: The American Case (Part One)', Verso Blog, 24 February 2016 [1985], available at: www.versobooks.com/blogs; Robert Brenner, 'The Paradox of Social Democracy: The American Case (Part Two)', Verso Blog, 26 February 2016 [1985]; Robert Brenner, 'The Paradox of Social Democracy: The American Case (Part Three)', Verso Blog, 29 February 2016 [1985].

21   The term 'controlled inclusion' is drawn from Oxhorn, 'Social Foundations', p. 228.

22   Oxhorn, 'Social Foundations', p. 225.

23   Quoted in Oxhorn, 'Social Foundations', p. 223.

24   Massimo Modonesi, *Revoluciones pasivas en América Latina*, Mexico City: Ítaca-UAM-Red Movimientos, 2017.

25   Brenner, 'The Paradox of Social Democracy'.

26   Michael Löwy and Robert Sayre, *Romanticism Against the Tide of Modernity*, Catherine Porter, trans., Durham: Duke University Press, 2001, p. 18.

27   Piva, '¿Cuánto Hay de Nuevo?', p. 141.

28   Pablo Stefanoni, 'América Latina: ¿un Momento Destituyente?', *Nueva Sociedad*, 311, 2024, pp. 4-16.

29   Eduardo Gamarra, 'Crafting Political Support for Stabilisation: Political Pacts and the New Economic Policy in Bolivia', in *Democracy, Markets, and Structural Reform in Latin America: Argentina, Bolivia, Brazil, Chile, and Mexico*, William C. Smith, Carlos H. Acuña and Eduardo Gamarra, eds, Miami: North-South Center Press, 1994; Catherine M. Conaghan, James M. Malloy and Luis A. Abugattas, 'Business and the "Boys": The Politics of Neoliberalism in the Central Andes', *Latin American Research Review*, 25(2), 1990, p. 3-30; James Dunkerley, 'Political Transition and Economic Stabilisation: Bolivia, 1982–1989', in James Dunkerley, *Political Suicide in Latin America: And Other Essays*, London: Verso, 1992.

30   Benjamin Kohl and Linda Farthing, *Impasse in Bolivia: Neoliberal Hegemony and Popular Resistance*, London: Zed Books, 2006, p. 121.

31   World Bank, *Bolivia Poverty Assessment: Establishing the Basis for Pro-Poor Growth*, New York: World Bank, 2005, p. 103.

32   World Bank, *Bolivia Poverty Assessment*, p. 3.

33   George Gray Molina and Gonzalo Chávez, 'The Political Economy of the Crisis in the Andean Region: The Case of Bolivia', in Andrés Solimano, ed., *Political Crises, Social Conflict, and Economic Development: The Political Economy of the Andean Region*, Northampton, MA: Edward Elgar, 2005, p. 86.

34   Jeffery R. Webber, *Red October: Left-Indigenous Struggles in Modern Bolivia*, Chicago: Haymarket, 2012, ch. 5; Forrest Hylton and Sinclair Thomson, *Revolutionary Horizons: Past and Present in Bolivian Politics*, First Edition, London and New York: Verso, 2007; Forrest Hylton and Sinclair Thomson, 'I. Insurgent Bolivia', *NACLA Report on the Americas*, 38(3), 2004, p. 15-19; Raquel Gutiérrez and Álvaro García Linera, 'El Ciclo Estatal Neoliberal y Sus Crisis', in Raquel Gutiérrez et al., eds, *Democratizaciones Plebeyas*, La Paz: Muela del Diablo, 2002; Álvaro García Linera, 'El Ocaso de un Ciclo Estatal', in *Democratizaciones Plebeyas*, Raquel Gutiérrez et al., eds, La Paz: Muela del Diablo, 2002; Álvaro García Linera, 'La crisis de Estado y las Sublevaciones Indígeno-Plebeyas', in Álvaro García Linera, Raúl Prada and Luis Tapia, eds, *Memorias de Octubre*, La Paz: Muela del Diablo, 2004; Álvaro García Linera, Marxa Chávez León and Patricia Costas Monje, *Sociología de los Movimientos Sociales en Bolivia: Estructuras de Movilización, Repertorios Culturales y Acción Política*, Second Edition, La Paz: Oxfam and Diakonia, 2005.

35   Webber, *Red October*, chs 6-7.

36   María Teresa Zegada et al., *La Democracia Desde los Márgenes: Transformaciones en el Campo Político Boliviano*, La Paz: Muela del Diablo, 2011, p. 44.

37   Zegada et al., *La Democracia*, p. 44-45.

38   Xavier Albó, *Movimientos y Poder Indígena en Bolivia, Ecuador y Perú*, Cuadernos de Investigación 71, La Paz: CIPCA, 2009, p. 83.

39   Zegada et al., *La Democracia*, p. 45.

40   Fran Espinoza, *Bolivia: La Circulación de sus Elites (2006-2014)*, Ciencias Sociales/Historia 36, Santa Cruz: Editorial El País, 2015, p. 135.

41   Linda C. Farthing and Benjamin H. Kohl, *Evo's Bolivia: Continuity and Change*, Austin, TX: University of Texas Press, 2014, p. 58.

42   Albó, *Movimientos y Poder Indígena en Bolivia, Ecuador y Perú*, 84.

43   On the role of 'resource nationalism' in Bolivia over the course of the twentieth century, see: Kevin A. Young, *Blood of the Earth: Resource Nationalism, Revolution, and Empire in Bolivia*, Austin: University of Texas Press, 2017.

44   Brent Z. Kaup, 'A Neoliberal Nationalization?: The Constraints on Natural-Gas-Led Development in Bolivia', *Latin American Perspectives*, 37(3), 2010, pp. 123-38; Brent Z. Kaup, 'Reiterated Problem Solving in Neoliberal and Counter-Neoliberal Shifts: The Case of Bolivia's Hydrocarbon Sector', *Theory and Society*, 44(5), 1 October 2015, pp. 445-70; Brent Z Kaup and Paul K Gellert, 'Cycles of Resource Nationalism: Hegemonic Struggle and the Incorporation of Bolivia and Indonesia', *International Journal of Comparative Sociology*, 58(4), 2017, p. 275-303; Bret Gustafson, *Bolivia in the Age of Gas*, Durham, NC: Duke University Press Books, 2020; Nicole Fabricant and Bret Gustafson, 'Moving Beyond the Extractivism Debate, Imagining New Social Economies', *NACLA Report on the Americas*, 47(4), 2014, pp. 40-5; Håvard Haarstad, 'Globalization and the New Spaces for Social Movement Politics: The Marginalization of Labor Unions in Bolivian Gas Nationalization', *Globalizations*, 6(2), 2009, pp. 169-85; Håvard Haarstad, 'FDI Policy and Political Spaces for Labour: The Disarticulation of the Bolivian Petroleros', *Geoforum*, Themed Issue: Globalising Failures, 40(2), 2009, pp. 239-48,; Håvard Haarstad, 'Cross-Scalar Dynamics of the Resource Curse: Constraints on Local Participation in the Bolivian Gas Sector', *The Journal of Development Studies*, 50(7), 2014, pp. 977-90; Derrick Hindery, *From Enron to Evo: Pipeline Politics, Global Environmentalism, and Indigenous Rights in Bolivia*, Reprint Edition, Tucson, AZ: University of Arizona Press, 2014.

45   Jeffery R. Webber, *From Rebellion to Reform in Bolivia: Class Struggle, Indigenous Liberation, and the Politics of Evo Morales*, Chicago, IL: Haymarket Books, 2011, pp. 84-98.

46   Salvador Schavelzon, *El Nacimiento del Estado Plurinacional de Bolivia: Etnografía de una Asamblea Constituyente*, Buenos Aires, Argentina: CLACSO, 2013; Salvador Schavelzon, *Plurinacionalidad y Vivir Bien/Buen Vivir: Dos Conceptos Leídos desde Bolivia y Ecuador Post-Constituyentes*, Buenos Aires: CLACSO, 2016; Sue A. S. Iamamoto, *El Nacionalismo Boliviano En Tiempos de Plurinacionalidad: Revueltas Antineoliberales, Asamblea Constituyente y Democracia Intercultural (2000-2009)*, La Paz: OEP, 2013.

47   Jorge Viaña, 'Estado Plurinacional y Nueva Fase del Proceso Boliviano', in Mabel Thwaites Rey, ed., *El Estado en América Latina: Continuidades y Rupturas*, Buenos Aires: CLACSO, 2012, pp. 376-77.

48   Boris Miranda, 'El Fin de las Logias y el Último Autonomista', *El Desacuerdo*, 29 September 2013.

49   Viaña, 'Estado Plurinacional', p. 377.

50   Álvaro García Linera, 'El Estado en Transición: Bloque de Poder y Punto de Bifurcación', in Álvaro García Linera et al., eds, *El Estado: Campo de Lucha*, La Paz: Muela del Diablo, 2010, pp. 15-16.

51   For an essay in the same volume that includes a less triumphal account of the same period, see: Luis Tapia, 'El Estado En Condiciones de Abigarramiento', in Álvaro García Linera et al., eds, *El Estado: Campo de Lucha*, La Paz: Muela del Diablo, 2010, p. 125.

52   Álvaro García Linera, *Las Tensiones Creativas de la Revolución: La Quinta Fase del Proceso de Cambio*, La Paz: Vicepresidencia del Estado, 2011.

53   Enrique Castañón Ballivián, 'Discurso Empresarial vs. Realidad Campesina: La Ecología Política de la Producción de Soya en Santa Cruz, Bolivia', *Cuestión Agraria*, 2, 2015, p. 73.

54   Viaña, 'Estado Plurinacional', p. 378.

55   Jeffery R. Webber, 'Revolution Against "Progress": Neo-Extractivism, the Compensatory State, and the TIPNIS Conflict in Bolivia', in Susan Spronk and Jeffery R. Webber, eds, *Crisis and Contradiction: Marxist Perspectives on Latin America in the Global Political Economy*, Chicago: Haymarket, 2015, pp. 302-33.

56   Viaña, 'Estado Plurinacional', p, 143.

57   Many of these figures had been signatories, alongside other left-indigenous oppositionists, of a manifesto published in June 2011, calling for a fundamental renewal of the 'process of change' (Various Authors, *Manifesto de la Coordinadora Plurinacional de la Reconducción: Por la Recuperación del Proceso de Cambio para el Pueblo y con el Pueblo*, La Paz, 2011). The manifesto famously elicited an acerbic pamphlet in response from the Vice President, denouncing what he took to be infantile ultra-leftism. Álvaro García Linera, *El 'ONGismo', Enfermedad Infantil Del Derechismo: (O Cómo La Reconducción Del Proceso de Cambio Es La Restauración Neoliberal)*, La Paz: Vicepresidencia del Estado Plurinacional de Bolivia, 2011.

58   Juan León Trujillo and Susan Spronk, 'Socialism Without Workers? Trade Unions and the New Left in Bolivia and Ecuador', in Eduardo Silva and Federico M. Rossi, eds, *Reshaping The Political Arena in Latin America: From Resisting Neoliberalism to the Second Incorporation*, Pittsburgh: University of Pittsburgh Press, 2018, pp. 141-48.

59 Andrés Arauz et al., 'Bolivia's Economic Transformation: Macroeconomic Policies, Institutional Changes, and Results', Washington, DC: Center for Economic and Policy Research, October 2019, p. 4.

60 Figures from CEPALSTAT, the statistical database of the United Nations Commission for Latin America and the Caribbean.

61 Fernanda Wanderley, *¿Qué Pasó con el Proceso de Cambio? Ideales Acertados, Medios Equivocados, Resultados Trastrocados*, La Paz: CIDES-UMSA, 2013; Carlos Arze and Javier Gómez, 'Bolivia: ¿El "Proceso de Cambio" Nos Conduce al Vivir Bien?', in Carlos Arce et al., eds, *Promesas En Su Laberinto: Cambios Y Continuidades En Los Gobiernos Progresistas de América Latina*, La Paz: CEDLA, 2013.

62 CEPB, *Bolivia en el Contexto Económico Mundial – 2013*, La Paz: Confederación de Empresarios Privados de Bolivia, 2014.

63 Arauz et al., 'Bolivia's Economic Transformation', p. 2.

64 Arauz et al., 'Bolivia's Economic Transformation', p. 13.

65 Arauz et al., 'Bolivia's Economic Transformation', p. 13.

66 Arauz et al., 'Bolivia's Economic Transformation', p. 14.

67 Cesar Daniel Vargas Diaz, Hernan Delgadillo Dorado and Eloy Wilson Villca Copali, 'The Fall in Gas Exports, International Reserves and Economic Growth in Bolivia', *International Journal of Economy, Energy and Environment*, 8(4), 2023, p. 95.

68 CEPALSTAT figures.

69 Arauz et al., 'Bolivia's Economic Transformation', p. 1.

70 Diaz, Dorado and Copali, 'The Fall in Gas Exports', p. 96.

71 CEPALSTAT figures.

72 CEPALSTAT figures. This is an eight-year average between 2015 and 2023, excluding 2020 because data is unavailable for that year.

73 Diaz, Dorado, and Copali, 'The Fall in Gas Exports'.

74 Diaz, Dorado, and Copali, 'The Fall in Gas Exports', p. 94.

75 CEPALSTAT figures.

76 Diaz, Dorado and Copali, 'The Fall in Gas Exports', pp. 93-94. It is also worth noting that there is a consistent problem of fuels being imported by the state at the international market price, subsidized for domestic consumption on the local market, and then purchased by black-market merchants for export, with the latter taking advantage of the differential between the subsidized Bolivian domestic price and the market price in neighbouring countries.

77 CEPALSTAT figures.

78 Jeffery Webber, 'Renovation in Bolivia?', *NLR Sidecar*, 6 February 2023, available at: www.newleftreview.org/sidecar.

79 Jeffery R. Webber and Forrest Hylton, 'The Eighteenth Brumaire of Macho Camacho: Jeffery R. Webber (with Forrest Hylton) on the Coup in Bolivia - Interviewed by Ashley Smith', *Verso Blog*, 15 November 2019, available at: www.versobooks.com/blogs.

80 Alberto Acosta, John Cajas Guijarrro and Hugo Jácome, 'Ecuador: Al Borde del Naufragio… Entre la Pandemia Sanitaria y el Pandemonio Neoliberal', Quito: Rosa Luxemburg Stiftung, Oficina Región Andina, March 2021, p. 3.

81 Webber, 'Renovation in Bolivia?'.

82   Fernando Mayorga, '"Elecciones Ya": ¿el MAS Recupera La Iniciativa?', *Nueva Sociedad*, 24 June 2020, available at: www.nuso.org; Pablo Ortiz et al., '¿Por Qué Volvió a Ganar el MAS?', *Nueva Sociedad*, 19 October 2020.

83   Pablo Stefanoni, 'Las Lecciones Que Nos Deja Bolivia', *Nueva Sociedad*, 5 March 2020. The elections were held late in 2020, but Arce did not assume office until early 2021, as is standard practice in the scheduling of Bolivian elections.

84   Fernando Molina, 'Luis Arce y el MAS: Gobierno Sin Hegemonía', *Nueva Sociedad*, December 2021; Fernando Molina, 'Las Antinomias Del MAS Boliviano', *Nueva Sociedad*, 14 April 2023; Fernando Molina, 'Evistas versus Arcistas', *Nueva Sociedad*, 26 September 2023.

85   Vladimir Mendoza, 'La Disputa Estratégica en Bolivia', *Jacobin Revista*, 21 April 2022, available at: www.jacobinlat.com; Vladimir Mendoza, 'El Proceso de Cambio en la Encrucijada', *Jacobin Revista*, 18 April 2023.

86   EIU, 'Bolivia: Country Report', London: Economist Intelligence Unit, 8 January 2024, p. 8.

87   Fernando Molina, 'Las "Arcenomics" No Escapan a La "Maldición de Los Recursos Naturales"', *Nueva Sociedad*, 27 February 2024.

88   EIU, 'Bolivia', pp. 6-7.

89   EIU, 'Bolivia', p. 6.

90   Fernando Molina, 'Bolivia: Un Golpe en Medio de La Tormenta', *Nueva Sociedad*, 5 August 2024.

91   Molina, 'Bolivia'.

92   Quoted in Molina, 'Bolivia'.

93   Molina, 'Bolivia'. For more perceptive commentary on the coup, see: Pablo Stefanoni, 'Bolivia: Claves de La Asonada Militar y Sus Coletazos', *Nueva Sociedad*, 27 June 2024; Angus McNelly, 'Spectacles of Crisis and Political Power Plays in Bolivia', *NACLA*, 28 June 2024, available at: www.nacla.org; Vladimir Mendoza, 'Bolivia: Ruido de Sables en Medio de la Crisis de Estado', *Jacobin Revista*, 28 June 2024.

94   EIU, 'Bolivia', p. 4; Mendoza, 'Bolivia'.

STARING INTO THE ABYSS: JAVIER MILEI AND THE ANARCHO-CAPITALIST ROAD IN ARGENTINA

RUTH FELDER AND VIVIANA PATRONI

As we write these notes, Argentina has been engulfed by a devastating combination of inflation and austerity. Disconcertingly, the government of self-proclaimed anarcho-capitalist Javier Milei (2023–2027) has moved assertively to impose structural reforms while using threats and violence as the main means to address dissent and social conflict.[1] He has also demonstrated an extraordinary disregard for the suffering his policies are inflicting on a population already battered by the effects of ten years of economic decline.

Milei's political style is based on a mix of authoritarianism, limited political competence and the creation of chaos. It has set the country on a course for crisis from day one. It is still difficult to know what the outcomes of this crisis might eventually be. Yet, there are two questions that may help to make sense of the current moment and to reflect upon potential emerging political scenarios. First, what structural conditions and recent tendencies have created the scenario where Milei's far right ideas have widespread electoral support? Second, how do we make sense of the first few months of the Milei government and its prospects? Milei's economic program relies on formulas that have been tried and ultimately proven wanting before. Yet while at some level his policies confront challenges that also have long historical roots in the country, they now do so under political conditions of what appears to be large social support. Milei's multiclass support, most notably among workers and especially precarious and informal workers, might give him political latitude that previous governments failed to secure. We explore these two questions with respect to Argentina – how could a country that was a prime example of the colossal failure of neoliberal orthodoxy and its prescribed reforms in the early 2000s now become a laboratory for an anarcho-capitalist experiment that can only promise more of the same?

Like several other Latin American countries, by the turn of the 21st century the Argentinean government sought to tackle the disastrous social consequences of the neoliberal reforms of the previous decade through the expansion of public spending and the reestablishment of the state's regulatory capacity in key areas of the economy. By then, extremely favourable conditions for the region's primary exports, combined with policy shifts, facilitated fiscal revenues that financed an unprecedented expansion of social programs. These programs were central to the early successes of the 'Pink Tide' of left and centre-left governments that spread across Latin America. In Argentina it was Peronism, the historical representative of the working classes in the country, that led a reform program addressing the worst of the legacy of neoliberalism which, in a paradoxical way, also saw their full development under another Peronist administration in the 1990s.[2] After 2008, however, declining commodity prices limited governments' fiscal room to continue to respond with the same effectiveness to workers' and lower income groups' expanding social and economic expectations. At the same time, different bourgeois factions previously weakened by the spread of social struggles against neoliberalism were regrouping and regaining the initiative.

Although Pink Tide political parties and alliances across the region continued to obtain electoral victories in the 2010s and early 2020s, a far-right backlash against them has also gained momentum. Consequently, growing polarization and alternation between political poles has become a significant trend across the continent. This is central to understanding the case of Argentina, as it moved abruptly out of the more progressive policies promoted by the Peronist government of Cristina Fernández de Kirchner (2007–2015) to elect, for the first time in free elections in the history of the country, a conservative government under the leadership of Mauricio Macri (2015–2019). The next elections then returned to power a more moderate coalition of sectors of Peronism and allies under President Alberto Fernández and Vice-President Cristina Kirchner in the 2019 election (2019–2023).

All in all, since the last years of Cristina Kirchner's government progressive forces in power in Argentina have been unable to recreate the favourable conditions for capital accumulation of the early 2000s, while being confronted with the growing dissatisfaction of both voters and investors. Progressive governments have attempted to contain crises by moderating the ambitions of their policies and searching for ways to broaden the basis of their support. Far from succeeding in the task, the strategy instead gave emerging and gradually more radicalized right-wing forces a platform that they have since used to gain political acceptance and win elections. Shifts between increasingly moderate centre left and progressive governments and an increasingly radicalized right represent not only pendulum swings in which the right attempts to revert the effects of progressive policies but also an expression of the limitations that these policies have had in addressing the structural consequences of neoliberal reforms. Meanwhile, the realities and prospects for most workers have entered a downward spiral that, as we discuss below, has further delegitimized the state and politics.

Milei represents the latest and most extreme version of this right turn in Argentina. His own account of the roots of the crisis confronting Argentina conforms with an extreme neoliberal orthodoxy: inflation as the malady of a fiscally irresponsible state, poverty as the result of the suffocation of the creative power of capitalism and economic underdevelopment as the natural outcome of over regulation. Milei's narrative evokes an imaginary conservative past of market rule, global integration and social discipline, an era when Argentina was supposedly an economic powerhouse. This partly explains why, as opposed to many other far right parties that have blamed economic globalization for the misfortune of the population of their countries, Milei has been a champion of the integration of Argentina into the global economy. Furthermore, while Milei and conservative groups in Argentina line up with many other far right parties, movements and organizations in blaming global 'woke' agendas for the supposed recognition of undeserved entitlements, his own extreme position on economic austerity and the rule of markets sets him apart from a number of right-wing actors of an otherwise similar political disposition.

This essay sets Argentina's far right experiment in the context of the country's history of social and class struggles, authoritarianism and, critically, the dynamics of growth and crisis which have characterized the country. While we explore the historical roots of these crises, our hope is that our inquiry will clarify the profound transformations Argentina has undergone in the new century. Understanding these new conditions is imperative to thinking through a way out of this far right dystopia.

ECONOMIC CYCLES AND POLITICAL SWINGS IN CONTEMPORARY ARGENTINA

Since the mid-20th century, Argentina has experienced periods of economic growth that inexorably ended in crises in which external balances became unsustainable, inflation accelerated and real incomes deteriorated. Foreign currency bottlenecks have been and continue to be at the heart of these cycles of growth and crisis. Revisiting the economic and political dynamic at their core seems essential to make sense of both Milei's rise to power and the future of his 'refoundational' program for the country.

The external, fiscal and macroeconomic crises that punctuate the economic trajectory of Argentina since the late 1940s make evident the heavy reliance on imports for economic growth and the insufficiency of export flows, mostly from agriculture, for generating the hard currency required to sustain the expansion of the economy. Drawing from longstanding debates over the political economy of Argentina, we find it useful to think of two forms of economic cycle.[3] A first type, the 'stop-and-go' cycle, occurs when the demand for dollars necessary to expand domestic manufacturing increases beyond what export earnings allow and makes currency devaluation unavoidable. The new exchange rate eases pressure on the balance of trade because it both increases the cost of imports, reducing demand for them, and makes exports more lucrative in domestic currency, encouraging their expansion. But the devaluation of the domestic currency also fuels inflation and recession because it increases the relative price of imports necessary for domestic manufacturing, as well as the domestic price of products that are also exported – which in the case of Argentina is mostly basic foodstuffs. Furthermore, through recessionary stabilization policies, the economy finds a new balance that makes possible the resumption of economic growth, but only to again reach a foreign currency bottleneck, necessitating another round of devaluation – the stop-and-go cycle.

The growing availability of foreign direct investment for industrialization since the 1950s and borrowing that began in the mid-1970s offered an alternative path of escape from the restrictions imposed by the recurrent balance of trade bottleneck. However, both of these sources of capital imply a constant outflow of hard currency either in the form of profit repatriation or interest payments. Moreover, as borrowing leads to an increase in the debt to GDP ratio and concern grows around the sustainability of it, the only way to secure new loans becomes through paying higher interest rates. The conditions are thus set for a downward spiral that reaches its bottom when no further loans are available, making currency devaluation inescapable, with acute economic crises and recessions following. This is the second type of economic cycle, often referred to as a 'go-and-crash' cycle. The concept aims to capture the gravity of the recessionary adjustment required not only to reduce the balance of trade deficit, as in the stop-and-go cycle, but now also to generate the trade surplus required to cover interest payments and profit remittances.[4]

During the decades when growth was based on import substitution, roughly between the 1940s and mid-1970s, stop-and-go cycles brought to the surface the intricate set of political and economic tensions behind capitalist accumulation in Argentina. Over this period, when devaluation reduced real wages and consumption, the response of those most affected by the policies put in place to stabilize the economy – the working classes broadly conceived and some sectors of the domestic bourgeoisie – was strong enough to force the government to reverse its policies. Starting in the 1960s growing transnationalized sectors of the economy shared with agricultural exporters a preference to address crises in the balance of payments through recessionary policies; but as soon as the worst of a crisis was over and political unrest mounted, they then favoured the beginning of a new expansionary cycle.[5]

The fact that economic cycles generated this political dynamic within and across classes can be explained in large part by the unique legacy resulting from the first period of Peronism (1945–1955), when it acted as a driver to reshape working class struggles.[6] Labour's high levels of organization and mobilization, combined with its critical role within the Peronist movement, transformed it into a colossal yet deeply contradictory political force. In the context of the short-lived elected governments and recurrent military coups which characterized Argentina between Perón's downfall in 1955 and his return in 1973, the Peronist labour movement was able to secure some significant gains for workers. Increasingly, however, the mobilization of workers was an expression of a deepening radicalization that sought to transform both trade unionism and Peronism more broadly, aiming to challenge their established hierarchies. Emerging demands for change were thus met with repression and resulted in growing levels of political violence. The return of Peronism to power, and the infighting between its right and left factions, unleashed a period of violence that was tragically only the preamble to the state terrorism which was to take hold of Argentina after the 1976 military coup.

This military regime embraced the neoliberal preference for greater economic openness and deregulation, the context for the go-and-crash cycles we have defined above. Trade liberalization in particular aimed at exposing domestic producers to international competition, thus limiting the possibility of acceding to labour's demands for higher wages through increasing prices. According to the military regime, this would help to suppress the power that the labour movement had managed to gain, and that had been at the core of distributive clashes and recurrent economic and political crises.[7] Above all, labour disciplining through bloody repression and the targeting of cadres within the more progressive segments of trade unionism was an essential component of this neoliberal advance guard in Argentina. In the aftermath of the defeat in the war over the Malvinas Islands with Britain, and the default on Argentina's foreign debt in the wider global debt crisis of

1982–83, the country returned to democracy in 1983. However, attempts to resume growth and employment creation by reverting what was then seen as the dictatorship's economic policy 'malpractice' failed, and neoliberal reforms gained further momentum starting in the 1990s.

Neoliberal reforms not only transformed the economy but also reshaped the dynamics of class struggles and weakened the power that the working classes had possessed to defend their wages under import substitution industrialization. To be sure, crisis and austerity policies did elicit mobilization and opposition from workers in this era, but neoliberalism increased working class heterogeneity and undermined traditional forms of workers' organizing. One of the most relevant aspects of these transformations has been the growing number of precarious workers and working poor, which has become an enduring feature of the country even in periods of economic growth.[8] Since then, the temporary resolution of the cyclical crises has never reconstituted the status quo ante. On the contrary, as cycles developed, they generated deeper political and economic crises. All in all, since the 1970s, workers' gains during periods of economic growth – when they existed – have been temporary, while their losses have become structural. And as we will discuss below, since 2013 the current cycle has taken a particular form, when even under conditions of economic stagnation the drain of foreign currency creates such pressure on external accounts that the 'crash' phase appears unending.[9]

As important as these dynamics were, while the transition to democracy limited the political appeal of right-wing authoritarian options, it also coincided with the consolidation of neoliberalism which, in turn, reduced the scope of what was understood as politically and economically feasible. This was the case even if, for critical periods, the neoliberal structural transformation was tempered by a commitment to addressing some of its devastating social consequences. The contradictory consolidation of some key democratic forms (that is, periodic elections and basic freedoms) has combined with hard limits to democratic deliberation around key state policies that – with some exceptions – have led to a gradual deterioration of working and living conditions for large segments of the population. After forty years of tension between democracy and neoliberalism, under Milei an authoritarian turn that resolves the contradictions between democratic forms and the rule of markets through suppressing basic democratic freedoms seems possible.

AFTER NEOLIBERAL REFORMS

In the early 1990s, Argentina had been the 'poster boy' for neoliberal reforms, only to fall into a vicious circle of economic crisis, deteriorating social indicators and conflict in the second half of the decade. This time, the cycle ended in the unprecedented crisis of 2001. By then, social mobilization made the usual resolution of the crisis through currency devaluation and austerity politically unfeasible. Politicians, technocrats and institutions seen as part of the architecture of neoliberalism became objects of widespread derision, vocalized as '*qué se vayan todos*' (all of them must go), the rallying cry of massive protests throughout the country. Contrasting sharply with what was to happen in 2023, the way out of this crisis came through the local version of the Latin American Pink Tide governments. Peronist President Néstor Kirchner (2003–2007) sought to overcome the crisis and rebuild the legitimacy of politics through a new set of state regulations. This audacity paid off. Under Néstor Kirchner's government, the country was able to resume economic growth, reduce poverty and unemployment while maintaining fiscal and external surpluses, and restructure its defaulted sovereign debt to alleviate its burden on the state.

But the recovery started showing its limitations in the second half of the 2000s, when fiscal and external bottlenecks resurfaced amidst the exacerbation of distributive struggles. Soon after the election of Cristina Fernández de Kirchner as president, the Argentinean economy suffered the impacts of the 2008 global financial crisis. The slowdown was short-lived, but the recovery that followed exhibited once again the features of a go-and-crash cycle. The government failed to reestablish conditions for sustained economic growth. Likewise, the expansion of social assistance programs became ineffective for addressing lagging job creation, labour precarity, social conflict and the intensification of distributive clashes. At the same time, disapproval of the government was growing on the basis that its discourse and practices restricted freedom and the rule of law only to buy the political support of the poor.[10] Cristina Kirchner succeeded in getting re-elected in 2011, but opposition intensified and converged into Cambiemos (Let's Change), a right-wing alliance led by Mauricio Macri who went on to win the 2015 presidential election.

Macri's rapid liberalization of the economy did not reverse the economic slowdown that had set in in the country. He succeeded though in addressing unresolved sovereign debt lawsuits, and thus the state regained access to international borrowing. But the spiraling growth of sovereign debt and the subsequent uncertainty about the state's capacity to service it soon restricted access to international credit. Inflation accelerated despite the lack of growth. Even though the International Monetary Fund (IMF) extended assistance with the largest loan in its history, Macri's conventional neoliberal policy package failed to deliver because of its own inconsistencies as well as the limits set by social resistance to austerity. Amidst widespread social discontent, in 2019 different sectors of Peronism and other opposition groups converged in the Frente de Todos (Everyone's Front, FdT), led by moderate Peronist Alberto Fernández, with Cristina Fernández de Kirchner as his vice-presidential candidate. In late 2019, they won the presidential election.

The Fernández government took power with a promise to rebuild the economy and restore workers' purchasing power, but the arrival of the Covid-19 pandemic forced it to change course. 'Pandemic policies' coincided with grim growth prospects due to the unfavourable international conjuncture, accelerating inflation and worsening the unsustainable external deficit left by the Macri government. As the economy fell into virtual paralysis, public spending to subsidize workers and businesses expanded beyond what many saw as fiscally responsible, yet still below what was necessary to prevent the lockdown having a devastating effect on a large number of precarious and unwaged workers.[11] The gap between the government's stated commitment to protecting society as a whole and reality left a painful and indelible mark in the memory of many workers. Moreover, public health measures that some saw as limits to their individual freedoms became one more factor contributing to the mistrust many people harboured against what they understood as unjustifiable state interference in their already difficult lives.

The state's response to the crisis and the profound inequalities that the lockdown made more visible eroded support for the government and contributed to further damaging the legitimacy of the state.[12] Some Cambiemos members, far right newcomers to politics including Javier Milei and a collection of conspiracist and aggressive fringe groups led demonstrations, social media campaigns and other actions against the lockdown. More broadly, these groups targeted government officials – including Vice President Cristina Kirchner, who suffered an attempt against her life – union leaders, feminist and human rights activists, among others. Evidence of the loss of support was seen in the result of the 2021 midterm elections, in which FdT came second to Cambiemos while far right groups competing for the first time won four seats in the lower chamber of Congress, including for Milei and his future vice-president, Victoria Villarruel.

Even though there was a mild economic recovery in 2021, inflation accelerated and produced an alarming deterioration in the purchasing power of wages. The government was then forced to tighten foreign exchange restrictions to avoid further devaluation pressures. By mid-2023, when economy minister Sergio Massa became the presidential candidate for the FdT (now renamed as Unión por la Patria, Unity for Homeland, UxP), government decisions became increasingly short-term and aimed more at improving Massa's electoral prospects than addressing any of the urgent economic problems facing the country.

By then, the evident failure to overcome the crash stage of the cycle by the governments of the two major coalitions that had ruled since the early 2010s intensified the crisis of political representation, as well as the willingness of the population to look for alternatives outside of conventional politics. Before moving to the Milei era, it is worth highlighting the tensions between the expectations of improvement to quality of life and the shortcomings of the economy since 2013. A decade after the Pink Tide governments implemented policies that had been able to boost forms of social inclusion and the expansion of consumption, these policies had reached their fiscal and political limits, while the impact of inflation on workers' income had deepened. Unsatisfied expectations and, more specifically, the feeling of becoming invisible to the state as deteriorating purchasing power, precarity and uncertainty spread through a very large segment of the population, helped to further damage the already weak legitimacy of the state. If these factors alone did not cause the turn to the far right, they created better conditions for its appeal. As we will discuss below, Milei came to power in circumstances where the status quo appeared to most people untenable but, at the same time, there seemed to be no alternative to it.[13] In other words, the far right in Argentina represents a rupture of the veil that blurred the magnitude of the political and social dislocations brought about by a crisis of neoliberalism. Yet, far from hastening neoliberalism's demise, its crisis has instead empowered neoliberal social forces to move assertively to expand neoliberalism's dominance. They have done so by both delegitimizing attempts to set political limits to capital while renewing their power to push harder, faster and more chaotically toward stricter market discipline.

More than at any point since the end of the last dictatorship in 1983, the shortfalls of political representation and the appeal of the far right's unconventional politics have now made transparent the underlying tension between neoliberalism and its mutations, and democratic practices and aspirations. As in many other countries, so far the outcome of these growing tensions in Argentina has been an incipient authoritarian turn – of which Milei is both an expression and a catalyst – accepted or at least overlooked by the general population. This disregard goes a long way in explaining the effectiveness of Milei's anti-democratic and violent discourse. Probably nothing exemplifies this authoritarian turn more vividly that his party's attempts to rehabilitate the record of the military's responsibility for 'crimes against humanity' during the 1976–1983 dictatorship. Likewise, as in the case of Bolsonaro in Brazil, Milei has not missed any opportunity to express his furious and wildly out-of-context anti-communism and to praise the canon of so-called 'Western values', rooted in the defence of private property and the patriarchal order, which still resonates with memories of the country's dictatorship. While such views echo key elements of fascism, Milei's anti-statism and the scant resources invested in grounding the party in a broad social movement has closer affinities to more recent forms of authoritarianism seen in Argentina and Latin America. Regardless of definitional debates, from the outset the Milei government has left no doubt as to its intention to deepen authoritarianism in Argentina through criminalization of protest, the elimination of state agencies and resources that guarantee the protection of human and civil rights, the rejection of 'gender ideology' and its celebration of cruelty as a prerogative of power.

THE NEW MILEI ERA

The unexpected 'outsider' comes to power

Milei's appeal lies in his ability to offer the hope that there could be a clean break from the status quo. He has denounced traditional politicians – the 'caste' (or elite) in his libertarian lingo – and the state as the instrument of their power, as being responsible for the economic woes of the country, from the power of the government to redistribute wealth to the perks politicians enjoy.

Even though Milei had not participated in elections until 2021, he was not without links to politics, much less large business in the country. Before becoming a member of Congress, he worked as an economics instructor and an advisor for politicians, banks, pension funds, media companies and business lobby groups, while publishing several general readership books and articles on economics and politics (with quite a few plagiarized passages). He has been a relentless advocate of the Austrian School of liberal economics and has belittled mainstream economic currents, including neoclassical economics and Keynesianism. His turn to electoral politics was also preceded by recurrent appearances on TV shows in which he combined unintelligible economic jargon with his histrionic and aggressive style, alongside almost a decade of being a bombastic influencer and anarcho-capitalist cosplayer who amassed a broad audience eager to engage with his rants about politics, the left and feminism. His performance in these roles has attracted followers in other Latin American countries and has helped him establish connections with other far right groups and organizations, among them Spain's Vox, Brazil's Bolsonaro family and the US-based Conservative Political Action Conference (CPAC), through which he expects to become a leader of the global far right.[14] His eccentricity has been another feature in the casting of a unique political character, as he matter-of-factly mentions that he talks with his dead dog and that he is part of a 'God-sent mission' to become the president and transform Argentina. Religious invocations have also been central to his public persona. He was raised as a Catholic but has repeatedly called Pope Francis a communist and decried the Social Doctrine of the Church. Without abandoning Catholicism, he has signalled his intention to convert to Judaism and join a current that brings together rigid religious norms and forms of ethno-nationalism.[15]

Pushing beyond the neoliberal trope of state inefficiency, Milei's anarcho-capitalist call has been to seek a path for the elimination of the state and with it the whole architecture of regulations that, in his view, have stifled the economy and the entrepreneurial spirit of Argentineans. Likewise, he sees social justice as abhorrent,[16] conflicting with individual freedom and tantamount to undeserved privileges, while advancing a ruthless repressive approach to social conflict. All in all, this combination of radical neoliberalism and conservative authoritarianism[17] has resonated with social frustration and trepidation around economic instability, urban insecurity and political corruption. Because of his appeal, right-wing groups – both conventional and unconventional, including traditional conservatives, neoliberals and vindicators of the 1976–1983 military dictatorship – have gravitated to Milei and his personal brand of libertarianism.[18]

By the time of the 2023 presidential election, the Fernández government was embattled by a major economic crisis, its inability to overcome its paralyzing internal disagreements and a right-wing opposition galvanizing the accumulation of resentments against the party in power. As the disastrous results of Macri government were also still fresh in people's minds, it was not the Cambiemos (now Juntos por el Cambio, Together for Change, JxC) candidate but Milei and his far right La Libertad Avanza (Freedom Advances, LLA) that managed to seize the moment, promising sweeping and somewhat implausible changes. It was in August of that year that the country took pause to grasp the full implications of the 30.04 per cent of votes that Javier Milei had attracted in the mandatory primary elections, known as PASO (Primarias Abiertas, Simultáneas y Obligatorias), in which all parties must participate if they want to run in general elections. The total votes obtained by the two JxC precandidates competing for the presidency was 28.28 per cent, some 60 per cent of which went to Patricia Bullrich. In the case of UxP, the two precandidates together totalled 27.27 per cent, with 78.48 per cent of that going to Massa. A centre-right alliance Hacemos por Nuestro País (We Do for Our Country) obtained 3.83 per cent of the votes and the left coalition Frente de Izquierda y de Trabajadores-Unidad (Workers' Left Front – Unity) 2.65 per cent.

Much to the (momentary) relief of those who continued to struggle to accept the rise of the extreme right as a potential electoral victor, Milei failed to make any gains in his share of votes in the general elections of October. Instead, Sergio Massa made significant progress, increasing his vote share to 36.69 per cent, a little over 9 per cent higher than that obtained by UxP in the primaries. In contrast, JxC oversaw a drain in votes, dropping some 3.5 per cent lower for a first round share of 23.81 per cent. Expectations thus grew that having looked into the abyss, the electorate was now ready to recalibrate its anger. As we now know, this was not to be. Milei won the run-off elections by capturing almost the entirety of the JxC coalition's votes, managing to win 55.69 per cent of the vote, defeating Massa on 44.3 per cent.[19] Milei attracted most JxC voters who were either willing to vote for anyone but Peronism, or who were politically and ideologically close to him. Significantly, LLA also did remarkably well in districts which had traditionally been Peronism's bastions.[20] This confluence of Peronist and anti-Peronist votes into Milei's far right camp expressed a reconfiguration of the political system in which a polarization between two coalitions (roughly speaking Peronism and its allies against an 'anti-populist' coalition) that had framed politics for almost two decades lost significance.

The first six months

Consistent with his anarcho-capitalist convictions, Milei made his first priority the elimination of the public deficit as the shortest path to fight inflation. In what he called the 'largest adjustment in history', he froze public sector wages, pensions and social assistance benefits, eliminated and/or left without budget several ministries and public agencies, fired a large number of public employees, stopped payments for key social programs, reduced and even paused federal transfers to provinces, and cancelled all public works projects. He also let the peso devalue by 118 per cent and lifted some price regulations. Predictably, devaluation triggered inflation that reached 25.5 per cent in December 2023, gradually slowing to 4.2 per cent by May 2024. Accumulated inflation during his first six months totaled 109.6 per cent. Aided by the impact of devaluation, he rapidly eliminated the fiscal deficit thanks to a 29 per cent real terms fall in public spending, explained in significant part by the 67 per cent cut to social services. Pensioners bore 32 per cent of this fall.[21] After the devaluation of the peso, the government adopted a crawling peg exchange rate regime, resulting in a growing exchange rate lag that has helped to slow down the rhythm of inflation but has negatively affected exports, fueled expectations of a future major devaluation and triggered warnings from capital, the IMF and orthodox economists.

Budgetary cuts and plummeting consumption resulted in a 5.3 per cent fall in economic activity during the first quarter of 2024. When compared with the same period of 2023, GDP shrank by 2.6 per cent.[22] This, in turn, has resulted in falling state revenues and intensified the need of further budgetary cuts. Labour and social indicators provide an alarming picture of the costs of these policies for workers. Real wages saw major losses against inflation, increasing only 58.4 per cent between December 2023 and May 2024 compared to the 109.6 per cent rate of inflation. Public sector workers, minimum wage earners and precarious workers have suffered the largest losses. For instance, while the average wage lost 14.9 per cent of its purchasing power, the legal minimum wage lost 28.8 per cent. Between the last quarter of 2023 and the first quarter of 2024, unemployment grew from 5.7 per cent to 7.7 per cent.[23] Poverty and extreme poverty, resulting from the combination of inflation and job destruction, reached 55.5 per cent and 17.5 per cent respectively, up from 40.1 per cent and 9.3 per cent in the first trimester of 2023.[24] The GINI index grew from 0.446 in the first trimester of 2023 to 0.467 in the first trimester of 2024, the worst measure of inequality since 2008.[25]

Austerity and the streamlining of the state have not, however, been the only drivers of government action. Rather, a broad refoundational economic, political, social, cultural and ethical agenda has informed its approach. Some arguments used to justify the dismantling of state agencies and budgetary cuts went way beyond organizational or budgetary efficiencies. Instead, they have become tools to dismantle any legal or institutional obstacle to the unrestricted rule of capital, advance the principle of individual self-reliance, stigmatize and punish those receiving some form of income or recognition through affirmative action from the state, and undermine workers' organizing.

This agenda was formalized in two main legal instruments. The first was an ambitious 'Decree of Necessity and Urgency' (DNU, Decreto de Necesidad y Urgencia),[26] the content of which was, very likely intentionally, made public on the anniversary of the 20 December 2001 social revolt against neoliberal austerity.[27] The day was furthered overshadowed by the Security Minister's threats to crush the demonstrations organized to commemorate it. The decree included the change or annulment of many laws and decrees, the privatization of state-owned companies, a labour reform erasing most individual and collective labour rights, and a protocol criminalizing protest, among many others. It raised widespread opposition on both procedural and substantive grounds.

While the controversies around the decree were running high, the government sent to Congress a bill pompously called the 'Law of Bases and Starting Points for the Freedom of Argentineans' (Ley de Bases y Puntos de Partida para la Libertad de los Argentinos, hereafter Bases law). It included the elimination of state agencies and programs, deregulation, reduction of export tariffs, privatizations, regressive reforms of the tax and pension systems, a new large investment incentive regime (RIGI, Régimen de Incentivos para Grandes Inversiones) that grants enormous advantages to international investors, reform of the energy sector, and the granting of extraordinary powers to the president to be able to sidestep Congress for at least two years in administrative, economic, financial and energy matters. As LLA has very few members of Congress, the debate of the bill was initially difficult, but opposition members, including many critical of the bill and alarmed at Milei calling Congress a 'rathole', nevertheless ended up lending their support to a shorter version of it that passed in June 2024.

Austerity, immunity to social pressure and the ability to gain support in Congress have been seen in a positive light by some domestic corporate organizations and figures, international oil and mining investors, international pundits and the IMF. Their expectation is that the government will be able to create better conditions for capital accumulation and profit making and, equally important, finally crush resistance to austerity. Yet, domestic exporters have refused to surrender their foreign earnings at the overvalued exchange rate, new international investments are yet to be seen, and the IMF has conditioned its assistance on further depreciation of the peso and liberalization of foreign exchange markets. Aware of the political implications of austerity, the IMF has also called attention to austerity's regressive impact and several transnational companies have already left the country or announced their intentions to sell their assets to domestic capitalists.[28]

By late May, doubts among these sectors and actors about the prospects of Milei's economic program (or lack of thereof) and especially his decision to let the exchange rate lag grow led to heightened exchange instability. It is safe to say that, in his attempt to show that the worst of the crisis is over, Milei has been acting in ways that are contradictory to his own economic ideas. Because he sees lower inflation as a central if not the only indicator necessary to maintain social support in a context of crumbling economic activity and deterioration of all labour and social indicators, he has resisted by all means possible a devaluation that would with certainty further accelerate price increases. What is still uncertain is for how long the government can sustain this strategy without access to the foreign borrowing or investment required to buttress the value of the domestic currency. So far, for all Milei's electoral protestations about communism and breaking all relations with communist countries, it has been only China that was willing to offer his government a chance by extending a currency swap and alleviating repayment fears. His bet now seems to be to wait for a Trump victory in the upcoming US presidential elections in November 2024, an outcome that in Milei's view would be critically beneficial. In his own version of reality, Trump would promptly push the IMF in the direction of extending new financing to Argentina to reward his active engagement as a leader of global standing in the promotion of far right ideas. As we know from previous experience, the combination of insufficient dollar reserves and the inability to find new sources of hard currency can only heighten the crash phase of the cycle. Moreover, there is still no indication as to how economic growth will resume and to what extent extractive enclave economies encouraged by the RIGI are going to be the drivers of growth. Furthermore, some of the privileges offered to international investors are likely to exacerbate rather than ease external bottlenecks as investors will not be under any obligation to park their foreign currency in the country and will enjoy major tax exemptions.

In sum, Milei's libertarian approach to the reorganization of the state has been effective in connecting with frustrations about its functioning and costs, but it should also raise questions about the future of its institutional and bureaucratic capacities to guarantee capital accumulation. These economic inconsistencies could over time represent challenges to the government. For now, the most effective dissent has been advanced by capital, whose doubts about the prospects of Milei's program are likely to force the government to further austerity in line with its own neoliberal disciplinary agenda. But this option is already eroding the social support on which he obtained the presidency. To the challenges that this erosion poses for Milei in maintaining his political base, we now turn.

Milei's allure

Clearly, threats, insults, unending conflicts and large doses of chaos all helped Milei to tap into, with uncanny precision, the veins of public discontent and direct it towards his own libertarian vision for Argentina. But we still need to ask why there was a public so receptive of his ideas, which in some cases spoke loudly and clearly to them (often promising sacrifice and punishment) while in other cases were simply nonsensical economic jargon.

Milei's narrative has had an extraordinary appeal because its malleable terms resonate with a diverse range of anger, grievances and aspirations.[29] In it, there is no reason to fear the power of libertarianism other than being a member of the corrupt and self-perpetuating 'caste'. This caste justifies its own existence as the promoter of social justice but perpetrates a tyrannical power over 'decent people'. Like caste, decent people is a vague category that includes hard-working individuals frustrated by the actions of the caste, even if they do not fully agree with all libertarian ideals, as well as those who pin their hopes in the anti-statist promise of freedom and order.[30] The policies implemented during the first six months in power have reflected this narrative faithfully, and have made progress in the moral refoundation of the Argentinean society, now freer from the supposed burden of social justice. With such lines, the government downgraded the status of state agencies including the Women, Gender and Diversity Ministry, the Environment and Sustainable Development Ministry and, tellingly, the Ministry of Labour – eliminating many of their functions, cutting their budget and firing most of their staff based on arguments about their irrelevance or negative impacts. The drastic reduction of social assistance programs for informal workers and their organizations and the firing of public sector workers have been celebrated as 'cleansing operations'. The use of inclusive language – seen as an imposition of global socialism – has been eradicated from the state, while the wider elimination of any reference to gender and sexual equality or environmental protection has been pursued in intergovernmental institutions.

Milei's narrative has been effective because it has resonated with sentiments that already existed within large segments of society. For a large number of individuals there is something fundamentally wrong with the status quo. More specifically, for many voters, Milei's call to individual sacrifice and reduced or null expectations of state support was an objective and accurate depiction of the reality in which they live. It also proved more realistic than the idea that progress would, somehow, in the near future make it possible to rebuild the social infrastructure created during the Pink Tide, as was implied in his opponent Massa's electoral campaign.

Anger and votes across classes

The exceptionality of Milei's movement is, without doubt, its resounding multi-class composition. This provides a telling contrast with the nature of the other two key political coalitions of the time: Peronism's association with the working classes and, until 2023 at least, the channelling of the middle and upper class votes by Cambiemos. In contrast, Milei won the support of more than half of the voters in all income brackets except for the highest income earners, where support was slightly below that (at 43.2 per cent). Available data from surveys indicates that 50.8 per cent of waged workers, 63.5 per cent of self-employed and 50.9 per cent of informal workers voted LLA in the second electoral round.[31]

A key grievance shared by many middle-class voters and some groups of workers has been the belief that there is an unbridgeable gap between their expectations of sustained improvements in their standard of living and what was possible under other governments. This perception has created heightened anxieties about their relative losses when compared to other groups. As in other countries, there has been a conviction that their economic misfortunes were connected to the existence of a state which extracts from them resources that are then misused in developing social programs and pensions that the country cannot afford and that the recipients do not deserve. From this point of view, Peronism, and in particular the Kirchners and their policies, are the culprits behind Argentina's prolonged 'agony'.

A critical area of multi-class social discontent against the state has been its recognition, at least in letter if not always in practice, of human and environmental rights, gender equality, sexual diversity and protection against ethnic discrimination. Many have seen these rights, and the movements and actors promoting them, as excessive and/or decadent. Particularly infuriating was an expanding set of regulations and, more to the point, of resources through which the state materialized this recognition. Milei's promise to do away with the public and legislative infrastructure erected to implement these rights struck a chord among a segment of the population. Resentful of what many among them perceived as misplaced entitlements, they saw in him the hope of finally giving voice to their own sense of victimization as the 'silent majority', oppressed for their views by a dominant discourse aligned with a global socialist agenda that delegitimizes their perceptions of right and wrong.

The electoral promise of reconstructing society to protect market values and individual freedoms, and the promise to punish those who have abused state power were, unsurprisingly, key drawing points for many middle and upper-middle class voters. The conventional right representing them had in a more veiled manner promoted this turn as well as an overall rejection of social justice. It was thus easy for its voters to turn to Milei in the runoff election. But his overwhelming success in attracting a majority of the working classes, including poor and precarious workers, is considerably more difficult to explain. Yet, the slow transformation of working-class political identities has been a long time in the making.

Without doubt, the limited outcomes of policy efforts to improve the living conditions and the prospects of this group of workers are central to understanding their recent political inclinations. As mentioned before, the consolidation of neoliberalism in the 1990s entailed momentous transformations in the configuration of the working classes in the country, principally through growing unemployment, informalization and precarization. Many of these informal and precarious workers organized to pursue their demands which transformed slowly from employment in the late 1990s and early 2000s to the recognition of informal, self-employed and unwaged workers as productive and their work as in no way marginal to capitalist accumulation since the 2010s.[32] Even though these organizations have been able to negotiate with the state and gain some recognition and assistance for their members, for many workers these options have only been a poor substitute for insertion into formal labour markets, not to mention that state support was not forthcoming for all of them.[33] Moreover, the efforts of these organizations to raise awareness about the disruptive potential of individualism and exploitative practices within the informal economy had to compete with glamourized versions of 'entrepreneurship' prominent among informal workers and often fostered by assistance policies. Thus, many informal workers have felt aggrieved by the state, increasingly identifying with the allure of free market ideology.[34] The inability of informal workers' organizations to fully comprehend these ideological and identity changes has limited the effectiveness of their collective action. Concepts like 'neoliberalism from below' can provide insights to understanding how neoliberal values are embedded in, and reproduced through, the ways informal workers secure their survival.[35] Milei's appeal has been precisely his capacity to tap into sentiments among these workers around practices that are already part of their everyday reality, developed as a survival strategy in light of an absent state. Following a neoliberal logic, his emphasis on individual effort, on the supremacy of markets and the denunciation of the intrusion of the state as exploitative and illegitimate has found a fit with these survival strategies that came to be conceived as 'entrepreneurship'.[36]

It is thus possible to understand how the threat of undermining state protections – either by eliminating labour protection or social programs – bears little or no weight for those living under the most precarious conditions. This is not just because these protections were of no significance in their daily life before Milei, but also because many of these workers see regulations and state spending as obstacles for their chances to improve their lot. Thus, the growing appeal of the far right's interpretation of Argentina's many failures among the poorest sectors of the population might be explained in this way. Yet, as the discussion about economic transformation in the first months of Milei government made clear, there is a substantial tension between the hope these workers have placed in Milei's ideas of freedom and their willingness to wait for positive outcomes. There is little evidence to believe that the social catastrophe the government has created in its initial efforts at implementing his anarcho-capitalist agenda is likely to be reversed any time soon and, for those who barely manage to survive, time is never on their side.

LOOKING AHEAD: SPACE FOR HOPE?

In closing, we thought it relevant to briefly address existing social contestation to Milei's initiatives. We do so because from it, whatever its shortcomings and limitations, is where more effective political and social responses are most likely to emerge. Calls to challenge the government's policies have abounded, which is unsurprising considering Argentina's history of social and labour movement organization and mobilization. However, thus far, these actions have not been particularly successful in setting limits to Milei's policies. Rather, Milei seems to be more concerned about doubts as to the viability of his economic program emerging from sectors of capital that do not include a concern for the material conditions workers must endure. Arguably, social struggles are unlikely to produce major policy reversals only a few months out from the election in which Milei gathered a solid majority of votes. What is still unclear, however, is whether challengers are strengthening their power for the future and, most importantly, finding new ways of building power and confronting the anarcho-capitalist experiment.

There were some very early, localized and somewhat spontaneous protests that did not have major repercussions. More massive and organized mobilizations followed soon after, starting with a general strike in January 2024, which was no minor factor in complicating the discussion of the Bases law in Congress. Thereafter, massive demonstrations marked International Women's Day and the anniversary of the 1976 military coup. Extraordinarily large, simultaneous local demonstrations in defence of public universities, whose functioning has been under threat due to budgetary cuts, took place in April, and forced the government to commit to lessen an initial budget cut equivalent to a 75 per cent in real terms. More recently, a protest against the vote for the Bases law in Congress was held in June and was met with heavy repression. There are some noteworthy features in these political events. First, protestors turned to the street in huge numbers across the country, including in many provinces and cities in which Milei's electoral performance had been exceptional. Second, they have involved the active participation and support of a cross-section of forces that had not always coordinated their responses previously. That labour movement organizations and left-wing political parties, alongside human rights, feminist and other organizations, have been able to unify around key issues is a promising development. Third, repression against these and other more localized demonstrations has been consistently escalating, with consequences that remain uncertain.

Beyond these massive demonstrations, there have also been multiple ways people and organizations have made clear their intention to confront the government's attack on workers and its plans to dismantle key institutions within the state. For example, in December 2023 the General Confederation of Labour (Confederación General del Trabajo) presented a legal challenge to the Decree of Necessity and Urgency's labour chapter, succeeding albeit temporarily in having the courts declare it unconstitutional. Workers have mobilized almost daily in their workplaces against dismissals and the erosion of their salaries, with this grassroots activism placing the official union leadership in a tight situation. Historically, organized labour's power of negotiation has been based not only in its capacity to mobilize but also its effectiveness at curtailing workers' responses where demanded. Both strategies have been pursued, depending on the circumstances, to preserve what labour leadership has conceived very narrowly as trade unionism's primary interests in the country. This moment is no different, even when one could argue that Milei's extreme position against unions leaves very little in the form of expectations for negotiation. Moreover, as real incomes continue to deteriorate and recession increases unemployment, a strategy of direct confrontation might become the only option available for unions, which is not without risks in a context of rising labour market insecurity, repression and the discrediting of workers' organizations.

Those who are dependent on social assistance have publicly exposed the government's numerous punitive actions against them, among the most reprehensible the decisions to reduce workfare programs and cancel the distribution of food to community kitchens, amidst rampant impoverishment and food insecurity, with the main purpose of undermining the primary sites of informal workers' organizing. There has also been an important presence of all major social movements alongside left wing parties and organizations in support of these demands. Although left-wing forces (broadly defined) have consistently underperformed electorally, they nevertheless remain a meaningful presence among social movements. Thus, the struggles of these movements might also provide the necessary medium to increase left-wing presence and the emergence of an effective anti-authoritarian force to challenge Milei.

This summary of challenges to the government and their prospects cannot be considered complete without reference to the fact that repression and the criminalization of protest and social conflict have been steadily escalating. In June protestors gathering around Congress to show their opposition to the approval of the Bases law were accused of plotting a coup d'état and some of them now face the prospect of long prison sentences. Changes to state intelligence agencies and their functions have made possible the widespread electronic surveillance of social networks, apps and websites to predict 'security risks', which opens the door for the monitoring of activists, organizations and movements on the argument that they are a threat to the state. Similarly, the government has drafted a bill that will overturn regulations that have prevented the military from performing police functions of domestic security and population control since the redemocratization of the country in 1983. This, no doubt, represents the government's profound aversion to any expression of opposition compounded by its impulse to negate the existence of basic rights like the right to protest. It also brings back spectres of the criminalization of activism and dissent that Argentineans have not seen since the end of the 1976–1983 dictatorship. The extent to which this will encourage or discourage people to mobilize is still an open question, but there are indications that the government may have managed to achieve the chilling effects it seeks at least for the time being. Increasing the costs of dissent and more effectively isolating public policy from social pressure is part of an ambitious plan to raze to the ground the bases upon which Argentinean traditions of organizing and mobilization have stood.[37] This is, in our view, a critical component of Milei's grand refoundational plan that, in unsettling ways, replicates previous dictatorial practices of buttressing and extending the centrality of the repressive arm of the state to enforce the working of free markets. This time the assault is taking place in a historical moment of particular political weakness for those forces that have historically fought authoritarianism and what it exposes about the needs of capital.

It is now hard to imagine the coming economic and political evolution of Milei's experiment. Making predictions in a country as politically and economically volatile as Argentina is a recipe for error, but there are some possible directions out of the current political conundrum. Frictions within the governing coalition may evolve into fractures between Milei's anarcho-capitalism and the authoritarian nationalism represented by Vice-President Villarruel, who has shown political ambition and acumen in distancing herself from some of Milei's egregious missteps and the political costs associated with them. It is not completely far fetched to think about the emergence of a reactionary nationalist response to Milei's anarcho-capitalism, in which Villarruel can coexist with some conservative factions within Peronism in a combination that may be appealing for sectors with a tradition of popular nationalism. Tensions within the government, combined with an incipient disillusionment about the direction of the change Milei is leading, also present opportunities for more democratic politics. Meanwhile, however, the more progressive sectors within Peronism are yet to engage in a critical examination of their own trajectory and prospects beyond nostalgia for the so-called 'victorious decade' of the 2000s.

Incipient as social struggles have been so far, they have been a way for people to corroborate the existence of a collective unwillingness to accept austerity and authoritarianism, which is crucial after the brutal defeat the Milei government represents for them. But more effective response requires not only demonstrations, no matter how massive they are, but also a renewal in the forms of organizing required to push back the advance the far right has managed to accomplish in sectors traditionally identified with more progressive politics. There needs to be a critical reassessment of how and why their existing political, organizational and discursive practices have undermined the ability of movements to prevent the rise of the far right and its appropriation of the badge of radicalism. Labour organizations in particular face the challenge of reinventing themselves and their forms of action to bridge the growing gaps between formal and informal workers, between those who receive state subsidies and those who do not, and between historical working-class collective identities and those connected to workers' individualization and 'entrepreneurization'. For all this to happen, broader political visions will be required through which the articulation of diverse demands can take place. This is most likely the moment's key challenge, as the kind of oppositional forces able to effectively offer viable alternatives to the cruel libertarian experiment have yet to emerge.

NOTES

We would like to thank our colleague Ana Logiudice for her insightful comments on an earlier version of this chapter.

1   In what follows, we use anarcho-capitalist and libertarian interchangeably, without engaging in the theoretical discussion about their precise meaning or distinction, given the fact that Milei himself uses both terms to describe himself.

2   As our discussion will show, since its founding in the mid-1940s, the Peronist party has undergone various iterations, often riddled by its own internal divisions and also tensions with its key bases of support within the organized labour movement. See, for example: Ricardo Sidicaro, *Los tres peronismos: Estado y poder económico 1946-1955, 1973-1976, 1989-1999*, Buenos Aires: Siglo Veintiuno Editores, 2002. On populism, see also note 6 below.

3   Oscar Braun and Leonard Joy, 'A Model of Economic Stagnation: A Case Study of the Argentine Economy', *Economic Journal*, 78(312), 1968, pp. 868-87; Javier Villanueva, 'Problemas de Industrialización con Restricciones en el Sector Externo', *Desarrollo Económico*, 4(14/15), 1964, pp. 171-82.

4   Jorge Schvarzer and Andrés Tavonanska, 'Modelos Macroeconómicos en la Argentina: del "Stop and Go" al "Go and Crush" [sic]', *Centro de Estudios de la Situación y Perspectivas de la Argentina*, Documento de Trabajo 15, 2008, p. 8.

5   Guillermo O'Donnell, 'State and Alliances in Argentina', *Journal of Development Studies* 15(1), 1978, pp. 3-33.

6   This period represents the first moment of populism in Argentina. In the country, populism acquired certain connotations, in particular its strong working-class orientation, in turn the reflection of the political and social significance organized labour already possessed in the country. Without exhausting all possible subtypes and variations, in the context of Argentina and Latin America more generally, we find it productive to think of populism as regimes reflecting some commitment toward redistributive policies, claiming to present the demands emerging from 'the people' and giving these demands legitimacy through the development of state institutions. Furthermore, the constitution of the people as antagonistic to those in positions of power is key in the construction of a political identity under populism, as is the connection that this identity allows people to develop among diverse and otherwise particularistic demands (See, in particular: Ernesto Laclau, 'Hacia una Teoría del Populismo', in *Política e Ideología en la Teoría Marxista. Capitalismo, Fascismo, Populismo*, Madrid: Siglo XXI Editores, 1978; and *On Populist Reason*, London: Verso, 2007). It has now become common place to use populism as a way of conceptualizing both centre-left and far right regimes, mostly because of its construction of alleged enemies to the people, or the presence of a charismatic leader. In our view, this strategy tends to confuse rather than clarify the contours of different political regimes. For example, while we think of the three Peronist administrations between 2003 and 2015 as befitting a definition of populism, we find it hard to consider Javier Milei to be leading a populist government.

7   Adolfo Canitrot, 'La Disciplina como Objeto de la Política Económica,' *Desarrollo Económico*, 19(76), 1980, pp. 453-75.

8   Ruth Felder and Viviana Patroni, 'Precarious Work in Recession and Growth: A New Structural Feature of Labor Markets in Argentina?', *Review of Radical Political Economics*, 50(1), 2018, pp. 44-65.

9   Jordán Daniel Ricchione, 'Del Stop & Go al Stop & Crash: Un Análisis de la Restricción Externa Argentina en el Período 2011-2019', Banco Central de la República Argentina, 2022.

10   Ernesto Semán, *Breve Historia del Antipopulismo: Los Intentos por Domesticar a la Argentina Plebeya, de 1810 a Macri*, Buenos Aires: Siglo XXI Editores, 2021.

11   Some numbers to illustrate this situation include that in 2022 only 40.2 per cent of workers had a formal job, while 51 per cent were informal (self-employed, beneficiaries of a social program, or worked without any kind of social security benefits). We discuss this in: Maisa Bascuas et al., 'Economía Popular y Políticas Estatales en la Pandemia y la Postpandemia', in Fernando Stratta and Miguel Mazzeo, eds, *La Economía Popular: Perspectivas Críticas desde Nuestra América*, Buenos Aires: Universidad de Lanús, 2024, pp. 207-26. Informal workers' average income was 48.2 per cent lower than workers in the private sector and 39.3 per cent below the average income of workers in the public sector. See: Eduardo Donza, 'Escenario Laboral en la Argentina del Post-COVID-19. Persistente Heterogeneidad Estructural en un Contexto de Leve Recuperación (2010-2022)', *Documento Estadístico-Barómetro de la Deuda Social Argentina*, Buenos Aires: Educa, 2023, p. 7.

12   Juan Grigera, 'Adding Insult to Injury: The COVID-19 Crisis Strikes Latin America', *Development and Change*, 53(6), 2023, pp. 1335-61.

13   On this topic, see: Rodrigo Guimaraes Nunes, *Bolsonarismo y Extrema Derecha Global: Una Gramática de la Desintegración,* Buenos Aires: Tinta Limon, 2024.

14   Pablo Stefanoni, *¿La Rebeldía Se Volvió de Derecha?: Cómo el Antiprogresismo y la Anticorrección Política Están Construyendo un Nuevo Sentido Común (y Por Qué la Izquierda Debería Tomarlos en Serio)*, Buenos Aires: Siglo XXI Editores, 2021.

15   For a more detailed portrait, see: Danielle Tomson, 'Who is the Real Javier Milei: Insights on Argentina's Anarcho-Capitalist President and his Unique Affection for Judaism', *Codastory*, 2 February 2024, available at: www.codastory.com.

16   Cecilia Camarano, 'Javier Milei: "El Concepto de Justicia Social es Aberrante, es Robarle a Alguien Para Darle a Otro"', *Ámbito,* 24 August 2023, available at: www.ambito.com.

17   Alberto Bonnet, 'El Ascenso de Milei en Argentina y las Nuevas Derechas Extremas desde América Latina', *Papel Político*, 29, 2024.

18   One of these groups is that of Vice-President Victoria Villarruel, an ultraconservative lawyer who expresses a more conventional lineage of the Argentinean religious, nationalist and pro-military right. She has been a prominent activist for the vindication of the military dictatorship and efforts to demand the release of those military members convicted of crimes against humanity, whom she sees as political prisoners.

19   Dirección Nacional Electoral, 'Resultados Electorales. Elecciones 2023', available at: https://resultados.gob.ar.

20   Adrián Piva, 'La Ultradererecha Gobierna en Argentina ¿el Fin de una Época?', *El Estado en Debate*, 3, 2024, pp. 58-73.

21   Eugenia Muzio, 'Los Seis Meses de Javier Milei en Diez Números', *Letra P*, 8 June 2024, available at: www.letrap.com.ar.

22   Hernan Nessi and Aida Pelaez-Fernandez, 'Argentina Enters Technical Recession as Job Losses Mount Under Milei', *Reuters*, 24 June 2024.

23   José Giménez, 'La Desocupación Aumentó al 7,7% en los Primeros Meses del Gobierno de Javier Milei: Cómo Evolucionó Este Indicador en los Últimos Años', *Chequeado*, 24 June 2024, available at: www.chequeado.com.

24   Martín Slipczuk y Matías Di Santi, '¿Cómo Evolucionó la Pobreza en la Argentina con Cada Presidente?', *Chequeado*, 4 June 2024.

25   Mariana Leiva, 'Creció la Desigualdad en la Argentina Durante los Primeros Meses del Gobierno de Javier Milei', *Chequeado*, 26 June 2024.

26   This type of presidential decree is restricted to exceptional circumstances in which urgency makes the regular process to pass laws impossible. Congress intervenes after the fact to support or reject it.

27   This was not the only decision made on an occasion with political significance. For instance, the name of the government palace's Women's Hall was removed on International Women's Day and an official video vindicating the dictatorship was released on the anniversary of the 1976 military coup, at the same time as hundreds of thousands mobilized to commemorate it.

28   Ricardo Quesada, 'Ya Hay 8 Grandes 'Multis' que Hicieron las Valijas en la Era Milei', *El Cronista*, 4 July 2024, available at: www.cronista.com.

29   On the far right narratives, see: Nunes, *Bolsonarismo*.

30   Esther Solano, Pablo Pavez and Thais Romá, 'El Votante Moderado de Milei: Entre la Esperanza y El Sacrificio', *Friedich Ebert Stiftung*, June 2024, available at: https://argentina.fes.de.

31   Julia Almeida, 'Who Votes for the Far Right in Latin America? A Fine-Grain Analysis of the Right-Wing Electoral Base in Brazil and Argentina', *Rosa Luxemburg Stiftung*, 18 December 2023, available at: www.rosalux.de; 'Cómo Fue el Voto a Massa y Milei Según la Condición Laboral,' *Pagina 12*, 21 November 2023, available at: www.pagina12.com.ar.

32   Maisa Bascuas et al., 'Rethinking Working-class Politics: Organising Informal Workers in Argentina', *Global Labour Journal,* 12(3), 2021, pp. 244-66.

33   Around six million workers are informal, while the largest organization bringing together these workers – the Popular Economy Workers' Union – has around a million members. See: Rosario Radaelli, 'Argentina Informal: Panorama de un Fenómeno que Llegó para Quedarse', *Pagina 12*, 6 May 2023.

34   Solano et al., 'El Votante Moderado de Milei', p. 10.

35   Verónica Gago, *Neoliberalism from Below: Popular Pragmatics and Baroque Economies*, Durham and London: Duke University Press, 2017.

36   Gago, *Neoliberalism from Below*.

37   Verónica Gago, 'El Gran Problema que Tenemos es Cómo Se Va Delineando que Libertad es Igual a Individualismo', interviewed by Diego Genoud, *elDiarioAR*, 3 August 2024, available at: www.eldiarioar.com.

THE RESISTIBLE RISE OF FASCISM: THE FAR RIGHT AND THE CRISIS OF THE GERMAN LEFT

INGAR SOLTY

The capitalist west has been haunted by a 'populist situation' for well over a decade now. A populist situation may be defined as a legitimacy crisis of the capitalist state which has the following four characteristics: a pervasive crisis of confidence in liberal democracy and its problem-solving capacities; strong anti-establishment sentiments among the population; the erosion of traditional large catch-all parties; and the transformation of historical party systems, which includes the emergence and often rapid growth of volatile new party projects.[1]

The populist situation has its roots in a pervasive crisis of global capitalism. This crisis is the foundation of the erosion of the liberal centre. It also structures the terrain on which both socialist strategies and the far right compete over diverging exit-strategies from the crisis. The crisis manifests itself across six dimensions. It is a crisis of: (1) capitalist accumulation; (2) social reproduction; (3) social cohesion, due to the polarization of society via the market and the fatal interplay between a capital-driven Fourth Industrial Revolution and the transformation of Keynesian welfare into neoliberal workfare states; (4) a crisis of liberal-parliamentary representation and democracy resulting from the first three crisis dimensions; (5) a crisis of ecological sustainability and climate; and (6) a crisis of the world order created by the US after 1945 and globalized since 1991, which is being challenged in the wake of the US–China high-tech rivalry.[2]

In light of the gravity of each of these crisis dimensions, the capitalist state, understood as the centralized bureaucratic apparatus burdened with the management of capitalism's systemic contradictions,[3] is in a mode of permanent ad-hoc firefighting. Global capitalism's crisis is also changing its deep structures. A new type of capitalism is emerging, which can be described as post-liberal both internally and in the international arena. The pervasiveness of crisis is due to the fact that crises that appear to have been averted in one dimension through the deployment of considerable state power resources flare up again in another dimension. For example, the global financial crisis that began in 2007 exposed the contradictions of neoliberal wealth inequality, financialization and finance-driven accumulation.[4] The eurozone crisis from 2010 onward revealed the contradictions of the neoliberal path of European integration.[5] The 'refugee crisis' of 2015 revealed the contradictions of neoliberal free trade imperialism[6] and its disastrous consequences: the hundreds of million-fold proletarianization of small peasants in the global South; a hyper-urbanized 'planet of slums';[7] ethnicized and confessionalized distribution struggles leading to state failures, ad hoc fire-fighting military interventions by the 'West', as in Libya in 2011, and geopolitical proxy wars, as in Syria. The 'refugee crisis' in turn proved to be an essential condition for the rise of right-wing authoritarian nationalism, especially in Europe, which uses refugees for racist propaganda. The Covid-19 pandemic crisis of 2020–2022 in turn exposed the contradictions of globalized just-in-time production, as well as those of neoliberal health care reforms. Two years later, the Ukraine war is another expression of the escalating crisis of the world order and acts as a catalyst for a new confrontation between a US-led bloc and a China-led bloc, with a few regional centres seeking to maintain multi-alignment between the two.

Europe was plunged into its populist situation as a result of 'internal devaluation' – austerity strategies that Western capitalist states pursued in response to the global financial and eurozone crises. The initial articulation of populism in Europe was a left wing one. In some contexts, new populist party projects were preceded by strong social movements. In southern Europe, for example, the so-called PIIGS states (as Portugal, Italy, Ireland, Greece and Spain were referred to at the time) saw extremely strong anti-austerity movements emerge as the main political articulation. These movements, in turn, formed the basis for the successes of new left-wing 'populist' parties such as Syriza in Greece, Podemos in Spain and the Left Bloc and Communist Party in Portugal.

These state power projects were the inevitable reaction to what could be described as the 'Portuguese conundrum'.[8] In Portugal, the 'Screw the Troika' protests of 2 March 2013 temporarily brought as much as a quarter of the population onto the streets. And yet, at the time even the strongest social movements did not lead to a reshuffling of the austerity-enforcing governments, let alone an end to austerity policies. It became obvious that in order to change politics, new projects of state power had to be formed. With a big bang, the emergence of Syriza and Podemos, and their obvious political necessity, ended the strategic horizontalism of 'changing the world without taking power',[9] which had dominated left-wing practice, especially in anti-capitalist social movements, in the two decades following the collapse of state socialism in the early 1990s. And when, at least in Portugal, a left-wing coalition eventually came to power, it successfully limited austerity, even if it was unable to push through substantial radical reforms.

The European periphery was, however, not alone in seeing the spread of populist appeals. While in the 'first-past-the-post' electoral systems of the US and Britain the two dominant parties appeared to be consolidated – with their electoral appeal actually increasing compared to the early 2000s – this merely masked the erosion of internal organizational cohesion in the US Democrats and the British Labour Party on the one hand, and the US Republicans and the British Tories on the other. While in continental Europe's proportional representation electoral systems left and right populist forces founded their own parties, in the US and British cases the dominant parties and their centrist elites instead came under tremendous pressure from grassroots revolts. From the left, the Bernie Sanders movement in the US, with the support of the Democratic Socialists of America, and Jeremy Corbyn's Labour Party revolt, with the support of the Momentum social movement, showed an immensely powerful, if ultimately unsuccessful, dynamic. On the right, Donald Trump successfully won not only the Republican Party nomination but also the presidency in 2016, against the conventional wisdom of political science;[10] while the UK's 2016 referendum on 'Brexit' from the European Union was approved following a successful right-wing mobilization.

In contrast to the experiences of southern Europe, the US and the UK, Germany appeared for a long time to be a haven of 'stability' in the 2010s, buoyed by timid revisions to the SPD and Greens' socially devastating and politically self-defeating Agenda 2010, as well as 120 billion euros in capital flight from southern Europe. Germany's political stagnation was symbolized by Chancellor Angela Merkel, who ruled in presidential style through her executive powers from 2005 until 2021, while all around her governments were being toppled as a consequence of populist revolts.[11] But within a decade Germany began to experience its own spread of populist forces on the political right, the pace of which outstripped many other countries in the capitalist core.

The federal government formed by the SPD (Sozialdemokratische Partei Deutschlands; Social Democratic Party of Germany), the liberal Green Party and the right-wing libertarian FDP (Freie Demokratische Partei; Free Democratic Party) in the fall of 2021, which deemed itself a 'progressive coalition', soon experienced a deep crisis of confidence, becoming historically unpopular. Soon, two thirds of the population were rejecting its policies. According to surveys, the so called 'traffic light' coalition lost between 19 and 23 percentage points in voter support as compared to the 2021 federal election result. In the state elections held on 1 September 2024 in the eastern German states of Saxony and Thuringia, they experienced a fiasco. In Saxony, the three governing parties together won the support of a mere 13.3 per cent of the electorate; in Thuringia their combined share of the vote dropped even lower to 10.4 per cent, ousting almost all representatives of the three parties from its parliament. It is hard to conceive a more drastic display of electoral disillusionment with the mainstream political establishment. Finally, the government collapsed in early November 2024 and early elections were called for February 2025, recalling the demise of the last two SPD-led governments of Helmut Schmidt in 1983 and Gerhard Schroeder in 2005.

However, the disdain into which the governing centrist parties have fallen has not ushered in new support for the mainstream conservative opposition. On the contrary, the CDU (Christlich Demokratische Union Deutschlands; Christian Democratic Union of Germany) and their Bavarian partner the CSU (Christlich-Soziale Union in Bayern; Christian Social Union in Bavaria) only gained around six per cent in the 2024 European elections. Moreover, opinion surveys suggest the CDU/CSU are not believed to offer any better solutions to social problems.[12] Trust in politics and its problem-solving capacities is at an all time low. There is a huge yearning for alternatives to 'business as usual'. This is the context in which populism has arrived in Germany.

THE MATERIAL ROOTS OF
GERMANY'S POPULIST SITUATION

A populist situation has been latent in German society since 2004, i.e. since Agenda 2010 and the Hartz laws, which deregulated the labour market and transformed the Keynesian welfare state into a neoliberal workfare regime. An erosion of neoliberal hegemony gave rise to Die Linke in the second half of the 2000s, although until 2022 Germany was not a 'downward mobility society',[13] but one where rampant fear of decline in social status predominated. Neoliberal deregulation of the labour market created a rift between the core workforce and a growing army of casual and agency workers in transnationalized, export-oriented industries. In the name of 'resilience', these workers functioned as the buffer for short-term layoffs and investment restructuring. The speed of the process in which atypical employment became typical employment showed the core labour force its future.[14] The pervasive fears of downward mobility and even social exclusion were reinforced by capital-driven digitalization and artificial intelligence, which now threatened even highly qualified professionals from journalists to lawyers to software programmers. The Hartz laws of the early 2000s acted like 'communicating vessels'[15] that disciplined the unemployed and the entire segmented German working class. In contrast to the US and Britain, where the wage-dependent 'middle classes' had already eroded from deindustrialization, weakened trade-union power and tuition fee-based education, Germany's working class maintained its 'middle class' lifestyle through the competitiveness of its manufacturing sector. Even though it was being eroded, workplace bargaining still sustained industrial union wages, as did the specific German system of tuition-free education and training for skilled workers.

By 2022, Germany had all the visible signs of an actually downwardly mobile society. The geopolitics leading to a new confrontation between blocs on Germany's eastern periphery was a major factor in setting the new conjuncture. The war in Ukraine formed a 'new asymmetrical transatlanticism' phase of European dependence on the US – especially for Germany – in terms of energy, reliance on the US domestic market, geopolitics and in the military-technopolitical realm. The Covid-19 pandemic had already promoted inflationary tendencies through the disruption of supply chains, and the Ukraine War, sanctions and counter-sanctions further weakened Germany and Europe. The western Europe–Russian symbiosis had provided a constant flow of cheap energy and had given a cost advantage to Germany's already strong industrial base. Russia, in turn, sought to utilize high returns on resource exports to diversify its economy and shift it to higher value-added production in digital economy. Cutting off Russian energy supplies to Germany created a new dependence on more expensive liquid natural gas, with around 80 per cent coming from the US and its more expensive shale fracking. German energy costs are now roughly three times higher than in the US and seven times higher than in China. More expensive energy, of course, means higher production costs not just for industry and transportation but also in housing, foodstuffs and everyday consumer goods. Energy costs inevitably threaten the competitiveness of capital and put further pressure on Germany and its low growth status, once more being referred to on occasion as the 'sick man of Europe'. Under this pressure, the government has focused on creating a business-friendly investment climate, maintaining competitiveness in relation to overseas rivals through high subsidies for transnational semiconductor corporations, corporate tax cuts, social spending cuts and state subsidies for industrial electricity prices. Moreover, it seeks to counter tightened labour markets and drive down labour costs, i.e., variable capital, through increased immigration of care workers and harsher workfare practices against the unemployed.[16]

The Ukraine war and the new austerity measures which were reinforced by April 2023's reform of the European Union fiscal compact – the most significant since it was adopted – are now leading to the impoverishment of broad sections of the population. Germans were used to reports from the US regarding the growing segment of the population living from paycheck to paycheck, but today this is also seen in Germany. Studies have shown that almost a third of the German population has no savings whatsoever to be able to respond to sudden shocks such as job loss, illness or spiraling living costs.[17] In 2023, almost two thirds of the wage-earning population spent their entire monthly income on covering living expenses,[18] and during the 2023 collective bargaining round even the most powerful segments of the working class employed in the metal industry only managed to at best prevent real income losses due to inflation.[19]

The war in Ukraine thus triggered sentiments of insecurity in an economically vulnerable and politically polarizing society. The 'traffic light' coalition and the conservative opposition share the belief that there is no alternative to the relative impoverishment of the popular classes and thus seek to mentally prepare the population for a 'lowering of expectations'.[20] Federal Economics Minister Robert Habeck's statement, according to which 'Germany is literally getting poorer',[21] is thus echoed by CDU opposition leader and Blackrock's former Europe chief Friedrich Merz, who, in 2023 said that 'we have probably … passed the peak of our prosperity'.[22]

Other policies of the SPD-led coalition have exacerbated the impacts of the Ukraine War on the economic insecurity of the general population. The government's self-declared goal was to push ahead with a 'green capitalist' transformation of the German economy, especially in the automotive industry, focused on accelerating decarbonization and electrification. To this end, it reallocated remaining pandemic emergency funds to a 60 billion euro 'climate and transformation fund'. In this way, the government also sought to circumvent the restrictions imposed by balanced budget amendments ('debt brake') to the German constitution.[23] Similar measures were also pursued in order to finance the additional 100 billion euros devoted to fulfilling NATO's requirement of military spending of at least 2 per cent of GDP. A November 2023 Federal Constitutional Court ruling, however, declared the 'climate and transformation fund' unconstitutional which, in turn, led to a termination of subsidies for electric cars. Given that in effect they had been a redistribution scheme by which workers' payroll taxes financed the 'conspicuous consumption' of the upper income bracket, the already disappointing sales of electric vehicles collapsed. This in turn led the EU and car companies to backtrack on the shift from the internal combustion engine to electric vehicles. The EU Commission's decision to follow suit with Trump and Biden's protectionism vis-à-vis Chinese electric vehicles (even against capital's hesitation resulting from fears of Chinese retaliation) was indicative of a botched industrial strategy.

The contradictions of this policy shift loom large. First, the EU's 'Green Deal' and decarbonization plan depend entirely on Chinese imports, from raw materials (silicon, lithium, etc.) to end products such as batteries and solar panels. Rebuilding independent solar panel production in Europe is a dangerous illusion. Given Chinese hyper-competitiveness, it would presuppose the systematic absorption of private accumulated wealth across Europe, the dismantling of Europe's 'iron cage of ordo-liberalism'[24] and the creation of a 'United States of Europe' wielding full sovereignty in economic policy. Only then could an all-European industrial policy systematically rebuild European solar panel production in relatively low-wage countries of Europe such as Romania and Bulgaria. Needless to say, class forces in Europe would never allow for such a dramatic change of direction. Second, the policy shift has reinforced the rise of far-right populism. What remains of Germany's decarbonization plans is a market-oriented carbon emission pricing which is almost doubling the price of a ton of CO_2 from 30 to 55 euros between 2023 and 2025. In combination with a heating law, it individualizes and ultimately shifts the costs of the climate crisis onto the working and lower income classes, even though they contribute the least to it. The burden is and will be felt by workers when buying groceries and gasoline, searching for affordable flights to summer vacation destinations, or replacing their heating systems in their badly insulated, unsellable homes in peripheralized regions. And while the government is forcing the proletariat to pay for the climate crisis in such an individualized way, its new protectionism against Chinese electric vehicles renders the working class unable to pay for the kind of things that would allow them to avoid these costs through artificially high prices. In other words, the SPD-led coalition government has, in an utterly irresponsible way, set climate policy in an antagonistic relationship to social justice.

As Bertolt Brecht famously noted, 'food is the first thing, morals follow on'. It is hardly surprising that the lower income classes in particular have turned their backs on the so-called 'progress coalition'.[25] However, unlike in the early 2000s, when an unpopular government under a social democratic chancellor who led the transformation of the Keynesian welfare state into a neoliberal workfare state facilitated the establishment of the new German left party Die Linke,[26] it is not the left that is benefitting from the 'populist situation.' On the contrary, it is the far right.

Specifically, it is the AfD (Alternative für Deutschland; Alternative for Germany) that is its sole beneficiary. According to polls ahead of the European elections in June 2024, it looked for a long time as if it would double its already strong result in the Bundestag elections from 10.3 per cent to well over 20 per cent. Support for the AfD has only been held back by the emergence of the BSW (Bündnis Sahra Wagenknecht; Sahra Wagenknecht Alliance). The BSW is a split from Die Linke and promotes an anti-establishment 'left conservatism' combining a traditional social democratic platform of redistribution in economic policy and a return to détente in foreign policy with a conservative stance on migration and right-wing rhetoric denouncing the 'woke' agenda of the 'lifestyle left'.[27] Still, the emergence of BSW has only slowed down the rise of the AfD, not stopped it.[28]

Meanwhile, the political centre's severely damaged climate policy is proletarianizing the far right. During the European elections of June 2024, the percentage of people voting for AfD who identified themselves as 'workers' in the exit polls shot up to 35 per cent, with a quarter of trade union members voting for the far right and its vocal opposition to Germany's climate policies. During the elections in Thuringia, 49 per cent of self-identifying workers and 51 per cent of those who considered themselves in an 'economically bad situation' voted for AfD, while in Saxony the numbers were 49 per cent and 45 per cent respectively.[29]

If a socialist had predicted that in 2021 voters would punish the new government in such a way but that Die Linke would *not* be the beneficiary, instead itself falling into a downward spiral threatening its very existence, that person would have been deemed a prophet of doom. But today the possibility of an Italianization of Germany – that is, the emergence of a country with capitalism but without a socialist party, or a 'demobilized class society' – is the most realistic scenario.[30] The political spectrum is narrowing down to a liberal centre that has lost hegemony and an emergent right-wing authoritarian nationalism that appears as the only 'systemic opposition'. While Karl Marx and Friedrich Engels still welcomed crises and the intensification of contradictions as historic moments to propel the labour movement and revolution, the various crises of capitalism since 2015 have made the left in Germany (and in Europe) weaker and weaker while the far right has been gaining in strength.

AUTHORITARIAN NATIONALISM AND
ISSUE OWNERSHIP IN GERMANY

The AfD appears to be an alternative to the system. It has successfully managed to present itself as the only opposition to the 'old parties' (*Altparteien* – a term taken directly from the Nazi Party's 'playbook' of the late 1920s). In responding to societal crisis and contradictions, the AfD performs as the only 'system alternative' and the only anti-establishment force. In doing so, it has benefited from its outsider status – in a way, taking the ground Die Linke had occupied between 2005 and 2010. The more propagandistically the bourgeois media of the centre writes against the AfD, the more they drive voters towards the far right, just as the PDS and later Die Linke also benefited from being constantly referred to in the bourgeois media as the successor of the East German communist SED party. The politically alienated sections of the population, who also feel socially powerless under capitalism, sense the hated establishment's fear of the AfD and they experience it as a form of self-empowerment to vote for it.[31]

And yet, in reality, the authoritarian nationalism of the far right does not embody an alternative program to the existing socio-economic system at all, neither in its theory nor practices.[32] Historically, traditional conservatism, as well as its fascist radicalization, has always been reactionary in the literal sense. As the US neoconservative intellectual David Horowitz once acknowledged, as a right-winger you know what you are against, namely equality and the left, but not necessarily what you are for.[33] Since the French Revolution, conservative thought and the political right have always reacted to existing social developments. Conservatism has never produced a coherent theory of society and the state. Conservatism therefore could be compatible with the authoritarian, monarchist or dictatorial state, but also with the neoliberal state of today.

In this sense, the right is a conformist pseudo-rebellion, and authoritarian nationalism revolts against the symptoms and contradictions of contemporary capitalism but not against its actual causes. For example, the AfD and the far right today mobilizes against migrants, asylum seekers and 'Islamic terrorists', but not against neoliberal trade and market liberalization policies which has destabilized the global South and has kept producing the causes of coerced migration. Nor does the far right mobilize against the climate crisis, one of the major causes of displacement today, and even denies that it exists. The same applies for its other key issues: it mobilizes against crime, but it reinforces the growing income and wealth inequality which is demonstrably the main driving force behind crime. It mobilizes against the emancipation of women but not for the expansion of free kindergartens and free care for the elderly, which would mitigate the inevitable struggles over the distribution of social reproductive labour. And finally, it claims to be the political force of local patriotism but overlooks the fact that market-driven policies are largely responsible for the desertion of rural areas and coerced internal migration for economic reasons.

Nonetheless, in Germany and beyond, the far right has emerged stronger than the left from the various moments of crisis since 2007. The more the populist and anti-establishment the political societal temper the more the 'pseudo-rebellious' far right appeals to voters. What can explain this?

In the political divisions that have formed from the eurozone crisis of 2010 to the Ukraine War crisis since 2022, the AfD has been able to claim 'issue ownership'.[34] It was able to appear, time and time again, as the main and even the only 'real opposition' to the prevailing unpopular policies of the German state. During the euro crisis, for example, the AfD was the most vehement advocate of 'market populism',[35] and backed letting the 'too big to fail' banks go bust and opposed the 'euro-bonds' meant to socialize bad debts in the European Economic and Monetary Union. In the Syrian refugee crisis, the AfD appeared as the only political force opposing Chancellor Angela Merkel's refugee policy. In contrast, the left appeared as a 'yes, but' opposition in referring positively to Merkel's 'we can do it' approach while demanding from government the financial means to actually manage the social integration of refugees.

The Covid-19 pandemic that began in 2020 further revealed the tactical mistakes and strategic limits of Die Linke's leadership. Across the 2000s, the left in Germany had made great political and intellectual efforts to develop, against neoliberal hegemony, a well-founded critique of neoliberalism and the associated commodification of the healthcare system, with privatization of hospitals and cuts to intensive care beds among the many symptoms of deteriorating provisioning. It also criticized austerity policies, which led to the drying up of public services, not least in health. A consequence was that, during the pandemic, health authorities were no longer able to trace chains of infection as a precondition to localized quarantine measures and limit blanket lockdowns. But instead of turning the coronavirus crisis into a political tribunal on neoliberalism and austerity, the left literally placed itself beside the sickbed of capitalism and worked to resuscitate the patient alongside the business and political classes. The left appeared as an appendix to the government on quarantine measures and 'lockdown'. Besides sacrificing its moral-intellectual capital on the care crisis in health, this issue positioning was particularly self-defeating as no political party in Germany was as internally divided on the lockdown as Die Linke. The criticism of pandemic management, the lockdown measures and the protests against them moved to the right (in the form of the 'Querdenker' movement). The right again occupied the position of the only anti-system party. Die Linke lost voters, and in some cases entire party district organizations (particularly in eastern Germany), to a new party, 'Die Basis', and steadily from there to the AfD.

The same destruction of hard-earned political capital accumulated by the left was incurred in their tactical decision to fall in line with the system with respect to the war in Ukraine – again to the advantage of the right. Against the hegemony of human rights interventionism in western states, the German left led the opposition and protests against NATO's Kosovo war in 1999, the Afghanistan war beginning in 2001 and the invasion of Iraq launched in 2003. Similarly, the left refused to support NATO's 2011 regime change operation in Libya as well as the later military operations in Mali and Syria.

The German left had, moreover, repeatedly warned against NATO's eastward expansion since 1991. Like several EU officials including the former Deputy EU Commission President and EU Commissioner for Eastern Enlargement,[36] the left in Germany had argued that it was a mistake to keep Russia out of the EU's 'Eastern Partnership'. Die Linke sharply criticized the George W. Bush administration's attempts to drag Ukraine into NATO during the alliance's summit in Bucharest in 2008, against the majoritarian will of the Ukrainian people and existing laws still in place at the time. In 2014, during the Euromaidan protests, Die Linke's leading politicians, notably Gregor Gysi from the right-wing of the party, emphasized that Ukraine had been economically, politically and ideologically divided by the tugging of East and West. Ukraine was being torn apart along the axis of Ukraine's competing oligarchs – the agrarian bourgeoisie leaning towards the West because of future export markets and the coal and steel industry bourgeoisie leaning towards the East because they feared EU association because of a lack of competitiveness vis-à-vis western European corporations.

But in 2022, the Die Linke leadership suddenly wanted nothing more to do with these historical positions. This was in part due to a loss of self-confidence and political disarray following the disastrous national election result of September 2021, which reduced Die Linke's vote share to only 4.9 per cent – on account of its ceasing to criticize the SPD and Greens in order to form a national coalition with them. It was also in part due to the unilateral Russian intervention in Ukraine in formal violation of international law. The entire leadership of Die Linke now deferred to NATO's discourse on the war while trying to maintain left-wing peace positions on a terrain that was being mined by the centrist government coalition and conservative opposition. But insofar as the left did nothing to counter the liberal narrative that Europe was threatened by a kind of Russian Hitler who would take over the continent in a genocidal fashion if weapons were not supplied to the Ukrainian government and there was no massive rearmament in the Cold War spirit of deterrence, it also lacked credibility. Because who in his right mind would argue against military spending when confronted with Hitler? The leadership of the left thus acted from a position of total defensiveness, from which it could never recover. But even during the Ukraine crisis, the AfD was able to present itself as a nationalist peace movement ready to replace Die Linke as the people's party.

THE AfD, AUTHORITARIAN NATIONALISM AND POLITICAL INSTABILITY

The rise of the AfD to the centre of national politics, and its position as by far the strongest force in the eastern federal states, holds immense potential for political destabilization even in the short term. With the AfD's electoral gains through 2024, it will be extremely difficult to form a government explicitly set against the right-wing election winners in all of these federal states. The CDU/CSU is still claiming to have a 'firewall' against working with the AfD. In Europe, however, some of its leading representatives, such as EU Commission President Ursula von der Leyen, already rely on Prime Minister Giorgia Meloni's Brothers of Italy party and France's Rassemblement National for political support and have argued that the 'firewall' runs to the right of Meloni.[37] So far, in eastern Germany where the AfD is openly fascist a coalition government is for now still out of the question. But AfD participation in a government coalition cannot be ruled out in the coming period.

The reason for this is the foreseeable instability of anti-AfD government coalitions. In several federal states of Germany, non-AfD coalitions would have to form in which the members have little in common in terms of ideology and program with some of the other parties. There is also little basis of trust established, and they will operate under considerable pressure from their own memberships. Joining forces with the 'ex-SED' Sahra Wagenknecht and 'Moscow's fifth column' BSW party is difficult to explain to the CDU base, as would be joining forces with the CDU for the political base of the BSW and Die Linke (and there has been no preparatory work for joint projects even among these two parties themselves). The forthcoming scenario is, therefore, largely already set in place. The AfD will tactically offer various governance procedures and policies to appear selfless and democratic. The pressure from the liberal media will be endless to form a three-party coalition against the AfD out of 'national responsibility' and for 'raison d'etat'. None of the parties will actually be able to escape this pressure out of self-interest. It is hard not to forecast a high degree of political instability in German politics, with a decline in the credibility of liberal parliamentarianism. The political flashpoints in the German political scene, with the AfD at the centre, are likely to spill over from parliamentary politics to the street.

The authoritarian nationalism of the far right presents itself in fundamental opposition to the status quo. An essential difference between historical fascism and the AfD is that the earlier movements of the far right from the 1920s could be seen as functional in some of its objectives for a capitalist class organized as a nation-state. However, under the superintendence of the American state, a global capitalism of transnational capital flows and institutions has emerged.[38] Nation-states support 'power blocs' in which transnationalized capital factions are dominant and, to some degree, states in global capitalism have also 'internationalized'. The state apparatuses that are most integrated into managing international capital flows, such as ministries of finance, central banks and industrial policy, have become even more dominant as the centres of economic and political power in states.[39]

Under the conditions of this global capitalism, however, the AfD is at odds with these key apparatuses of the state and the interests of the transnational capital they align with. As long as the AfD does not say 'yes' to the euro (a key resource for German-based capital in world markets) or 'yes' to NATO (as the military arm for securing world markets for western capital), the AfD cannot be a political arm of Bosch and Siemens, Bayer and BASF, or Volkswagen, BMW and the rest. This poses crucial questions: will contemporary fascist movements adapt to the prevailing power relations and dominant capital? Will they do so because they have few principles and little ideological coherence? Or do capital actors possibly adapt to fascist movements instead?

Since the US election victory of Donald Trump and the UK's Brexit referendum 2016, the far right has shown itself increasingly able to exercise real power in the capitalist centres and influence the levers of power. It was thus possible to study 'what "unruly" right-wing authoritarian nationalists do when they rule'. But even in power, the far right has so far been unable to implement its economic nationalist ideas and break the dominance of transnational capital in favour of domestic markets and national owners of capital. In the US, the economic nationalist program of Trump and his key strategist Steve Bannon was contained by the power and interests of internationalized American capital.[40]

In Germany, the mastermind of the AfD's *völkisch* wing, Götz Kubitschek, has imposed a 'ban on imitation' on his party in order to avoid being co-opted by the ruling class. Nevertheless, under the conditions of political advancement, adaptation processes in the extreme right in Europe cannot be denied. After the European parliamentary elections in June 2024, the leading right-wing parties of Giorgia Meloni from Italy and Marine Le Pen from France excluded the AfD from the joint group in the European Parliament in order to be able to cooperate better with the traditional conservatives. Marine Le Pen's commitment to the EU, the eurozone and NATO was also the result of a strategy to present herself as reliable for reasons of state.

The adaptation in the right-wing authoritarian-nationalist camp is accelerated by the issue of war, with Le Pen in France and Meloni in Italy eventually coming to back NATO support for Ukraine in its war – in contrast to the AfD. The Israeli war on Gaza has also enabled the far right's further integration into the governance structures of the west. Here, the strategic importance of anti-Muslim racism, which is the driving force of the far right in Europe, also makes it possible for the far right to refer positively to so-called 'Judeo-Christian civilization'. For the AfD, the only path to power is its 'Meloni-ization'.

Furthermore, in the context of new bloc confrontations between the western states and others, especially between the US and China, there is a partial renationalization of capitalism taking place, notably around green technologies, the most advanced computer chips and electric vehicles.[41] With the renationalization of capital, however, central concepts and practices of the extreme right of the late 19th and early 20th century are also experiencing a resurgence. This begins with European 'de-risking' through a revival of protectionist politics (and rightly seen by Chinese elites as an American attempt to de-couple Europe from China). It also entails a merging of state and economic power, not least in the new symbiosis of armaments and industrial policy in Europe to re-establish corporate 'national champions'.[42] This is a political terrain on which the authoritarian nationalism of the AfD could comfortably find a place, demanding competitiveness and productive capacities for the good of 'the people and the nation'.

SOCIALIST WEAKNESS, FAR RIGHT STRENGTH

The liberal centre is stuck in a dilemma. States are tasked with developing sustainable exit strategies to manage capitalism's crises and contradictions. But both the instabilities of capitalism and political interventions themselves can lead to an erosion of hegemony which might be filled by new – including populist – political forces. The crisis of liberal centrism entails a fundamental and inevitable contradiction faced by states as to the political management of economic and social instabilities. States are far from 'ideal collective capitalists' in resolving political divisions over economic policy, as both Nicos Poulantzas and Jürgen Habermas argued from different theoretical approaches. Paradoxically, periods of social instability and crisis tend to cause political party systems to fragment and fray in precisely those historic situations in which a political solution to the contradictions dominating the political scene requires a politically unified bourgeoisie coordinating with the power and financial resources of the state.[43] As a result, liberal-parliamentary systems are just as likely to produce tendencies of dysfunctionality in such conjunctures. The erosion of the centrist 'catch-all parties' increases the fragmentation of party systems, with the result that these parties transform their organizational apparatuses into a logic of self-preservation focused on short-term tactics to maintain their own power.

Populist discourses emerge in such conjunctures as political parties are less and less able to develop political visions and exit strategies that sustain their respective constituencies, let alone society as a whole. This increases the alienation of the population from the political class and its parties, who begin to appear in late neoliberalism as a separate caste that is out of touch with the population. The crisis of representation and liberal democracy thereby intensifies, and visions of a better tomorrow shift to the promises from billionaires, venture capitalists and Silicon Valley of wild market utopias featuring space colonization, transhumanism, cryptocurrencies, and the like. Societal and political approaches to addressing public issues, as well as liberal parliamentarism in general, is devalued.[44] Nobody can expect anything from the state anymore that improves daily life, only harassments such as having to wear a mask in public during a pandemic or the promise of state sovereignty over borders or punitive tariffs. The loss of a public centre of gravity, moreover, reinforces the spread of individual coping strategies alongside demands for authoritarian nationalisms not trapped by conventional and corrupt liberal democratic politics.

In such a confluence of contradictions and specific crises, the hegemonic appeal of the liberal centre erodes, but so too does belief in the common good and redistributional agendas that have always been the sources of energy and organization for socialist and left-wing movements. Fear of downward mobility, cynicism and pervasive pessimism with regards to the future have historically been the 'social raw material' of fascism.[45]

As Poulantzas argued in his critique of Marx's theory of Bonapartism and the Comintern's understanding of fascism, fascist movements experience their rise in historical situations in which social conditions are in such a state of disarray and crisis that they have become intolerable and therefore politically unsustainable for broad sections of the population. While at the same time, egalitarian and inclusive ways out of the crises favoured by socialist movements are marginal or seem unrealistic for broad sections of the working class.[46]

In these historical situations, with the pervasive feeling that there are no longer enough resources to save everyone, ideological mechanisms of drawing boundaries of exclusion take effect.[47] Such lines of demarcation between the 'deserving' and the 'undeserving' are drawn outwards in terms of race and downwards in terms of class. Unlike in the late 19th and early 20th century, the grievances of the working classes are no longer addressed through non-state institutions of immediate proletarian solidarity but rather mediated through the nation state, which individualizes the working class as individual citizens with codified vested rights. When there is apparently not enough for inclusive egalitarianism, 'privileges of the established'[48] emerge as the ideological basis for defending one's own status against other social groups. These other groups have historically been granted fewer rights because they are either latecomers without comparable citizenship rights or because they are regarded as less valuable in the sense of a 'producerist ideology' as they have not submitted themselves, either adequately or at all, to the merciless rules of the market.[49] In this sense, right-wing extremism is a pseudo-revolt, because ironically its subjects call on the state to protect them for having conformed to the symbolic values of capitalist society. The fascist promise is that there can still be enough for all the 'deserving' market subjects if only ruthless action without 'naïve left-wing humanist sentimentality' is taken against the 'hungry mouths' from the outside (Greece, Syria, Ukraine, etc.) and within (the unemployed, the lazy, the 'nonconformists'). In these times of perceived scarcity, the left, which assumes the natural equality of people, loses out to the political right, which has historically always justified existing forms of inequality and unequal treatment through various legitimizing assumptions of unchangeable biological or cultural inequality.[50] Meanwhile, the far right thrives on the notion that through anti-discrimination policies and the like, the left seeks to protect certain preferred minorities or disadvantaged social groups from the mercilessness of the market to which everyone else has to conform. If those minorities or social groups are also the ones that used to be considered inferior, either 'racially', sexually or socially (workers, especially unemployed workers), or used to be 'illegal' and against 'traditional values' (such as gay and trans people), then the far right can orchestrate a backlash on behalf of those who purportedly are the expression of 'the people' or a 'silent majority'. '*Deutschland, aber normal*', 'Germany, but normal' has been a key election slogan of the AfD.

There exists, then, in Germany and other states in Europe, a political correlation between the weakness of socialist and left-wing social forces located in inclusive and pluralist politics, and the organizational ascent of fascist and anti-pluralist forces. It is by no means a coincidence that the July 2015 financial strangulation of the Greek left-wing government of Syriza by the Troika (comprised of the European Union, European Central Bank and International Monetary Fund) and the heated politics of the 'refugee crisis' of August 2015 followed on from one another. The victory of the position of the CDU's Wolfgang Schäuble as German Finance Minister and key pivot point of the EU ruling class finalized the cross-Europe defeat of a solidary-inclusive exit strategy from the euro crisis and symbolized the death of all hopes for a new 'Social Europe'. The vacuum left behind by the left was then largely filled by right-wing authoritarian nationalism on the back of the racist mobilization against criminal refugees from the Arab world and North Africa, a continuous campaigning source for fascist rejuvenation in Germany and Europe. The weakness of the left forms a foundation for the strength of the right, as revealed in election results for the left and the extreme right in Europe ever since 2015.[51] The successes of the left around Bernie Sanders and Jeremy Corbyn ultimately remained a flash in the pan or were eclipsed by the victories of the right (Trump, Brexit). The success of the left-wing alliance NUPES in France in the summer of 2024 was also conceivable only in strategic collusion with the Macronist neoliberal centre, which then stabbed the left in the back, colluding with the extreme right.

Neoliberalism's polarization of societies through market forces nurtured political polarization.[52] The political polarization that has followed, however, has not formed in antagonisms over alternative economic policies, let alone public ownership, especially because neoliberalism depoliticized economic issues leading to market-compliant 'post-democracies'.[53] In a populist situation characterized by socialist weakness, political polarization therefore articulates itself through the 'superstructure' of the judicial system, education, culture, and so forth. Societal divisions form around 'pseudo-conflicts' over 'trigger points' such as, for example, 'gender-sensitive' language in public documents, 'veggie days' in school and workplace canteens, parking spaces for cars and bike lanes. Political energies are directed at these issues. And the sovereignty of the state which is lacking in the economic fundamentals of capitalism is shifted towards borders and against visible targets like asylum seekers and migrants.[54] Politics thus takes the form of a 'hyperpolitics' of new social and political cleavages with respect to social and cultural modernization.[55] The pervasiveness of such 'culture wars' further erodes the coherence of socialist movements. They are issue cleavages largely between fractions of the petty-bourgeois middle classes and segments of the working class with academic degrees often in 'white-collar' occupations. These splits within the broad working class make it increasingly difficult for socialist class politics to create new fronts of solidarity and class consciousness to confront the new fascism and revive viable anti-capitalist alternatives.

Strategies against the AfD today are caught between a revival of the popular front politics of the 1930s, and a rehabilitation of social fascism theory and practice that differentiates the left from other anti-fascist forces. In retrospect, the latter has been seen as responsible for the fact that the anti-fascist workers' movement did not succeed in preventing the victory of fascism from the 1920s through to the rise of Hitler to power. A policy that identifies the main enemy in the SPD, Greens and FDP is criticized against this background. Sahra Wagenknecht, for instance, caused outrage across many progressive quarters when she described the Greens as the 'currently most dangerous party in the German Bundestag' in a speech.[56]

But the resurgence of popular front politics also raises strategic questions. The anti-fascist mass demonstrations across Germany in the spring of 2024 were supported by many left-wing organizations. But when left-wing demonstrators marched side by side with Federal Chancellor Olaf Scholz and Foreign Minister Annalena Baerbock in Potsdam, for example, they gave the impression of an all-party coalition against the AfD. This added to the aura of the far-right party as system-oppositional.

The strategies of the social democratic and liberal centre are characterized by a 'helpless anti-fascism'[57] reliant on popular education practices of propaganda and repression. The policies of the liberal centre are now also providing the political terrain in which the social roots of fascism are taking hold. Anti-fascist fronts must, therefore, be carefully constructed. Local and regional alliances against the right, especially in eastern Germany, show opponents of the AfD – ordinary citizens, administrators, teachers, businesses – that they are not alone. At the national level, the problem remains that the vacuum of the left is being filled by the right. The lack of a forceful and visible egalitarian-inclusive exit strategy from the mounting contradictions of global capitalism is the space in which fascism continues to thrive. The development of a third socialist pole beyond both the neoliberal centre and right-wing authoritarian nationalism is therefore the real anti-fascism of action. The strategic challenge appears to be the conundrum that the success of such a socialist alternative presupposes the credibility of its message that there is enough for everyone even if the forces of socialism are currently unable to actually deliver egalitarian outcomes practically.

NOTES

1   Karin Priester, *Rechter und linker Populismus*, Frankfurt/New York: Campus, 2012, p. 16.
2   Ingar Solty, *Der postliberale Kapitalismus. Renationalisierung – Krise – Krieg*, Cologne: Papy Rossa, 2024.
3   Nicos Poulantzas, *State, Power, Socialism*, London: Verso, 1978.
4   Greg Albo, Sam Gindin and Leo Panitch, *In and Out of Crisis*, London: Merlin, 2010.
5   Bernd Röttger, *Neoliberale Globalisierung und eurokapitalistische Regulation*, Münster: Westfälisches Dampfboot, 1997; Patrick Ziltener, *Strukturwandel der europäischen Integration*, Münster: Westfälisches Dampfboot, 1999; Ingo Stützle, *Austerität als politisches Projekt*, Münster: Westfälisches Dampfboot, 2013.
6   Ellen Meiksins Wood, *Empire of Capital*, London/New York: Verso, 2005.
7   Mike Davis, *Planet of Slums*, London/New York: Verso, 2006.
8   Ingar Solty, 'Is the Global Crisis Ending the Marriage of Capitalism and Liberal Democracy?', in Maximilian Lakitsch, ed., *Political Power Reconsidered*, Zürich et al.: LIT, 2014, pp. 161-204.
9   John Holloway, *Change the World Without Taking Power*, London: Pluto, 2002.
10   Trump thus contradicted the 'Duverger Law', according to which politicians in America's first-past-the-post electoral systems who are too far to the left or the right may enthuse their base during primary elections but, like Barry Goldwater in 1964 or George McGovern in 1972, must surely lose national elections because they are too radical for the centre, allegedly where elections are decided. See: Maurice Duverger, *Party Politics and Pressure*, New York: Crowell, 1972.
11   Ingar Solty, 'German De-Unification. Gerhard Schröder, Angela Merkel and the Liberal Roots of German Neofascism', *Monthly Review*, 72(6), 2020, pp. 44-60.
12   Robert Vehrkamp and Silke Borgstedt, *Die Mitte stärken*, Berlin: Bertelsmann-Stiftung, 2024.
13   This is the original title in German of Oliver Nachtwey, *Germany's Hidden Crisis*, London: Verso, 2018.
14   Klaus Dörre, 'Functional Changes in the Trade Unions. From Intermediary to Fractal Organization?', *International Journal of Action Research*, 7(1), 2011, pp. 8-48.
15   Klaus Dörre and Tatjana Fuchs, 'Prekarität und soziale Desintegration', *Z. Zeitschrift Marxistische Erneuerung*, 16(3), 2005, pp. 20-35.
16   Solty, *Der postliberale Kapitalismus*.
17   Sebastian Franke, '30 Prozent der Deutschen ohne jegliche Ersparnisse', *ING Economic and Financial Analysis*, 7 December 2022.
18   Sparkassen- und Giroverbände, *S-Mittelstand-Fitnessindex*, Berlin, 13 September 2022.
19   Thorsten Schulten, *Tarifpolitischer Jahresbericht 2023*, WSI-Tarifarchiv der Hans-Böckler-Stiftung, February 2024.
20   Sam Gindin, 'The Crisis in American Labor. Interview by Chris Maisano', *Jacobin*, 8 February 2013.
21   Quoted in Birgit Marschall, 'Der Preis, den Deutschland bezahlen muss', *Rheinische Post*, 27 April 2022.
22   Sandra Saatmann, 'Friedrich Merz: "Höhepunkt des Wohlstandes liegt vorerst wohl hinter uns"', *WELT*, 11 April 2022.

23   Stephen Gill, 'The Emerging World Order and European Change: The Political Economy of European Union', in Ralph Miliband and Leo Panitch, eds., *The New World Order: The Socialist Register 1992*, London: Merlin Press, 1992, pp. 157-96.

24   Magnus Ryner, 'Europe's Ordoliberal Iron Cage: Critical Political Economy, the Euro Area Crisis and Its Management', *Journal of European Public Policy*, 22(2), 2015, pp. 275-94.

25   Christian Teevs, 'Ampel verliert besonders bei Menschen mit gerinerem Einkommen', *Der SPIEGEL*, 11 April 2024.

26   Ingar Solty, 'The Historic Significance of the New German Left Party', *Socialism and Democracy*, 22(1), 2008, pp. 1-34.

27   Sahra Wagenknecht, *Die Selbstgerechten*, Frankfurt: Campus, 2021.

28   Ingar Solty and Sebastian Friedrich, 'Sahra Wagenknecht's Party Is Here to Stay', *Jacobin*, 20 September 2024.

29   All data from Infratest dimap exit polls, available at: www.tagesschau.de.

30   Klaus Dörre, 'Umkämpfte Globalisierung und soziale Klassen: 20 Thesen für eine demokratische Klassenpolitik', in Mario Candeias, Klaus Dörre and Thomas E. Goes, *Demobilisierte Klassengesellschaft und Potenziale verbindender Klassenpolitik*, Berlin: Rosa-Luxemburg-Stiftung Materialien 23, 2019, pp. 11-56.

31   Accordingly, as exit polls showed in both the 2024 European elections and the state elections in Thuringia and Saxony, the AfD still receives roughly half of its support in elections from people who do not vote for it out of conviction and a more or less coherent right-wing extremist worldview, but out of disappointment with the other parties.

32   Sebastian Friedrich, *Die AfD. Analysen – Hintergründe – Kontroversen*, Berlin: bertz+fischer, 2019, pp. 133-44.

33   David Horowitz, *Radical Son: A Generational Odyssey*, New York: Touchstone, 1998, p. 392.

34   John R. Petrocik, 'Issue Ownership in Presidential Elections, with a 1980 Case Study', *American Journal of Political Science* 40(3), 1996, pp. 825-80.

35   Thomas Frank, *One Market Under God*, New York: Anchor, 2000.

36   Günter Verheugen and Petra Erler, *Der lange Weg zum Krieg: Russland, die Ukraine und der Westen – Eskalation statt Entspannung*, München: Heyne, 2024.

37   Nick Alipour, 'Jens Spahn: Die Brandmauer in Europa verläuft rechts von Meloni', *Euractiv*, 21 May 2024.

38   Leo Panitch and Sam Gindin, *The Making of Global Capitalism. The Political Economy of the American Empire*, London/New York: Verso, 2012.

39   Robert W. Cox, *Production, Power and World Order: Social Forces in the Making of History*, New York: Columbia, 1987.

40   Ingar Solty, 'What Do "Unruly" Right-Wing Authoritarian Nationalists Do When They Rule', in Michelle Williams and Vishwas Satgar, eds., *Destroying Democracy*, Johannesburg: Wits University Press, 2021, pp. 71-96.

41   Ingar Solty, *Die neue Blockkonfrontation. Hochtechnologie – (De-)Globalisierung – Geopolitik*, Munich: isw-Report, 2023.

42   Judith Dellheim, Claude Serfati and Ingar Solty, *Sicherheitspolitik contra Sicherheit: Zur Symbiose von Rüstung und Industrie in der Europäischen Union*, Berlin: Rosa-Luxemburg-Stiftung Manuskripte Neue Folge 24, 2020.

43   Nicos Poulantzas, *State, Power, Socialism*, London/New York: Verso Classics, 2000, p. 113.

44   Thomas Wagner, *Robokratie*, Cologne: Papy Rossa, 2015.

45   Oskar Negt, 'Trabanten des Kapitals: Angstrohstoff – der jüngste Angriff auf die Lebenszeit', *Der Freitag*, 14 May 2004.

46   Nicos Poulantzas, *Fascism and Dictatorship*, London: New Left Books, 1974.

47   Beverly J. Silver, *Forces of Labor*. Cambridge: Cambridge University Press, 2003.

48   Wilhelm Heitmeyer, *Deutsche Zustände Vol. 10*, Frankfurt: Suhrkamp, 2010.

49   Chip Berlet and Matthew N. Lyons, *Right-Wing Populism in America: Too Close for Comfort*, New York: Guilford Press, 2000.

50   Ingar Solty, 'links/rechts', in Wolfgang Fritz Haug et al., eds., *Historisch-kritisches Wörterbuch des Marxismus*, Vol. 8/II, Hamburg: Argument, 2015, pp. 1153-68.

51   Cornelia Hildebrandt, 'After the Defeat: New Challenges for the Radical Left After the European Elections', *Transform Network Blog*, 6 July 2019, available at: www. transform-network.net.

52   Ingar Solty, 'Market Polarization Means Political Polarization: Liberal Democracy's Eroding Centre', in Leo Panitch and Greg Albo, eds, *New Polarizations, Old Contradictions: The Socialist Register 2022*, New York: Merlin Press, 2022, pp. 53-72.

53   Colin Crouch, *Post-Democracy*, Cambridge: Polity Press, 2004.

54   Steffen Mau, Thomas Lux and Linus Westheuser, *Triggerpunkte. Konsens und Konflikt in der Gegenwartsgesellschaft*, Berlin: Suhrkamp, 2023.

55   Anton Jäger, *Hyperpolitik. Extreme Politisierung ohne politische Folgen*, Berlin: Suhrkamp, 2023.

56   Georg Ismar, 'Wagenknecht greift Grüne an – und liebäugelt mit Parteigründung', *Die Welt*, 21 October 2022.

57   Wolfgang Fritz Haug, *Der hilflose Antifaschismus*, Frankfurt: Suhrkamp, 1967.

RADICAL REMUNICIPALIZATIONS: REMAKING AND RECLAIMING PUBLIC SERVICES

DAVID A. MCDONALD

Debates about privatization have raged in academic journals for decades, largely polarized into two camps: for and against. There is, however, a newer and more refreshing conversation on the block that challenges this stale dichotomy – remunicipalization. Also known as 'reverse privatization' or 'insourcing', remunicipalization refers to processes of returning services back to public ownership and management after a period of private sector control.

More than 1,600 cases of remunicipalization in over 70 countries have been documented in services such as water, electricity, health care, transportation and waste management.[1] It can happen at various scales, for diverse reasons, and often involves a complex web of state institutions and non-governmental actors, representing one of the most intriguing shifts in public policy and grassroots activism of the last 20 years.[2]

Paradoxically, remunicipalization can be simultaneously expansive and narrow in scope. Expansive because many municipal services are immensely important to our social, economic, cultural and ecological welfare. While it may be a cliché, water is indeed 'life', and alongside other basic services such as electricity and transportation they are of vital importance to humanity. Having essential services such as these owned, socialized and operated publicly rather than privately can make an enormous difference to people's lives.

Remunicipalization is also expansive in the sense that it can be linked to larger political projects. As the literature on 'new municipalism' demonstrates, political activism at the local level has been re-animated in the past few decades, partly in response to the downloading phenomena of the neoliberal era and partly because municipal is the level of government that people can most readily engage in[3] (although it is not an entirely 'new' phenomenon of course[4]). Bringing services back into public hands can be part of these municipal struggles and is sometimes a catalyst for broader political action.

Remunicipalization thus represents an important opportunity for progressive change: an opening of new political and economic terrain for socialist strategy and struggle (as per the theme of this issue of SR). Emerging 'out of the everyday but diverse local politics of social reproduction and a faltering neoliberalism', remunicipalization projects 'have much to offer a transformative and democratic left project',[5] creating opportunities for progressive socialist politics in ways that can address the multiple crises of climate, health and access to essential services.

But remunicipalizations can be remarkably narrow in scope as well. This is because most remunicipalization projects involve a single service in a single municipality, sometimes with very limited objectives (such as saving money). As Cumbers and Paul[6] are equally quick to note, 'there is nothing inherently progressive about remunicipalization'. It represents a 'systemic pushback against privatisation, but also an uncertain conjunctural political moment where many pathways are possible'. Some remunicipalizations are merely pragmatic and can swing back to the private sector at any time. Some are arguably worse than privatization, with control of essential services handed over to crony state capitalists and authoritarians, or in ways that conceal the commodifying effects of neoliberal state management. Even relatively progressive forms of remunicipalization can lull us into thinking they are more transformative than they really are. These potential 'closures' are just as important to identify as the 'openings' that remunicipalization offers, forcing us to carefully assess the potentials for moving towards more equitable and democratic forms of public services.

This essay provides an overview of this variegated terrain of remunicipalization while also attempting to advance debates on what radical/socialist forms of remunicipalization could look like, beginning with a brief historical review of remunicipalization in the *longue durée*, comparing contemporary efforts to (re)claim public services with similar struggles over a century ago.

BACK TO THE FUTURE?

The rapid industrialization of European and North American cities in the early 1800s was accompanied by a dramatic growth of networked services, provided almost universally by the private sector. Small and large firms sprung up to provide water, gas, transportation, waste management, health care and electricity services for growing productive and consumptive needs.[7] Where economies of scale and capital intensity mattered, there tended to be large players – with some of the most important private utility companies in operation today owing their existence to this period, such as Suez, United Water and General Electric.[8] More localized services such as waste removal and healthcare were typically managed by small, sometimes informal, private providers, although consolidations quickly became the norm.

This laissez-faire approach to service development began to change in the mid to late 1800s with a push to municipalize facilities, whereby local state authorities took ownership and control of private services. This trend spread throughout Europe and North America and carried into the 1940s.[9] The overarching rationale for municipalization was that service provision by multiple providers was illogical and wasteful, particularly with natural monopolies such as water, gas and electricity, where it made little economic or regulatory sense to have multiple infrastructures. Outbreaks of cholera and other public health concerns added to the pressure. The British Parliament passed a series of public health measures, the first in 1848, mandating local authorities to take action, after which the municipalization movement in that country came to encompass an extraordinary range of public services, including slaughterhouses, cemeteries, crematoria, libraries, refuse and sewage disposal services, and even a sterilized milk depot.[10]

This enthusiasm for state ownership nevertheless hid competing and often antagonistic ideological motivations for municipal takeover. On the left, some advocates of 'municipal socialism' advanced a strong anti-capitalist sentiment, ridiculing the 'robber barons' of the day and tapping into a 'widespread anti-monopoly sentiment' that 'flowed easily into calls for public production and distribution of basic goods and service'.[11] But just how socialist this movement was remains disputed. Many critics saw these initiatives as far too compromised to create fundamental social and economic change, with no less a detractor than Vladimir Lenin declaring the municipalization trend to be incapable of bringing about larger socialist transformation.[12] These revolutionary critics disdained the gradualist municipal politics of the Fabians, rejecting the parliamentary road to socialism that they said these utility enterprises represented.

To the right were reform movement liberals who argued for municipalization on efficiency grounds, in part to combat the municipal socialism movement. John Stuart Mill, for example, took up the cause of water reform in Britain, criticizing what he saw as the wastefulness of fragmented private supply.[13] Similar arguments were made in the United States, where the commitment to municipal services was more a response to the corruption and ineffectiveness of private companies than any ideological strategy.[14] These pro-capitalist municipalizers were exemplified by the '*goo goos*' (short for 'good government') of Chicago in the early 1900s, whose chief interest was to introduce 'business-like efficiency into city government'.[15]

This marketized form of municipalization was as much an attempt to promote private capital accumulation as it was to challenge it, with many policy makers seeing rationalized forms of public ownership of services as an effective way to enhance overall market growth. As MacKillop notes in the case of early water infrastructure in Los Angeles, 'public investments furthered private interests on a grand scale', as land developers pushed for public service extension to open new frontiers of accumulation.[16]

From the 1930s onwards, and escalating rapidly in the 1940s, there was a winding down of the municipalization movement and a scaling up of publicly owned services to the national and regional levels.[17] Much of this consolidation took place in sectors where new technologies and modes of governance made large, networked services possible, such as with electricity and health care, while water stayed mostly at the municipal level due to transportation costs.

Meanwhile, non-essential services such as municipal cinemas and restaurants disappeared altogether, often vilified for stifling entrepreneurship, leaving the field open to private enterprise. In effect, the emergence of *national* Fordist states took the wind out of *municipal* public service sails, advancing capital accumulation on increasingly national and global scales while squashing the potential for more radical redistributive initiatives locally.

By the 1970s, the pendulum had swung back towards private sector participation. This shift is well documented, but it is useful to highlight two important ways in which the current neoliberal moment differs from that of the liberal era that originally ushered in private services in the 1800s. Despite having been 'hollowed out' from four decades of austerity[18] neoliberal governments today are far more robust than their laissez faire cousins a century ago, with the potential to develop and maintain networked services in ways that were technically and politically inconceivable in the early 1900s, including a new range of governance technologies (such as smart meters) and a broader set of financial and informational resources to draw on. Further, the public sector itself has been fundamentally transformed by neoliberal practice and ideology, with many public agencies being run like private businesses, employing market-based management techniques, salary structures and performance evaluations.[19] As such, the breadth of what constitutes a 'public' service has been considerably expanded over the past century.[20]

CONTEMPORARY REMUNICIPALIZATION

By the late 1990s it was becoming clear that this second wave of privatization had not lived up to its promises of cheaper and more transparent service delivery. As long-term contracts came to an end, many were either not renewed or cancelled prematurely. Dozens of such remunicipalization cases were documented in the early 2000s, with the number then increasing dramatically after 2010. This was the year that Paris' water services were remunicipalized, which received considerable public and academic attention.[21]

It is impossible to know with certainty how many services have been remunicipalized in the past two decades, in part because many examples are small and likely to go unreported (e.g. bringing snowplowing back in-house). Furthermore, there is a lack of resources available to systematically track all forms of remunicipalization. The most notable efforts have come from a team of academics at the University of Glasgow in collaboration with the Transnational Institute and Public Services International (as part of the GLOBALMUN project)[22] who have identified more than 1,600 cases (as mentioned above) while continuing to update their database.[23]

Importantly, contemporary remunicipalization is a truly global phenomenon, with cases from Ghana, Kazakhstan, Turkey, Hungary, Argentina, Guinea, Tanzania, Malaysia, Bolivia and beyond. It is also multi-sectoral, with remunicipalizations taking place in water, health care, transportation and wide range of other services. It should also be noted, however, that the bulk of documented examples are concentrated in handful of countries (notably Germany, France and the United States) and sectors (notably water and electricity), limiting our understanding of other sectors and regions,[24] highlighting the need for further research.[25]

As impressive as this is, it should not be forgotten that privatization persists. Basic forms of divestiture and public-private partnerships of various stripes continue to take place – notably in so-called 'emerging' economies.[26] At the same time, new forms of private sector influence and marketization of the public sector have become more pronounced – notably via financialization.[27] Reliable data on these trends is also limited – the World Bank no longer systematically tracks privatization – but the scope and scale of privatization has arguably increased in some regions and sectors, making it important to continue monitoring these trends.

As to why remunicipalization is happening, every case is unique but there are common threads that emerge among them, typically involving the failure of a privatization project due to one or more of the following issues: rising prices, growing inequalities, worsening service quality, lack of investment in infrastructure, lack of transparency in decision making, high costs of regulation, increasing levels of corruption, and exorbitant profit-taking.[28]

Not all cases of remunicipalization are due to private sector failure, however. In some instances, remunicipalization is done out of necessity, either because private companies have decided not to renew their contracts or because there are an insufficient number of bidders on a privatization tender. In some of these cases governments have been caught off-guard, unprepared for re-starting what can be a massive financial and administrative undertaking, highlighting the importance of being alert to the possibility of remunicipalization to avoid rushed decisions on major infrastructural matters (such as the cases of Hamilton, in Canada, and Buenos Aires, Argentina, where policy makers and activists alike had to scramble to work out new public water and sanitation systems).[29] Even governments in favour of privatization can find themselves in this position, particularly in low-income countries and sectors such as water and sanitation where financial risks have deterred private companies from taking contracts.[30]

DIFFERENT TYPES OF REMUNICIPALIZATION

The types of remunicipalization that have emerged are equally varied. Although it is impossible to say what percent of remunicipalizations fall into which categories, due to informational gaps, there is sufficient evidence to identify distinct typologies. Debates remain about the complex ideological nature of these different remunicipalization forms, but there is growing agreement as to their general characteristics.[31]

The first type of remunicipalization receives relatively little attention but is important to highlight. Categorized as *autocratic state capitalism*, these types of remunicipalization are characterized by reversals of privatization undertaken by relatively undemocratic, market-oriented governments as part of a more general shift towards state control of strategic sectors and enterprises in capitalist economies. In these cases, remunicipalization is driven as much by political and social objectives as economic ones, ranging from attempts to enhance national sovereignty to regulating and disciplining citizen behaviour. This form of remunicipalization is not necessarily anti-capitalist in its orientation. Rather, it can be seen as a strategic reversal of privatization, under certain conditions, with the aim of achieving targeted social goals while expanding market-like operational characteristics, such as full cost recovery and financially driven performance indicators to enhance other market functions in the economy.

One example of such a remunicipalization is to be found in Malaysia's water sector.[32] After a period of privatization, constitutional amendments were made in 2006 which allowed the federal government to seize all assets previously owned by local water operators whether public or private. The intent was to fast-track public investment where the private sector had failed to do so, while at the same time regaining control over a critical resource for regional development planning. The liberalization of water management and distribution was seen to have eroded the ability of Malaysia's de facto one-party state to engage in pro-Malay (*Bumiputera*) development policies for the country's ethnic Malay majority.[33] Hungary provides another example, with the conservative nationalist government of Viktor Orbán introducing a top-down form of remunicipalization in 2010. This move was designed to reverse the post-Soviet privatization binge of the 1990s, based on the argument that private service providers were overcharging citizens.[34] The Hungarian economy as a whole remains largely market oriented but remunicipalized public services have become 'extremely centralised' for the 'national interest'.[35]

There are other examples of autocratic forms of remunicipalization which may offer additional insights, as in Almaty (Kazakhstan), Antalya (Turkey), Bamako (Mali), and Conakry (Guinea).[36] The growth of state capitalisms in general, and the potential for privatization reversals in China in particular, may see these figures rise.[37] A lack of empirical data precludes deeper analysis.

A second category of remunicipalization is *market managerialism*, intentionally aimed at promoting markets and advancing capital accumulation. But in these cases the rationale for putting services back into state hands is more narrowly economistic, intended largely to enhance the efficiency of service provision. Grounded in a neo-Keynesian reading of context-specific market failures – insufficient competition, lack of regulatory capacity on the part of the state – private-sector service delivery is seen to be less efficacious than state delivery and thus a drag on the economy.[38] In these cases, remunicipalization is seen as a necessary, if temporary, measure to reduce operating costs and ensure sufficient investment in services to expand local production and consumption.

As with the arguments of the *'goo goos'* of a century ago, a specific type of government is required to provide these remunicipalized services. The objective here is an entrepreneurial state: one with cost recovery, internal competition and marketized forms of managerial incentives guiding their operation. These forms of remunicipalization can be seen as part of a broader shift towards 'new public management' (and its more recent iterations),[39] resulting in a 'broadening and blurring of the "frontier" between the public and private sectors', combined with a 'shift in value priorities away from universalism, equity, security and resilience towards efficiency and individualism'.[40] Remunicipalized water services driven by this logic can be characterized as quasi-commercial entities, focusing on market-based performance indicators, a 'preference for more specialized, "lean", "flat" and autonomous organizational forms', and a 'widespread substitution of contract or contract-like relationships for hierarchical relationships'.[41] They may be public in name, but these marketized forms of remunicipalization can serve to deepen, not weaken, the commercialization of public services.[42]

Concerns with marketized forms of remunicipalization are exacerbated by the almost ubiquitous growth of corporatization over the past three decades, notably water and electricity utilities that are owned and operated by the state but function at arm's length from government with separate legal status and ringfenced finances.[43] Not all corporatized water services are commercial in their orientation, but ringfencing does make it easier (even necessary) to focus on the financial bottom line, with utility managers frequently remunerated or incentivized according to the surplus/deficit of their 'business unit'.[44] In some cases, these public water providers are even more commercial than their private counterparts, aggressively pursuing 'surplus' to satisfy their new operational mandates. Critics see this as the proverbial wolf in sheep's clothing, offering a façade of public ownership while propagating market ideology.[45]

An example of such a remunicipalization is that of Dar es Salaam in Tanzania. After a brief and disastrous experience with a private concession in the water sector in 2003, the World Bank reversed its policy recommendations to the Tanzanian government, promoting instead the creation of a new public water operator in 2005.[46] The Dar es Salaam Water and Sewerage Corporation has since managed to extend coverage and improve some aspects of service delivery – 'proving that public water services can be managed well by the state, and can outperform the private sector in many ways'.[47] But the newly corporatized entity has become much more market-oriented than before, enforcing cost recovery on the poor and 'failing to meet its obligations in the lowest income areas of the city'.

The largest number of market-oriented remunicipalizations have been in the United States, in the very 'heartland of capitalism'.[48] Many of these remunicipalizations are driven by fiscally conscious municipal managers who decide to bring services back in-house simply because it is cheaper to do so by removing the costs of monitoring and tendering as well as eliminating profit-taking by private firms. The corollary to this is that decisions to outsource are equally pragmatic, resulting in pendulum-like swings between public and private service operations depending on which option is cheaper.

Politics plays a part in these remunicipalizations but ideological opposition to privatization is not a primary driver. As Warner and Aldag note: 'We do not find support for remunicipalization [in the United States] as a political project'; it is 'a pragmatic market management project'.[49] Similar types of remunicipalization can be found in Europe.[50]

A third type of remunicipalization can be broadly defined as *social democratic*. These are the most celebrated forms of remunicipalization on the part of NGOs and labour unions and are common in Western Europe and Latin America.[51] In these cases, remunicipalization is seen as an opportunity to challenge the hyper-commodification of privately-run services while promoting public values that go beyond notions of individualized marginal pricing. There is also a push for better horizontal integration of public services and the promotion of public solidarity within and across sectors – including cross-subsidizations – in contradistinction to the ringfencing associated with commercialized forms of public service delivery. These demands are also typically accompanied by calls for new forms of social engagement in public services that promote meaningful citizen participation.

In other words, the social democratic position does not see the push for remunicipalization as a return to a pre-privatization status quo, but rather as an opportunity to upend the bureaucratized, top-down and inequitable forms of public services common in the Keynesian era. Such a shift in governance requires a broad coalition of state and non-governmental actors to enact change (although they remain state-driven), and also comes with further demands for more environmentally sustainable forms of public service provisioning.

The remunicipalization of water services in Paris is the archetype for this perspective, with the introduction of social tariffs aimed at making water services more affordable for low-income households, the promotion of upstream water management with farmers to reduce runoffs into the water supply, and the creation of a 'water observatory' that brings together users, elected officials, researchers and academics in decision making. The Paris plans also came with solidarity programmes for other public water operators in France and elsewhere to promote and improve public water services internationally.[52] Terrassa, Spain, has seen similar initiatives with its remunicipalized water operator.[53]

But as positive as these changes have been, it cannot be forgotten that these social democratic forms of remunicipalization are not explicitly anti-market in their objectives and continue to operate within a broader capitalist framework. Calls for decommodification, for example, require scrutiny. Social democratic service operators can make significant improvements to equity but they cannot reverse or escape the influence of the commodification process writ large.[54] As a provider of a single service in a single city, a remunicipalized service operator is as much a product of the broader dynamics of commodification as any other public or private company. It can choose to price services in ways that are aimed at meeting social needs, but its overall operations will still be shaped by the exchange values of human and capital resources in a capitalist market economy, with local businesses demanding rates that are competitive with other municipalities.

In other words, the best a social democratic service operator can do is work around the margins of the market. It cannot alter its fundamental mechanisms and should be frank with itself (and its users) about the limits this political orientation places on its ability to change the ways that a local service is shaped by larger global economic forces, particularly when it comes to financing ambitious social, political and environmental objectives.

There are also remunicipalization movements and organizations that are driven by explicitly *anti-capitalist* sentiments. These groups share many of the same goals as their social democratic counterparts – such as improved services and enhanced democratic control – but reject the possibility of a reconciliation between social justice and capitalism, pointing to the many ways in which market economies colonize our broader lifeworlds.[55]

These anti-capitalist voices are not uncommon in remunicipalization movements, but they are seldom in the ascendency, with anti-capitalist protagonists having yet to realize an actual remunicipalization victory in the 21st century. This lack of success is not surprising in a world of neoliberal hegemony, but it is exacerbated by the fact that anti-capitalist voices also tend to be highly fragmented, struggling to find a unified vision of what a 'socialist' service should look like, driven as much by a rejection of old-style communist command economies as they are by opposition to market provisioning of public goods and needs. A growing commitment to grassroots voices, transparent decision making and smaller-scale infrastructure development provides some cohesiveness to this grouping. But as with anti-capitalist political movements more broadly, there is as much that pulls them apart as binds them together when it comes to (re)building public services.

Just how widespread these anti-capitalist positions are when it comes to remunicipalization debates is difficult to say given the dearth of detailed case study evidence. Nevertheless, anti-market voices are particularly evident in European and Latin American remunicipalization movements, with networks such as the European Water Movement and Red Vida encompassing a wide range of radical positions (including that of the next category, autonomism). Former Soviet bloc countries have also witnessed remunicipalization efforts from new and old socialist voices,[56] and the anti-capitalist academic literature on 'public' services in general continues to grow.[57]

Finally, there are *autonomist* advocates of remunicipalization that are leery of both capitalist and socialist forms of change. There are overlaps here with the other categories (such as demands for equity and environmental sustainability), but this grouping distinguishes itself through its emphasis on community-driven service solutions grounded in a local socio-ecological context with little or no direct state involvement. Water is arguably the most common sector for these voices to be heard, in part because of traditional and artisanal community-led delivery systems, but arguments for autonomy can be found in energy, health and education as well.[58]

Technically these are not remunicipalization movements, per se, because they are generally opposed to centralized and bureaucratized forms of state delivery (regardless of its ideological orientation). But given their commitment to reclaiming and rebuilding publicly controlled and publicly managed forms of services, and the increasing trends towards the co-production of services by state and community organizations, they are an important component of the remunicipalization debate.[59]

Significantly, there are no actual cases of autonomous remunicipalization, although there are many long-standing examples of community-run systems which have never been privatized or municipalized and which are fiercely defended as such.[60] But autonomist voices are present in a variety of remunicipalization movements, fighting to end privatization and re-claim community control. Typically, these groups and individuals work in coalition with other progressive organizations, but as with anti-capitalist remunicipalization voices are seldom the dominant force.

Autonomist voices are most prevalent in remunicipalization networks in Latin America and Europe, where notions of a 'commons' and 'citizen control' are widespread.[61] But reclaiming and rebuilding autonomous service provision has proven difficult in practice, made harder by the highly centralized and institutionalized realities of most contemporary service systems. The very nature of modern networked systems cuts against the horizontal and localized aspirations of autonomous provision, making these goals perhaps the hardest of all to realize in a state-driven world of public services.

A SOCIALIST REMUNICIPALIZATION?

What, then, might a socialist form of remunicipalization look like? The question is a loaded one, given long-standing and intensely contested notions of what socialism means. There are also the inherent limits of what can be done at the local level. Lenin was right,[62] of course, in highlighting the fact that it is not possible to have socialism in a single city, let alone a single service, and the same limitations apply to remunicipalization today.[63]

It is not my aim to provide a concrete definition of socialist remunicipalization here. The intent is to indicate the possibilities for remunicipalizations that are more explicitly anti-capitalist than the social democratic varieties outlined above, as well as being more democratic and alert to social diversities and ecological crises than were the socialist experiments of the 20th century. World order is also more complex in the intersections of markets, states and ecology than it was a century ago, with capital manifesting itself in ways that are both place-based and global, allowing for multiple points of engagement and resistance, alongside opportunities to develop alternative forms of social provisioning. A remunicipalized service can create substantive change and be part of a larger shift in political consciousness, acting as a wedge to open paths of transformation that challenge market mechanisms and disrupt flows of capital. Socialist remunicipalization is therefore as much the process of extending collective community control as it is the product of service provisioning.

The work of Cumbers and Paul[64] is useful here, arguing that we need to see remunicipalization as part of the conjunctural terrain of the larger contradictions and failures of neoliberalism. As such, remunicipalization is a 'dynamic' phenomenon set within a 'fluid set of political and social relations…which can lead to new configurations and political alliances'.[65] While it would be 'premature to proclaim a new post-neoliberal regime emerging' they argue that remunicipalization 'has the potential to challenge not only neoliberal governance processes but also deeper underlying organic features of capitalist social relations. This is because its emergence illuminates the central contradiction between profit/exchange value on the one hand and use value/basic social needs on the other'.[66]

In other words, socialist forms of remunicipalization cannot be prescribed in advance, will differ from place to place, and must go beyond the constrained social democratic goals that animate many of the progressive remunicipalization debates today. Social democratic reforms are important and necessary transitional demands but they are not an end goal. If stopped at the social democratic stage, these reforms remain entrapped in the contradictions and limits of a marketized public sphere.

In the medium term, socialist forms of remunicipalization must aim to reclaim 'greater democratic control over the production and utilization of surplus value', as per Harvey's arguments for reclaiming the 'right to the city'.[67] In the longer run the objective should be to move the production and distribution of public services beyond their principal role of facilitating private capital accumulation, while working towards a system of public service provision driven by non-commodified principles, aiming to fulfil use values instead of exchange values.[68]

These transformative changes will not happen overnight. Regardless of how quickly legal and institutional reforms can be put in place in a remunicipalized service, deep-seated functional practices and bureaucratic values are slow to adjust and require continual political effort and activism. The key to building more equitable, democratic and sustainable state-led public services in the medium term is balancing progressive administration with meaningful social engagement. Skilled public sector employees and frontline workers are essential to the reform of public services, but even the most well-intentioned professionals cannot create more egalitarian forms of public services on their own. Nor are social movements yet 'strong enough or sufficiently mobilized to force through this solution', not having 'converged on the singular aim of gaining greater control over the uses of the surplus – let alone over the conditions of its production'.[69] Creating transformative change with public services will require a combination of an effective and progressive state alongside a broad coalition of community, labour, NGO and other non-state actors prepared to demand non-marketized forms of public services 'if the dispossessed are to take back the control which they have for so long been denied'.[70]

There are, of course, cases where working with and within the state is not possible, either because the state is too autocratic or simply non-existent. In these instances, community-led services can and have proven to be an effective substitute to privatization. However, idealized notions of autonomous forms of public services in which all forms of state are rejected in favour of non-hierarchical self-organization can be deeply problematic.[71] Although the general principles of decentralization and local autonomy have been long part of socialist politics, it is essential to frame the energy and creativity of grassroots movements in relation to state structures in the (re)building of meaningful public services. Capturing and remaking states is a daunting task, but much of the anti-state commons literature 'evacuates completely any responsibility to think about how counter-hegemonic projects can contest the dominance of the state and the public realm by neoliberal forces'.[72] This can mean abandoning the most effective tool we have for addressing the social, economic and ecological crises associated with unequal public services. Radical remunicipalization, in other words, is inescapably a project that will be struggled for and disputed on the terrain of the state.

NEW OPENINGS FOR RADICAL REMUNICIPALIZATIONS

Advancing radical forms of remunicipalization will require action on multiple fronts. One is theoretical. An unfortunate outcome of the privatization debate has been the creation of a simplistic binary: private is bad, public is good. As we have seen with the realities of remunicipalization, public can come in many shapes and sizes, some of which are deeply problematic.

Indeed, the very notion of publicness is itself a creation of the market, with nineteenth century capitalists accepting – even demanding – a public sphere that would legitimate the emergence of private interests and yet also facilitate capital accumulation.[73] The limits of this liberal public sphere inherently constrain the potential of radical remunicipalization in a market economy. Recognizing these conceptual and spatial tensions will not resolve the problem, but it does force a theoretical reckoning with the very meaning of what constitutes a (local) public service and highlights the need to go beyond social democratic reforms to explore new practises of democracy and community control.

For activists and progressive policy makers this conceptual reframing requires new tactics and language, different from those employed to fight privatization. Being anti-privatization does not in itself constitute a pro-public vision. Political activism has been remarkably successful at identifying the problems of privatization and instigating remunicipalization, but it does little to help develop concrete alternatives beyond the notion that 'public is better'. Promoting radical forms of remunicipalization therefore requires a distinct set of pro-public arguments that engage with the complex and constantly shifting terrains of a global market economy as well as the equally complex notions of what constitutes 'public'. As Cumbers and Paul note: 'Too often, the left is busy fighting the last war, whilst the right and forces of capital, untroubled by ideological purity, reassemble.'[74]

Activists cannot assume that the same tactics and language of anti-privatization will translate easily to a pro-public movement. There must be a willingness to (strategically) criticize public services to make them better. This need not demonize front-line staff that do their best to provide services in a world of public sector austerity, but it is essential to call out racist, hierarchical or opaque practices and decision making as an essential step towards creating new types of public services that are not mere replicas of some supposed 'golden age' of welfarism. Criticizing public services runs the risk of feeding into a pro-private agenda, but transparent and open self-reflection is essential if we are to develop new discursive terrains.

Nor will the arguments for remunicipalization be as singular and universal as they have been in the fight against privatization. Criticisms of the latter have been consistent around the world and across sectors. Remunicipalization, by contrast, is about rebuilding entirely new systems, with different priorities in different places. Some communities may demand direct participation in decision making, for example, while others may be unconcerned with such engagement. As such, there are no easy slogans that can bring together advocates of remunicipalization in ways that have been possible in the fight against privatization.

Finding time, energy and resources for a parallel but separate struggle will also be a challenge. The unions, NGOs and community organizations that are at the forefront of the remunicipalization movements also tend to be the ones fighting privatization (and a myriad of other issues) making it difficult to stretch already overextended individuals and organizations.

Research has a role to play here as well. Progressive policy intellectuals have too frequently focused on positive examples of social democratic forms of remunicipalization and celebrated these as examples of why remunicipalization works (the current author included). More research is needed on how these efforts could be more transformative and reach beyond the service in question. We also need to better understand problematic forms of remunicipalization, including 'failed' attempts (instances where efforts to bring services back in house were unsuccessful, or where post-remunicipalization reforms have not produced what policy makers and activists had hoped for).[75] It is difficult to know how many such cases exist, but casting a wider net into new geographic and sectoral terrains could provide insights into impediments to remunicipalization, and new strategies and tactics for activist struggles that can help avoid these problems.

Detailed research and activism in sectors other than water and electricity is also required. Comprehensive and multifaceted assessments of remunicipalizations in health, transport, waste, housing and other essential services are needed to better understand their unique challenges, as well as the synergies they may have with other sectors to help build cross-sectoral modelling. Institutional, financial and cultural norms can differ dramatically from water to health care to waste management, with no guarantee of shared objectives or strategies. Gains in one area can also mean losses in another, requiring a deeper appreciation of how individual remunicipalizations can influence service delivery as a whole, including cross-border impacts between jurisdictions.

There should also be a thematic expansion of research. Studies to date have tended to focus on relatively generic assessments of the social, economic and political dynamics of remunicipalization: for example, are prices more affordable; is decision-making more participatory; and have services improved? There is a lack of research tackling questions and approaches to equitable provisioning that account for gender, indigeneity, and racialization.[76] For example, what role do women play in remunicipalization struggles? How are racialized communities impacted by the return of services to public hands? Are Indigenous voices being heard in the debates? Do working conditions improve for front-line workers? How these questions relate to efforts to create 'socialist' forms of remunicipalization is a critically important line of inquiry.

Research into energy democracy and local provisioning has demonstrated that well-intended public service reforms can have negative social, economic and cultural outcomes, making it important to disaggregate the benefits from remunicipalization even while insisting on universal access to services irrespective of class and identity.[77] Socialisms that have been blind to these racialized and gendered dynamics are far too common. Efforts to create radical forms of remunicipalization must not fall into the same trap. Working with local communities to build these research capacities and agendas is critical.

None of this is intended to diminish the remarkable accomplishments of the hundreds of struggles against privatization of local services and demands for remunicipalizations of the past 20 years. But it is necessary to highlight the complex institutional and ideological terrains of the state upon which remunicipalizations unfold, and to underscore the need to be alert to the inherent limits placed on all social and economic reforms in capitalist economies. No single act of remunicipalization is going to usher in a socialist era. However, paying attention to the practical and theoretical constraints of being 'public' in a market economy, while setting explicitly non-market goals, can help to advance more radical forms of remunicipalization and contribute to the development of political imaginaries aimed at meeting fundamental human needs.

NOTES

1   Dario Cibrario and Andrew Cumbers, 'Remunicipalisation: Breaking through as Public Policy', *PSI – the Global Union Federation of Workers in Public Services*, 31 October 2022, available at: www.publicservices.international.

2   Martin Pigeon et al., *Remunicipalisation: Putting water back into public hands*, Amsterdam: Transnational Institute, 2012; Emmanuele Lobina and David Hall, 'Water privatisation and remunicipalisation: international lessons for Jakarta', Rapport PSIRU, soumis à la Central Jakarta District Court Case No, 527, 2013; Emmanuele Lobina, 'Water remunicipalisation: Between pendulum swings and paradigm advocacy', in Sarah Bell et al., eds, *Urban Water Trajectories (Vol. 6)*, New York: Springer, 2016, pp. 149-61; Satoko Kishimoto et al., 'Our public water future: The global experience with remunicipalisation', Transnational Institute (TNI)/Public Services International

Research Unit (PSIRU)/Multinationals Observatory/Municipal Services Project (MSP)/European Federation of Public Service Unions (EPSU), 2015; Satoko Kishimoto et al., 'The Future is Public: Towards Democratic Ownership of Public Services', Transnational Institute (TNI)/Public Services International Research Unit (PSIRU)/Multinationals Observatory/Municipal Services Project (MSP)/European Federation of Public Service Unions (EPSU), 2020.

3   Greig Charnock, 'Barcelona en Comú: urban democracy and "the common good"', in Leo Panitch and Greg Albo, eds, *Socialist Register 2018: Rethinking Democracy*, 2017; Emilia Arpini et al., 'New municipalism in South America? Developing theory from experiences in Argentina and Chile', *Urban Studies*, 60(11), 2022, pp. 2290-2306; Bertie Russell et al., 'Strategies for a new municipalism: Public–common partnerships against the new enclosures', *Urban Studies*, 60(11), 2022, pp. 2133-57; Siddharth Sareen and Katinka Lund Waagsaether, 'New municipalism and the governance of urban transitions to sustainability', *Urban Studies*, 60(11), 2022, pp. 2271-89; Matthew Thompson, 'What's so new about New Municipalism?', *Progress in Human Geography*, 45(2), 2021, pp. 317-42.

4   Maureen Mackintosh and Hilary Wainwright, eds, *A Taste of Power: the Politics of Local Economics*, London: Verso, 1987, p. 2.

5   Andrew Cumbers and Franziska Paul, 'Remunicipalisation, Mutating Neoliberalism, and the Conjuncture', *Antipode*, 54(1), 2022, pp. 212-13.

6   Cumbers and Paul, 'Remunicipalisation', pp. 213.

7   William Emmons, 'Private and Public Responses to Market Failure in the US Electric Power Industry, 1882–1942', *The Journal of Economic History*, 51(2), 1991, pp. 452-54; Martin Melosi, *The Sanitary City: Environmental Services in Urban America from Colonial Times to the Present*, Baltimore: Johns Hopkins University Press, 2000; Sam Bass Warner, *The Private City: Philadelphia in Three Periods of Its Growth*, Philadelphia: University of Pennsylvania Press, 1987.

8   Mark Granovetter and Patrick McGuire, 'The making of an industry: electricity in the United States', *The Sociological Review*, 46(S1), 1998, pp. 147-73; Dominique Lorrain, 'La firme locale–globale: Lyonnaise des Eaux (1980–2004)', *Sociologie du travail*, 47(3), 2005, pp. 340-61.

9   D.E. Booth, 'Municipal socialism and city government reform: the Milwaukee experience, 1910–1940', *Journal of Urban History*, 12(51), 1985, pp. 225-35; John Kellett, 'Municipal socialism, enterprise and trading in the Victorian city', *Urban History*, 5, 1978, pp. 36-45.

10   Shelton Stromquist, *Claiming the City: a Global History of Workers' Fight for Municipal Socialism*, London: Verso Books, 2023.

11   Gail Radford, 'From municipal socialism to public authorities: institutional factors in the shaping of American public enterprise', *The Journal of American History*, 90(3), 2003, p. 807.

12   Vladimir Lenin, 'The agrarian programme of social-democracy in the first Russian revolution, 1905-1907', 1907, available at: www.marxists.org.

13   John Stuart Mill, '1851. The Regulation of the London Water Supply', in John M. Robson, ed., *The Collected Works of John Stuart Mill, Volume V – Essays on Economics and Society Part II*, Toronto: University of Toronto Press, London: Routledge and Kegan Paul, 1967.

14   Radford, 'From municipal socialism'.

15   Richard Morten, 'Public Transportation and the Failure of Municipal Socialism in Chicago, 1905-07', *Illinois History Teacher*, 9(1), 2002, pp. 28-36.

16   Fion MacKillop, 'The Los Angeles 'oligarchy' and the governance of water and power networks: The making of a municipal utility based on market principles (1902–1930)', *Flux*, 60(61), 2005, pp. 23–34.

17   Robert Millward, 'The 1940s Nationalizations in Britain: Means to an End or the Means of production?', *The Economic History Review*, 50(2), 1997, pp. 209-34.

18   Jamie Peck and Adam Tickell, 'Neoliberalizing Space', *Antipode*, 34(3), 2002, pp. 380-404.

19   Rhys Andrews et al., 'Corporatization of public services', *Public Administration*, 100(2), 2022, pp. 179-92; Germà Bel et al., 'The costs of corporatization: Analysing the effects of forms of governance', *Public Administration*, 100(2), 2022, pp. 232-49.

20   David A. McDonald, *Meanings of Public and the Future of Public Services*, New York: Routledge, 2023.

21   Pigeon et al., *Remunicipalisation*; Emmanuele Lobina, 'Calling for progressive water policies', in Satoko Kishimoto, Emmanuele Lobina and Olivier Petitjean, eds, *Our Public Experience: The Global Experience with Remunicipalisation*, Amsterdam: Transnational Institute, 2015, pp. 6-18; Kishimoto et al., 'Our public water future'; Kishimoto et al., 'The Future is Public'.

22   See: www.gla.ac.uk/research/az/globalremunicipalisation/.

23   Cibrario and Cumbers, 'Remunicipalisation'.

24   Kishimoto et al., 'Our public water future'; Kishimoto et al., 'The Future is Public'.

25   David A. McDonald, 'Landscapes of Remunicipalization: A Critical Literature Review', *Urban Affairs Review*, 0(0), 2024.

26   Sylvia Cesar, 'Privatization of water: Evaluating its performance in the developing world', *Annals of Public and Cooperative Economics*, 90(1), 2019, pp. 5-23; Jamie Davidson, 'Opposition to privatized infrastructure in Indonesia', *Review of International Political Economy*, 28(1), 2021, pp. 128-51; Ahmet Zaifer, *Privatization in Turkey: Power Bloc, Capital Accumulation and State,* Leiden: Brill, 2022.

27   Rhodante Ahlers and Vincent Merme, 'Financialization, water governance, and uneven development', *Wiley Interdisciplinary Reviews: Water*, 3(6), 2016, pp. 766-74; Alex Loftus et al., 'The political economy of water infrastructure: An introduction to financialization', *Wiley Interdisciplinary Reviews: Water*, 6(1), 2019.

28   Antonio Estache and Emili Grifell-Tatjé, 'Assessing the impact of Mali's water privatization across stakeholders', ECARES Working Paper 2010-037, 2010; Food and Water Watch, 'The Public Works: How the Remunicipalization of Water Services Saves Money', *Fact Sheet*, December 2010, available at: www. foodandwaterwatch.org; David Hall et al., 'Public resistance to privatisation in water and energy', *Development in Practice*, 15(3-4), 2005, pp. 286-301; David Hall et al., 'Replacing failed private water contracts', PSIRU report, London: University of Greenwich, 2010, available at: http://gala.gre.ac.uk; David Hall et al., 'Re-municipalisation in the early twenty-first century: Water in France and energy in Germany', *International Review of Applied Economics*, 27(2), 2013, pp. 193-214; Anne Le Strat, 'Discussion: The remunicipalization of Paris's water supply service: a successful reform', *Water Policy*, 16(1), 2014, p. 197; Edouard Pérard, 'Water supply: Public or private?: An approach based on cost of funds, transaction costs, efficiency and

political costs', *Policy and Society*, 27(3), 2009, pp. 193-219; Alberto Ruiz-Villaverde and Miguel García-Rubio, 'Public Participation in European Water Management: from Theory to Practice. Water Resources Management', 31(8), 2017, pp. 2479-95; Mildred Warner, 'Reversing Privatization, Rebalancing Government reform: Markets Deliberation and Planning', in M. Ramesh, Eduardo Araral Jr, and Xun Wu, eds, *Reasserting the Public in Public Services: New Public Management Reforms*, New York: Routledge, 2010, pp. 30-48; Hellmut Wollmann et al., 'From public service to commodity. The demunicipalization (or remunicipalization?) of energy provision in Germany, Italy, France, the UK and Norway', in Hellmut Wollmann and Gérard Marcou, eds, *The Provision of Public Services in Europe, Between State, Local Government and Market*, Cheltenham/Northampton: Edward Elgar, 2010, pp. 168-90.

29   Alex Loftus and David A. McDonald, 'Of liquid dreams: a political ecology of water privatization in Buenos Aires', *Environment and Urbanization*, 13(2), 2001, pp. 179-99; Martin Pigeon, 'Who takes the risks? Water Remunicipalisation in Hamilton, Canada, in Martin Pigeon et al., eds, *Remunicipalisation: Putting water back into public hands*, Amsterdam: Transnational Institute, Kingston: Municipal Services Project, 2012, pp. 74-89.

30   Karen Bakker, *Privatizing Water: Governance failure and the world's urban water crisis*, Ithaca: Cornell University Press, 2010.

31   Bart Voorn, 'Country, sector and method effects in studying remunicipalization: a meta-analysis', *International Review of Administrative Sciences*, 87(3), 2021, pp. 440-60; Raymond Gradus and Tjerk Budding, 'Political and institutional explanations for increasing re-municipalization', *Urban Affairs Review*, 56(2), 2020, pp. 538-64; Daniel Albalate et al., 'Extent and dynamics of the remunicipalisation of public services', *Local Government Studies*, 50(4), 2024, pp. 1-14; McDonald, 'Landscapes of Remunicipalization'.

32   Rory Padfield et al., 'Uneven development and the commercialisation of public utilities: A political ecology analysis of water reforms in Malaysia', *Utilities Policy*, 40(June), 2016, pp. 152-61; Martin Pigeon, 'Soggy Politics: Making Water "Public" in Malaysia', in Martin Pigeon et al., eds, *Remunicipalisation: Putting Water Back Into Public Hands*, Amsterdam: Transnational Institute, Kingston: Municipal Services Project, 2012, pp. 90-104; Yen Hua Teo, 'Water services industry reforms in Malaysia', *International Journal of Water Resources Development*, 30(1), 2014, pp. 37-46.

33   Chan Khoon, 'Privatizing the welfarist state: health care reforms in Malaysia', *New Solutions: A Journal of Environmental and Occupational Health Policy*, 13(1), 2003, pp. 87-105; Chan Khoon, 'Re-inventing the welfarist state? The Malaysian health system in transition', *Journal of Contemporary Asia*, 40(3), 2010, pp. 444-65; Nepomuceno Malaluan, 'The Public in Asia Power', in David A. McDonald and Greg Ruiters, eds, *Alternatives to Privatization: Public Options for Essential Services in the Global South*, New York: Routledge, 2012, pp. 256-83.

34   Tamás Horváth, 'From Municipalisation to Centralism: Changes to Local Public Service Delivery in Hungary', in Hellmut Wollmann, Ivan Koprić and Gérard Marćou, eds, *Public and Social Services in Europe: From Public and Municipal to Private Sector Provision*, London: Palgrave, 2016, pp. 185-200.

35   Horváth, 'From Municipalisation to Centralism', pp. 193, 198.

36   Emmanuele Lobina, 'Calling for progressive water policies', in Satoko Kishimoto, Emanuele Lobina, and Olivier Petitjean, eds, *Our Public Experience: The Global Experience with Remunicipalisation*, Amsterdam: Transnational Institute, 2015, pp. 6-18; World Bank, 'Guinea - Third Water Supply and Sanitation Project', Washington, DC: World Bank, 2006.

37   Zhangkai Huang et al., 'The reversal of privatization in China: A political economy perspective', *Journal of Corporate Finance*, 71(102115), 2021.

38   Joseph Stiglitz, 'The Economics Role of the State: Efficiency and Effectiveness', in Thomas Hardiman and Michael Mulreany, eds, *Efficiency and Effectiveness in the Public Domain: The Economic Role of the State*, Dublin: Institute of Public Administration, 1991, pp. 37-59.

39   Stephen Osborne, 'The New Public Governance? Public Management Review', *Public Management Review*, 8(3), 2006, pp. 377-88.

40   Christopher Pollitt, *The Essential Public Manager*. Buckingham: Open University Press/ McGraw Hill, 2003, p. 474.

41   Pollitt, *The Essential Public Manager*, p. 27.

42   John Clarke, *Creating Citizen-consumers: Changing Publics and Changing Public Services*, Thousand Oaks: Pine Forge Press, 2007.

43   Andrews et al., 'Corporatization of public services'.

44   David A. McDonald, 'To corporatize or not to corporatize (and if so, how?)', *Utilities Policy*, *40*, 2016, pp. 107-14.

45   Marcela López, *Corporatization and the Right to Water in Colombia: Conflicts, Citizenship and Social Inequality*, New York: Routledge, 2022.

46   Martin Pigeon, 'From Fiasco to DAWASCO: Remunicipalising Water Systems in Dar es Salaam, Tanzania', in Martin Pigeon et al., eds, *Remunicipalisation: Putting Water Back Into Public Hands*. Amsterdam: Transnational Institute, Kingston: Municipal Services Project, 2012, pp. 40-57; Elliot Rooney, 'Failed privatisation in urban water utilities: Can PuPs pick up the pieces? Reviewing evidence from Dar es Salaam, 2005–2018', *Geoforum*, *152* (103998), 2024.

47   Pigeon, 'From Fiasco to DAWASCO', p. 41.

48   Mildred Warner, 'Pragmatic Publics in the Heartland of Capitalism: Local services in the United States', in David A. McDonald, ed, *Making Public in a Privatized World: The Struggle for Essential Services*, London: Zed Books, 2016, pp. 175-96.

49   Mildred Warner and Austin Aldag, 'Re-municipalization in the US: A pragmatic response to contracting', *Journal of Economic Policy Reform*, *24*(3), 2021, pp. 229; See also: Mildred Warner and Amir Hefetz, 'In-Sourcing and Outsourcing: The Dynamics of Privatization among US Municipalities 2002-2007', *Journal of the American Planning Association*, 78(3), 2012, pp. 313-27; Mildred Warner et al., 'Pragmatic municipalism: US local government responses to fiscal stress', *Public Administration Review*, 81(3), 2021, pp. 389-98.

50   Magnus Jansson et al., 'Drivers of outsourcing and backsourcing in the public sector— From idealism to pragmatism', *Financial Accountability & Management*, 37(3), 2021, pp. 262-78; Bart Voorn et al., 'Re-interpreting re-municipalization: finding equilibrium', *Journal of Economic Policy Reform*, 24(3), 2021, pp. 305-18; Daniel Albalate and Germà Bel, 'Politicians, bureaucrats and the public–private choice in public service delivery: anybody there pushing for remunicipalization?', *Journal of Economic Policy Reform*,

24(3), 2021, pp. 361-79; Judith Clifton et al., 'Re-municipalization of public services: trend or hype?', *Journal of Economic Policy Reform*, 24(3), 2021, pp. 293-04.

51   Nicola Capone, 'Acqua e libertà: La lunga marcia per la ripubblicizzazione del servizio idrico', *Teoría e storia del diritto privato*, 4(29), 2011; Christine Jakob and Pablo Sanchez, 'Remunicipalisation and workers: Building new alliances', in Satoko Kishimoto, Emanuele Lobina, and Olivier Petitjean, eds, *Our Public Water Future: The Global Experience with Remunicipalisation*, Transnational Institute (TNI)/Public Services International Research Unit (PSIRU)/Multinationals Observatory/Municipal Services Project (MSP)/European Federation of Public Service Unions (EPSU), 2015, pp. 76-89; Piergiorgio Novaro and Jacopo Bercelli, 'Water services are the bridgehead for a return to publicly owned utilities in Europe. A comparative analysis', *Water Resources Management*, 31(8), 2017, pp. 2375-87; Satoko Kishimoto, 'Why the remunicipalisation movement is growing', *IPPR Progressive Review*, 26(1), 2019, pp. 51-9; Angela Pohlmann and Arwen Colell, 'Distributing power: Community energy movements claiming the grid in Berlin and Hamburg', *Utilities Policy*, 65(101066), 2020; Massimiliano Agovino et al., 'Corporate governance and sustainability in water utilities. The effects of decorporatisation in the city of Naples, Italy', *Business Strategy and the Environment*, 30(2), 2021, pp. 874-90.

52   Le Strat, 'Discussion'; Vanessa Turri, 'Remunicipalisation of water services in Europe. Comparative study of the Neapolitan and Parisian cases', *Water Policy*, 24(12), 2022, pp. 1842-58.

53   Mar Satorras et al., 2020, 'Reinventing public water amid Covid-19 in Terrassa,' in David A. McDonald, Susan Spronk and Daniel Chavez, eds, *Public water and COVID-19: Dark clouds and silver linings,* Amsterdam: Transnational Institute, Buenos Aires: CLACSO, 2020, pp. 61-84; Míriam Planas Martín et al., 'Remunicipalisation in Catalonia: Strategies and Responses', *Development*, 65(2-4), 2022, pp. 228-36.

54   Jacob Smessaert et al., 'The commodification of nature, a review in social sciences', *Ecological Economics*, 172(106624), 2020; Christoph Hermann, *The Critique of Commodification: Contours of a Post-capitalist Society*, Oxford University Press, 2021.

55   Philipp Terhorst et al., 'Social movements, left governments, and the limits of water sector reform in Latin America's left turn', *Latin American Perspectives*, 40(4), 2013, pp. 55-69; Hug March et al., 'The deadlock of metropolitan remunicipalisation of water services management in Barcelona', *Water Alternatives*, 12(2), 2019, pp. 360-79; Carlos Santos, 'Open questions for public water management: Discussions from Uruguay's restatization process', *Utilities Policy*, 72(101273), 2021; Cumbers and Paul, 'Remunicipalisation'; Martin Sarnow and Norma Tiedemann, 'Interrupting the neoliberal masculine state machinery? Strategic selectivities and municipalist practice in Barcelona and Zagreb', *Urban Studies*, 60(11), 2022, pp. 2231-50.

56   For Bulgaria, see: Georgi Medarov and David A. McDonald, 'Which way will the winds blow? Post-privatisation water struggles in Sofia, Bulgaria', *Water Alternatives*, 12(2), 2019, pp. 438-58.

57   Hug March et al., 'The deadlock of metropolitan remunicipalisation'; Nasya Razavi, *Water Governance in Bolivia: Cochabamba since the Water War*, Abingdon: Routledge, 2022; Beltran Roca and Jon Las Heras, 'Trade unions as retaining walls against political change: A Gramscian approach to remunicipalisation policies in a Spanish City', *Capital & Class*, 44(1), 2020, pp. 3-25; Cumbers and Paul, 'Remunicipalisation'; McDonald, *Meanings of Public.*

58   Carles Sanchis-Ibor et al., 'Collective irrigation reloaded. Re-collection and re-moralization of water management after privatization in Spain', *Geoforum*, 87, 2017, pp. 38-47; Sören Becker et al., 'Between coproduction and commons: understanding initiatives to reclaim urban energy provision in Berlin and Hamburg', *Urban Research & Practice*, 10(1), 2017, pp. 63-85; Bagué Tova, 'La remunicipalización del servicio de abastecimiento urbano de agua: instituciones y común', *Revista de Antropología Social*, 26(2), 2017, pp. 427-48; Gabriel Weber et al., 'De-privatisation and remunicipalisation of urban services through the pendulum swing: Evidence from Germany', *Journal of Cleaner Production*, 236(117555), 2019.

59   Mackintosh and Wainwright, *A Taste of Power*; Rhodante Ahlers et al., 'Informal space in the urban waterscape: Disaggregation and co-production of water services', *Water Alternatives*, 7(1), 2014, pp. 1-14; Joost Fledderus et al., 'Restoring trust through the co-production of public services: A theoretical elaboration', *Public Management Review*, 16(3), 2014, pp. 424-43.

60   Elinor Ostrom, *Governing the Commons: The Evolution of Institutions for Collective Action*, Cambridge University Press, 1990; Ahlers et al., 'Informal space'; Paul Trawick, 'Against the privatization of water: An indigenous model for improving existing laws and successfully governing the commons', *World Development*, 31(6), 2003, pp. 977-96.

61   Davide Mazzoni and Elvira Cicognani, 'Water as a commons: An exploratory study on the motives for collective action among Italian water movement activists', *Journal of Community & Applied Social Psychology*, 23(4), 2013, pp. 314-30; Susan Spronk et al., 'Struggles for Water Justice in Latin America: Public and "Social-Public" Alternatives', in David A. McDonald and Greg Ruiters, eds, *Alternatives to privatization: Public options for essential services in the global South*, New York: Routledge, 2012, pp. 421-52; Madeleine Bélanger et al., 'Work of the Ants: Labour and Community Reinventing Public Water in Colombia', in David A. McDonald, ed., *Making Public in a Privatized World: The Struggle for Essential Services*, London: Zed Books, 2016, pp. 26-42; Razavi, *Water Governance in Bolivia*.

62   Lenin, 'The agrarian programme'.

63   See also: Gregory Albo, 'The limits of eco-localism: scale, strategy, socialism', in Leo Panitch and Colin Leys, eds, *Socialist Register 2007: Coming to Terms with Nature*, 43, 2007.

64   Cumbers and Paul, 'Remunicipalisation'.

65   Cumbers and Paul, 'Remunicipalisation', p. 211.

66   Cumbers and Paul, 'Remunicipalisation', p. 205.

67   David Harvey, 'The right to the city', *New Left Review*, 53, 2008, pp. 37-38.

68   For longer discussion, see: McDonald, *Meanings of Public*.

69   Harvey, 'The right to the city', p. 39.

70   Harvey, 'The right to the city', p. 40.

71   David A. McDonald, 'Finding common (s) ground in the fight for water remunicipalization', *Community Development Journal*, 54(1), 2019, pp. 59-79.

72   Andrew Cumbers, 'Constructing a global commons in, against and beyond the state', *Space and Polity*, 19(1), 2015, pp. 62-75.

73   McDonald, *Meanings of Public*.

74   Cumbers and Paul, 'Remunicipalisation', p. 204.

75   March et al., 'The deadlock of metropolitan remunicipalisation'; Susan Spronk and Emilie Sing, 'The struggle for public water in Marseille, France', *Water Alternatives*, 12(2), 2019, pp. 380-93; Razavi, *Water Governance in Bolivia*, 2022; David A. McDonald and Erik Swyngedouw, 'The new water wars: Struggles for remunicipalisation', *Water Alternatives*, 12(2), 2019, pp. 322-33.

76   Although exceptions include: Hernández Ran and Claudia Tomic, 'Speeches and practices after the remunicipalisation process of Santiago Sochiapan, Veracruz', *Aegaeum*, 1(1), 2006; Gerardo Alatorre Frenk, 'Flowing movement: Building alternative water governance in Mexico', *State of Power 2018*, Transnational Institute, 5 January 2018, available at: www.tni.org; Razavi, *Water Governance in Bolivia*.

77   Sean Sweeney, 'Conflicting Agendas: Energy Democracy and the Labor Movement', in Denise Fairchild and Al Weinrub, eds, *Energy Democracy Advancing Equity in Clean Energy Solutions*, Washington, DC: Island Press, 2017, pp. 113-38; Antonio Gabriel La Viña et al., 'Navigating a trilemma: Energy security, equity, and sustainability in the Philippines' low-carbon transition', *Energy Research & Social Science*, 35, 2018, pp. 37-47; Elizabeth Allen et al, 'Women's leadership in renewable transformation, energy justice and energy democracy: Redistributing power', *Energy Research & Social Science*, 57, 2019, pp. 1-9.

THE DEMOCRATIC AND TRANSFORMATIVE POTENTIAL OF PUBLIC BANKS

THOMAS MAROIS AND SUSAN SPRONK

We are living in a time of multiple crises. The latest calculations from science agencies reveal 2023 as the warmest year for the planet as measured by average temperature since global record-keeping began, and 22 July 2024 as the hottest single day on earth ever recorded. Current predictions suggest that global warming will only accelerate.[1] We are still reeling from the aftermath of the Covid-19 pandemic. The pandemic delayed progress towards closing the overall global gender gap by more than 30 years.[2] Much of the global South has been immersed in a debt crisis of a breadth and depth not seen since the early 1980s.

Addressing these crises, and making progress toward a more egalitarian, equalizing and green global development model, will entail mobilizing a huge mass of capital to convert and transform existing infrastructure and manufacturing plants and to build new ecologically responsible productive capacities. To date, the financialized world market has responded primarily by market ecology measures of price and tax incentives and subsidies. This approach has failed at the pace, scale, or on the terms required for the necessary reshaping of the circuits of capital, a failure well-documented by socialist and ecological researchers and activists, and further underscored by the United Nations.[3]

However, while these critiques have been telling, there is also the need to address alternatives given left movements have been struggling in even pushing reform agendas ahead. This essay argues that there is no pathway to financing green *and just* transitions that does not take on the terrain of the world's myriad of publicly-owned and -controlled banks. While governments across the global North have committed in principle to increasing the amount of green financing, raising this finance and making sure that the resources are channelled into investments that promote collective and egalitarian policy processes remains a crucial ongoing struggle. Governments both North and South need to make more effective use of their existing capacities and resources. But this involves a confrontation over the neoliberal policy regime and the limits of capitalist states. In the world of climate finance, public banks are a necessary – but not by themselves sufficient – potential form of counter-power, offering an alternative that could contribute to the decarbonization, democratization and definancialization of actually-existing market economies.[4]

It is worth underscoring that while none of what public banks do is outside of global financial capitalism and its structural confines, they are not stagnant institutions but open to contestation.[5] Nor are public banks inherently progressive entities, but they can be reclaimed for public purposes and potentially democratically governed by community, collective and social movement forces in the interests of green and socially just transitions.

In the absence of democratic and social controls over public banks, private corporate interests will continue to intensify pressures to subordinate the institutional and interventionist capacity of public banks to profit maximization. Political projects to reclaim and democratize public banks, by contrast, can help to reverse the neoliberalization of social reproduction and build the capacity of workers, women, racialized and marginalized communities to resist market-oriented structural adjustment and to explore decommodified – even anticapitalist – alternatives.[6]

The agenda of this essay is to begin by illustrating the important – and most often neglected – scale of contemporary public banking capacity, and by locating public banks within a history of socialist thinking on the transformation of banking and finance. In turn, we then explain why public banks are central to an ecologically-just transition by providing examples of emergent movements and practices among them that can contribute to definancialization and to cracking open spaces for struggles over the democratization of capitalist economies.

PUBLIC BANK ASSETS

Public banks are financial institutions that are often, but not always, owned by national states (so 'state-owned' banks). Yet sub-national and municipal public authorities and public enterprises also own banks, making them public. Banks can also be made public via legally binding public interest mandates and meaningful public governance. That is, a bank can be public through ownership, mandate, governance or any combination of these factors.[7] As illustrated below, there are many institutional types of public banks, including central banks, multilateral banks and postal banks, as well as retail, universal and development banks at national and sub-national scales.

Public banks have a long history.[8] The first emerged over 600 years ago, a municipal bank founded in Barcelona in 1401 – the Taulat de Cuitat.[9] But historical data on public banking numbers and assets are sparse. Public banks achieved their zenith in the 1970s (outside the soviet economies). At that time, they controlled 40 per cent of the largest banks' assets in the developed world, and in the developing world, 65 per cent of the largest banks were public.[10] During four decades of subsequent neoliberalization, public banking declined with many examples privatized. But today public banking is experiencing a resurgence, exemplified by new institutions such as the Canada Infrastructure Bank, opened in 2017, and the Scottish National Investment Bank, opened in 2020. Across the US, there are multiple state-level legislative processes underway to create new public banks. In 2023, Congresswomen Rashida Tlaib (MI-12) and Alexandria Ocasio-Cortez (NY-14) introduced the second version of the Public Banking Act, much of it premised on democratic governance. In 2024, the Environmental Protection Agency of the US government awarded $5 billion to the Coalition for Green Capital to create a new national green bank.

Yet the scale of public banks has long been underappreciated. In 2012, the World Bank estimated that public banking assets were worth around $2 trillion, while a 2017 OECD climate finance report pointed to 250 public development banks with assets of around $5 trillion.[11] In 2019, the United Nations Inter-Agency Task Force on Financing for Sustainable Development affirmed the OECD report's assessment.[12] However, new research conducted within the Finance in Common Summit (the network of public development banks) framework has dramatically improved empirical estimates, identifying over 530 public development banks in existence as of 2024 (excluding commercial banks) with $23 trillion in assets, accounting for about 10 to 12 per cent of annual global investments.[13]

Nevertheless, most multilateral agencies continue to underestimate the number and scale of public banks by counting only public 'development' banks. Our approach, however, is to identify total combined public banking assets held within commercial, development and universal forms of public banks. In brief, public commercial banks are retail deposit-taking institutions that lend to households, corporations and governments, providing a full range of day-to-day banking services (savings, chequing, credit cards, mortgages and so on) through branch and online networks. Public development or investment banks mostly do not provide daily financial services or accept personal deposits, but rather specialize in large-scale and long-term projects and on-lending to other banks. Their sources of funding usually come from government, international development agencies and bond issuances.

Public universal banks perform both commercial and development banking functions, marrying deposit taking with investment making.

As of mid-2024, there are 914 public commercial, development and universal banks and financial institutions at the national and sub-national scales.[14] These public banks hold $55 trillion in combined assets. Put in context, public banks control assets 10 per cent greater than the 2023 GDPs of the US, China and Germany *combined*. Furthermore, the total number of assets held by these banks increased by $6 trillion from 2020 to 2024.[15] And if you add to these banks the multilateral development banks (like the World Bank and Asian Development Bank) and the apex domestic entities (the central banks), then there is a total of 1115 public financial institutions worldwide that command over $91 trillion as of 2024.[16] Public banks are of a material scale that must not be ignored by progressive forces.

Our primary concern in this essay is with the national, sub-national and smaller regional public banks – institutions that have not garnered near the same attention as the large multilateral and central banks. National and sub-national public banks are ubiquitous, diverse and closer to local and national communities than their multilateral corollaries. The financial capacity of this set of 900 plus public banks far outstrips that of the multilateral banks (which have about $4.5 trillion in assets in 2024). They include sub-national banks, such as municipal public banks like the commercial Banco de Ciudad de Buenos Aires in Argentina (est. 1878), the German North Rhine-Westphalia (NRW, est. 2002) development bank, and the Canadian commercial provincial bank the Alberta Treasury Branch (est. 1938). At the national scale, they include development banks like India's National Bank for Agriculture and Rural Development (NABARD, est. 1981), the Fiji Development Bank (est. 1967) and Brazil's BNDES (est. 1952). Based on our research and expertise, the more inspiring examples of progressive public banks already functioning in the public interest are located at the local and national scales. There is potential for these banks to function as pro-public entities working to advance the collective interests of communities.

SOCIALIST THINKING ON BANKING AND FINANCE

Socialist researchers have often struggled to understand public banks within specific social formations and capitalist development or as a potential financial alternative. Critical political economy and Marxian studies have thoroughly explored the structural effects of capitalist development and finance.[17] Yet this research has been 'slow to develop its theoretical treatment of banking' in general, and of public banking in particular.[18] One of the problems has been the assumption that all banks are privately owned entities. In his magisterial

The Limits to Capital, David Harvey leaves us only with the note that 'banks are also private institutions in competition with each other'.[19] Such limiting assumptions even extend to discussions of contemporary climate finance. Brett Christophers' incisive critique of the limits of profit imperatives in renewable power generation proceeds as if all energy investors are private when they are clearly not, and often benefit from public banks of various kinds.[20]

A great deal of socialist writing on finance has also tended to focus on higher level abstractions of money capital within the circuit of capital.[21] These studies have analyzed how the amassing of ever-larger pools of available money capital enables more aggressive accumulation and competitive processes, often at the expense of workers. They build on Marx's insights on how with the consolidation of capitalism the credit system became 'a new and terrible weapon in the battle of competition' and was transformed into an 'enormous social mechanism for the centralization of capitals'.[22] Hilferding further drew socialists' attention to the credit system, emphasizing how the system 'socializes other people's money for use by a few' to accelerate capitalist production by overcoming barriers to investment.[23]

Since the 1990s, there has been an explosion of debates and studies on the financialization of the global economy. In the late 1990s, Paul Sweezy identified the 'financialization of the capital accumulation process' as integral to late monopoly capitalism.[24] John Bellamy Foster later identified how financialization creates instability and crises. Costas Lapavitsas, Paulo dos Santos and Ben Fine have provided fine-grained analyses of structural changes in the financial incomes of large firms within leading capitalist states and resulting crisis tendencies.[25] These studies illustrate that one of the consequences of financialization is that (private) banks have developed new ways to extract income from households and workers through financial services. Fine emphasizes how economic and social reproduction are more deeply and structurally tied to the financial system, intensifying the processes of neoliberal restructuring.[26] Others have turned their attention to the devastating consequences of financialization in sectors such as food systems, water and housing, as well as the forms particular to the global South, such as the rich discussions around subordinated financialization.[27]

Yet despite socialists' many contributions to our understanding of finance and financialization, not many have meaningfully grappled with concrete alternatives at the level of banking and credit systems.[28] A few examples suffice to make the point. Stephen Maher and Scott Aquanno demonstrate that contemporary finance is a necessary but contradictory process whose crises are often worked out through the development of new forms of financialization, yet they leave to others the work of specifying what types of banks and credit functions would be necessary to confront intensified financialization. Adrienne Roberts highlights the problems of contemporary approaches to understanding the role of gendered narratives in mainstream finance and development tropes, but does not reflect on what kinds of responses and institution are needed to create the conditions in which women and gender non-conforming folks could empower themselves. David McNally analyzes the links between global money and the bloody histories of colonial conquest and slavery, but says little about the struggles of contemporary public banking movements seeking economic justice for racialized and marginalized communities. Both Peter Newell as well as Gareth Bryant and Sophie Webber offer much-needed clarity on the need for an increase in climate finance at a massive scale, but their proposals only tinker at the margins of existing private sector and smaller-scale institutional arrangements with little appreciation for existing public sector financial capacity, which is a necessary component of any wider systemic transformation.[29] More also needs to be done to excavate the diverse untold stories of radical left financial programmes, both in and out of government.

This lacuna in contemporary socialist thinking and practice is unfortunate, given that revolutionary movements of the early twentieth century took it as given that any project of societal transformation requires exerting democratic control over finance. Nationalizing the banks was a prime objective. For example, Lenin was deeply concerned with the role that banks can and must play in the Russian Revolution. As he wrote in October 1917:

> Capitalism has created an accounting apparatus in the shape of the banks, syndicates, postal service, consumers' societies, and office employees' unions. Without big banks socialism would be impossible. The big banks are the 'state apparatus' which we need to bring about socialism, and which we take ready-made from capitalism; our task here is merely to lop off what capitalistically mutilates this excellent apparatus, to make it even bigger, even more democratic, even more comprehensive. Quantity will be transformed into quality. A single State Bank, the biggest of the big, with branches in every rural district, in every factory, will constitute as much as nine-tenths of the socialist apparatus. This will be countrywide book-keeping, country-wide accounting of the production and distribution of goods, this will be, so to speak, something in the nature of the skeleton of socialist society.[30]

Lenin further wrote in December 1917 that workers' control depends on controlling the banks:

> The first step towards the emancipation of the people from this penal servitude is the confiscation of the landed estates, the introduction of workers' control and the nationalisation of the banks. The next steps will be the nationalisation of the factories, the compulsory organisation of the whole population in consumers' societies, which are at the same time societies for the sale of products, and the state monopoly of the trade in grain and other necessities.[31]

Reflecting on the Paris Commune, he went on to state that 'we have learned much since the Commune, and we would not repeat its fatal errors, we would not leave the banks in the hands of the bourgeoisie'.[32] The mistake of not taking over financial power was powerfully dramatized by Brecht in his play on the Paris Commune. He delved into communard debates on whether to leave the Bank of France independent (and thus ultimately in the hands of the counter-revolutionaries) or to seize its assets to push forward revolutionary aspirations. You do not need to see the play to know it ends badly.

Bank nationalizations also figured prominently in national independence struggles and various developmentalist projects of the twentieth century. Post-revolutionary governments in China and Cuba nationalized the banks.[33] While diverse in cause and outcome, nationalist movements in Algeria, Costa Rica, Egypt, India, Korea, Libya, Tanzania and Vietnam took existing banks under state control and/or established new public banks in order to achieve greater domestic political autonomy.[34] In the global South, resisting imperial expansion and establishing national sovereignty requires the ability to issue debt in local currency, and thus gain control over domestic lending.[35] It should therefore be of no surprise that today renewed activism for economic and political sovereignty among First Nations peoples in Canada include calls for creating a new Indigenous Development Bank.[36]

As Marx famously argued, to only think about the world is wholly inadequate since the point is to change it. This adage is truer now than ever in the face of the extinction-level challenge of financing a global green and just transition. We urgently need to rapidly expand the body of critical problem-driven and praxis-oriented emancipatory research on how to address both the depth and scale of the climate crisis – one that provides an actionable alternative to the dominant pro-private narrative.[37] Building on existing public banking capacities may be one entry point to alternatives.

NO GREEN TRANSITIONS WITHOUT PUBLIC BANKS

Mainstream strategies for financing climate transitions, embodied in the United Nations' 2030 Sustainable Development Goals (SDGs), over-rely on private investors as the solution. This stems from deep-seated and class-based beliefs in the power of markets and private capital to resolve all social, economic, political and ecological problems.[38] This bias shaped the 2015 Financing for Development 'Addis Ababa Action Agenda' and, more significantly, the World Bank's 'Billions to Trillions' development finance plan of the same year, which advocated for market-based and private-sector led development and climate solutions.[39]

Driven by shareholders' demands for maximum profit, private investors are structurally unequipped to finance the world's green infrastructure needs. No amount of de-risking for private investors through 'blended finance' or the formation of public-private partnerships will move the needle at the pace, scale, or on the terms needed.[40] There are structural reasons for this. Private corporations that commit resources at the start of the circuit of capital (be it green or otherwise) must augment their money investments either through the sale of some product or via returns on financial transactions. Failure to do so results in investment losses or business collapse. Private corporate entities are thus profit maximizers due to fiduciary duties to increase shareholder returns.[41] Climate action, socially just transitions and equitable development only matter to the extent that they produce shareholder returns, that is, that they increase surplus value. As such, environment, social and governance commitments that hamper profit are quickly sacrificed in the interest of the bottom line.[42] Despite evidence to the contrary, those interested in maintaining the status quo continue to argue for the expansion and intensification of private investment into green capitalism.[43]

Yet cracks in the edifice are growing. The United Nations recognizes that the international financial architecture has been 'unable to support the mobilization of stable and long-term financing at scale for investments needed to combat the climate crisis and achieve the SDGs'.[44] The United Nations Conference on Trade and Development (UNCTAD) argued that, as of 2023, $30 trillion would be needed over the following eight years in order to meet SDG targets, highlighting the role that public development banks must play in financing a Global Green New Deal.[45] A recent op-ed summarizing research published by the G20 – co-written by none other than former Chief Economist of the World Bank and US Treasury Secretary Larry Summers – suggested that the turn to blended finance has been 'disastrous' and has slowed investment in development to a trickle.[46]

Private investors have badly underperformed, even at sheer quantity. Table 1 shows tracked global climate finance data from 2017 to 2022. In 2022, private investors provided $463 billion (or just under 33 per cent) of total climate finance (almost all of which came from commercial institutions and corporations). Public institutions, however, accounted for $730 billion, or almost 52 per cent. More than four-fifths of this amount came from public banks, financial institutions and enterprises.

Table 1: Global climate finance by household, private and public sources (billions USD)[47]

Source	2022	2021	2020	2019	2018	2017
Households/individuals	222	147	59	51	65	41
Private investors*	463	418	274	252	215	227
Public institutions**	730	549	332	337	261	340
Total	**1415**	**1114**	**664**	**639**	**540**	**608**

* Includes commercial financial institutions; corporations; funds; institutional investors; and others.
** Includes bilateral development financial institutions; export credit agencies; government; multilateral climate funds; multilateral development financial institutions; national development financial institutions; public funds; state-owned enterprises and financial institutions.

In other words, public institutions are far outperforming private investors in climate investments. This record is despite the fact that private investors hold about 80 per cent of the over $281 trillion in total global financial assets (public and private).[48] Moreover, private climate finance is concentrated in the sectors with the highest return, such as energy and transport, and in wealthier zones of the world economy – that is, they invest practically nothing in the highly indebted countries of the global South or in rural areas and poorer municipalities in the global North.[49] Practically speaking, moreover, public banks and financial institutions already possess the institutions, material capacity and investment trajectories needed to lead on global green transitions.

Given their potential public purposes and social development mandates, public banks are also uniquely positioned to play a key role in pushing for a pro-labour and gender equity transformative approach to financing for development. This is especially the case in the provision of essential infrastructure and services, such as those related to housing, transportation, household electricity, health, education, water and sanitation, and climate change adaptation.[50] Significantly, public spending on physical infrastructure reduces the burden on women and allows them to devote more time to both paid work and leisure activities. Social spending that promotes gender equality in education and health improves productivity and income throughout the economy, and most importantly, enhances well-being. For example, improved water supply and sanitation, especially in lower-income countries, reduces the time spent searching for water as well as time lost to illness, important factors that increase the burden of unpaid work in these countries.[51] Improved transport connectivity reduces time spent supplying the household and facilitates access to essential services and labour markets.[52]

If mandated to do so, public banks can respond to the call of feminist civil society organizations and trade unions that have been advocating for investment in public goods and services since the early days of neoliberal structural adjustment.[53] International worker organizations, such as Trade Unions for Energy Democracy, Public Services International and the Services Employees International Union, as well as national examples like the Canadian Union of Public Employees and the Korean Public Service and Transport Workers' Union, have taken increasingly strategic positions on public banks for advancing workers' rights and aspirations, including pro-worker green transitions.

PRO-PUBLIC PUBLIC BANKING CAN BE BUILT ON

Public banks are not inherently pro-public entities. But neither do they present immutable barriers to realizing green and just transitions. Quite the opposite. There is a plethora of promising practices in the public banking world that are the result of the struggles of workers, women and racialized communities which might further collectivist aspirations to build a more sustainable and livable world. A few examples might serve as indicators of what pro-public public banking advocates can build on.

In 2016, a municipally owned hydropower plant located in Norway, Helgeland Kraft, was awarded 'Public Winner' of the Architecture and Sustainability category at the Architizer A+ Awards.[54] The power installation is considered the world's most beautiful hydropower plant. Its public owners were motivated by a desire to build a power station that was visually appealing and adapted to its surroundings, in order to encourage visitors and build support for public renewable energy. The public regional development bank, the Nordic Investment Bank (NIB, est. 1975), co-financed the project via a public-public collaboration. The project reflects the relatively early turn of the NIB to financing sustainable transitions, a turn that was codified in the bank's updated Sustainability Policy in November 2021. In the words of NIB

Head of Sustainability and Mandate, Luca De Lorenzo, the policy 'reflects that we are running out of time, and that we really need to step up efforts to decarbonise the energy sector. So, we are taking a very clear stance, we will not finance any fossil fuel-based energy generation.'[55] The NIB is not alone, as there are a range of public banks in the Nordic countries, including municipal banks, that provide local governments infrastructure financing at long-term and affordable rates.[56]

FONPLATA is a public regional development bank formed by Argentina, Bolivia, Brazil, Paraguay and Uruguay in 1971, and it has been engaged in an innovative public-public partnership to promote the universalization of water and sanitation services in the Greater Buenos Aires region of Argentina.[57] Following the renationalization of the water authority in the context of Argentina's financial meltdown in 2001, the government sought to expand services to poor and marginalized areas. They did this via the integration into the service area of the periphery that had been neglected by the previous private operators of the authority. In order to meet the dual goals of expanding services and creating jobs for marginalized communities – and in the context of the unemployed workers' movement – the public water company hired local worker cooperatives to help with the work of digging trenches, laying the pipe, and so on. In its initial years, the Water + Work and Sewage + Work programs were financed by the national treasury. In 2019, they secured a loan from FONPLATA to finance their continuation. The loan promotes the socio-economic goals of the previous program, including expanding the number of household connections and creating local employment by hiring local cooperative members. The terms of the loan also promote gender equality goals by stipulating that half of the jobs created by any new cooperatives joining the program must go to women.

In Turkey, the sub-national public development bank, Iller Bank (or Ilbank; Bank of the Provinces, est. 1933) has its roots in financing municipal reconstruction and development following the 1919 to 1923 Turkish War of Independence.[58] Ilbank is owned by local authorities (the municipalities and provinces) and supports mid-size municipality and village infrastructure and development. By law, Ilbank receives a recurrent source of monthly capital injections equal to two per cent of the total tax incomes of the provincial authorities and municipalities. Its lending is further bolstered by retained earnings and borrowing from foreign institutions. For example, Ilbank has received World Bank and European Investment Bank funding for Turkey's national 'Sustainable Cities' projects. Ilbank specializes in providing appropriate, long-term financing to cities. According to one Ilbank staff member involved in municipal water finance, 'no one can compete since no one dares to lend more cheaply' – including private financiers.[59] While there are substantive benefits of a purposively designed public bank, the research on Ilbank also highlights the importance of ensuring effective, accountable and transparent governance.

A critical dynamic view of public banks holds that 'publicness' is not only or solely determined by quantitative ownership levels.[60] That is, to be 'public' does not necessarily mean that an institution is owned by government. Rather 'publicness' is a socio-historical determination that must consider mandate, mission and governance arrangements in the service of contested notions of the public good. Historical functions shape ownership form. Such is the case with certain worker-owned banks that, while privately owned by their members or constituents, have an evident public purpose.

In Japan, we see this in the Rokin Labour Banks (RLBs), founded in 1953. Yasunori Nishida, President of the National Association of Labour Banks, states that the 'Labour Banks were founded … as financial institutions for and by working people'.[61] There are thirteen independent commercial RLBs and a central coordinating body, the Rokinren Bank.[62] The RLBs are neither owned by government authorities nor governed by the state, but they have a legally-defined public purpose to contribute to the 'improvement of the economic status of workers' and to do so without being profit-maximising entities.[63] They are further distinguished from for-profit banks by their social links to trade unions and worker-led democratic governance. The RLBs, moreover, collaborate with public agencies to deliver public policy objectives, such as affordable housing. They have the institutional and material capacity to do this given they command assets of around $190 billion, based on a constituency of about 12 million individuals who bank with them.[64] In 2019, the RLBs introduced the Labour Bank SDGs Action Guidelines to incorporate environmental, social and governance (ESG) factors into bank decisions.[65]

In Costa Rica, the Banco Popular y de Desarrollo Comunal (BPDC) is a 100 per cent worker owned bank that is also run by and for the working class of the country. Founded in 1969, the idea was to fight usury and to democratize credit for workers. The BPDC is a public-like universal bank, meaning it engages in both daily financial services and development projects. It is the third (sometimes fourth, depending on the day) largest bank in Costa Rica, with over $6.6 billion in assets.[66] It is likely the world's most democratic bank, with its mandate determined by an elected Workers' Assembly. The Workers' Assembly was formalized in public law in 1986, constituting the bank's highest decision-making forum.[67] Ten social and economic sectors (artisanal; communal; cooperative; self-managed; independent; teachers; professional; as well as the confederated, non-confederated, and solidarity syndicates/trade unions) designate 290 representatives to the Assembly. In turn, the Workers' Assembly designates four representatives to serve on the seven-member National Board of Directors. The other three members are appointed by the national government. The BPDC not only institutionalizes democratic decision-making – it also subjects its decisions to gender equity requirements. In all major decision-making forums in the bank, from the local and regional committees to the national level, at least half the participants and appointees must be women. Moreover, the Workers' Assembly is responsible for integrating recommendations made by the Permanent Commission for Women, a separate oversight body within the bank.

Overall, the BPDC is guided by three strategic missions (gender equity, accessibility and environmental responsibility) and a triple bottom line (the economic, the environmental and the social), which were the outcomes of a nation-wide consultation the mid-2010s.[68] The BPDC is, it must be said, a profit-maximising bank that competes directly with private banks and other public banks in the country. However, at the same time, it uses these financial returns to fund its not-for-profit social bank arm and to provide concessional lending for community development projects, such as social housing, communal water infrastructure, energy efficiency and biodiversity.[69]

TOWARDS DEFINANCIALIZATION AND DEMOCRATIZATION

None of these – or any other – public banking cases are free of contradictions. Rather, these and other diverse cases from the global North and South illustrate that public banks have the financial and institutional capacity to promote public policy goals and social justice ends. So, too, do public banks have the resources necessary to finance green transitions in distinct global contexts. But in whose interests will public banks act? How can we ensure that green transitions will be just? Just as public banks can shield workers, women, the poor and the environment from financialized market imperatives, they can also be made to shield finance capital, investors, carbon capital and elites from any threat to their wealth and privilege.[70] For public banks to internalize pro-public interests, social forces must be at least as well organized (if not far better) than pro-private forces.

The future of pro-public public banking will depend on popular classes' ability to definancialize and democratize these institutions. Financialization has intensified the interconnectedness of capitalist social relations and circuits of capital, so that the essence of life-making and social reproduction is ever more subordinated to the interests of private accumulation. Neoliberal state restructuring has sought to 'de-politicize' economic decision-making by insulating the state apparatuses regulating finance and money from democratic pressures in ways that working classes and marginalized communities have yet to successfully resist and reverse. The task of socialist and progressive forces is, then, to reverse the neoliberal financial revolution by building pro-public financial capacities that can direct banking functions toward collective democratic interests and, in particular, to addressing the climate emergency.

Definancialization can be materially advanced through public banks. For those of a more Keynesian orientation, definancialization means confronting global (private) finance to roll back excessive financialized motives, markets, actors and institutions.[71] This move is necessary, but it is only a start. Socialist strategies need to be more ambitious, seeking to build capacity to control flows of capital, slow them, direct them and, ultimately, to collectively own them. Definancialization should not have the political and policy agenda of merely shrinking the total mass of finance capital or as simply re-regulating global markets. Rather, definancialization should be understood as building 'the pro-public financial capacity to democratically overwhelm the undemocratic and exploitative motives and practices of financialized capitalism over social reproduction'.[72]

Outright public (and public-like, as in cooperative and community) ownership is the only viable and realistic option at present.[73] Strategically, building pro-public public banking capacity also avoids a direct frontal confrontation with the most powerful fraction of capital today, finance capital. That is a struggle that we are at present ill-prepared to win. Yet public banks already exist and persist within the public sphere. If we are able to summon the collective power necessary to (re)set the mandate of public banks, we have the potential to definancialize them. And by doing so, we open up new and critical pathways to economic democracy.

Democratization must therefore be advanced at one and the same time in and through public banks. Harvey succinctly identifies the problem: 'the raw money power wielded by the few undermines all semblances of democratic governance'.[74] Reversing this structural trend means building capacity for people to demand of the state 'public goods for public purposes'.[75] Channeling investments to address social need rather than profit requires social control over public banks and their investments. Public bank democratization 'is about the rights of citizens, workers, women, popular classes, and the most marginalized to command a representative, meaningful, free, prior, informed, binding, and accountable say over how public banks use public resources to tackle common challenges'.[76] It is about advancing economic democracy, meaning institutionalizing the collective ability to bring societal needs to the foreground of economic planning.[77] Public banks can advance this goal by combining economic and financial power with political power, and they can do so democratically.

Nothing in what we have written should be taken as naively asserting that public banks will achieve pro-public ends merely for being 'publicly owned'. We have had to rethink public banks (just as we have the institutions that deliver public services more broadly) as dynamic entities that often institutionalize difficult contradictions.[78] In this Marxian-informed view, public banks 'are institutionalized social relations that reflect historically specific relations of power and reproduction between the banks, other firms, the state, and labor in general'.[79] This conceptual framework allows for the 'qualitative integration of agency and power struggles into an analysis of how change occurs at the level of banking institutions'.[80] In consequence, public banks are understood as being only as good or as bad as contending social forces make them, albeit within the confines of gendered, racialized and class-divided capitalist societies and a financialized world market. Yet to rethink public banks as dynamic and contested institutions within the public spheres of states within capitalism is to open up real possibilities, if not inevitabilities. A dynamic rethinking of public banks provides both a theoretical and practical alternative capable of financing pro-public green and just transitions.

In terms of strategy, there are practical yet transformational strategies that need collective action. First, educate. Critical scholars, activists, trade unionists, civil society organizations and social forces must explore and understand the material and institutional public banking capacity within their communities. Second, engage. Public banks, especially at the sub-national and national scales, are not 'out there'. They are in our communities and are often governed by people around us. Municipalities can propose useful programmes, environmental groups and social justice organizations can demand meaningful safeguards, trade unions can ask for a seat at the governing table, and so on. Fundamentally, pressure must be put on public banks' public owners to democratize the institutions and green their mandates. Third, resist. Behind the pro-public potential of public banks lurks pro-private interests that are well-organized and -resourced. The resurgent neoliberal agenda of de-risking private finance and of advancing public-private partnerships needs to be critiqued and countered. In our view, this is best done by advancing critically-informed and forward-thinking transformative green and just proposals for public banks. There is no green future that will not pass through the world's public banks, but the struggle remains as to who will stand to benefit.

NOTES

1   World Meteorological Association, 'July Sets New Record Temperatures', 13 August 2024, available at: https://wmo.int/media/news/july-sets-new-temperature-records.
2   World Economic Forum, 'The Global Gender Gap Report', 17 December 2019; and 12 June 2024, available at: www.weforum.org.
3   Peter Newell, *Power Shift: The Global Political Economy of Energy Transitions*, Cambridge: Cambridge University Press, 2021; Gareth Bryant and Sophie Webber, *Climate Finance: Taking a Position on Climate Futures*, Newcastle upon Tyne, UK: Agenda Publishing, 2024; United Nations, *Our Common Agenda Policy Brief 6: Reforms to the International Financial Architecture*, May 2023.
4   Thomas Marois, *Public Banks: Decarbonisation, Definancialisation and Democratisation*, Cambridge: Cambridge University Press, 2021.
5   Thomas Marois, 'A Dynamic Theory of Public Banks (and Why It Matters)', *Review of Political Economy*, 34(2), 2022, pp. 356-71.
6   Lucia Pradella and Thomas Marois, eds, *Polarising Development: Alternatives to Neoliberalism and the Crisis*, London: Pluto Press, 2015.
7   Marois, *Public Banks*.
8   Devin Case-Ruchala, 'An Old, Novel Idea: Introducing G-Pub, an Original Dataset of Public Bank Formation', *Review of International Political Economy*, 31(4), 2024, pp. 1271-97.
9   Laura Miquel Milian, 'The Taula de Canvi of Barcelona: Success and Troubles of a Public Bank in the Fifteenth Century', *Journal of Medieval Iberian Studies*, 13(2), 2021, pp. 236-53.
10 Eduardo Levy Yeyati et al., 'A Reappraisal of State-Owned Banks [with Comments]', *Economía (Washington, D.C.)*, 7(2), 2007, pp. 209-13.
11 World Bank, *Global Financial Development Report 2013: Rethinking the Role of State in Finance*, Washington: The World Bank, 2012, p. 120; OECD, *Investing in Climate, Investing in Growth*, Paris: OECD Publishing, 2017, p. 273.
12 UN IATF, *Financing for Sustainable Development Report*, New York: United Nations Inter-Agency Task Force on Financing for Development, 2019, p. 143.
13 See: Finance in Common Summit, available at: https://financeincommon.org/summit.
14 BankFocus, online database inquiry, 5 August 2024, *Moody's Analytics BankFocus*, 2024, available at: https://login.bvdinfo.com/R0/BankFocus.
15 These calculations are based on 2020 Bank Focus data, cited in Marois, *Public Banks*, p. 43.
16 BankFocus online database inquiry, 2024.
17 David Harvey, *The Limits to Capital*, Oxford: B. Blackwell, 1982; Leo Panitch and Sam Gindin, *The Making of Global Capitalism: The Political Economy of American Empire*, London: Verso, 2012.
18 Costas Lapavitsas and Paulo L. Dos Santos, 'Globalization and Contemporary Banking: On the Impact of New Technology', *Contributions to Political Economy*, 27(1), 2008, p. 34; Thomas Marois, 'A Dynamic Theory of Public Banks (and Why it Matters)', *Review of Political Economy*, 34(2), 2022, pp. 356-71.
19 Robert Guttmann, *How Credit-Money Shapes the Economy: The United States in a Global System*, New York: M.E. Sharpe, 1994; Mike Hall, 'On the Creation of Money

and the Accumulation of Bank Capital', *Capital and Class*, 16(3), 1992, pp. 89-114; Lapavitsas and Dos Santos, 'Globalization and Contemporary Banking'; Paul M. Sweezy, *The Theory of Capitalist Development: Principles of Marxian Political Economy*, New York: Monthly Review Press, 1970 [1942]; Harvey, *The Limits to Capital*, p. 247.

20   Brett Christophers, *Why the Market will Never Solve the Climate Crisis*, London: Verso. 2024.

21   Harvey, *The Limits to Capital*; François Chesnais, *Finance Capital Today: Corporations and Banks in the Lasting Global Slump*, Boston, MA: Brill, 2016; and Thomas Marois, *States, Banks and Crisis: Emerging Finance Capitalism in Mexico and Turkey*, Cheltenham, UK: Edward Elgar, 2012.

22   Karl Marx, *Capital, Vol. III*, London: Penguin, 1990 [1976], p. 778.

23   Rudolf Hilferding, *Finance Capital: A Study of the Latest Phase of Capitalist Development*, trans. by Morris Watnick and Sam Gordon, London: Routledge, 2006 [1910], p. 180.

24   Paul M. Sweezy, 'More (or Less) on Globalization', *Monthly Review*, 49(4), 1997, p. 3.

25   John Bellamy Foster, 'The Financialization of Capital and the Crisis', *Monthly Review*, 59(11), 2008, pp. 1-19; Costas Lapavitsas, 'Financialised Capitalism: Crisis and Financial Expropriation', *Historical Materialism*, 17, 2009, pp. 114-48; Paulo dos Santos, 'On the Content of Banking in Contemporary Capitalism', *Historical Materialism*, 17, 2009, pp.180-213; Ben Fine, 'Locating Financialisation', *Historical Materialism*, 18, 2010, pp. 97-116.

26   Fine, 'Locating Financialisation'.

27   Jennifer Clapp and S. Ryan Isakson, *Speculative Harvests: Financialization, Food and Agriculture*, Winnipeg: Fernwood, 2018 ; Nadine Reis, Germán Vargas Magaña and Santiago Vélez Villegas, 'Water, Finance and Financialization: A Review', *Water Alternatives*, 17(2), 2024, pp. 266-91; Susanne Soederberg, ed., *Risking Capitalism*, Bingley: Emerald, 2016; Ilias Alami et al., 'International Financial Subordination: A Critical Research Agenda', *Review of International Political Economy*, 30(4), 2023, pp.1360-86.

28   For exceptions, see: Marois, *States, Banks and Crisis*; Marois, *Public Banks*.

29   David McNally, *Blood and Money: War, Slavery, Finance, and Empire*, Chicago, Illinois: Haymarket Books, 2020; Stephen Maher and Scott M. Aquanno, *The Fall and Rise of American Finance: From J.P. Morgan to Blackrock*, London: Verso, 2024; Adrienne Roberts, 'Gender, Financial Deepening and the Production of Embodied Finance: Towards a Critical Feminist Analysis', *Global Society*, 29(1), pp. 107-27; Newell, *Power Shift*; Bryant and Webber, *Climate Finance*.

30   Vladimir I. Lenin, 'Can the Bolsheviks Retain Power?', in *Collected Works*, Moscow: Progress Publishers, 26, 1972, pp. 87-136.

31   Vladimir I. Lenin, 'How to Organise Competition?', in *Collected Works*, 26, 1972, p. 407.

32   Vladimir I. Lenin, 'The Russian Revolution and Civil War They Are Trying To Frighten Us With Civil War', in *Collected Works, 26*, 1972, pp. 28-42.

33   Becky Chiu and Mervyn K. Lewis, *Reforming China's State-owned Enterprises and Banks*. Cheltenham, UK: Edward Elgar Publishing, 2006; Central Bank of Cuba, available at: www.bc.gob.cu.

34   Bank nationalizations can equally constitute a form of working–class subordination by capital via the socialization of private investors' risks and debts within specific historical and class formations. See: Thomas Marois, 'Emerging Market Bank Rescues in an Era of Finance-Led Neoliberalism: A Comparison of Mexico and Turkey', *Review of International Political Economy*, (18)2, 2011, pp. 168-96.

35   Peter Gowan, *The Global Gamble*, London: Verso, 1999.

36   FNFMB (First Nations Financial Management Board), *RoadMap Project Chapter 4: Unlocking Economies*, 2022.

37   Milan Babic and Sarah E. Sharma, 'Mobilising Critical International Political Economy for the Age of Climate Breakdown', *New Political Economy*, 28(5), pp. 758-79.

38   Bertrand Badré, *Can Finance Save the World? Regaining Power Over Money to Serve the Common Good*, Oakland, CA: Berrett-Koehler Publishers, 2018.

39   Adrian Murray and Susan Spronk, 'Blended Financing, Canadian Foreign Aid Policy, and Alternatives', *Studies in Political Economy*, 100(3), 2019, pp. 270-86; Marois, *Public Banks*.

40   Eurodad, 'Financing for Development and the SDGs: An Analysis of Financial Flows, Systemic Issues and Interlinkages', Eurodad, 2018, available at: www.eurodad.org; Bryant and Webber *Climate Finance*; Christophers, *Why the Market Will Never Solve the Climate Crisis*.

41   TNI, '"Green" Multinationals Exposed: How the Energy Transition is Being Hijacked by Corporate Interests', Transnational Institute, 2023, available at: www.tni.org.

42   EPSC, 'Financing Sustainability: Triggering Investments for the Clean Economy', *EPSC Strategic Notes*, issue 25, Brussels: European Political Strategy Centre, European Commission, 8 June 2017.

43   See, for example: 'World Bank Group Timeline', available at: https://timeline. worldbank.org/en/timeline/eventdetail/3381; The Global Commission on the Economics of Water, available at: https://watercommission.org; The Glasgow Financial Alliance for Net Zero, available at: www.gfanzero.com.

44   UN, *Our Common Agenda*.

45   UNCTAD, 'SDG Investment: Trends Monitor, United Nations Conference on Trade and Development', Issue 4, Geneva: UNCTAD, September 2023; UNCTAD, *Trade and Development Report 2019, 'Financing a Global Green New Deal'*, Geneva: UNCTAD, 2019.

46   Lawrence H. Summers and N.K. Singh, 'The World is Still On Fire', *Project Syndicate*, 15 April 2024.

47   CPI, *Global Landscape of Climate Finance: 2023,* London: Climate Policy Initiative, 2023, updated 12 January 2024.

48   Marois, *Public Banks*, p. 40.

49   CPI, *Global Landscape*; Bryant and Webber, *Climate Finance*.

50   FiC Joint CSO Statement, 'Public Development Banks Must Deliver on the World We Want', 10 November 2020, available at: www.eurodad.org; David A. McDonald, Thomas Marois and Susan Spronk, 'Public Banks + Public Water = SDG 6?', *Water Alternatives*, 14(1), 2021, pp. 117-34; Thomas Marois, 'The Potential of Public Banks to Fund Local Quality Public Services: A Policy Brief for Workers and Trade Unions', Geneva: Public Services International, 2023.

51   UN Women, *World Survey on the Role of Women in Development 2014: Gender Equality and Sustainable Development*, New York: United Nations, 2014.

52   Stephanie Seguino, *Financing for Gender Equality in the Context of the Sustainable Development Goals*, Discussion Paper No. 11, Geneva: UN Women, 2016.

53   Gita Sen and Caren Grown, *Development, Crises and Alternative Visions: Third World Women's Perspectives*, London: Earthscan, 1988; Corina Rodríguez and Masaya Llavenaras Blanco, eds, *Corporate Capture of Development: Public-Private Partnerships, Women's Human Rights, and Global Resistance*, London: Bloomsbury Academic, 2023.

54   Nordic Investment Bank, 'World's Most Striking Power Plant Wins Architecture Prize,' 28 September 2016, available at: www.nib.int.

55   NIB, 'NIB to Update Its Sustainability Policy', Helsinki: Nordic Investment Bank, 2021, available at: www.nib.int.

56   Petri S. Juuti, Riikka P Juuti and David A. McDonald, 'Boldly Boring: Public Banks and Public Water in the Nordic Region', *Water International*, 47(5), 2022, pp. 791–809.

57   Melina Tobías and Devin Case-Ruchula, 'The Hard Work of Progressive Public Lending: FONPLATA and Financing the Sustainable Development Goals in Buenos Aires', in David A. McDonald, Thomas Marois and Susan Spronk, eds, *Public Banks and Public Water in the Global South*, London: Routledge, 2025.

58   Ali Rıza Güngen, '"No One Can Compete since No One Dares to Lend More Cheaply!": Turkey's Ilbank and Public Water Finance', *Water International*, 47(5), 2022, pp. 771-90.

59   Güngen, '"No One Can Compete"', p. 774.

60   Marois, 'A Dynamic Theory'.

61   Rokin Labour Bank (RLB), *Annual Report 2022*, Tokyo: National Association of Labour Banks, 2022, p. 3, available at: https://all.rokin.or.jp/en.

62   Akira Kurimoto and Takashi Koseki, 'Rokin Banks: 70 Years of Efforts to Build an Inclusive Society in Japan Through Enhancing Workers' Access to Finance', Paper No. 76, Geneva: International Labour Organization, 2019, p. 12.

63   RLB, *Annual Report 2022,* p. 7.

64   RLB, *Annual Report 2022*.

65   See: RLB, 'Labour Bank SDGs Action Guidelines', March 2019, available at: https://all.rokin.or.jp/file/The%20Labour%20Bank%20SDGs%20Action%20Guidelines.pdf.

66   Susan Spronk, Karina Valverde and Thomas Marois, 'Democratic Patient Finance: The Banco Popular and Community-Based Water Operators in Costa Rica', in David A. McDonald, Thomas Marois and Susan Spronk, eds., *Public Banks and Public Water in the Global South*, London: Routledge, 2025.

67   Marois, *Public Banks*, p. 211.

68   Marois, *Public Banks*, pp. 214-5.

69   Spronk et al., 'Democratic Patient Finance.'

70   Marois, *Public Banks*, p. 147.

71   Ewa Karwowski, 'Towards (De-)Financialisation: The Role of the State', *Cambridge Journal of Economics*, 43(4), 2019, pp. 1001-27.

72   Marois, *Public Banks*, p. 154.

73   Thomas Hanna, *The Crisis Next Time: Planning for Public Ownership as an Alternative to Corporate Bank Bailouts*, Washington: The Democracy Collaborative, 2018; Lavinia Steinfort and Satoko Kishimoto, eds, *Public Finance for the Future We Want*, Amsterdam:

Transnational Institute, 2019.

74   David Harvey, *The Enigma of Capital and the Crises of Capitalism*, London: Profile Books, 2010, p. 220.

75   David Harvey, *Rebel Cities: From the Right to the City to the Urban Revolution*, London: Verso, 2012, p. 88.

76   Marois, *Public Banks*, p. 186.

77   Gregory Albo, 'The World Economy, Market Imperatives and Alternatives,' *Monthly Review*, 48(7), 1996, pp. 6-22; Henri Lefebvre, *Marxist Thought and the City*, trans. by Robert Bononno, Minneapolis: University of Minnesota Press, 2016[1972], p. 132.

78   Gregory Albo, 'The Public Sector Impasse and the Administrative Question,' *Studies in Political Economy*, 42(1), 1993, pp. 113-127; David A. McDonald and Greg Ruiters, eds, *Alternatives to Privatization: Public Options for Essential Services in the Global South*, New York: Routledge, 2012.

79   Marois, *States, Banks and Crisis*, p. 29.

80   Marois, *States, Banks and Crisis*, p. 29.

IS IT RACE OR RACISM? WHY BINARY EXPLANATIONS FOR INEQUALITY HAVE FAILED BLACK AMERICANS

TOURÉ F. REED

In late September 2023, scholar and public intellectual Ibram X. Kendi was swept into a maelstrom of controversy. Specifically, Kendi was accused of misappropriating funds in his capacity as director of Boston University's Center for Antiracist Research. The charges received a great deal of attention because since the 'racial reckoning' that followed the brutal murder of George Floyd, Kendi – a *New York Times* best-selling author, recipient of the 2016 National Book Award (for 2015's *Stamped from the Beginning*), favorite photo-op for Democratic politicians, and MacArthur Genius grant recipient – has been among the best known contemporary black American antiracists.

Given the accolades he has garnered, it should not surprise that Kendi would also become one of the most prominent academic beneficiaries of racial justice oriented corporate largess. The ubiquitous calls for a racial reckoning during the 'Great Awokening' of 2020 translated into a flood of corporate sponsorship for racial justice initiatives. In February of 2023, the McKinsey Institute for Black Economic Mobility reported that between May 2020 and October 2022, corporations had pledged some $340 billion to racial justice initiatives – with just sixteen Fortune 1000 Corporations accounting for 93 per cent of these pledges.[1]

After his appointment as head of the Center for Antiracist Research, Kendi would help raise $55 million – with contributions coming from more than 3,000 donors, including $10 million from Twitter's Jack Dorsey, $1.5 million coming in from biotech firm Vertex and T.J. Maxx respectively, and $25 million from an anonymous donor.[2]

Although Kendi has been accused of mismanaging the centre's funds, I am agnostic on this matter if for no other reason than it is not yet clear that Kendi did anything wrong.[3] The aim of this piece, then, is far removed from a desire to join the pile-on questioning Kendi's managerial competence.

Rather, Kendi's evolving perceptions of inequality offer a useful window onto an unsatisfying binary that has long driven liberal and even popular understandings of the root causes of enduring disparities.

Since the 2016 Democratic primaries, racial justice discourse has condensed around the insistence that Democratic social policies have failed to eliminate disparities because liberals have refused to recognize racial inequality as an evil distinct from class inequality. The political utility of this problematic claim is transparent. Hillary Clinton and the Democratic National Committee (DNC) gravitated toward frameworks such as implicit bias and systemic racism as explanations for entrenched racial inequalities in order to both marginalize Bernie Sanders as a so-called 'class reductionist' and to deflect attention from the policy contributions of the centrist 'New Democrats' to incarceration and disparities in homeownership and income. As the Covid-19 pandemic only strengthened support among Democratic voters for Sanders's signature issues – Medicare for All, in particular – liberals, corporate media, major corporations and university administrators tightened their embrace of a racial justice framework that insisted on divorcing disparities from capitalism. Prominent antiracist thinkers such as Robin DiAngelo, Ta-Nehisi Coates and Ibram X. Kendi have played an important role in this project. In branding efforts that are best suited to nurturing personal growth as if they were programs capable of engendering structural transformation, these and other liberal antiracists have tended to attribute lingering inequalities to an aggregate of white bad actors – references to systemic or structural racism notwithstanding – rather than the product of a system, capitalism, whose very structure produces material inequalities that cross the boundaries of race, sex, sexuality, etc.[4]

From the vantage point of intellectual and political history, perhaps the most striking thing about the now commonplace contention that Democratic policymakers' class reductionism – expressed in a preference for class-based, rather than race-based, analyses and remedies for inequality – is at the heart of liberals' decadeslong failure to eliminate disparities is that the claim is simply wrong. To be sure, postwar liberalism failed to end what we generally call racial inequality, even if fair housing legislation along with workplace antidiscrimination laws and initiatives have helped to improve the material conditions of the black white-collar professionals, public sector employees and service sector workers who were/are well-positioned to ride the wave of the post-industrial economy. Nevertheless, as I have argued elsewhere, modern liberalism's inability to eliminate disparities is not owed to liberals' *alleged* 'class reductionism' but to their *real* 'race reductionism'. Rather than situating racial inequalities within American political-economy (or late capitalism), liberal policymakers' and intellectuals' perceptions of and responses to lingering disparities have generally oscillated between two racialist poles: *race*, in the form black people's alleged cultural deficiencies (underclass tropes) or *racism*, in the form of white people's alleged cultural deficiencies (the so-called 'original sin' of racism).

Ironically, despite the now dominant insistence to the contrary, class-oriented analyses of racial disparities have been largely displaced from *realpolitik* discourse on inequality, as policymakers and 'serious scholars' since the Kennedy administration have generally viewed black poverty as exceptional to capitalism. This tendency, as I will discuss below, has been disproportionately, though not exclusively, detrimental to African Americans.

Kendi's public persona and the fanfare surrounding him give the impression that his work represents a radical departure from liberal orthodoxies; however, the substance of his project deviates little from acceptable liberal discourse on racial inequality. Kendi's historical and political analyses also proceed from a binary frame – though, officially, not the race-racism frame. Specifically, he views 'racial inequity' and its fixes through the lens of *racism* and *antiracism*. Kendi defines racism, reasonably in my view, as the belief in 'a racial hierarchy' or any concept that regards one group as inferior or superior to another.[5] I have argued elsewhere that the belief in biological or quasi-biological races may be a more broadly useful definition of racism than Kendi's, insofar as this cultivated belief serves as the ideological and cultural basis for both reifying inequalities that are the product of social relations and the insistence that racial groups are distinguished from each other by discrete interests. Nevertheless, he and I share the view that European explorers, conquerors, slaveholders and the intellectuals and governments that supported them invented race (in the late-18th century in my view, in the 15th century in Kendi's) to treat social hierarchies as if they were the product of nature or divinity.[6]

Kendi ultimately contends that racism is the product of racist policies, which engender racist attitudes. Here too, at the most basic level, he is onto something. Consider, for example, the racial attitudes nurtured by redlining. Between the dawn of the 20th century and the mid-1930s, the real estate industry and the Federal Housing Administration's (FHA) Homer Hoyt – the former chief economist of the National Association of Real Estate Boards – identified a neighborhood's racial composition as one of many factors determining property values.[7] Enshrining best business practices into law, discriminatory FHA mortgage policies did not simply deny blacks and other so-called racial undesirables access to government subsidized mortgages. The statute lent coherence and force to the devaluation of homes in 'white neighborhoods' that were either in proximity to African American communities or, worse yet, in which black residents had 'invaded'. In practice, such policies cultivated among white homeowners a logical, if despicable, racial hostility toward African Americans and other non-whites whose mere presence – irrespective of any other redeeming qualities – threatened white homeowners' most prized investment.

To be sure, discriminatory laws, like FHA mortgage policy, were not handed down from on high. Much like the 17th century Virginia statute that reserved permanent bondage for Africans and American Indians while exempting English indentured servants from chattel slavery,[8] powerful constituencies – be they plantation owners or the real estate and banking industries –determined the policies that reified blacks' and other non-whites' social inferiority. Still, the impetus for such policies cannot be reduced to Kendi's racist and anti-racist binary, which obscures a foundational matter. The powerful burgesses who shaped the Thirteen Colonies' laws in the 17th and 18th centuries and the interests who shaped early 20th century real estate valuations were not merely invested in racial domination; rather, they invented and codified racial distinctions into law (in the case of colonial America) or they utilized extant racial taxonomies (20th century housing policies) to establish politically viable and ultimately contextually contingent means of *economic exploitation*. Indeed, this is why roughly 90 per cent of homeowners living in redlined communities were white.[9]

Though elements of Kendi's definition of 'racism' and his formal perspective on the relationship between race and policy are not without value, his definitions for 'racists' and 'antiracists' along with his related tendency to equate racial disparities with racist policies are less compelling. As others have noted, Kendi applies racism so liberally that he, ironically, divests the word of much of its explanatory power. According to him, 'a racist policy' is any policy that produces a disparity. 'A racist', in his view, is one who endorses racist policies. 'Racist ideas' inform and, thus, buttress racists' commitments to policies that produce disparities by attributing inequities to the engrained or intrinsic characteristics of the alleged inferior and superior racial groups.[10]

Drug sentencing disparities might appear to affirm the utility of Kendi's definition of racist policies. For example, the 1997 Congressional US Sentencing Commission found that while whites constituted the majority of crack users, blacks accounted for 90 per cent of individuals prosecuted for crack possession under federal drug laws. These sentencing disparities undoubtedly contributed to blacks' overrepresentation among the inmate population. But if one considers the fact that, during the 1990s, the black murder rate was roughly four times their share of the total population (eight times higher than whites' murder rate), would it still be reasonable to attribute blacks' overrepresentation among the inmate population *simply* to the racism embedded in the criminal justice system? Since it is also true that African Americans were the majority of victims of violent crime and property thefts perpetrated disproportionately by blacks, should we conclude that antiblack racism motivated both the 84 per cent of black voters who, in 1996, cast ballots endorsing Bill Clinton's tough on crime political agenda and two-thirds of the members of the Congressional Black Caucus who voted for the 1994 Omnibus Crime Act , which – as we all know today, but was evident then, too – impacted blacks disproportionately?[11] Simply put, blacks' overrepresentation among inmates during the 1990s is not reducible to racism in the criminal justice system.

When confronted with the myriad inequalities and undemocratic dispositions that shape the material world, Kendi ultimately responds with a multiplicity of subgroupings of racism and by extension racists including: 'biological racism', 'ethnic racism', 'cultural racism', 'segregationist racism', 'assimilationist racism', 'class racism', and a host of other racist subgroupings that word count constraints will not permit me to list.

The bottom line is that, whatever the particulars, in Kendi's view racism in its many forms is the ultimate source of inequalities that impact blacks disproportionately but not exclusively. Thus, at this stage of Kendi's intellectual and political life, he champions the *racism* half of the race-racism binary that has long driven liberal discourse and public policy aimed at addressing inequality.

According to Kendi, antiracism is the only real fix for pervasive disparities. But what is antiracism? Kendi contends that antiracism is first and foremost policies that 'lead to racial equity'. Such policies must be buttressed by 'antiracist ideas' that reject the notion that inequities are rooted in racial group characteristics and instead identify disparities as unimpeachable evidence of racism.

What might antiracist policies look like? Well, in a 2019 *Politico* thought piece, Kendi argued that America might finally 'fix the original sin of racism' by ratifying an antiracist amendment to the Constitution. The proposed amendment 'would make unconstitutional racial inequity over a certain threshold as well as racist ideas by public officials'. The amendment would establish and 'permanently fund the Department of Antiracism (DOA)', whose 'trained experts on racism … would be responsible for preclearing all local, state and federal public policies to ensure' they would not yield racial disparities.[12]

Donald Trump's third year in the White House seemed a peculiar moment to propose an antiracist constitutional amendment, as Trumpism should have eliminated all doubt about the political vulnerabilities of even extant affirmative action initiatives. Indeed, despite the fact that the beneficiaries of antidiscrimination policies include more than half the US adult population, affirmative action's susceptibility to sometimes disingenuous political attacks can be traced, in some part, to the sway of anti-statism and the related politics of resentment engendered by bipartisan acceptance of precarity for all. Of course, this acceptance comes with the exceptions of those deemed too big to fail and an increasingly narrow sliver of so-called protected classes. One might, therefore, wonder if Kendi's decision to assign the acronym DOA to his proposed government agency announced that he too was aware that this project was dead on arrival.

Perhaps because his political project casts improbable reforms that are incapable of generating wide political support as the best hope for radical change, Kendi remains among the most influential champions of the corporate-approved antiracism movement. However, his reflections on his pivotal if not transformative senior year of high school reveal that, in the early 2000s, Kendi embraced very different sensibilities about race, racism and inequality. In his best-selling primer, *How to Be an Antiracist*, Kendi confesses that he, much like Barack Obama, had been uncertain about the value of school during adolescence. While Kendi was a dedicated and skilled athlete, the confidence he had on the basketball court did not initially carry over into the classroom. Young-Kendi was, thus, riddled with self-doubt about his intellectual abilities, as he succumbed to pervasive racist stereotypes about black men.[13] Despite his intellectual insecurities and uneven academic performance, Kendi tells us he was a competent, if eccentric, orator. And it is the oratorical muscle he flexed at a competition in early 2000 that not only bolstered Kendi's academic confidence, but crucially offers a clear window onto the contrast between Kendi's perspectives on racial inequality at the dawn of the 21st century and his antiracist intellectual and political project today. Simply put, young-Kendi, like most of his contemporaries twenty-five years ago, tended to attribute inequality to *race* rather than *racism*.[14]

In his last year of high school, Kendi won speech competitions sponsored by his school and the county. In January 2000, he would deliver a rousing speech to the Prince William County Dr. Martin Luther King, Jr. Oratorical Contest – an event sponsored by the historically black Delta Sigma Theta sorority. Reimagining Martin Luther King Jr's 'I Have a Dream Speech' for the new millennium, young-Kendi's address centered on the alleged cultural deficiencies of black Americans. 'Now one hundred thirty-five years' after emancipation, he said, 'the Negro is still not free. Our youths' minds are still in captivity!'. He continued, 'They think it's okay to be those who are most feared in our society! … They think it's okay not to think! … They think it's okay to climb the high tree of pregnancy! … They think it's okay to confine their dreams to sports and music!"[15]

The minds of black youth and adults remain 'captive', young-Kendi declared, 'because they somehow think that the cultural revolution that began on the day of [King's] dream's birth is over. How can it be over when *many times* [emphasis added] we are unsuccessful because we lack intestinal fortitude'. 'How can it be over', he continued, 'when our kids leave their houses not knowing how to make themselves, only knowing how to not make themselves? How can it be over if all of this is happening in our community?'[16]

Today, Kendi is 'flush with shame' about what he describes as the 'racist speech [he] gave' as a teen, and wonders whether he projected onto 'his people' his own low self-esteem or if the low regard he had for 'his people' informed his poor sense of self. Irrespective of whether young-Kendi's speech revealed his own self-loathing, his address was pregnant with the racialist tropes that dominated discourse on inequality from the 1980s through the Obama presidency. It is important to keep in mind, however, that Kendi's speech did not disparage black people, per se. In fact, young-Kendi was careful to caveat his victim blaming. He used the third-person plural (they) to describe black Americans' deficiencies as readily as he used the first-person plural (we/our) to assert kinship. Likewise, when he stated that '*many times* we are unsuccessful because we lack intestinal fortitude', he was not suggesting that *all* blacks lacked gumption; he was implying *some* did. Kendi's audience understood this distinction, as he reports that the African American attendees and judges enthusiastically applauded his address. If young-Kendi's speech were disparaging *black people*, then why did his audience take to it with such zeal?[17]

Young-Kendi's speech resonated with his black audience because it was *not* driven by racial self-hatred. Whether he knew it at the time, young-Kendi was rehearsing 'underclass' tropes that had become mainstream by the end of the 1980s and hegemonic by the Clinton years. The term 'underclass' was coined in the 1960s; however, it would not gain popular usage until the 1980s. Though 'class' appears in the compound word 'underclass', the term functions to divorce economic inequalities from the capitalist processes that generate them. The underclass construct described a stratum of poor blacks and certain Hispanic populations in expressly *culturalist*, but fundamentally *racialist*, rather than class, terms. Indeed, underclass ideology traced poverty to poor people's alleged cultural dysfunction. Extrapolating from anthropologist Oscar Lewis's culture of poverty thesis, proponents of underclass ideology claimed that 10–20 per cent – not all – of the urban black and Latino poor were in the grip of a self-perpetuating cycle of pathological behaviors, characterized by welfare dependency, drug and alcohol dependency, promiscuity, a disregard for education, and criminal activity. [18]

President Reagan's attacks on means-tested programs, such as Aid to Families with Dependent Children (AFDC) and the Food Stamp Program, were frequently wed to lurid tales of irresponsible, profligate minorities whom he alleged were bleeding the nation dry one out-of-wedlock pregnancy and pink Cadillac at a time.[19] While President Bill Clinton's appearances at black churches and on the Arsenio Hall Show (hosted by the eponymous popular African American talk show host) gave some hope that the centrist-Democrat might end Reagan's racist, underclass-informed war on poor people, Clinton's 1992 platform left little doubt that the Democratic party of the 1990s owed more to Reagan than Franklin Roosevelt or Lyndon Johnson. Citing the work of black sociologist William J. Wilson, Clinton echoed Reagan's concerns about crime, welfare dependency and the prevalence of female headed households in ghetto communities. Clinton was careful to attribute the root causes of ghetto underclass behavior to deindustrialization.[20] However, instead of pursuing a legislative agenda centered on bolstering the manufacturing sector or promoting unionization, Clinton targeted the so-called underclass with jail via the Omnibus Crime Act (1994), limited their access to federal financial assistance via the Personal Responsibility and Work Opportunity Reconciliation Act (1996) and razed their homes via HOPE VI (1998).[21]

As neoliberalism foreclosed state remedies to the economic inequalities that were at the heart of the social problems that impacted majority black and brown communities disproportionately, *realpolitik* discourse on disparities among black Americans coalesced more and more around underclass tropes. Simply put, the attachment to racialist explanations for inequality expressed by young-Kendi and embraced by his black audience were hardly unique.

From the 1980s through the Obama Presidency, black Americans across the political spectrum echoed concerns about the web of social pathologies that allegedly ensnared many –though not all – blacks. Surging rates of murder, drug-gang related violence, property theft, welfare dependency, and 'baby mama drama' all comprised the standard litany of alleged black social dysfunction.

By the 1990s, the high rates of gun-related homicide among black men triggered alarm among elected officials and black voters alike, as African Americans were overrepresented among both perpetrators and victims. Scholarship, then and now, revealed a strong correlation between violent crime and poverty;[22] however, by the early-1990s those who insisted on viewing violent crime through the lens of political economy were regularly accused of enabling, if not coddling criminals. Since 2016, centrist Democrats such as Secretary of State Hillary Clinton and President Joe Biden have railed against systemic racism. In the 1990s, however, First Lady Hillary Clinton's and Senator Joe Biden's public addresses in support for the Violent Crime Control and Law Enforcement Act were actively dismissive of the systemic or structural roots of crime and inequality.

In her now infamous 'super predators' speech, First Lady Clinton warned that drug cartels were producing a distinct breed of violent criminals. 'They're not just gangs of kids anymore', she said. 'They are often the kinds of kids that are called super-predators … no conscience, no empathy.' According to Clinton, the immediate threat these savage brutes posed to law abiding citizens required a swift and harsh response from law enforcement. 'We can talk about why they ended up that way," she said, "but first we have to bring them to heel".[23] If Joe Biden's case for the crime act was more colorful than Clinton's, the First Lady and the Senator were united in the belief that the systemic roots of crime were irrelevant. As Biden asserted on the floor of the US Senate:

> It doesn't matter whether or not the person that is accosting your son or daughter or my son or daughter, my wife, your husband, my mother, your parents, it doesn't matter if they were deprived as a youth. It doesn't matter whether or not they had no background that enabled them to become socialized into the fabric of society. It doesn't matter whether or not they're the victim of society. The end result is they're about to knock my mother over the head with a lead pipe, shoot my sister, beat up my wife, take on my sons.

Biden concluded 'so, I don't want to ask what made them do this. They must be taken off the street.'[24]

During Hillary Clinton's and Joe Biden's presidential campaigns, criminal justice reform activists reminded voters of the pivotal role played by the underclass-informed super predator trope in centrist Democrats' case for the 1994 crime act. What has garnered less attention and inspired even less reflection, however, is underclass ideology's sway over *black* popular discourse on inequality during the same period. As both Republicans and Democrats discouraged racial minorities and other working people from turning to the state for material redress; as draconian policing and mass incarceration – the warehousing of the reserve army of labour – were among the few available remedies for the social consequences of depressed wages and concentrated poverty in America's post-industrial cities; and as neoliberalism ushered in the return of scientific racism and Social Darwinism by other names; black *realpolitik* and cultural sensibilities shifted to the right – again, just as neoliberal political orthodoxies would ravage black America.

In a 1990 *Washington Post* interview centered on a recent surge in so-called black-on-black murder rates in Washington DC, Reverand Jesse Jackson asserted that the fix lay squarely on the shoulders of blacks for the fratricide running rampant in black communities. Drawing, as he often did, on a sports analogy, Jackson said:

> When a basketball team keeps missing free throws, they don't blame the conditions or the rules of the game or unfair officiating. They work on analysis, timing, technique, trajectory. Well, when our team keeps making babies out of wedlock, keeps having crack-addicted babies, keeps on killing each other, it's time for analysis.[25]

Jackson discouraged blacks from turning to the government for assistance, asserting, instead, that African Americans needed to take personal responsibility for their own problems.

> It's all well and good to talk about oppression, but we've got to rid ourselves of that with which we want our oppressors to be rid of. We've got to go to the question of introspection, without being defensive or feeling that to talk honestly about these issues somehow compromises the race.[26]

Honest discussion, of course, meant divorcing symptoms of economic inequality – like violent crime – from their political-economic context by blending the racialist language of 'fratricide' and 'black-on-black crime' (which announced camaraderie) with underclass-informed tales of racial group cultural dysfunction.

A few years later, comedian Chris Rock would echo Jackson's sentiments in his breakout routine, 'the difference between black people and niggas'. Rock began by asking the audience: 'who's more racist, white people or black people?' Answering his own question, Rock declared: 'Black people. Ya know why? Because we hate black people, too!' After asserting 'there's a Civil War going on in [mid-1990s] America' between 'black people and niggas', Rock railed against 'niggas" penchant for gunplay, duplicity, criminality, willful embrace of ignorance, welfare dependency and the collective acceptance of child abandonment along with the related perception of 'taking care of [one's own] kids' as exceptional.[27]

Rock's reflections on the, then, pending welfare reform of the Personal Responsibility and Work Opportunity Act are especially instructive: 'Every time you see welfare in the news, they always show black people. Black people don't give a fuck about welfare. Niggas are shaking in their boots.'[28] Rock went on to exclaim that hard-working, tax-paying black men and women hate the irresponsible 'niggas on welfare' who support their children on the taxpayer's dime. Harmonizing with sentiments expressed by then Senator Joe Biden and First Lady Hillary Clinton, Rock's bit rejected the value of situating the symptoms of poverty within their social context. Instead, he presumed that welfare recipiency was itself a scarlet letter announcing the beneficiaries' depravity.

> It ain't all black people on welfare. White people are on welfare, too. But we can't give a fuck about them. We just gotta do our own thing. We can't be like 'oh they fucked up we can be fucked up'.[29]

Like young-Kendi's reimagining of King's 'I have a Dream Speech', Rock's 'black people vs niggas' routine ultimately recast a class divide among African Americans as a racial one. Indeed, Rock insinuates that white welfare recipients and black welfare recipients, the latter presented as 'niggas', shared common traits, distinguishing both from 'black people'.

Rock's racialized characterizations of poor blacks offer a window onto the pervasiveness of such explicitly class-free accounts of inequality. Indeed, one would find the same themes running through superficially sympathetic but fundamentally reactionary depictions of ghetto life in films of the era such as: Stephen Milburn Anderson's *South Central* (1992), the Hughes Brothers' *Menace II Society* (1993), John Singleton's *Boyz N the Hood* (1991) and *Baby Boy* (2001), and the 2009 film *Precious* produced by, among others, Lee Daniels, Tyler Perry, and Oprah Winfrey.

If one is underwhelmed by the imprint of these tropes on black film and comedy, it would be worth reflecting on the centrality of underclass tropes to President Barack Obama's so-called post-racial presidential bid and presidency. Indeed, Obama's 2004 DNC address discouraged blacks from expecting government to fix all of their problems while encouraging them to be more engaged parents; his 2008 race speech, 'A More Perfect Union' not only suggested that older blacks, like Reverend Jerimiah Wright, were trapped in a feedback loop of psychological traumas inflicted upon them by a Jim Crow era that had long since passed, but he also insinuated that overly permissive welfare policies undermined black family formation and contributed to social dysfunction; and, of course, his 2008 'Father's Day Speech' lectured African American fathers about the importance of personal responsibility, asserting that the failure of too many black men to instill values of excellence, empathy, hope and self-reliance in their children was a key contributor to ghetto social malaise.[30]

Obama's disposition to scold inner-city minorities did not preclude the helping hand of government. However, when combined with the Jedi-mind-trick-like assertion in this his 2004 DNC address that inner-city residents did not expect government to solve *all* of their problems, Obama's embrace of underclass ideology signaled to Democrats and even conservatives that he, like Bill Clinton before him, had little interest in redressing the material roots of inequality – a reality that was, ironically, softened by Obama's folksy references to seemingly more benign black archetypes such as the loveable but lazy 'Cousin Pookie'.[31]

It is worth noting that while Chris Rock and Obama's rehearsals of underclass tropes helped catapult them to super-stardom and the White House respectively, comedian Bill Cosby's infamous 2004 'Poundcake' speech – delivered at the NAACP's 50th Anniversary of the *Brown* Decision –tarnished his then lofty reputation, even as his remarks paralleled those of Jackson, Rock and Obama. Indeed, Jackson, Obama, Rock and Cosby each described the same landscape of black social pathologies. However, Cosby deigned to say the unspoken part out loud. Whereas Rock and Obama avoided formal reference to *economic class* via racial slur (niggas) and archetype ('Cousin Pookie'), Cosby explicitly assigned the hegemonic underclass tropes to poor and working-class blacks.[32]

To be clear, scholars left little doubt as to the economic background of the so-called underclass, even as the culturalist frame itself practically uncoupled black poverty from its political-economic roots (wage and trade policies, deindustrialization, the postwar transformation of American cities, the long consequences of discriminatory mortgage policy and the retreat from quality public housing, etc.). The popular usage of underclass tropes, however, was much fuzzier on the alleged causal relationship between the dysfunctional behavior of poor African Americans and poverty. In the hands of the black 'folk', the class background of underclass archetypes was often obscured by a language of racial group fraternity expressed by team metaphors and a tendency to oscillate between the first and third person plural. It was further obscured by the related disposition to wed calls for collective responsibility to a narrative that traced the ultimate source of contemporary social ills not to late capitalism's disproportionate impact on blacks – exacerbated by the racial limits of New Deal and postwar liberalism – but to the *psychological damage* whites inflicted upon blacks via *sui generis* racial institutions such as slavery and Jim Crow. This is to say, Cosby may have rehearsed the same litany of underclass tropes as nearly everyone else at the time; however, his decision to say 'the quiet part' out loud was unique, as was the popular backlash to his articulation of otherwise commonplace tropes.

The racial justice sensibilities that have been dominant since 2020 are, in many ways, a welcome departure from the underclass-informed narratives that characterized discourse on inequality for most of the past 40 years. However, though the popularity of antiracist primers by Kendi and others may give the impression that a transformation of 'race relations' is on the horizon, the revivalist spirit driving contemporary antiracism is but another iteration of the race-racism binary that has permitted policymakers since the Cold War to look past the capitalist roots of racial disparities. To the detriment of blacks and, frankly, all other poor and working-class Americans, bipartisan commitment to racialist interpretations of inequality has left the US electorate – blacks among them – with no other framework with which to make sense of unemployment, poverty, welfare dependency, crime and so on. Underclass ideology, with its identification of black cultural pathologies as a major source of lingering disparities in the aftermath of civil rights legislation, not only helped justify cuts to public goods such as public assistance and even public education, but it also informed the case for tough on crime policies.

While antiracism has helped shift discourse on inequality away from allegations of dysfunctional black culture, antiracist frameworks generally attribute racial inequalities to the aggregate of white bad actors rather than anything reasonably understood as structural contributors. Thus, much like underclass ideology, the dominant antiracist discourse offers a means of making sense of historic and extant inequalities that abstracts them from capitalist class relations – hence the swell, fleeting or not, of corporate sponsorship for Kendi's and other antiracist initiatives and programs since the summer of 2020.

Any serious effort to redress racial inequalities necessitates that we view them through the lens of class. Why? The most obvious reason is that black people are human beings. Human beings have certain material needs, among them food, protection from the elements and water. In an advanced capitalist society, these basic needs might only be met with money and by extension well-paying jobs. If our goal is to improve the lives of the masses of black Americans rather than to grow the ranks of the black millionaire and billionaire class, we must commit ourselves to improving employment and housing for African American working-class people. Blacks' small share of the US electorate along with the heterogeneity of class interests found among African Americans themselves make plain that efforts to improve the material conditions of most blacks will require interracial political coalitions centered on improving the lives of all poor and working-class Americans.

None of this is to suggest that antidiscrimination policies have run their course. Since racial discrimination can and often does have a devastating effect on people's lives, antidiscrimination policies are necessary. The eventual elimination of affirmative action is, thus, among the many threats posed to a democratic society by the Trump-appointed conservative supermajority on the US Supreme Court. But to insist on the necessity of policies like affirmative action is not to imply that they are sufficient.

The Civil Rights Acts of 1964 and 1968 have, indeed, mitigated racial inequalities by opening pathways for appropriately credentialed blacks to enter the middle and upper classes. By dismantling the formal barriers that had placed well-paying jobs and decent housing beyond the reach of qualified minorities, antidiscrimination laws have, unquestionably, contributed to the relative income gains blacks have made over the past half century. Nevertheless, affirmative action and fair housing legislation have failed to eliminate disparities because automation, the slow death of the union movement and public sector retrenchment have contributed to the decline in real income for the bottom 80 per cent of American workers. As sociologist Robert Manduca has shown, between 1968 and 2016, black household income increased from the 25th to the 35th percentile, as median white household income moved from the 54th to the 57th percentile. Had blacks not made *any* relative progress over this period, the ratio of median black to white household income would have fallen from 57 per cent to 44 per cent between 1968 and 2016. Of course, had wages remained constant, the black-white family income ratio would have risen from 57 per cent to 70 per cent.[33]

It is reasonable to attribute neoliberalism's disproportionate impact on blacks, in part, to the historic legacy of racist policies and practices. But it is important that we situate African Americans' historic and contemporary experiences within the broader currents of American political economy. The Civil Rights Acts of 1964 and 1968 and the Voting Rights Act of 1965 were signed into law more than a decade into the period of what would eventually be known as deindustrialization. Thus, even before the Civil

Rights Movement's greatest legislative victories had cleared the formal racial barriers to black upward mobility, the very pathways working-class whites had traveled from the tenements to the suburbs had already begun to close.

Had this legislation been passed a generation earlier, it is likely that the racial wealth gap would either not exist or would at least be far less pronounced.[34] Still, neither poor African Americans' alleged cultural deficiencies (race) nor whites' pathological commitment to white-skin privilege (racism) is the primary culprit, today. The uncomfortable truth is that the elimination of racial disparities requires socialist policies – a right to a job at a living wage, labour laws that facilitate collective bargaining, taxpayer funded tuition-free higher education and national healthcare.

The overly narrow, Human Resources friendly Diversity Equity and Inclusion (DEI) initiatives that have been the bread and butter of scholars like Kendi and DiAngelo are not just incapable of redressing racial disparities,[35] they have in fact compounded an obvious political problem. By deflecting attention from the capitalist roots of pervasive inequalities, DEI, along with reparations, and even Black Lives Matter have narrowed the purview of unacceptable human suffering to so-called identity groups. In a context in which the American middle-class has been on the decline for nearly five decades, electoral math – if not human decency – should make plain the counterproductive nature of this approach. Indeed, liberals' and progressives' commitment to race reductionist frameworks have predictably played into the American right's well-rehearsed efforts to stoke the flames of racial animus, as constructs like 'white privilege' seem to imply that neoliberalism's white victims are either collateral damage or deserving of their fate in the criminal justice system or the unemployment line.[36]

To say that the road to a progressive American politics is uncertain is an understatement. President Trump's Federalist Society-approved Supreme Court Justices have already struck blows against affirmative action, abortion rights, voting rights and the administrative state – altering, for perhaps a generation, the parameters of what is politically feasible. Short term, our best hope is that Vice President Kamala Harris and her running mate, Tim Walz, will win the 2024 presidential election, providing progressives with breathing room that might facilitate political organization. To be clear, I am not suggesting that a Harris presidency would likely usher in a return to New Deal liberalism or, better yet, socialism. But the fact that Harris has picked a pro-labour progressive as her running mate gives reason to believe that she sees the error of Hillary Clinton's ways and understands the importance of pushing a working-class political agenda.[37] If we want to improve the lives of poor and working-class African Americans, we must move beyond race reductionism. Our decades-long commitment to viewing and addressing enduring inequalities through the race-racism binary has not and cannot serve the needs of poor and working-class African Americans, precisely because it insists on viewing racial inequality as exceptional to capitalism.

NOTES

1   Megan Armstrong, Eathyn Edwards, and Duwain Pinder, 'Corporate Commitment to Racial Justice: An Update', McKinsey Institute for Black Economic Mobility, 21 February 2023 available at: www.mckinsey.com.

2   Mike Damiano and Hillary Burns, 'Kendi Raised Millions with Promises to Conquer Racism. What Went Wrong?', *Boston Globe*, 30 September 2023.

3   Kendi has been accused of mismanaging more than $40 million of the Boston University Center for Antiracist Research's funds. However, when all is said and done, most of the $47 million is still on hand. The Center for Antiracist Research has provided meaningful funding for scholars engaged in a variety of race-related research projects.

4   Ta-Nehisi Coates, 'The Case for Reparations', *The Atlantic*, 15 June 2014; Keeanga Yamahtta Taylor, 'Ibram X. Kendi's Anti-Racism', The New Yorker, 21 October 2023; Nathan Robinson, 'What's So Bad about Robin DiAngelo', *Current Affairs*, 19 July 2021; Robin DiAngelo, *White Fragility: Why It's So Hard for White People to Talk About Racism*, Boston: Beacon Press, 2018, pp. 148-54; Touré F. Reed, *Toward Freedom: The Case Against Race Reductionism*, New York: Verso Books, 2020, pp.146-58.

5   Ibram X. Kendi, *How to be an Antiracist*, New York: One World, 2024, Chapter 1, Kindle.

6   Kendi, *How to be an Antiracist*, Chapter 3, Kindle.

7   Amy E. Hillier, 'Redlining and the Home Owners' Loan Corporation', *Journal of Urban History*, 29(4), 2003, pp. 396-97, 414-15.

8   Kathleen M. Brown, *Good Wives, Nasty Wenches, and Anxious Patriarchs: Gender, Race and Power in Colonial Virginia*, Chapel Hill: UNC Press, 1996, Chapter 4, Kindle.

9   Race was not the lone factor determining how either the Home Owner's Loan Corporation (HOLC) or FHA established a neighborhood's property values or lending risks. Indeed, even as 95 per cent of black homeowners lived in redlined communities, whites constituted 92 per cent of homeowners in such communities. If race were the primary factor determining HOLC and FHA ratings, black redlined communities would have been more prosperous on average than their white counterparts. However, as Price Fishback et al. have found, white redlined neighborhoods tended to possess stronger economic characteristics than black redlined communities, amplifying the role played by class in shaping HOLC and FHA ratings. None of this is to deny the racist barriers to black homeownership created by the FHA's discriminatory lending policies. Rather, the rating systems used respectively by HOLC and FHA, were informed by racial and economic concerns that cannot be fully distilled from each other. Price V. Fishback et al., 'The HOLC Maps: How Race

and Poverty Influenced Real Estate Professionals' Evaluation of Lending Risk in the 1930s', *The Journal of Economic History*, 83(4), 2023, pp. 1021-22, 1033.

10   Kendi, *How to be an Antiracist*, Chapter 1, Kindle.

11   Marie Gottschalk, *Caught: The Prison State and the Lockdown of American Politics*, Princeton: Princeton University Press, 2014, Chapter 6, Kindle; Alexia Cooper and Erica L. Smith, 'Homicide Trends in the United States, 1980-2008', US Department of Justice, available at: https://bjs.ojp.gov/content/pub/pdf/htus8008.pdf; "How Groups Voted in 1996', Roper Poll, available at: www.ropercenter.cornell.edu; Danielle Kurtzleben, 'Understanding the Clintons' Popularity with Black Voters', NPR, 1 March 2016.

12   Ibram X. Kendi, 'Pass an Antiracist Constitutional Amendment', *Politico*, 2019.

13   Though I am a little more than a decade older than Kendi, my peers and I also struggled with similar doubts during our time at high school in the late 1980s. I can, therefore, appreciate the resonance of Kendi's work, as his prose often conveys a feeling of vulnerability and humanity that connects with a broad readership. Unfortunately, the accessibility of Kendi's work is also owed to the fact that he – like Robin DiAngelo – presumes that personal transformation will translate into societal transformation. Yes, education is indispensable to any political movement; however, successful, transformative political movements – from abolition, to the American union movement, to the black American Civil Rights Movement – were comprised of coalitions bound together by mutual interest rather than the kind of noblesse oblige that antiracism calls for.

14   Kendi, *How to be an Antiracist*, Introduction, Kindle.

15   Kendi, *How to be an Antiracist*, Introduction, Kindle.

16   Kendi, *How to be an Antiracist*, Introduction, Kindle.

17   Kendi, *How to be an Antiracist*, Introduction, Kindle.

18   Adolph Reed Jr, *Stirrings in the Jug: Black Politics in the Post-Segregation Era*, Minneapolis: University of Minnesota Press, 1999, pp. 179-80.

19   Gillian Brockwell, 'She was stereotyped as the welfare queen. The truth was more disturbing, a new book says', *Washington Post*, 21 May 2019.

20   William Julius Wilson, *The Truly Disadvantaged: The Inner City, the Underclass, and Public Policy*, Chicago: University of Chicago, 1987, pp. 4, 16-18; 'A Visit with Bill Clinton: The Conflict Between the "A student" and the "pol"', *The Atlantic*, October 1992.

21   Reed, *Toward Freedom*, New York: Verso Books, 2020, p. 135.

22   James Forman, Jr. 'Racial Critiques of Mass Incarceration: Beyond the New Jim Crow', *New York University Law Review*, 87, February 2012, pp. 114-16, 131-36; John Clegg and Adaner Usmani, 'The Economic Origins of Mass Incarceration', *Catalyst*, 3(3), 2019, available at: www.catalyst-journal.com.

23   Robert Mackey and Zaid Jilani, 'Hillary Clinton Still Haunted by Discredited Rhetoric on Superpredators', *The Intercept*, 25 February 2016.

24   Andrew Kaczynski, 'Biden in 1993 Speech Pushing Crime Bill Warned of "Predators on our Streets" Who Were "Beyond the Pale"', *CNN*, 7 March 2019; 'Fact Check: Hillary Clinton, not Joe Biden, Used the Term Super Predator in the 1990s', *Reuters*, 26 October 2020.

25   William Raspberry, 'Black-on-Black Violence Jackson's Answer', *Washington Post*, 1 February 1990.

26   Raspberry, 'Black-on-Black Violence Jackson's Answer'.

27   Chris Rock, *Bring the Pain*, directed by Keith Truesdell, CR Enterprises
      Production Partners, 1996, 29:29-37:01, available at: www.youtube.com/
      watch?v=coC4t7nCGPs&t=2452s.

28   Chris Rock, *Bring the Pain*, 34:10-35:35.

29   Chris Rock, *Bring the Pain*, 35:18-36:20.

30   'Transcript: Barack Obama's Father's Day Remarks', *New York Times*, 15 June 2008;
      'Transcript: Barack Obama's Keynote Address at the 2004 Democratic National
      Convention', *PBS News Hour*, 27 July 2004.

31   Nia-Malika Anderson, 'Cousin Pookie is back! And yes, he is still sitting on the
      couch', *Washington Post*, 20 October 2014.

32   Bill Cosby, 'Pound Cake' speech, delivered at the NAACP 50th Anniversary of US
      Supreme Court's decision in *Brown vs. Board of Education*, 17 May 2004, available at:
      www.blackpast.org.

33   Robert Manduca, 'Income Inequality and the Persistence of Racial Economic
      Disparities', *Sociological Science*, 5, 2018, pp. 191-97.

34   Since the racial wealth gap is largely concentrated among the top 10 per cent of
      earners in each racial group, policy focus on so-called racial wealth ensures that our
      discourse on persistent inequalities is class-skewed and downplays income inequality's
      pivotal role in generating disparities. Bucking the trend, economists Dionissi Aliprantis
      and Daniel Carroll have shown that the labor income gap has in fact been the driving
      force behind contemporary wealth disparities. According to Aliprantis and Carroll, by
      1977 the labor income gap eclipsed the impact of 'initial inequality' on racial wealth
      disparities. By 1990, the labor income gap accounted for roughly 80 per cent of the
      racial wealth gap. The researchers ultimately argue that had the black-white income
      gap been closed in 1962, the racial wealth gap would have been largely eliminated
      by 2007 – translating into a black-white wealth ratio of about 90 per cent. Dionissi
      Aliprantis and Daniel Carroll, 'What's Behind the Persistence of the Racial Wealth
      Gap?', *The Federal Reserve Bank of Cleveland: Economic Commentary*, 28 February 2019,
      available at: www.clevelandfed.org.

35   As sociologists Frank Dobbin and Alexandra Kalev have shown, the efficacy of
      diversity training is often short-lived and largely confined to those who are already
      receptive. Conversely, such efforts may exacerbate racial animus among those who
      are circumspect about diversity training but have been compelled by employers
      to 'suffer through' such initiatives. Dobbin and Kalev do not dismiss the utility of
      diversity training; however, they suggest that pairing such efforts with mentoring
      and teamwork would be much more effective at chipping away at discriminatory
      attitudes and barriers. Frank Dobbin and Alexandra Kalev, 'Why Diversity Programs
      Fail', *Harvard Business Review*, July-August 2016; Dobbin and Kalev, 'Why Doesn't
      Diversity Training Work: The Challenge for Industry and Academic', *Anthropology
      Now*, 10(2), September 2018, pp. 49-53.

36   'White privilege' creates a number of analytical problems. First, it detracts attention
      from the action of discrimination, which has to be the race-based mechanism
      influencing lingering disparities. Second, it equates disproportionality with totality,
      equating whiteness with economic privilege and blackness with poverty. Third, those
      who use the term ultimately treat freedom from discrimination as a 'privilege', as this
      is the advantage all whites possess over blacks and other people of color across class

tiers. On this third point, it is worth considering that not long ago, political activists, racial liberals and progressives had generally understood freedom from discrimination as the bare minimum. By treating freedom from discrimination as a privilege, 'white privilege' unwittingly reimagines the political floor as the ceiling. See: Hadass Silver, 'Inventing "White Privilege": Pseudo-progressivism in American Political Discourse', *American Political Thought: A Journal of Ideas, Institutions, and Culture*, 11(4), 2022, pp. 438, 445-49, 459-61.

37   Branko Marcetic, 'The Tim Walz VP Pick Shows America's Politics are Changing', *Jacobin*, 6 August 2024; Thomas Adams, 'Tim Walz Is a First! A Union Member and Not a Lawyer', *Common Dreams*, 8 August 2024, available at: www.commondreams.org.

THE US LEFT'S NEW LABOUR MOMENT AND THE RANK-AND-FILE STRATEGY

NICK FRENCH

'It was the best of times, it was the worst of times' might be a fitting epigraph for a reflection on the state of the US socialist left today. After a brief moment in early 2020, when it seemed conceivable that self-described democratic socialist Bernie Sanders might win the Democratic Party nomination for president, the resurgent left's electoral wings have been clipped. Amid an atomizing and deadly global pandemic, and in the wake of an inspiring but short-lived wave of protests against racial injustice, lifelong centrist Joe Biden ascended to the presidency. Ambitious national legislative goals, like Medicare for All, a Green New Deal and free college for all dropped off the agenda.

Socialists, *Jacobin* founder Bhaskar Sunkara wrote in early 2022, were 'large enough to be a political presence in parts of the country – and a subculture for thousands of activists – but far too disorganized and powerless to carry out [our] political program'.[1] Much the same could be said today. That's not to say there are no bright spots: socialists have gotten a toehold in Congress, as well as won elected office at the local and state level across the country. And although it is down from its height, as of early 2024 the Democratic Socialists of America still boasted over 75,000 members – though, to be clear, its activist base is much smaller. The socialist left, as Sunkara acknowledges, is not going away anytime soon.

Probably most exciting, though, are the promising signs of life in the US labour movement, which has seen union density and its overall political relevance decline continuously over the past several decades. Since the pandemic, more workers have been going on strike; unions have made breakthroughs with new organizing in higher education and, to a much lesser degree, at corporate behemoths Starbucks and Amazon; and reform movements toppled corrupt and collaborationist leaderships in the International Brotherhood of Teamsters and the United Auto Workers

(UAW). The latter victory in turn led to a historic strike at the 'Big Three' US automakers, which reversed years of concessions and won major gains on pay and labour standards in the growing electric-vehicle sector. The UAW is now building on the momentum of its strike win with an ambitious campaign to organize non-union auto shops in the southern United States.

These developments have been a source of optimism for those of us on the left who see the organized working class as the force with both the interest and the capacity to win major reforms of the sort Sanders championed, and as the potential agent of a socialist reconstruction of society. Many on the post-2016 US left have wagered on the prospect revitalizing and remaking the labour movement into a militant, democratic force, which is in turn an essential step in working-class people developing their capacities and willingness for class struggle. The recent organizing and strike victories give us some tangible reasons to hope that prospect might become a reality.

THE CRESTING OF THE SANDERS WAVE

The US left's current turn toward labour has to be understood in the context of the electoral insurgency that began with Bernie Sanders' 2016 presidential run. Sanders' surprisingly successful primary challenge to presumptive Democratic nominee Hillary Clinton – and Clinton's ultimate triumph and then surprising loss to Donald Trump in the general election – led to a surge of people joining the Democratic Socialists of America (DSA), which had endorsed Sanders in the primary.

The organization, which had been founded in 1982 and boasted around 6,000 members prior to Sanders' campaign, saw its numbers begin to grow rapidly.[2] The group's membership received another big boost in 2018 with DSA-endorsed Alexandria Ocasio-Cortez's (or 'AOC', as she is often called) surprising congressional primary victory against Joe Crowley in New York City and Rashida Tlaib's election in Detroit. But DSA members started to run for and win elected office at the local and state level across the country too. The DSA was just one force among many in this progressive electoral insurgency, though the largest explicitly socialist one; other organizations, notably Sanders' group Our Revolution, Justice Democrats, the labour-union-based Working Families Party and the climate-oriented Sunrise Movement also helped elect left-leaning candidates to Congress and at lower levels of government.

Local chapters of the reborn DSA engaged in a variety of activities, from popular political education to mobilizing members for protests and picket-line solidarity, to tenant organizing and mutual-aid projects. Yet the organization probably became best known for its electoral work, which served as its centre of gravity. Between 2017 and 2020, many organized in particular around the prospect of supporting a 2020 Bernie Sanders primary run; after Sanders launched his campaign, much of DSA went 'all in' on supporting it, phone-banking and door-knocking for Sanders and attempting to use excitement around the campaign as an opportunity for recruitment and political education.

Despite a handful of early primary victories that made Sanders the candidate to beat, by the end of March 2020 former vice president Joe Biden had all but clinched the nomination. At the same time, the Covid-19 lockdowns threw a wrench in much of the organizing momentum of DSA and affiliated groups like Sunrise, which had seen Sanders' campaign as an opportunity to advance its ambitious Green New Deal program.

The historic wave of Black Lives Matter protests against racist police violence over the summer of 2020 briefly energized the left, putting questions of historic racial and economic injustices at the forefront of public consciousness and politicizing a new cohort of radicals. Yet it produced very little in the way of lasting institutional change or shifts in the dominant political orientation of either the Democratic or Republican parties.

With Joe Biden's election to the presidency that November, a certain chapter in the post-2016 left's history came to a close. However, the DSA and its electoral project have continued to advance in important respects: working in coalition with allies like Justice Democrats, the Working Families Party, and a handful of progressive unions, socialists added to their congressional delegation in 2020 with the election of Jamaal Bowman in New York and BLM activist Cori Bush in Missouri, and have also continued to rack up wins in state and local office. Bowman and Bush were, however, ousted in Democratic Party primaries this summer – thanks in large part to huge donations from the pro-Israel lobby that was enraged by their criticism of Israel's brutal campaign in Gaza. Yet elsewhere, democratic socialists have built a particularly strong beachhead in the New York State legislature, where they have eight members. The DSA also continued to grow its dues-paying membership for a time, even with the blows of the Sanders loss and the disorganizing effect of the lockdowns, peaking at around 95,000 members in early 2021. The group now stands at about 78,000 members, roughly its level in early 2020.

At the same time, the ambitions of the left at the height of the Sanders campaigns – the hope that a Sanders win (or near-win) might lead to the passage of major social-democratic reforms like single-payer health care or the Green New Deal, or even spark a fundamental recalibration of the American political system – seem to have been dashed, or at least put on ice. Even as socialists and their sometimes-allies on the progressive end of the Democratic Party have gradually increased their numbers, their ability to move the dial in Congress and state legislatures remains very limited. The result has been what Oliver Eagleton has aptly dubbed 'the dismal rise of the lobbyist left', which he sees as afflicting left-populist movements in the UK and continental Europe as well.[3] In the United States, it has meant socialist standard-bearer Sanders attempting to '"forge an uneasy alliance with Joe Biden" in chairing the Senate budget and health committees', Eagleton writes. Consequently, 'Sanders has seen his campaign pledges – most notably the Green New Deal – metamorphose into Biden's imperial agenda: militarised competition with China, backed by subsidies for green capital and increased fossil fuel extraction'. One can make similar arguments about the trajectory of figures like AOC, who, according to a May 2024 *New York Times* profile, 'has emerged as a tested navigator of [Congress's] byzantine systems ... We're witnessing a skilled tactician exiting her political adolescence and coming into her own as a veteran operator'.[4]

Yet for all the maneuvering of Sanders, AOC and their allies in Congress, the major reforms they championed prior to Biden's presidency have been either sidelined or advanced in distorted or badly watered-down form. Take, for instance, the fate of the American Climate Corps, which was shrunk from a New Deal–style program of mass public employment into a meager Clintonesque job-training effort.[5] One of the greatest pieces of evidence of the electoral left's weakness, perhaps, is its failure to get Biden, his successor Kamala Harris, or most of the Democratic Party to end, or even meaningfully temper, its support for Israel's genocide in Gaza.

But as Eagleton suggests, this 'lobbying turn' is itself borne of the left's lack of a mass social base, and in particular its isolation from the historic source of socialist movements' strength: the organized working class. Nevertheless, and to its credit, since the US left's 2016 rebirth many socialists have been working to advance an analysis and strategy that speaks to this problem.

THE PROMISE OF THE RANK-AND-FILE STRATEGY

Resolving this lack of a basis for socialist power is central to the strategic perspective that has come to be known as 'the rank-and-file strategy' (RFS). In the past few years, DSA members and others on the left have begun pursuing this strategy in a number of ways and have turned to focusing their energies on labour activism more broadly, especially since the end of the 2020 Sanders campaign.

There have been no small number of debates within DSA and the broader left about the proper orientation to labour, concerning both whether the

RFS is an adequate perspective on the labour movement and about how to effectively carry it out. Here I want to assess the prospects for the RFS provided by the current moment, as well as the most important ongoing debates about socialists' strategic orientation to the labour movement. I argue that the current labour insurgency provides a crucial opening for socialists to advance the RFS, which will likely be necessary for the left to make serious breakthroughs in electoral and legislative projects that have, in many ways, stalled.

The rank-and-file strategy attempts to address two problems that have afflicted the socialist left in the US since the late twentieth century. The first is that the working class, despite occasional sparks or even explosions of activity, is largely quiescent, in no small part because the main institutions that have historically organized working-class people to fight collectively for their interests – labour unions – have for decades put up little resistance and represent a shrinking proportion of the workforce.

The second, related problem is that US socialists are mostly isolated from the working class, and in particular from *organized* workers in the unions.[6] That is a major problem for a political project based on the proposition that the working class is the social force with both the interest in winning a postcapitalist society and the capacity to do so. Much the same is true, however, even for the prospects of winning limited reforms of the kind represented by FDR's New Deal and the social-democratic compromises of capitalism's postwar 'Golden Age'.[7] The generous welfare states established in much of Europe, for instance, were made possible by left political parties based in massive and powerful labour movements, whose electoral heft and ability to engage in organized disruption forced elites to make concessions.

In response to these problems, the RFS says that socialists should rebuild a social base in the rank and file of unions with the aim of helping to raise worker militancy and consciousness. Unions emerge naturally in capitalist society as expressions of workers' efforts to resist exploitation, and are therefore 'where both class formation and class conflict begin', as Kim Moody put it in the 2000 pamphlet that introduced the RFS.[8] From there, socialists should attempt to transform sclerotic or ossified unions into democratic, fighting institutions, and to use workplace fights as the basis for developing a broader political vision and organization among workers – the sort of socialist vision and organization ultimately needed for a large-scale transformation of society.

At the core of the RFS is the simple idea that unions, insofar as they are democratic institutions of class war, play the functions of organizing collective resistance to capitalist exploitation and raising worker consciousness. For this reason, the RFS emphasizes a socialist presence among the rank and file. It is from within the rank and file that challenges to complacent or corrupt union leaderships originate, and it is the activity of rank-and-file workers organizing democratically to confront employers that can plant the seeds of deeper challenges to the capitalist control and ownership of production, beyond unions' official purview of ordinary collective bargaining.

To this end, the RFS calls for socialists to '[build] the rank-and-file movements and organizations that are fighting for a more effective, democratic, and inclusive union in the context of the main fight with the bosses', Moody says. That is a key part of the broader project of building, and connecting unions to, class-wide labour and political organizations, including socialist organizations.

The RFS rests on an analysis of unions as being essentially beset by certain internal tensions. On the one hand, as mentioned above, they are organic expressions of workers' interest in resisting exploitation, the form in which workers come together under capitalism to collectively fight back against employer demands. In this regard, unions are spaces where workers gain experience in and develop their capacities to engage in class struggle. That is why Friedrich Engels called them 'schools of war', and why socialists see building labour fights as a central task.[9]

On the other hand, insofar as they are embedded within capitalist social relations, unions remain dependent on the profitability of the firms that employ their members. Unions can fight employers for higher wages, more generous benefits and more humane working conditions – but these fights must be kept within certain bounds, since demanding too much can threaten firm profitability and competitiveness and thereby risk their members' jobs. Since unions seek to demand concessions from capitalists without pushing them to the wall, they generally become institutions that mediate conflict between workers and employers, attempting to negotiate a *modus vivendi* between the two. This dynamic in turn produces certain interests on the part of elected leaders and paid staff, whose positions lead them to prioritize the union's successful negotiation of contracts for members and the preservation of the union as an institution.

Yet union leaders' and staffers' desire to be able to smoothly carry out collective bargaining and maintain institutional stability often leads them to restrain or discourage the rank-and-file militancy that is the ultimate source of unions' power, and which also 'schools' workers in class combat. This conflict of interests generates the kind of process of 'bureaucratization' that Robert Michels famously attempted to explain in *Political Parties*, and that Claus Offe and Helmut Wiesenthal later analyzed perceptively in 'Two Logics of Collective Action'.[10]

Here we can see why RFS advocates think it is crucial for socialists to get involved in the rank-and-file of the labour movement, and sometimes to be involved in struggles against union officials. For one thing, rank-and-file rebellions are necessary correctives to the structural pressures that union leaders and staff find themselves under. For another, battles that pit the activity of rank-and-file workers directly against the boss, through strikes and other forms of disruptive confrontation, can plant the seeds of further-reaching fights against capitalists' control of production.

SOCIALISTS AND THE RFS TODAY

The rank-and-file strategy has been advocated by many in DSA since its post-2016 surge. It was officially adopted as the organization's perspective on the labour movement at the DSA's 2019 national convention, and the commitment has been reaffirmed at subsequent biannual conventions.

The DSA is not a monolith, of course, and its recent history has been one of fierce and sometimes acrimonious debates between competing caucuses and political tendencies. The fight to get the organization to adopt and implement the RFS has largely been led by the Bread and Roses caucus, which was founded in 2019. This caucus brought together younger activists, many of whom had been activated by the 2016 Bernie campaign or by *Jacobin* magazine, with a number of organizers of an older generation associated with the Labor Notes media and organizing project, which has helped seed and support union reform efforts since its founding in 1979, and the socialist organizations International Socialists and Solidarity, both with roots in the Trotskyist tradition. I will say a little more about those groups below.[11]

For Bread and Roses, the RFS was part of a broader strategic orientation that saw insurgent electoral campaigns like Sanders' presidential runs as necessary but insufficient for building democratic socialism. The hope was that, alongside left-wing electoral efforts, social-movement mobilization, and the building of explicitly socialist organizations like the DSA, rank-and-file work would help build the kind of consciousness-raising battles against capital that would be required for a successful socialist political project. As the group put it in its 'Where We Stand' document:

The most critical task for socialists is to help develop a labour movement that is militant, left-wing, and democratic. Working-class people's greatest strength is in the workplace because capitalists depend on the exploitation of labour to make their profits. And the workplace brings workers of all backgrounds together and generates common interests that can be the basis for powerful movements.[12]

That said, other tendencies and caucuses in the DSA have been supportive of the rank-and-file strategy and similar ideas over the years, including Reform and Revolution (formed out a split from Socialist Alternative), Tempest Collective (including many former members of the International Socialist Organization) and Communist Caucus. The RFS's fiercest opponents in the DSA have probably been the now-defunct caucus Collective Power Network, which led the charge against adopting the approach ahead of the DSA's 2019 convention;[13] at the most recent national convention in 2023, members from the more electorally focused Groundwork and Socialist Majority Caucuses unsuccessfully argued against language proposed by Bread and Roses that prioritized building relationships with rank-and-file workers over relations with union officials.

DSA members have attempted to implement the rank-and-file strategy through a diverse array of tactics, including through forming national networks of socialist activists in different unions (such as DSA Teamsters) as well as mobilizing members and elected officials to support major strikes and union contract campaigns (like UAW's 2023 'stand-up strike' and the ongoing Starbucks organizing drive and contract negotiation).

The DSA's two most distinctive labour efforts, however, have probably been the Emergency Workplace Organizing Committee (EWOC), on the one hand, and on the other hand the project of encouraging members to get rank-and-file union jobs in select industries, with the aim of organizing from the shop floor. EWOC, jointly launched by the DSA at the beginning of the pandemic with the historically left-wing United Electrical, Radio and Machine Workers of America (UE), is a largely volunteer-run effort that assists non-union workers who are looking for assistance in organizing their workplaces. Although hardly a panacea for the continuing decline of union density in the US, the project has racked up dozens of union wins, particularly at smaller workplaces, and its model of what labour scholar Eric Blanc has called 'worker-to-worker organizing' may be a necessary complement to the traditional staff-led model of new organizing.[14]

Since it is focused on new organizing in mostly smaller shops, however, EWOC largely does not speak to the RFS's central aim of reforming the existing labour movement – something that is surely necessary (if insufficient) for carrying out energetic new organizing at a big enough scale.[15] In this respect, the DSA's attempts to get members to 'industrialize' in various unions are essential. This has taken a number of forms, including efforts by both the national organization and individual chapters to create 'pipelines' into certain unionized occupations and industries: UPS Teamsters, nursing, K–12 public education, telecommunications and electrical work, to name a few. Some socialists have taken up the call to get union jobs on their own initiative. And last year, some DSA members and fellow travelers helped form the Rank & File Project, an organization working to train and funnel social-justice-minded organizers into select unions in locations across the country. In summer 2024, the group wrapped up its first cohort of the 'Rank and File School', training recruits in the basics of organizing and preparing them for union reform work.[16]

Precisely because of the fierce headwinds faced by the left's electoral project and the 'lobbyist turn' of some of its leading figures, this kind of work is more important than ever. The forward march of the Sanders insurgency, I would argue, has been halted by two major obstacles. The first is that progressive forces lack the *leverage* required to wrest major concessions from elites – the kind of concessions that would be represented by Medicare for All or a federal jobs guarantee. Without the capacity to engage in the kind of mass disruption, say, that frightened politicians and sections of capital into acceding to the Second New Deal (which included the New Deal's most far-reaching pro-worker reforms), the reforms that made up Sanders' 2020 platform are probably dead in the water.[17] And that's not even to mention further-reaching visions of economic democracy.

But for the time being, that obstacle is largely theoretical. The Sanders wave crashed against the rocks of a more immediate obstacle: he couldn't get enough votes. Part of the explanation is the concerted opposition of establishment Democrats and much of the corporate media, who were able just in time to organize a consolidation of the crowded Democratic primary field around Biden. This opposition was not insurmountable, though. The reason Sanders could not *overcome* hostile establishment forces was because he simply could not convince enough voters – especially the disaffected poor and working-class voters he was most counting on – that he had a feasible program and path to realizing it.

In a postmortem reflection on Sanders' big defeat in the Super Tuesday primaries in March 2020, Paul Heideman aptly summarized the problem:

What's now clear is that the Sanders campaign isn't simply attempting to change what's at stake in an election, but also to change the ways most people make decisions about politics. This is an extraordinarily difficult task.

In the long term, accomplishing this requires building alternative institutions for people to rely on for information ... Unions, once, were an important source of information for voters. People's social lives can also provide cues. Among white evangelicals and many black Democrats, churches are an important source of political cues. In order to win, the Left needs to rebuild social and political institutions that can compete with party elites.[18]

Without such institutions, the left has little hope of convincing a sufficient number of people to get behind a socialist (or even social democratic) candidate or agenda.

In short, socialists' electoral and legislative agendas have come up against the barriers of both a lack of structural leverage and a low level of consciousness. These are the problems that the rank-and-file strategy aims to resolve, by transforming the labour movement into a powerful institutional expression of class struggle and at the same time rebuilding a base of socialists among the organized working class. If socialists have been discussing the RFS since Sanders' 2016 campaign gave the American left new life, then, it is maybe in the post-Sanders era that the need for the RFS is clearest.

GREEN SHOOTS OF LABOUR INSURGENCY AND OPENINGS FOR THE LEFT

It is one thing to have an idea of what is to be done; it is another to be in a position to do it. Thankfully, events in the labour movement over the past few years suggest openings for socialists pursuing the rank-and-file strategy.

For one thing, unions' public favourability is at a historic high, with an October 2023 poll finding that 71 per cent of Americans approve of labour unions.[19] The number of workers who say they would join a union if given the chance is also relatively high: the Economic Policy Institute estimated that, in 2023, at least 48 per cent of non-union workers would vote to unionize their workplaces if they could.[20] We shouldn't read too much into polls, but they do seem to reflect an increasingly militant mood among the working class, as labour journalist Alex Press put it back in 2021.[21] 2023 saw thirty-three major work stoppages (work stoppages involving at least 1,000 workers that last for at least one shift during the workweek), the highest number since 2000.[22] This heightened militancy is no doubt in part due to the tight labour market created by the pandemic, as well as government policy that has uncharacteristically prioritized low unemployment.

We should be sober about these figures. They are still well down from historic highs: there were 570 major work stoppages in 1952, for example, and the unionized proportion of the workforce peaked at over 30 per cent in the 1950s. Union density is continuing to decline, dropping to a new low of 10 per cent in 2023. A number of inspiring and high-profile union victories, however, suggests that these green shoots of militancy could grow into something greater.

These victories included the 2022 union win at Amazon's JFK8 warehouse that revealed the chink in the logistics giant's armor, and the emergence of a number of other organizing efforts: a string of wins by Starbucks Workers United at coffee shops across the country, leading to the union now bargaining its first contract with the company; an explosive wave of organizing in higher education, which saw over 40,000 academic workers unionize in 2023 alone;[23] continuing progressive activism among public K-12 schoolteachers, especially the wave of victorious wildcat strikes in Massachusetts, and the Chicago Teachers Union (CTU) establishing itself as a local political powerhouse with the 2023 elevation of former rank-and-file CTU organizer Brandon Johnson to the mayor's office, among other electoral wins; reformers helping topple the administration of James P. Hoffa in the Teamsters and the subsequent achievement of major contract gains for UPS workers; and the dramatic rise of the reform movement in the UAW, resulting in the historic concession-reversing strike against the Big Three US automakers and an ambitious new campaign to organize non-union auto shops in the US South. The new UAW was also among the first big US labour unions to call for a ceasefire in Gaza.

Socialists can't afford to be Pollyanna-ish about these events. All of them have seen setbacks and deserve critical analysis. For instance, Amazon workers at JFK8 have yet to win their first contract, nor have warehouse workers at any of the company's other facilities been able to replicate the success in winning a union election (though the Teamsters are having some success in unionizing subcontracted delivery drivers); the task of organizing Amazon seems both as necessary and as daunting as others.[24] And after a historic union win this spring at the Volkswagen factory in Chattanooga, Tennessee, the UAW lost its election at the Mercedes-Benz plant near Vance, Alabama. The union's new international leadership is also now facing a corruption probe stemming from clashes among top officers.

It would be easy to list more ominous signs. If there is reason to be hopeful about recent developments, there is also plenty of reason to worry that labour's forward momentum might stall out and that it might not result in the hoped-for reversal of union decline (let alone any kind of movement toward socialism). Still, much of what is happening in the labour movement now would have been regarded as highly improbable by most observers just a few years ago. This insurgency suggests a growing openness to labour organization and militancy of the kind that socialist RFS proponents hope to foster and take advantage of. In some cases – particularly Teamsters and UAW reform and public-school-teacher activism – they are actually products of the rank-and-file strategy avant la lettre.

Teamsters for a Democratic Union, the rank-and-file reform caucus that helped elect new president Sean O'Brien in 2022, was founded in the 1970s, in part, by socialists who had taken jobs in the freight industry to build a base and agitate for democracy and militancy in the union. Unite All Workers for Democracy (UAWD), the reform group that successfully pushed for direct elections of top officers and eventually elected new president Shawn Fain and allies to the UAW International leadership, was the latest in a string of reform efforts dating back to the '60s and '70s, which also involved socialists who had industrialized into auto jobs. UAWD activists drew inspiration and guidance from this earlier generation of reformers, as well as allies in the TDU. Socialist activists also played a key role in the reform of the CTU that set the stage for its historic 2012 strike, and in the union's effort to build a progressive electoral vehicle in the city, United Working Families (the group responsible for electing Johnson as mayor in 2023). Labor Notes has played a central role in these efforts. Started by socialists in the same milieu that was taking jobs in the Teamsters, UAW and elsewhere during the New Left's 'turn to industry,' many of them from the International Socialists group, Labor Notes' goal has been to 'put the movement back in the labour movement', as its tagline says. It has aimed to report on and assist with rank-and-file activism and union reform projects of all kinds, and to build connections between union militants across unions and sectors. Although it does not explicitly identify as socialist, the mission of Labor Notes is part of the broader RFS project of transforming unions into fighting institutions.

If measured by the success of affiliated reform movements, Labor Notes has certainly had an important impact. But it is also perhaps revealing of the current moment that the group's biennial convention has in the past few years become a must-attend event for labour activists. The 2018 Labor Notes conference had over 3,000 attendees, while its most recent conference in 2024 had 4,700 registered participants, with thousands more turned away due to lack of space. Bernie Sanders himself gave a keynote address at the event in 2022; Shawn Fain gave the closing remarks this year.

All told, despite the serious challenges, it's not unreasonable for socialists to wager on deepening and expanding reform victories in large unions like the UAW and spreading them to other unions. And the militant mood that seems to be bubbling up in at least some sections of the working class means there may be opportunities to wage a greater number of transformative workplace fights – fights that build worker consciousness by, to quote former Labor Notes editor Jane Slaughter, 'teach[ing] us that we do have power, and giv[ing] us practice in the organizing it will take to change the balance of power beyond the workplace, in society'.[25]

There is case to be made, too, that socialists should try to strike while the iron is hot. The tight labour market that has fueled this militancy – and the outrage felt by workers at the indignities they suffered during the Covid-19 pandemic while being called 'essential' – won't last forever.

STRATEGIC DEBATES ON THE LABOUR LEFT

As alluded to above, the rank-and-file strategy is not uncontroversial, even among leftists who acknowledge the importance of revitalizing the labour movement and building a base within it. Since DSA's 2016 rebirth, there has been no shortage of debates between RFS advocates and those who see that perspective as overly narrow, self-marginalizing, or otherwise inadequate. Reviewing those debates is helpful for understanding what the RFS recommends in today's context and why.

Some of the major disputes between critics and proponents of the rank-and-file strategy concern the tactical emphases of RFS proponents. Points of frequent disagreement include the strategy's emphasis on the need for socialists to take jobs as rank-and-file workers rather than as union staff; its related critique of the union bureaucracy; and its tendency to prioritize reform of existing unions over new organizing efforts. All of these fault lines have shown up, for instance, in internal debates in the DSA over whether to endorse the rank-and-file strategy and how to interpret it.

Some objections to the rank-and-file strategy appear to stem from conflating tactical recommendations or particular threads of analysis with the strategy itself. That is not to deny that the RFS recommends socialists take rank-and-file jobs, or that it involves a critique of union officialdom's role in the working class, or that it gives union reform efforts a special centrality. But all of these elements flow from the deeper analysis outlined earlier, and they belong to a broader framework that sees a diversity of tactics as necessary to building the labour movement and, ultimately, working-class power.

The RFS does not say that union leaders or staffers are 'bad' or unnecessary, or that socialists should in general refuse to take leadership positions or union staff jobs. Indeed, rank-and-file reform efforts aim at taking over and transforming unions, which typically requires unionists committed to democracy and militancy to, at strategic junctures, ascend to leadership and take on full-time organizing positions. But an analysis of the structural constraints under which unions operate leads to an emphasis on rank-and-file activism.

The underlying analysis of unions as two-sided social institutions – serving to both foster and contain class conflict – also helps illuminate the priority that the RFS gives to union reform work. New organizing is of course vital to stopping and reversing the labour movement's disintegration.

Organizing growing leviathan Amazon is particularly urgent, as it threatens to undermine the hard-fought gains of unionized workers at UPS – a big reason that the post-Hoffa Teamsters are now devoting considerable resources to organizing the company. But the dynamics of bureaucratization have meant that most labour leaders have not been willing to spend substantial resources on attempting to organize new members, instead preferring to pad their unions' investment portfolios.[26] Nor have they generally been able or willing to wage and win the kinds of ambitious battles that make unions look like sufficiently attractive propositions to non-members. In short, it seems that most unions need to be reformed *before* they will put the needed effort into new organizing. Recent events in the United Auto Workers appear to be bearing this out.

These issues are of course related to debates around democracy: reformers seek greater internal democracy as both a means of reforming unions and as an end in itself, with the aim of bringing rank-and-file members more centrally into the decision-making and activity of their unions. But some on the left have also raised questions about the value of union democracy: Are more democratic unions actually more militant and/or effective? Are unions with more internal democracy more likely to engage in aggressive organizing or strike? Do they win better contracts?

More democracy is certainly not a guarantee of greater militancy or effectiveness, and there are plenty of examples of internally undemocratic, 'top-down' unions that wage aggressive, winning campaigns. Is there a general connection in either direction? Each side of the debate can point to some empirical evidence, though the topic deserves more systematic study.[27] There are good theoretical reasons to predict, however, that excessively autocratic unions will stifle member initiative and participation and ultimately hinder the organization's ability to bring the full weight of their collective power against capital. A union, Judith Stepan-Norris and Maurice Zeitlin write in their classic study of the exceptionally democratic, Communist-led unions in the CIO, 'not only can but also should be both an "army" and a "town meeting"'.[28]

But from the perspective of the rank-and-file strategy, there are deeper reasons to care about union democracy. An immediate goal of the RFS is to rebuild unions so they can fight and win. A less immediate but more fundamental aim is to turn unions into sites where workers develop the consciousness and capacity required for a project of social transformation. Sam Gindin and Leo Panitch, reflecting on the aftermath of the 2016 Sanders campaign, captured well what is needed in this regard. The Sanders campaign, they said, open[ed] space for a new politics that can become 'rooted' in the sense of being grounded in working-class struggles but committed to the radical transformation of the generally exhausted institutions of the labour movement. This ranges across turning union branches into centres of working-class life, leading the fight for collective public services, breaking down the oligarchic relationship between leaders and led, contributing to building the broadest member capacities, emphasizing the importance of expressing a clearer class sensibility, and even becoming ambitious enough to introduce socialist ideas.[29]

A PATH FORWARD?

The socialist electoral project in the US has run into certain roadblocks, which can only be overcome if the left builds a base in, and helps to transform, the organized labour movement. The rank-and-file strategy is an approach to doing just this. Looking at the sparks of insurgency in labour today, as well as unions' overall public favourability, I suggest that the time is ripe for the socialist interventions in the labour movement that the RFS calls for. As socialists have increasingly turned their attention to labour, they have continued to debate tactics and strategy, with many challenging elements of the RFS. Assessing some of the key debates helps bring out the defining features, and strengths, of the rank-and-file perspective.

But this discussion only scratches the surface of the issues the nascent socialist labour left in the US needs to confront. One of the biggest questions for the RFS is how to widen shop-floor fights into class-wide struggles, and how rising worker militancy can find political expression. Can socialists help transform unions not only so that they start organizing with real vigor and take the fight to employers on the shop floor, but also so that they begin to unite behind a program of redistribution, greater public ownership and democratic control of the economy? What would that program look like in its specifics? And how can unions go about forging the kind of large-scale working-class political organization – that is, a party – that can advance it within the state?

The political direction of the reformed UAW suggests both promising developments and potential pitfalls in this regard. Shawn Fain's administration has not been afraid to take bold progressive political stances, both those having to do more directly with union members' interests and those expressing a wider solidarity. These have included the demand for a just transition to electric vehicles, support for a thirty-two-hour workweek and – in a remarkable break with the union's past staunch support for Israel – becoming one of the first major unions to call for a ceasefire in Gaza. Yet just a month after signing onto the ceasefire call, Fain endorsed Joe Biden for president even as the latter was sending tens of billions of dollars worth of weapons to Israel to carry out its genocide. When Biden dropped out in July 2024, the UAW quickly and enthusiastically announced its support for his replacement on the ticket, Vice President Kamala Harris.

There is an obvious logic to these decisions. From the perspective of the interests of UAW members, US labour generally, and that of Palestinian lives, a Donald Trump presidency would almost certainly be worse than a second Biden term or a Harris presidency. Biden, it should be noted, has been unusually publicly supportive of the UAW, walking its picket line during the Big Three strike in 2023 and inviting Fain as a special guest to the 2024 State of the Union address – though these moves should probably be understood as an attempt to shore up electoral support in key Midwest battleground states like Michigan in response to a popular strike, and after Fain delayed endorsing Biden longer than Democrats could typically expect of a UAW president. The lesser-evil logic at work here just goes to show that labour's political ambitions and room for maneuver will be limited so long as it does not have a political vehicle of its own to champion its interests and articulate and advocate a broader egalitarian vision.[30]

Hope for the left may lie in socialists helping to build a rising tide of militancy that can be channeled into efforts to build a new party. Otherwise, unions' attempts to intervene in politics may end up simply repeating the 'insider' turn that the socialist electoral project has taken post-2020, with similarly disappointing results.

NOTES

1   Bhaskar Sunkara, 'The Left in Purgatory', *Jacobin*, 44, Winter 2022.

2   Joseph M. Schwartz, 'A History of Democratic Socialists of America 1971-2017: Bringing Socialism from the Margins to the Mainstream', Democratic Socialists of America, July 2017, available at: www.dsausa.org.

3   Oliver Eagleton, 'The Dismal Rise of the Lobbyist Left', *New Statesman*, 30 September 2023, available at: www.newstatesman.com.

4   Gaby Del Valle, 'The Alexandria Ocasio-Cortez You Don't Know', *New York Times*, 4 May 2024.

5   Daniel Goulden, 'We Need a Real Green Jobs Program to Fight Climate Change', *Jacobin*, 4 October 2023.

6   This is somewhat controversial, as the extent to which we judge leftists to be isolated from the working class depends on how exactly we define the working class. See, for example: Chris Maisano, 'Don't Overstate the Divide Between the Campus and the Working Class', *Jacobin*, 13 December 2022. But even if we define the working class a bit 13more capaciously, it is clear that the socialist left is small in numbers and its support confined mostly to the college educated.

7   See, for example: Michael Goldfield, 'Worker Insurgency, Radical Organization, and New Deal Labor Legislation', *American Political Science Review*, 83(4), 1989, pp. 1257–82.

8   Kim Moody, 'The Rank and File Strategy: Building A Socialist Movement in the U.S.', Solidarity, 2000.

9   Friedrich Engels, *The Condition of the Working Class in England*, 1845, available at: www.marxists.org.

10   Robert Michels, *Political Parties: A Sociological Study of the Oligarchical Tendencies of Modern Democracy*, New York: Routledge, 1999; Claus Offe and Helmut Wiesenthal, 'Two Logics of Collective Action: Theoretical Notes on Social Class and Organizational Form', *Political Power and Social Theory*, 1(1), 1980, pp. 67-115.

11   To be clear, many members of the Labor Notes and IS/Solidarity milieux active in the DSA are not and have never been Bread and Roses members. But Bread and Roses has played an important role in connecting this tradition with the post-2016 DSA.

12   Bread and Roses, 'Where We Stand', available at: https://breadandrosesdsa.org/where-we-stand/. Full disclosure: I am a founding member of the Bread and Roses caucus. See also: Jane Slaughter, 'The Political Revolution Goes to Work', *Socialist Forum*, Fall 2018, available at: https://socialistforum.dsausa.org; Meagan Day and Micah Uetricht, *Bigger Than Bernie: How We Can Win Democratic Socialism in Our Time*, New York: Verso, 2020.

13   The 2019 convention in particular sparked a flurry of polemics over the rank-and-file strategy. Bread and Roses collated many entries in the debate at: https://breadandrosesdsa.org/archive/convention-2019/follow-the-debates/.

14   Eric Blanc, 'Worker-to-Worker Organizing Goes Viral', *New Labor Forum*, 33(1), 2024, pp. 77-83.

15   Although it can have some impact: workers who organize into existing unions sometimes push to reform them, and new worker organizing via EWOC might push other unions to take new organizing more seriously.

16   Full disclosure: I am currently a part-time staffer for the Rank & File Project.

17   To be sure, the Biden administration has been notably progressive on a number of fronts, which might be partly credited to the rising influence of the left. On the whole, though, I don't think the Biden administration's moves toward a more populist (and nationalist) economic policy represent a meaningful change in workers' fortunes. See: Nick French, 'Assessing Bidenomics', *Dollars & Sense*, 373, July/August 2024; Sam Gindin, 'Bidenomics and the Left', *Nonsite*, 44, 20 October 2023.

18   Paul Heideman, 'When Liberals Lose Elections, They Blame the Voters. Leftists Can't', *Jacobin*, 4 May 2020.

19   'New Poll Shows 7 in 10 Americans Support Labor Unions', American Federation of Government Employees, 16 October 2023, available at: www.afge.org.

20   Heidi Shierholz et al., 'Workers Want Unions, But the Latest Data Point to Obstacles in Their Path', Economic Policy Institute, 23 January 2024, available at: www.epi.org.

21   Alex N. Press, 'US Workers Are in a Militant Mood', *Jacobin*, 15 October 2021.

22   'Major Work Stoppages in 2023', Bureau of Labor Statistics, Press Release, 21 February 2024, available at: www.bls.gov/news.release/pdf/wkstp.pdf.

23   Ryan Quinn, 'Higher Ed Workers Seek to Coordinate Nationally', *Inside Higher Ed*, 26 March 2024, available at: www.insidehighered.com.

24   For a discussion of the challenges, see: Sam Gindin, 'A Generational Challenge: Taming Amazon, Renewing Labour', *The Bullet*, 20 May 2024, available at: www.socialistproject.ca.

25   Jane Slaughter, 'Labor Notes: Forty Years of Troublemaking', *Labor Notes*, 29 January 2019, available at: www.labournotes.org.

26   Labour researcher Chris Bohner has shown that, despite representing an ever-smaller share of the US workforce, unions' financial outlooks are in many cases rosier than ever, thanks in part to a refusal to spend big on strikes or new organizing. See, for example: Chris Bohner, *Labor's Fortress of Finance: A Financial Analysis of Organized Labor and Sketches for an Alternative Future: 2010-2021*, Radish Research, Fall 2022, available at: www.radishresearch.org.

27   See, for example, the exchange between Chris Bohner and Dave Kamper in *Jacobin*: Chris Bohner, 'Direct Elections for Labor Leaders Make for More Militant Unions', *Jacobin*, 5 December 2023; Dave Kamper, 'Union Democracy Is a Value, Not a Strategy', *Jacobin*, 31 January 2024; Chris Bohner, 'No Union Democracy, No Union Revitalization', *Jacobin*, 25 February 2024.

28   Judith Stepan-Norris and Maurice Zeitlin, *Left Out: Reds and America's Industrial Unions*, New York: Cambridge University Press, 2002, p. 59. For a classic statement of the strategic importance of union democracy, see: Mike Parker and Martha Gruelle, *Democracy Is Power: Rebuilding Unions from the Bottom Up*, Labor Notes, 1999.

29   Leo Panitch and Sam Gindin, 'Class, Party, and the Challenge of State Transformation' in Leo Panitch and Greg Albo, eds, *Socialist Register 2017: Rethinking Revolution*, 2017, pp. 35-58. It is worth comparing the perspective advanced here with the essential work of labour strategist Jane McAlevey, one of the greatest influences on the thinking of the US labour left today. McAlevey's views, which emphasize the importance of activating and developing the capacity of rank-and-file union members for shopfloor fights, aligns in many ways with the rank-and-file strategy. But McAlevey, whose background was as a professional organizer for the Service Employees International Union (SEIU), tends not to discuss union reform, or the potential for a disconnect between the interests of union leaders and staff, on the one hand, and the rank and file on the other. She also has relatively little to say about how union organizing can serve as the basis for a broader socialist project and is critical of the role of more ideological 'activists'. For a summary and critique of her approach, see: Mike Parker, 'Review: *No Shortcuts: Organizing for Power in the New Gilded Age*', *Labor Notes*, 19 October 2017; Sam Gindin, 'The Power of Deep Organizing', *Jacobin*, 8 December 2016.

30   The political situation in the post-Hoffa Teamsters makes for an interesting, although certainly not more auspicious, contrast with the new UAW. President Sean O'Brien has made overtures to Donald Trump, going so far as to speak at this year's Republican National Convention while praising both Trump's running mate J.D. Vance and Missouri GOP Senator Josh Hawley; the Teamsters have also made large donations this election cycle to both the Republican National Committee and the Democratic National Committee. O'Brien also asked to speak at the Democratic National Convention in August, but his request was ignored by the party. In September, the Teamsters announced that they weren't making an endorsement in the presidential election.

THE CLIMATE MOVEMENT, THE SUFFRAGETTES AND THE MEANING OF MILITANCY

FEYZI ISMAIL

Countless popular comparisons have been made between the climate protesters of today and the suffragettes, who at the turn of the 20th century used direct action, civil disobedience and increasingly militant tactics to fight for the right to vote for women.[1] The mainstream media has drawn parallels with the suffragettes ever since climate protest exploded onto the global scene in 2018. More interestingly, the climate movement itself has embraced the comparison. The suffragettes formed the Women's Social and Political Union (WSPU) in 1903 under the slogan 'deeds not words' and vowed to secure the vote by any means, including attacking property. When Extinction Rebellion (XR) emerged in 2018, they adopted the slogan.

The suffragettes' most famous tactic was window smashing, which they aimed to turn into a political point: 'the argument of the broken pane of glass is the most valuable argument in modern politics',[2] contended WSPU co-founder Emmeline Pankhurst, highlighting the value placed on property over women's lives. XR have also smashed a few windows in their time – legitimate, they argue, given the scale of the crisis. In early 2023, seven women activists – dressed up as suffragettes no less, and wearing patches that read 'better broken windows than broken promises'[3] – were given suspended sentences for breaking the glass on the front of the London headquarters of Barclays bank, responsible for financing $167 billion worth of fossil fuel projects between 2016 and 2021.[4] The activist group Just Stop Oil, too, have borrowed from the suffragettes with the targeting of art galleries and sporting events. In late 2023, Just Stop Oil activists broke the glass on Velazquez's *Rokeby Venus* in the National Gallery, explicitly referencing suffragette Mary Richardson's slashing of the painting with a meat cleaver in 1914 to protest government hypocrisy over women's right to vote and the treatment of Emmeline.[5] The analogy has not been lost on the movement.

We should understand the range of tactics that the suffragettes and the wider suffrage movement used – on the one side, direct action involving property destruction, the disruption of public events and attacks on individual politicians and, on the other side, mass demonstrations, deputations to parliament and other forms of collective action, including support for strikes – as two traditions of militancy within the movement.[6] These traditions were tested most rigorously with the outbreak of World War I. Whereas one tradition of militancy began to reflect an elitist politics that thoroughly capitulated to the war, rejected an engagement with the mass labour unrest of the time and abandoned mass mobilization, the other tradition had the potential to organize people into a wider struggle, bring down the government and raise economic and social concerns beyond the vote, particularly for the working class. In both traditions, the politics informed the tactics: the former came to reflect a conservative politics, while the latter reflected a socialist orientation.

There are, of course, intense debates on the radical end of the climate movement concerning strategy and tactics: the extent to which we should concentrate on the sphere of production as opposed to consumption; the effectiveness of tactics ranging from direct action to mass mobilization; the role of the state in directing a transition away from fossil fuels; and whether property destruction strengthens or undermines the capacity of the movement to escalate, to name a few.

Perhaps the most popular reference to the suffragettes in the discussion around climate movement strategy is Andreas Malm's *How to Blow Up a Pipeline*, in which he makes the case for property destruction. Only a few pages of the short tract are devoted to the suffragettes, but it is a contentious reading of history.[7] Malm argues that the WSPU's campaign of property destruction 'went hand in hand with mass mobilization'.[8] In fact, the WSPU's focus on property destruction came at the *expense* of the mass movement and of working-class struggle. Not only had the rallies, demonstrations, public meetings and other forms of collective action been largely sidelined in favour of individual acts of heroism, there was also no role for the working classes: the WSPU leadership wanted the vote to be handed down to women, argued against strikes during a colossal upsurge of industrial struggle[9] and ultimately relied on authoritarianism, substitutionism and violence as a strategy, which contradicted and weakened the democratic legitimacy of the suffrage movement as a whole.

While much of the climate movement draws inspiration from the suffragettes, claiming the historical victory over the right to vote as a vindication of its tactics, the crucial difference is the climate movement's insistence on nonviolent direct action, which the WSPU categorically moved away from. Militant tactics were roundly criticized by other sections of the suffrage movement, notably the National Union of Women's Suffrage Societies (NUWSS), which was several times bigger than the WSPU, the Women's Freedom League (WFL), which split from the WSPU in 1907, and the radical suffragists, who participated in both the NUWSS and WSPU processions in London. The tactics of the climate movement have also been criticized, not so much for their militancy but for reflecting the middle-class sensibilities of a section of the professional class, whose separation from material production, according to Matt Huber, makes them neglectful of working-class concerns.[10] The crucial questions, then, are whether the strategy and tactics of the WSPU – property destruction in particular – were effective in securing the vote for women and whether the current tactics of the climate movement, focused on nonviolent direct action, represents an alternative.

The experience of the WSPU reveals that neither calls for property destruction nor the insistence on strategic nonviolence serve to strengthen the climate movement. Although their respective tactics appear conflicting and contradictory, the WSPU's militancy and the militancy of the current climate movement share at least three features: a denial of the need to find broad popular support in wider society; a rejection of an engagement with political parties and politics in general; and an underestimation of the power of the working class to stop production and thereby transform society. While the WSPU leadership was not interested in a wider emancipatory project, under the current climate and ecological emergency, we have no such luxury. If we are to respond to this emergency, it will have to mean the reorganization of the economy away from capitalist social relations, and a strategy that brings us closer to freedom from exploitation of both people and planet.

TWO TRADITIONS OF MILITANCY

Historians of the suffrage movement in Britain often make the distinction between the 'militant' suffragettes and the 'constitutional' suffragists.[11] But militancy did not belong solely to the WSPU. While the WSPU was certainly the most notorious organization of the suffrage movement of the early 20th century and undoubtedly 'revitalized a genteel and moribund women's suffrage movement'[12] that was dominated by the NUWSS and its methods of drawing-room meetings and lobbying parliament, the movement as a whole was complex and varied. Indeed, there was a 'vital debate within the suffrage movement itself – and the wider political culture of which it was a part – about the scope, meaning and utility of militancy'.[13] At the time, as now, the deployment of militant tactics in the form of property destruction was assumed to reflect a radical, even revolutionary, politics. Scrutiny of the politics that accompanied the militancy of the WSPU, however, reveals a flawed political strategy that not only antagonized potential support but was also not threatening to ruling class interests.

In its early days, when the WSPU was close to the Independent Labour Party (ILP) and its socialist roots, the suffragettes worked for ILP candidates in elections, and were keen to attract working-class women, particularly from the East End of London. This changed in 1906, when during the Cockermouth by-election, the WSPU declared that it would remain independent of any party. This was significant because it signalled a break from organized labour and the WSPU's links with northern socialism, and was a factor in the WFL subsequently splitting from the WSPU. Eventually, the new election policy of the WSPU was that all government candidates would be opposed, particularly those of the Liberals, but also including those socialist candidates in the Labour Party who supported women's suffrage. The WSPU leadership had also become increasingly concerned about the work being undertaken in London's East End – mass mobilization on a working-class basis – by Sylvia Pankhurst, Emmeline's middle daughter. Moving the WSPU from Manchester to London in 1906 was partly designed to put an end to this work.[14] It was at this time that tactical differences within the organization began to appear, eventually culminating in rival strategic visions. Emmeline and her oldest daughter Christabel Pankhurst – co-founder of the WSPU and its chief tactician – resigned from the ILP in 1907.

The WSPU had initially used a range of tactics in its campaigning, from direct action to mass demonstrations. The first notable use of militant tactics was in 1905, two years after the organization was established. Christabel and fellow suffragette and former textile worker Annie Kenney publicly questioned Liberal Party politician Sir Edward Grey at a Liberal rally in Manchester's Free Trade Hall, unfurling a banner in the middle of his speech, asking: 'will the Liberal government give women the vote?'.[15] They were promptly thrown out and arrested, and chose imprisonment rather than paying a fine. It was a turning point for the suffrage movement and for the WSPU. Such action was unprecedented and defied prevailing norms about the role of women in British politics, drawing more women into the suffrage movement and the WSPU itself.[16] The leadership wanted the national attention garnered by such disruptive tactics and the WSPU was beginning get the lion's share of press and publicity. But the militancy had to escalate if the publicity was to be sustained.

In 1907, they stormed parliament. In 1908, they organized what became known as Women's Sunday, at the time the biggest demonstration to date – some half a million people turned up and tens of thousands of women marched to Hyde Park.[17] Yet they were still not granted the vote. The first stones were hurled at 10 Downing Street shortly after Women's Sunday.[18] Two years later, stemming from a combination of understandable frustration over the lack of progress, in particular the failure of the 1910 Conciliation Bill which proposed granting propertied women the right to vote, and increasing state repression, the suffragettes officially resorted to more violent forms of direct action.[19] On 18 November 1910, three hundred women marched on parliament to protest the failure of the Bill to be heard and for six hours were confronted with horrific police brutality: they were beaten, kicked and sexually assaulted, and at least two women died of their injuries.[20]

The suffragettes named it Black Friday and it was in its wake that the leadership made a decisive turn: they began with a series of determined window-smashing campaigns, vandalized statues and paintings, exploded letterboxes, chained themselves to railings and fought the police. When they were arrested and imprisoned, and not recognized as political prisoners by the authorities, many suffragettes went on hunger strike, suffering the most ruthless forms of force feeding.[21] This kind of protest tends to travel in one direction. The more the Asquith government refused to pay attention to votes for women, the more desperate the actions became.[22] And yet, while on the one hand they steered clear of 'hard economic targets'[23] such as factories, on the other, they refused to relate to the mass labour unrest. After the failure of the third Conciliation Bill in 1913, the suffragettes escalated to arson attacks on empty buildings and placing bombs on trains and in railway stations.

Christabel justified the escalation of militancy in 1910 by arguing that the tactic of the demonstration had been exhausted. Women's Sunday in particular was the pinnacle of constitutional agitation.[24] There was also a practical consideration that explained the shift in tactics. In the context of mounting police violence, getting arrested quickly – which is what tended to happen following a broken pane – was preferable to being battered for hours at a demonstration before getting arrested. Nevertheless, militant direct action precluded the mass involvement of working-class women in the movement because it was primarily undertaken by women who could afford arrest and prison, or bail, as was the case with Emmeline and other wealthier women.[25] Christabel moved to Paris to avoid arrest, directing the organization from there. Emphasising individual bravery over collective action, the tactics began to reflect the class position of the leadership.

To fully appreciate the political development of the WSPU, it is crucial to consider the other tradition of militancy within the suffrage movement – whether suffragette or suffragist – that relied on the power of the working class. A number of the women's suffrage groups that emerged in the 1860s, including in the Lancashire mill towns where large numbers of women worked, joined the NUWSS. Radical suffragists, many of whom had worked in the mills themselves, would go on to form the Lancashire and Cheshire Women Textile and Other Workers' Representation Committee in 1903, months before the formation of the WSPU, aligning themselves with Labour and pushing for labour and suffrage representation in parliament. It was logical that they worked with the cotton unions to improve conditions for women workers, not merely for the abstract right to vote, since almost half of the 200,000 women cotton workers in the area were organized in a trade union.[26] Jill Liddington and Jill Norris, who detail the lives of prominent radical suffragists in *One Hand Tied Behind Us*, argue that there were many in the suffrage movement who believed the vote could only be won by building a mass movement of working women, firmly based in the cotton unions.[27]

During the new unionism of the late 1880s, Esther Roper and Eva Gore-Booth, in particular, helped organize factory gate meetings, pushed through motions at union branches and worked with local trades councils. Later, working within the North of England Society for Women's Suffrage in Manchester, they applied those skills to the suffrage campaign, organizing deputations to parliament and mass petitions.[28] They were drawing on an earlier generation of socialists such as Emma Paterson, who had argued that suffrage reform must include votes for women, and that women must also organize themselves in trade unions.[29] The radical suffragists politicized women workers and drew them into the suffrage campaign but also persuaded the Labour Representation Committee – predecessor to the Labour Party – to support the idea of women's suffrage.

Although they worked with the WSPU while it was based in Manchester, the radical suffragists saw the tactics of the WSPU as self-destructive: Selina Cooper, for example, who had worked in the mills since she was ten and became a socialist, did not believe 'that the elitist actions of a few militants could ever carry the weight of the demands of the mass of organized working women'.[30] Working-class suffragists also felt at odds with the donations rolling into the WSPU and that 'militancy for its own sake merely alienated' the support they had built amongst textile workers.[31] Yet the radical suffragists were also running out of steam a few years into their campaign, largely because they were isolated in Lancashire and Cheshire and were unable to influence parliament or the Trades Union Congress at the national level.[32] None were particularly interested in national politics.[33] Moreover, the North of England Society's Liberal financial backers felt uneasy about the radical suffragists' emphasis on labour.

Meanwhile in London, the East London Federation of Suffragettes – who took on the name after splitting with the WSPU in 1913 – also understood that building support for the vote required connecting the issue to the realities of everyday life for the mass of women. They established deep roots in the area. One obvious concern was work – wages, working conditions and the misery of unemployment. They publicized appalling conditions at work in their weekly newspaper *The Woman's Dreadnought* and helped lobby managers and local politicians. In response to regular attacks by the police in the East End, the Federation formed a People's Army, inspired by the Irish Citizen Army. Their other major concern was housing, over which the Federation organized a 'No Vote, No Rent'[34] strike designed to pressure both landlords and the government. Here was a militant tactic that working-class women were using collectively to potentially win concrete gains.

The Federation organized with working-class women to address a whole range of practical concerns – from substandard housing and the lack of childcare to inadequate food and irregular work – but also joined calls against the war. On the eve of war in June 1914, Sylvia went on hunger strike to press for a deputation of working women to petition Prime Minister Asquith for the vote. The deputation was initiated by a demonstration of thousands in East London and then elected by a series of large public meetings. A number of accounts, not least Sylvia's own, suggest that following the deputation, Asquith's hostility to women's suffrage began to wane.[35] It was not that the Federation was against throwing stones and smashing a few windows – Sylvia and others were arrested for this as late as 1913 – but these actions did not dominate their strategy. The focus was instead the mass participation of working women and men in improving their conditions with a view towards self-emancipation.

When war broke out, the Federation stepped up: they opened several milk distribution centres and cost-price restaurants to stave off hunger, a nursery where working women could safely leave their children and a co-operative toy factory where local women could earn a wage and learn a trade. The toy factory attempted to pay fair and equal wages and provide decent working conditions. All of this was central to Sylvia's understanding of socialism from below and making the vote relevant to working-class women by 'linking it with the problems that they wanted to change'.[36] Maintaining popular support for their activities had always been crucial for the Federation, and when Emmeline and other leaders were arrested and put on trial for conspiracy in 1912, Sylvia concentrated on consolidating suffragette activity in London to win back public support, including visiting picket lines and organizing some of the biggest demonstrations since Women's Sunday in 1908.[37]

THE CENTRALITY OF THE WORKING CLASS

The turn towards the WSPU's brand of militancy took place during the biggest wave of working-class militancy since the new unionism of the 1880s, which began to raise wider political and economic questions. Mass agitation and campaigning activities were rather more able to connect with the 'Great Unrest' – the 'unprecedented explosion of trade union militancy'[38] between 1910 and 1914 when millions of people across essential industries went on strike over wages, working conditions and union recognition. Women and girls in unorganized sectors and workplaces in London and elsewhere took inspiration from dockers, miners, gas and transport workers across the country and came out on strike.[39] Whereas the WSPU explicitly spurned making connections with labour, there is evidence of at least tenuous links between the wider suffrage and labour movements, and the potential that existed for fighting women's oppression and working-class exploitation as part of the same struggle.[40] It was the *combined militancy* of the suffrage, labour and other movements that posed the greatest threat to the ruling class.

The overriding idea that sustained the WSPU's tactics was that the real dividing line in society was not class, but sex.[41] All men, including working-class men, were sexist and neither the socialists nor the ILP were any better, having failed to prioritize equality between men and women.[42] The leadership felt that the WSPU could grow to the point where it wouldn't need the ILP, and this could only be done by appealing to women of all classes. This analysis accepted conventional views that women's natural roles were in the maternal and domestic spheres: women would be better able to raise children and take care of the household if they had the vote.[43] Yet it would somehow also prevent the sexual oppression of women and increase wages. Implicit in this politics was not only 'an acceptance by the WSPU leaders of the existing political system and its values'[44] but a rejection of the working class as an agent of change and of working-class organization. By 1914, the WSPU's newspaper *The Suffragette* was explicitly calling for a Tory government.

Run by an increasingly small number of loyalists, the WSPU was operating in relative isolation from mass politics and could not engage with the struggles of working people. Beyond the distinction between suffragettes and suffragists, it is well known that one of the main divides within the suffrage movement was along class lines: between those who saw the vote as an end in itself and those who understood the right to vote as instrumental. Thousands of working-class women wanted the vote, but made immediate connections between the political demand – what the vote meant for participation in political and public life – and their own economic reality. They understood the vote to be significant because of its value in opening up a struggle that could transform their living and working conditions.

These were not concerns for middle- and upper-class women in the movement, and certainly the strategy of the WSPU leadership was focused on the vote as a panacea, mobilizing arguments that narrowly focused on political equality with men. Crucially, the vote was to be won on an equal basis with men, which meant inclusion in the system based on the right to vote through property and therefore the exclusion of a sizeable proportion of working-class women and men from the vote. The property qualification had been a complex and intense source of debate within the suffrage movement and within the Labour Party – between those arguing for universal adult suffrage and the outright abolition of the property qualification, and a section of women suffragists arguing for limited enfranchisement based on property as a first step towards adult suffrage.[45] The socialist position was that anything less than the principle of universal suffrage was unacceptable; at the same time, it was used by the right to postpone the whole question: 'adult suffrage or nothing'.[46] While some argued that opposing limited franchise simply meant the status quo, others rejected this, arguing that a limited franchise would delay enfranchisement for the working class.

Christabel had come to dismiss the value of working-class women in the movement and, along with Emmeline, believed that the vote had to be handed down to working-class women; they were incapable of fighting for it themselves. Christabel argued that 'their [working women's] lives were too hard, their education too meagre to equip them for the struggle' and that instead of using 'the weakest for the struggle … we want picked women, the very strongest and most intelligent'.[47] If there was no value in working-class women in the movement, then there was no value in the agency of working-class women to exert their collective power, and collective action was not going to be central to either strategy or tactics.

However, at no time was the growing conservativism of the WSPU more apparent than in their response to the outbreak of World War I. Emmeline and Christabel capitulated. Now the interests of women and the vote itself were of lesser importance than the interests of the nation. *The Suffragette* became *Britannia*, the organization called for conscription and argued against socialism.[48] Lloyd George – hated by the WSPU for the bulk of his time as Chancellor of the Exchequer before the war – became one of the WSPU's heroes as minister of munitions, then secretary of state for war and later prime minister. Emmeline accepted substantial funds from Lloyd George to organize a demonstration in 1915 in defence of women's right to serve in war work, including in munitions factories.[49]

British women were indeed an indispensable pillar of the war effort. But this nationalist logic was foundational to the evolution of the WSPU into a xenophobic organization. The leadership became rabidly anti-German: it called for all official organizations to be purified of German blood and, although anti-German sentiment was not uncommon during the war, 'the extremes to which the WSPU took it was'.[50] All pacifists were traitors and the only thing that mattered was national interest. Christabel argued that the 'old delusion, class war, is exploded. The interests of the Nation are one and indivisible. The true, the natural and the divinely intended human grouping is according to nations.'[51]

As the war dragged on, the WSPU, which now had the financial backing of leading capitalists, launched a campaign against industrial militancy, any opposition to the war and Bolshevism. In 1917, it changed its name to the Women's Party, whose program was in 'no way based on sex antagonism'.[52] It had little to offer working-class women who were ravaged by the war's devastation. By the end of the war, Emmeline was travelling around the country rallying support for British imperialism and warning audiences about the dangers of Bolshevism. Ten years later, she became a candidate for MP for the Tories. Christabel moved to the US to become an evangelical Christian. Mary Richardson – the suffragette who slashed the *Rokeby Venus* – ended up joining the British Union of Fascists under Oswald Mosley and ran its women's section. Other prominent WSPU members, such as Sophia Duleep Singh, a descendant of Indian royalty as granddaughter of Maharaja Ranjit Singh, also ended up throwing themselves into the war effort.[53]

By abandoning the working-class origins of the WSPU, 'in many ways, Christabel and Emmeline Pankhurst represented the most conservative components of the whole suffrage movement'.[54] Christabel thought strikes unnecessary and during the war advocated the burning of socialist books. In contrast, Sylvia solidarized with other movements and causes, looking to find connections. It was when she spoke alongside James Connelly in the Royal Albert Hall in 1913, in defence of Irish workers who were locked out of their workplaces for joining the Irish Transport and General Workers Union (ITGWU) – and despite the fact that ITGWU leadership supported women's suffrage – that Christabel summoned her to Paris and informed her that the WSPU would have nothing to do with what was then the East London Federation of the WSPU. The differences in their respective approaches were now explicit. The Federation had already been working relatively autonomously for several years, but neither Emmeline nor Christabel appreciated Sylvia's increasing profile and popularity. The name of the organization was changed to the East London Federation of Suffragettes, much to the annoyance of the WSPU, and it continued to be run on democratic principles.

The WFL also supported strike action, mainly of women workers, and became actively involved in these struggles, arguing that women's franchise was not the sole remedy to women's oppression but rather connected to changing the wider economic and social system and the emancipation of the class. The WFL stopped short of becoming a socialist organization, though its leader Charlotte Despard described herself as a socialist. She argued against the war, remaining committed to the suffrage cause throughout it. Teresa Billington-Grieg, also a prominent socialist in the WFL, wrote a scathing critique of the WSPU, claiming that the leadership would be afraid of a revolution.[55]

After the war, there were organizations that continued to campaign. The WFL campaigned for full equality with men in other respects, including pay, work and under the law. The NUWSS became the National Union of Societies for Equal Citizenship. The East London Federation of Suffragettes went furthest to push the suffrage issue to its political limits and became the Workers' Suffrage Federation in 1916, supporting not only universal suffrage but the Easter Rising in Ireland against British rule. In 1918, it became the Workers' Socialist Federation. Openly socialist and internationalist, it was an integral part of opposition to the war and the revolutionary left, and publicly supported the Bolsheviks in Russia.[56] These organizations represented the fact that, to many working-class women and men in the suffrage movement, the vote was secondary to the struggle for emancipation but could be used as a concrete demand to mobilize around.

THE POWER OF MASS MOBILIZATION

As the actions of the WSPU became increasingly detached from the mass movement for the right to vote, fewer and fewer women were willing to participate. Although large donations continued to pour in, the rate of new memberships, for example, began to decline from 1909, with a dramatic fall of at least 42 per cent in the fiscal year 1913–14.[57] According to Andrew Rosen, 'the arson campaign itself was undoubtedly the most important single factor that fostered the decline'.[58] The sabotage strategy became more about causing maximum inconvenience for the government – but in tandem with imposing maximum inconvenience on the wider public in order that more individuals would put pressure on the government – and less about winning popular support. The WSPU's early indifference towards political parties was also a rejection of politics that could shape mass public opinion.

The downplaying of the importance of mass mobilization, however, was also reflected in the growing lack of internal democracy within the organization. In seeking absolute loyalty with their strategy and tactics, Emmeline and Christabel began to undermine the democratic structures of the WSPU. In 1907, Emmeline cancelled the annual conference and abandoned the WSPU constitution, arguing along with Christabel that militant tactics necessitated an autocratic structure: 'an army does not elect its generals'.[59] Eventually they rejected discussion and consensus altogether, preferring instead to dictate policy from the headquarters to the branches.[60] The organizational crisis in 1907 that led to the split establishing the WFL meant that democratic questions were being discussed much more widely outside the WSPU, and the WFL was explicit about operating on a democratic basis with internal elections. Many women in the WSPU, however, particularly those who would go on to leave, cited the contradiction between fighting for democratic reforms while participating in an undemocratic organization.[61]

The militancy also necessitated a level of conspiracy. Whereas in the past, the WSPU had announced demonstrations, declared intentions to engage in action ahead of time and explained strategy to members, increasingly actions had to be kept secret. This became all the more necessary, and understandably so, as repression increased.[62] There is also evidence that a number of women had expressed doubts about the tactics but remained active in the organization out of personal loyalty.[63] Prominent figures also left the WSPU at various points, including Elizabeth Garrett Anderson, citing the window-smashing campaign, and Dora Montefiore, over the lack of democracy.

In 1912, Frederick and Emmeline Pethick-Lawrence, who formed part of the core leadership that built the WSPU, were ousted from the organization by Emmeline Pankhurst on the grounds that they disagreed with the call for arson. The Pethick-Lawrences supported militancy but only on a large, open scale, whereas arson had to be done in secret and was intended precisely to avoid arrest, not to win public support. Though they left wanting to avoid damage to the WSPU, their departure had a profound effect on the organization, not least because it left WSPU policy in the hands of Christabel alone. Rosen notes that 'the process of the previous six years whereby persons of some independence of thought had been progressively eliminated from the inner councils of the Union had now reached its logical climax, with the achievement of a complete autocracy'.[64] As Paul Foot astutely observes, without the democratic structures in which to debate such tactics, force of personality decided.[65]

The WSPU had failed to force the government to grant women the vote 'not necessarily because the tactics were too extreme, but because they lacked broad appeal and yet were not sufficiently coercive to compel concessions'.[66] The bulk of the activities of the East London Federation of Suffragettes, on the other hand, was focused on pushing for mass, collective action through the self-activity of working people around material questions, and the further suffering that many experienced as a result of the war. For the Federation, all of this work was strictly not about charity but 'about building a strong, mass movement of working women who could and would demand their rights'.[67] Without a mass movement to keep the leadership accountable, the WSPU's tendency towards authoritarianism and substitutionism was inescapable.

Even if a number of brave individuals were willing to make sacrifices, the outcomes were limited. The government could not be seen to be capitulating to what they regarded as terrorism, and so the response was even greater repression. Moreover, property destruction had given the government an excuse to withhold the vote. This was particularly the case from 1912 in response to the arson and bombing campaigns. The war had also changed the suffragettes. It could be argued that not only was the WSPU leadership not in a position to renew the campaign of militancy in the form of property destruction after the war, but rather that at the beginning of the war, they had in fact been in no position to continue it. It had reached its limits, and the war had intervened to expose those limits.

The duration of World War I separated suffragette militancy, which ceased entirely in 1914, and the granting of the vote in 1918. It was not primarily the suffragettes' property destruction campaign that secured the vote for women, but a combination of objective and subjective factors centred around war and revolution and the participation of women in production. The whole of the establishment was clearly rattled by the spectre of revolution in Russia, Germany and elsewhere in Europe. Enfranchisement for a section of older, propertied women, was a small price to pay to avoid stirring up revolutionary fervour. Moreover, that so many soldiers and sailors who fought in World War I did not have the right to vote – those who made up much of the 40 per cent of men excluded from the vote under the property qualification – yet were willing risk death on government orders, made withholding the franchise from them untenable.

The war brought unprecedented numbers of women into production and, therefore, changed the position of women in society irrevocably. More than a million women were organized in trade unions. Women who were working in the factories, in the fields and in transport throughout the war were also indispensable to the war effort; this new reality, along with the upcoming election, made the whole question of electoral reform an urgent issue. Though a number of these women would not qualify for the vote until 1928, when universal suffrage was introduced, their role demolished the myth that women were incapable of work that was traditionally done by men. If, after the experience of the suffragettes and the entire suffrage movement, there were any doubts about whether women were capable of fighting, including for better pay and conditions at work, alongside men, those too were weakened.

THE CLIMATE MOVEMENT AND
THE SECOND CRISIS OF LIBERALISM

History reveals that the WSPU's militancy had a number of detrimental effects on the wider suffrage movement: it undermined the ability of the mass of the population to participate in and strengthen the movement as a whole; it allowed the government to drive a wedge between activists and the wider population; it took activists out of the movement through regular spells in prison; it alienated much existing and potential working-class support; and it hindered activists within and outside the movement from making connections between different struggles. To foreground this history is not to use the suffragettes as an argument against civil disobedience, mass arrests or even property destruction *tout court*; context can necessitate any and all of these tactics. It is certainly not to argue for patience in bringing about change, as politicians asked of the suffragettes. But without a mass movement, property destruction could not be sustained in the long-term, and without a central role for the working class, the disruption could not be leveraged towards more fundamental change.

The suffrage movement encompassed groups and individuals with a wide range of ideological differences, from a handful of Tories and many middle-class reformers to working-class women and men, and those influenced by socialist ideas. These differences were reflected in equally significant tactical differences. There are clear similarities between the courageous individuals fighting for suffrage over a century ago and those in the climate movement who now face arrest, fines and long prison sentences for sounding the alarm in an attempt to force the government to act. The activists in these groups – XR and Just Stop Oil the most prominent among them – form part of a wider climate movement that encompasses distinct and competing ideologies and associated tactics.[68]

If the winning of the vote was, in reality, inseparable from – and, in fact, secondary to – the potential contained within the *struggle* for the vote, then any transition on the climate front needs to contain within it the struggle for wider social and economic change. This change must be drastic enough, in both speed and scale, for it to instigate continuous transition, not just away from fossil fuels, but towards an entirely different society based on democratic control. For this to happen, the radical end of the climate movement must deploy tactics that make it possible to grow the movement as much as possible and relate to wider struggles beyond the climate movement – the struggles that working people are already engaged in. The suffrage and labour struggles at the turn of the century began to do this, but ultimately failed to coalesce into a unified and unassailable force against the ruling powers.

The crises that led to World War I endure in different forms, only now unfolding under conditions of climate breakdown. Thus, when George Dangerfield in his classic *The Strange Death of Liberal England* described how the combination of the suffrage, trade union and Irish rebellions of the pre-war years constituted a serious threat to liberalism in England, it was an argument about the balance of class forces in the context of multiple crises. What began to tip the balance in favour of working-class control was the fact that the rebellions were taking place concurrently. Had the tenuous links between them been strengthened and had the war not intervened, liberalism may not have been resurrected in the virulent form of neoliberalism. With neoliberalism exhausted[69] and the warnings ever starker about impending climate and ecological catastrophe, strategic questions are pressing.

The circumstances in which significant change can come about are when the establishment is confronted with a large, militant and mobilized social force that has broad support in the population and when it fears for the future stability of the regime. As one element of this, direct action can at times dramatically illustrate the power of an argument and the strength of feeling amongst large swathes of the population. XR have created a number of these moments, and two in particular in 2019: in April, they occupied and blockaded bridges, buildings, stations and busy streets for 11 days, with the action centred around a pink boat lodged in the middle of Oxford Circus in central London displaying the words 'Tell the Truth'.[70] There were 1,130 arrests. Immediately following these actions, sympathetic MP Jeremy Corbyn, then leader of the opposition, brought a motion to parliament to officially declare a climate and environment emergency. It was passed unopposed in the House of Commons.[71] In October, they organized a 2-week 'international rebellion', co-ordinated with more than 60 countries, bringing over 30,000 people onto the streets of London.

Yet it is also true that certain forms of direct action can be counterproductive. As part of the October 2019 actions, when two XR activists disrupted the journeys of thousands of commuters at Canning Town station in London by jumping on top of a train in the middle of morning rush hour, it reflected not only inexperience but an ignorance of the realities of working people.[72] Moreover, it exposed the disregard for democracy within the organization: an online poll conducted by XR on social media revealed that 72 per cent of the more than 3,700 respondents opposed the action,[73] yet it went ahead.

At the end of 2022, XR issued a controversial statement entitled 'We Quit', declaring that 'building collective power, strengthening in number and thriving through bridge-building is a radical act'.[74] True enough, but subsequent national actions have been relatively muted. XR seemed to recognize the need to engage the public, but proposed a shift in tactics with no serious ideas about how to build public support in a systematic way. While what they dubbed 'The Big One' in April 2023 brought some 50,000 people onto the streets, despite claims of wanting 100,000, and while 2024 has involved hundreds of smaller local activities across Britain, XR appears to have run its course.

In contrast, Just Stop Oil – which split from XR in 2022 while remaining comradely with the group – remain devoted to nonviolent direct action and have continued with disruptive tactics. High-profile actions in 2024 involved throwing orange corn flour over Stonehenge and spraying orange paint onto private jets stationed at Stansted airport. Probably their most famous action has been throwing cans of tomato soup on Van Gogh's *Sunflowers* in the National Gallery in 2022, ostensibly to make a link between the cost-of-living crisis and the cost of oil – that neither people nor the planet can afford business-as-usual. Although their actions have diversified and their targets have become more imaginative – galleries, sporting events, English Heritage sites – they have largely remained in the same register. Even if the actions are more targeted, against fossil fuel infrastructure, for example, what animates Just Stop Oil is a steadfastness to the tasks of educating the public and persuading the government.

Indeed, for much of the climate movement, direct action has been predicated on the assumptions that the public is not aware, or at least not sufficiently aware, of the climate crisis and that the government is open to persuasion. Yet the evidence is that the public is acutely aware; poll after poll shows keen awareness of and anxiety around climate change among huge majorities.[75] Direct action has plausibly contributed to this awareness, but the perceived lack of action on the part of the public stems from the fact that people feel powerless to confront the enormity of planetary breakdown and unconfident about exerting their class power, within or outside the confines of the trade union movement. Just Stop Oil have attempted to engage with workers in fossil fuel industries, supported picket lines and participated in mass demonstrations organized by other movements. Nevertheless, the question of popularity – not only whether the public is sympathetic to the movement, but whether they can *participate* in it in ways that improve their lives – is not irrelevant but in fact central to the challenges ahead.

Spokespeople for the movement have claimed that the objective is not popularity, citing Martin Luther King Jr and the suffragettes as 'unpopular', rather than divisive; according to one, 'this isn't the X factor, public support would be nice, but women didn't get the vote by voting'.[76] Not only does this contradict the stated desire to change public opinion, but it also reveals that building a mass movement is not the purpose of action. Now that the current Labour government has agreed to suspend all new oil and gas licences, Just Stop Oil wants it to sign a legally binding fossil fuel treaty; after that, 'we can all go home and … there is no more disruption'.[77] The objective here is policy change, coupled with a rejection of politics – both right-wing *and* left-wing – and political parties. This was nothing short of confusing during the Corbyn years, reducing politics to a series of voluntaristic actions based on moralism.[78] Citizens' assemblies, organized by sortition rather than on the basis of experience, ideas and internal democracy, where deliberation is reduced to a small group of individuals advised by experts, remains a core XR demand. Class interests, and the need to build a labour movement based on the objective power of the working class, are absent. In short, the tactics of the climate movement reflect an indifference towards popular support, politics and the primacy of production.

The most influential theoretical basis from which the tactics of nonviolent direct action are drawn is the work of Harvard academic Erica Chenoweth and former US state department official Maria J. Stephan. In their most prominent work, Chenoweth and Stephan survey over 323 violent and nonviolent resistance campaigns between 1900 and 2006 and conclude, in a selective manner with little analysis of class dynamics and the reasons for the uprisings, that nonviolence is twice as likely to succeed.[79] While it is true that high levels of participation contribute to success, their analysis is technical, not political. Chenoweth's widely cited claim that the mobilization of 3.5 per cent of the population is all that is needed for regimes to crumble – a figure that XR had seized upon[80] – was later qualified as not necessarily being prescriptive.[81] Resistance groups, armed or otherwise, are not, in general, interested in mere 'policy objectives'.[82] Applied to the climate emergency, the notion of policy change fails to capture the gravity of what we face.

Principled nonviolence – the rejection of the use of violence towards achieving political objectives under all circumstances – also underestimates the repression of direct action by the state, with the 2023 Public Order Act being one such weapon to imprison mounting numbers of climate and other activists.[83] In fact, direct action and civil disobedience have the potential for maximum impact when carried out alongside mass action in a strategic fashion, where the mass movement and working-class struggle dominate.[84] While the climate is a major concern for working-class people – and at times is catapulted to the forefront of struggle – at the same time, many working-class people, through force of circumstance, tend to be motivated by more immediate concerns that may not be directly related to the climate: wages, working conditions, or even more abstract issues such as British involvement in or support for foreign wars, occupations and genocide. These struggles, reflected in the climate struggle itself, also embody a profound democratic deficit in society.

We have on the streets worldwide an unprecedented antiwar, pro-Palestine upsurge, where Israel's war and US backing for it has come to symbolize and further expose the deep contradictions between the imperialist powers that support genocide and the criminalization of those demanding its cessation. The Palestine movement has changed electoral calculations in Britain, France and elsewhere, in however a modest way. It has infused a sense of urgency into global politics, reflected in the explosion of protest in the last two decades, which has created conditions of possibility.[85] For much of the global population, society has become untenable; major protests are underway in Kenya, Nigeria, Bangladesh and elsewhere in the global South over the cost of living, wages, corruption and resulting repression.

Palestine and the wider Middle East is one aspect of the global context, which includes NATO's proxy war in Ukraine against Russia and increasing confrontation with China. The social movements and strike waves around the world have to greater or lesser extents raised questions about alternatives to the existing system of carnage. If we take seriously the proposition that capitalism is the source of the crisis, then destabilising the capitalist system and challenging imperialism – including in relation to the question of Palestine – is a climate objective and must be part of the strategy for the climate movement. In the history of capitalism, it is democratic movements that ultimately threaten property. But we need not only a movement capable of the physical destruction of property, as happens in revolutionary moments, but one that threatens the power of the propertied classes, and for this we need a combination of movements making common cause with one another

– coordinated, solidarizing and ready to escalate. If many of the same people demonstrating over Palestine recognize the climate as a concern, then a victory for the Palestine movement is a victory for the climate movement.

Beyond this, an organizational form is needed that connects the movement and the class and develops an understanding of what it means to challenge the system. At this point, we need not just for coal, oil and gas to be left in the ground, but the wholesale transformation of society, which even the IPCC acknowledges. The unprecedented rise of protest in defence of Palestine, coming off the back of the biggest strike wave in a generation in Britain, are signs that many understand what is at stake.

CONCLUSION

The courage, commitment and organization of WSPU activists is indisputable. The suffragettes animated the women's suffrage movement, rallied untold numbers to the cause and many people, including working-class women who were committed to militancy, made huge sacrifices. The same applies to climate activists today. But admiration for the militants and solidarity with the cause must not impede a sober evaluation of whether the strategy or tactics are effective. When the Representation of the People Act was signed at the end of World War I, it was a victory amid unimaginable destruction and loss of life. Not only was it 'a sad and hollow victory, an anti-climax to a long campaign',[86] but the subsequent history of the vote is one in which it has been undermined.[87]

Time has run out for hollow victories. If we want nothing short of the planet, then we need a strategy and tactics that has a chance at winning, based on a certain reading of history. If tactics are to be experimented with alongside and within the mass movement, then building the mass movement is essential. And while there are numerous historical examples of mass movements that have won over political questions, workers have a strategic position like no other in society. In a context where the magnitude of the climate crisis raises questions of fundamental change, and therefore various forms of militancy, including industrial action, the job of radicals is surely to relate to and find ways of supporting action undertaken by the working-class, reinforcing its capacity to challenge the structures of power.

Tactics must not divide the climate movement, but for this we need clarity over strategic questions: it matters that the concerns of working-class people are central to the climate movement; it matters who is in power and how we relate to political parties; it matters what position the climate movement takes on pressing questions of war and imperialism, as in the current movement in defence of Palestine; and it matters the extent to which the movement supports striking workers, particularly during strike waves. The question is how to make society ungovernable, how to threaten dominant class interests through solidarity and collective action – on the streets and in the workplaces – and through those struggles how we can start to gain control. As the world hurtles towards greater and greater devastation, we urgently need a strategy and tactics for fundamental change, but it needs to be one that starts with the struggles that are already being fought.

NOTES

1   This contribution focuses on the climate movement in the British context, given the history of the suffragettes in Britain, but the arguments can be applied more generally. It was the *Daily Mail* that first used the nickname 'suffragette' as a derogatory play on 'suffragist' to describe WSPU activists, but they embraced the label.

2   Diane Atkinson, *Rise Up, Women! The Remarkable Lives of the Suffragettes*, London: Bloomsbury Publishing, 2018, p. 288.

3   '"Better broken windows than broken promises" – Extinction Rebellion women break windows at Barclays HQ in Canary Wharf', Extinction Rebellion, 7 April 2021, available at: https://extinctionrebellion.uk.

4   'Banking on Climate Chaos: Fossil Fuel Finance Report 2022', Rainforest Alliance, Banktrack, Indigenous Environmental Network, Oilchange International, Reclaim Finance, Sierra Club and Urgewald, 30 March 2022, available at: www.bankingonclimatechaos.org.

5   For video footage of the action, see: https://twitter.com/ExtinctionR/status/1721549936011976708. See also: Louise Coyne, 'Just Stop Oil Attack the Rokeby Venus: How the Group is Using the Suffragettes' Disruptive Tactics to Shape Public Opinion', *The Conversation*, 6 November 2023. Available at: www.theconversation.com.

6   This point belongs to Katherine Connelly and the ideas introduced in: 'The Suffragettes, Black Friday and Two Types of Window Smashing', *Counterfire*, 18 November 2010, available at: www.counterfire.org. She later developed these ideas in a brilliant and informative alternative history of the suffragettes: *Sylvia Pankhurst: Suffragette, Socialist and Scourge of Empire*, London: Pluto Press, 2013.

7   For a blunt critique of Malm's use of the suffragettes as an example to be followed, see: Mike Haynes, 'Forget the Pipelines: Blowing Up Bad History – the Peculiar Story of Andreas Malm and the Suffragettes', *Historical Materialism blog*, n.d., available at: www.historicalmaterialism.org.

8   Andreas Malm, *How to Blow Up a Pipeline*, London: Verso, 2020, p. 41.

9   In 1910, Christabel wrote that strikes should be replaced by 'the political method, whereby the elected representative of the employers, of the workers and of the public at large discuss and arrive at a settlement'. Cited in: Les Garner, *Stepping Stones to Women's Liberty: Feminist Idea in the Women's Suffrage Movement, 1900-1918*, London: Heinemann Educational Books, 1984, p. 52.

10   Matt Huber, *Climate Change as Class War*, London: Verso, 2022, p. 31.

11 Sandra Holton argues that this distinction makes little sense in the context of much overlap between the NUWSS and the WSPU in the early years of the latter and a degree of cross-membership at a local level. Similarly, June Purvis argues that militancy for the suffragettes encompassed a broad range of both legal and more illegal, violent actions. See: Sandra Stanley Holton, 'Did Militancy Help or Hinder the Granting of Women's Suffrage in Britain?', *Women's History Review*, 28(7), 2019, pp. 1227-33; June Purvis, 'Did Militancy Help or Hinder the Granting of Women's Suffrage in Britain?', *Women's History Review*, 28(7), 2019, pp. 1200-17.

12 Laura E. Nym Mayhall, 'Defining Militancy: Radical Protest, the Constitutional Idiom, and Women's Suffrage in Britain, 1908-1909', *Journal of British Studies*, 39(3), 2000, p. 341.

13 Mayhall, 'Defining Militancy', p. 342.

14 The other reasons for the move, according to Jill Liddington and Jill Norris, were that the WSPU could put more effective pressure on the Liberal government, and break both the WSPU's dependence on the ILP and its links with the radical suffragists. See: *One Hand Tied Behind Us: The Rise of the Women's Suffrage Movement*, London: Rivers Oram Press, 1984, p. 204.

15 Paul Foot, *The Vote: How It Was Won and How It Was Undermined*, London: Penguin, 2005, p. 195.

16 Foot (*The Vote*, p. 199) notes some of the figures: in 1907, suffragettes collectively spent 191 weeks in prison; in 1908, 350 weeks. Membership doubled in 1908. The WSPU organized more than 100,000 meetings in the first 6 years of its existence, filling the largest venue in the country, the Albert Hall, thirteen times.

17 On Women's Sunday, see: 'The suffragettes in Hyde Park', Royal Parks website, 8 March 2022, available at: www.royalparks.org.uk/read-watch-listen/suffragettes-hyde-park. After Women's Sunday, held on 21 June 1908, a number of mass demonstrations organized by the WSPU took place throughout the country that year. In July alone, there were crowds of 150,000 in Manchester and 100,000 in Leeds, in addition to another 20,000 in Clapham Common in London. See: Andrew Rosen, *Rise Up, Women! The Militant Campaign of the Women's Social and Political Union 1903-1914*, London: Routledge, 1974, p.109.

18 Mary Leigh and Edith New had taken this initiative without direction from the WSPU leadership and were sentenced to two months in prison, alongside common criminals. Purvis ('Did militancy help or hinder?', p. 1203) uses this example to argue that the WSPU leadership was not autocratic, since women were using their agency to choose which actions they would undertake. But this arguably began to change as the militancy intensified and members had to follow stricter orders, and become more secretive.

19 The cross-party Conciliation Committee for Women's Suffrage was composed of 54 MPs in favour of women's enfranchisement, put together in 1910 by two *Daily News* journalists Henry Brailsford and H.M. Nevinson. Brailsford did not agree with the WSPU's tactics but was outraged at the government's use of force feeding. The Conciliation Committee introduced three private-member Conciliation Bills in parliament – in 1910, 1911 and 1912 – proposing to grant propertied women the right to vote. While the WSPU called temporary truces while the Bills were debated, after each Bill's failure, it ramped up the militancy.

20 The deputation of suffragettes was part of a 'Women's Parliament' meant to challenge the legitimacy of parliament at Westminster. The government attempted but failed to

cover up the police brutality and Winston Churchill, then Home Secretary, refused to permit an inquiry into what happened. See: Vicky Iglikowski-Broad, 'Suffragettes and the Black Friday protests: 18 November 1910', The National Archives Blog, 18 November 2019, available at: https://blog.nationalarchives.gov.uk.

21   Atkinson, *Rise Up, Women!*, 2018; Sarah Jackson and Rosemary Taylor, *East London Suffragettes*, Cheltenham: The History Press, 2014. The torture of force feeding led a number of women to attempt suicide in prison, including Zelie Emerson, who was Sylvia Pankhurst's dear friend, and Emily Wilding Davison, who is known for stepping in front of the King's horse at the Epsom Derby in 1913, tragically dying of her injuries. To avoid the embarrassment of having the death of a suffragette on their hands, in 1913 the Liberal government introduced the Temporary Discharge of Prisoners Act (1913) – what became known as the 'Cat and Mouse Act' – allowing prisoners who had been force fed to be temporarily released in order to recover their health, only to be rearrested and sent back to prison once they did so.

22   Rosen (*Rise Up, Women!*, p. 179) notes that 'the militant campaign had never been static – militancy had always taken on progressively more extreme forms…'. Christabel herself argued in her autobiography *Unshackled: The Story of How We Won the Vote* that 'mild militancy was more or less played out' (cited in Rosen, *Rise Up, Women!*, p. 131).

23   Garner, *Stepping Stones*, p. 49. Rosen (*Rise Up, Women!*, p. 244) notes that 'arson might have been more effective if commercial and industrial targets had been chosen more frequently', whereas the private homes that were targeted only inconvenienced very few people.

24   As Women's Sunday had failed to persuade Asquith, Christabel had written in the WSPU newspaper *Votes for Women* that 'no larger meeting is conceivable … if the holding of public meetings were our last resource, our case would indeed be helpless' (Rosen, *Rise Up, Women!* p. 106).

25   Though Emmeline did spend considerable time in prison on several occasions, particularly in 1912 and 1913, with the escalation of militancy.

26   Foot, *The Vote*, p. 192.

27   Liddington and Norris, *One Hand*, pp. 15-16.

28   Along with Sarah Dickenson, Sarah Reddish and other activists, one mass petition launched on 1 May 1900 involved, in addition to a series of mass meetings, the patient collection of signatures from house to house in the evenings, speaking with women who were home from work and preparing the evening meal. The petition revealed the widespread support for the franchise amongst women textile workers – together with a number of sympathetic men – with almost 30,000 signatures collected by the time it was taken to parliament. See: Liddington and Norris, *One Hand*, pp. 143-7.

29   Foot, *The Vote*, p. 183.

30   Liddington and Norris, *One Hand*, p. 19.

31   Liddington and Norris, *One Hand*, p. 210.

32   Foot, *The Vote*, p. 193; Liddington and Norris, *One Hand*, p. 162.

33   Liddington and Norris, *One Hand*, p. 275.

34   Jackson and Taylor, *East London Suffragettes*, p. 143.

35   Jackson and Taylor (*East London Suffragettes*, p. 78) note that *The New Statesman* suggested at the time that the deputation marked a distinct step forward in the suffrage campaign.

36 Connelly, *Sylvia Pankhurst*, p. 49.

37 Foot, *The Vote*, p. 218; Connelly, *Sylvia Pankhurst*, p. 47. For a comprehensive account of Sylvia's life, see also: Rachel Holmes, *Sylvia Pankhurst: Natural Born Rebel*, London: Bloomsbury Publishing, 2020.

38 Ralph Darlington, 'The Pre-First World War British Women's Suffrage Revolt and Labour Unresent: Never the Twain Shall Meet?' *Labour History*, 61(5-6), 2020, p. 467.

39 Barbara Drake, *Women in Trade Unions*, London: Virago, 1984.

40 Darlington, *Labour History*, p. 468.

41 Christabel later developed this basic position into notions of good and evil, including that 'sexual disease spread by prostitution was the evil responsible for society's worst ills' (Rosen, *Rise Up, Women!*, p. 196).

42 There was, however, also some truth in the impression that socialists were no better on the question of female suffrage, with a number of prominent leaders of the Social Democratic Federation (SDF), Britain's first socialist party, who were against it. This is despite the fact that the official manifesto of the SDF called for universal suffrage. See: Foot, *The Vote*, p. 188. The Industrial Syndicalist Education League (ISEL) was also dismissive of women's franchise. See: Darlington, *Labour History*, p. 474.

43 The WSPU did, however, mobilize some of the first arguments around wages for housework, though these were marginal to their overall demands. They referenced the economic value of domestic work and highlighted the reality of women's unpaid labour, which was a contribution to feminist arguments more generally. Though the WSPU did not challenge the 'separate spheres' theory and there were few details on how wages were to be paid and by whom (Garner, *Stepping Stones*, p. 51), the idea of separate spheres was not an uncommon position within the suffrage movement, given the prevailing ideas of the time.

44 Garner, *Stepping Stones*, p. 52.

45 When Keir Hardie and the Lancashire and Cheshire Women Textile and Other Workers' Representation Committee conducted separate surveys, their investigations revealed that 80 per cent of people who would be enfranchised by a limited bill were working class. See: Liddington and Norris, *One Hand*, p. 180-81.

46 Foot, *The Vote*, p. 206.

47 Connelly, *Sylvia Pankhurst*, pp. 58-9. When the East London Federation of Suffragettes was formed in 1913, Sylvia published her response in the first issue of the Federation's newspaper, *The Woman's Dreadnought*: 'Some people say that the lives of working women are too hard and their education too small for them to become a powerful voice in winning the vote. Such people have forgotten their history' (Jackson and Taylor, *East London Suffragettes*, p. 58). At the launch of the Federation, she argued 'we must get members to work for themselves and let them feel they are working for their own emancipation' (Garner, *Stepping Stones*, p. 81).

48 It should be noted that the initial reaction of the WSPU to the war was broadly in agreement with much of the rest of suffrage movement, which blamed the war on 'the male characteristic of physical force' (Garner, *Stepping Stones*, p. 55).

49 Atkinson, *Rise Up, Women!*, pp. 515-16. Atkinson notes that the procession resembled those of the past that the WSPU had organized, with 90 brass bands, 125 contingents and hundreds of banners, rallying some 60,000 women.

50 Garner, *Stepping Stones*, p. 56.

51   Garner, *Stepping Stones*, p. 57.

52   Garner, *Stepping Stones*, p. 59.

53   Her life and involvement in the suffrage movement is detailed in Anita Anand's highly readable *Sophia: Princess, Suffragette, Revolutionary*, London: Bloomsbury Publishing, 2015.

54   Garner, *Stepping Stones*, p. 105.

55   Teresa Billington-Greig, *The Militant Suffrage Movement: Emancipation in a Hurry*, London: Frank Palmer, 1911, p. 113.

56   The WSF was also involved in negotiations that led to the formation of the British Communist Party. Garner, *Stepping Stones*, p. 79 and p. 85; Jackson and Taylor, *East London Suffragettes*, p. 125 and p. 163.

57   Rosen (*Rise Up, Women!*, p. 212) also notes that 'it is probable that the Union ceased to publish new members' fees after 28 October 1913 in order to avoid publicizing the WSPU's rapidly decreasing ability to attract converts'.

58   Rosen, *Rise Up, Women!*, p. 212.

59   Garner, *Stepping Stones*, p. 29.

60   Mayhall, *Journal of British Studies*, p. 347.

61   According to Garner (*Stepping Stones*, p. 47), 'the whole history of the WSPU is littered with breakaways by women who could not tolerate the dictatorship of the Pankhursts'. Estimates about how many women left the WSPU in the split are debated, with lower figures at 20 per cent of the WSPU membership. Nevertheless, the 1907 split that established the WFL and the 1913 split that consolidated the East London Federation of Suffragettes are the most significant, signalling major tactical and strategic differences.

62   Secrecy is needed where repression is high, but inevitably excludes large numbers, who would not be in the know, and therefore has a tendency towards elitism.

63   Rosen (*Rise Up, Women!*, p. 170) notes that 'Christabel's growing belief in the political efficacy of destroying property had certainly not yet permeated the WSPU as a whole'.

64   Rosen, *Rise Up, Women!*, p. 178.

65   Foot, *The Vote*, p. 222.

66   Rosen, *Rise Up, Women!*, p. 243.

67   Jackson and Taylor, *East London Suffragettes*, p. 114.

68   Insulate Britain also briefly made headlines when they were formed in late 2021 by XR activists. They managed to make direct links between the climate crisis and soaring energy bills for the vast majority, but after 6 months, declared their own actions – a handful of protests blocking motorways over a 2-month period – a failure. Many activists associated with the organization have since been sentenced to prison. The climate movement in Britain, of course, constitutes a number of strands, including a range of environmental NGOs, think tanks, corporate projects around carbon trading and green innovation, trade union initiatives, legal activism and specific campaigns targeted against fossil fuel infrastructure. In 2019, the Youth Strike 4 Climate movement, coordinated by the UK Student Climate Network (UKSCN) and Fridays for Future founded by Greta Thunberg, also brought tens of thousands of school students out on strike. On 20 September 2019, they called a general strike challenging workers to join them and mobilized an estimated 300,000 people across Britain. The tactic of the strike by school students sent a powerful message to the government and the wider public, but the network disbanded in 2020, in part due to

the pandemic. Direct action now currently dominates the radical end of the climate movement in Britain, despite increasingly repressive legislation.

69   Neil Davidson, *What Was Neoliberalism? Studies in the Most Recent Phase of Capitalism, 1973-2008*, Chicago: Haymarket Books, 2023; Gary Grestle, *The Rise and Fall of the Neoliberal Order*, Oxford: Oxford University Press, 2022.

70   See: 'We Were the Boat: The Inside Story of an April Icon', Extinction Rebellion, 15 April 2020, available at: https://extinctionrebellion.uk.

71   See: '"The Most Important Issue of Our Time," Opposition Calls to Declare Climate Emergency', UK Parliament news, 1 May 2019, available at: www.parliament.uk. The motion was proposed also as a result of the school strikes launched by Youth Strike 4 Climate.

72   During their trial, the prosecutor claimed that the activists disrupted the journeys of 48,000 people. See: Jack Wright, 'Extinction Rebellion Activists Who Scaled a Tube at Canning Town at Rush Hour Before Being Dragged Off and Roughed Up by Commuters Admit: "We Got It Wrong" as Judges Spares Them Jail But Warns, "You Went Too Far"', *Daily Mail*, 18 March 2022. Although the activists involved apologized, others in XR defended the action. One activist associated with the action claimed desperation over climate breakdown and didn't know 'what else to do'. See: Matthew Taylor, '"It Has Been Polarising": Tube Protest Divides Extinction Rebellion', *The Guardian*, 17 October 2019.

73   Jane Wharton, 'Most Extinction Rebellion Activists Did Not Want to Disrupt the Tube', *Metro*, 17 October 2019.

74   See: 'We Quit', Extinction Rebellion, 31 December 2022, available at: https://extinctionrebellion.uk.

75   See: Madalina Vlasceanu et al., 'Addressing Climate Change with Behavioral Science: A Global Intervention Tournament in 63 countries', *Science Advances,* 10(eadj5778), 2024; 'Three-Quarters of Adults in Great Britain Worry About Climate Change', Office for National Statistics, 5 November 2021, available at: www.ons.gov.uk; 'The World's Largest Survey on Climate Change is Out – Here's What the Results Show', UNDP Climate Promise, 27 June 2024, available at: https://climatepromise.undp.org.

76   See: '"Do Just Stop Oil's Tactics Actually Work?" | Part 1/3', Just Stop Oil YouTube channel, 16 August 2024. According to Roger Hallam, founder and one of the chief ideologues of both XR and Just Stop Oil, majorities are not needed, only a few thousand people and the rest will follow. See: Roger Hallam, *Common Sense for the 21ˢᵗ Century: Only Nonviolent Rebellion Can Now Stop Climate Breakdown and Social Collapse*, self-published, 2019, p. 22.

77   See: '"Do Just Stop Oil's Tactics Actually Work?"'.

78   Hallam argues that the movement should use 'words like honour, duty, tradition, nation, and legacy' at every opportunity. See Hallam, *Common Sense*, p. 60.

79   Erica Chenoweth and Maria J. Stephan, *Why Civil Resistance Works: The Strategic Logic of Nonviolent Conflict*, New York: Columbia University Press, 2011, p. 15.

80   Kyle R. Matthews, 'Social Movements and (Mis)Use of Research: Extinction Rebellion and the 3.5% Rule', *Interface*, 12(1), pp. 591-615, 2020.

81   Erica Chenoweth, 'Questions, Answers, and Some Cautionary Updates Regarding the 3.5% Rule', *Carr Center Discussion Paper*, 2020.

82   Chenoweth and Stephan, *Why Civil*, p. 13.

83   See: 'An Open Letter to All Celebrities Who Publicly Support Just Stop Oil from Eight Women Currently Imprisoned in Bronzefield', Just Stop Oil, 7 August 2024, available at: https://juststopoil.org. Hallam has now also been sentenced to 5 years in prison along with four other activists. Just Stop Oil is campaigning in their defence under the banner #WholeTruthFive. See: https://juststopoil.org/2024/07/18/whole-truth-five-sentenced-to-4-5-years-at-southwark-crown-court/

84   Feyzi Ismail, 'Memo to Just Stop Oil and Everyone Risking All to Save the Planet: We Need a Rethink', *The Guardian,* 7 December 2022. For one of the most convincing cases of the centrality of working-class struggle to addressing the climate crisis, see: Huber, *Climate Change as Class War.*

85   Vincent Bevins, *If We Burn: The Mass Protest Decade and the Missing Revolution,* London: Wildfire Books, 2023.

86   Garner, *Stepping Stones,* p. 103.

87   Paul Foot's *The Vote* is surely one of the finest political histories of the struggle for the vote, and of how both the vote and democracy were undermined under capitalism.

THE CONTEMPORARY HISTORY OF THE US PALESTINE SOLIDARITY MOVEMENT

ARUN GUPTA

During the heady days of Occupy Wall Street (OWS) in the fall of 2011, protesters would chant, 'All day, all week, occupy Wall Street' while marching around the financial district in Lower Manhattan.[1] In Portland, Oregon, during the summer of 2020, when the George Floyd movement protests raged for more than 100 days in a row, crowds of black-clad gas-masked demonstrators would chant, 'Stay together, stay tight, we do this every night'.[2] During the spring of 2024, when encampments in solidarity with Gaza spread to about 120 US university and college campuses, students would chant, 'Disclose, divest, we will not stop, we will not rest'.[3]

These three slogans reveal the nature of US-based left movements in the first quarter of the twenty-first century. Foremost, the slogans indicate an imperative to act. Action is not a tactic. It is the end. The tactic – a public camp, social media-driven protest, nonstop demonstrations – is the organization and creates the revolutionary agent. The tactic is memeable and viral. These movements achieve success by creating an innovative moment in which a protest tactic captures media attention, briefly puts state power on the defensive and then spreads rapidly. Rarely is there a developed strategy or defined leadership, organization is minimal if any and protests tend to ossify quickly and veer toward maximalism. The porous, opaque and unstructured nature of these movements leaves them open to cooptation and opportunism. These movements are either outright anarchist, as with OWS, or have significant anarchist elements. But, being voluntarist, ephemeral and in constant flux, they tend to be more anarchic than anarchist. Activists claim decision-making is horizontal and uses consensus, but in practice those with the most cultural and social capital wield the most influence. In other words, they replicate the hidden power structures that Jo Freeman described in her landmark essay 'The Tyranny of Structurelessness'.[4]

I term these 'spontaneous protests', but in a specific manner. After OWS began, social movement historian Frances Fox Piven said that anyone who called the protests spontaneous doesn't understand them. Piven was correct that there was a history of ideas, individuals and organizations from which Occupy emerged. At the same time, however, movements like Occupy, George Floyd and Palestine solidarity have attracted millions of new participants in short order and with little organizational infrastructure. The theoretical underpinning of these movements is similar to that of the Industrial Workers of the World (IWW). In the early 1900s, the IWW sought to organize all workers regardless of race, gender, citizenship or work into 'One Big Union'.[5] The Wobblies lionized regular agitation and 'striking on the job'.[6] They would fight for concessions but refused to compromise with bosses. Their goal was not to win employment contracts, but rather to grow powerful enough to seize the means of production and operate the economy themselves, democratically and for social ends.

While the Wobblies had little of the allergy to organization and structure endemic to 'spontaneist' movements today, they share important similarities. For example, if public space is substituted for the shop floor, then there are clear parallels between the Global Justice Movement (GJM) that emerged in 1999, Occupy Wall Street and the Wobblies. OWS and the GJM refused to compromise with the state, especially police; they sought to unite everyone in protests that would build until they overwhelmed 'the system'; and then 'the people' would employ direct democracy to run society along anti-corporate if not anti-capitalist lines. Instead of strikes, the GJM had 'convergences', where everyone would gather to protest capitalist summits such as those of the International Monetary Fund (IMF), World Economic Forum and World Trade Organization (WTO). Occupy camped in prominent public spaces and used general assemblies, where 'the new world was being built in the shell of the old' (a riff on a saying attributed to Antonio Gramsci).[7] If the Wobblies were guilty of wishful thinking, many activists today indulge in magical thinking. They lack theory and a vision of the ideal society, instead believing that once capitalism collapses, we will naturally revert to an anarcho-communitarian society where resources and power would be distributed equitably and consensually.

OWS lacked strategy and, famously, even specific demands, but it had an impact.[8] In 2011, when President Barack Obama sought a 'grand bargain' with Republicans to reduce the national debt by cutting Social Security and Medicare, Occupy flipped the script from austerity to income and wealth inequality.[9] It popularized discussion of class and class power through its framework of 'the 1%' and 'the 99%'. OWS opened the door to low-wage worker organizing such as the Fight for $15 campaign, and paved the way for Bernie Sanders' 2016 presidential campaign, which in turn spurred the meteoric growth of the Democratic Socialists of America and helped revive socialism as a political and intellectual force among American youths, who in 2024 were more likely to view it positively than they did capitalism.[10]

These movements are part of the context in which the US-based Palestine solidarity movement (PSM) evolved over the last three decades. It developed a network of Palestinian, Muslim and anti-Zionist Jewish groups that took the lead in organizing against the Israeli genocide in Gaza that began in October 2023. Students took centre stage in the spring of 2024, when university crackdowns on campus protest encampments backfired and galvanized public support. The student camps were direct descendants of OWS in that they were continuous protests in public space, employing a disruptive tactic that went viral and thereby influencing national politics. There were important differences as well. Unlike Occupy, the students had demands; there were leaders, even if decision-making was often spur of the moment; many students were involved in Palestine solidarity organizations before they set up camp; and many were wary of the media, as reflected in the discipline they showed in messaging. While the students faced considerable police violence, as the Occupy protesters had, they also had to contend with McCarthyite political and legal repression.

In April 2024, I interviewed dozens of student protesters at New York University, the New School, Fashion Institute of Technology, Columbia University and City College of New York, all of which are in Manhattan. Students demanded transparency in university endowment investments, which are often secretive and can be enormous – $13.6 billion for Columbia and $50.7 billion for Harvard.[11] Students called for universities to divest from companies implicated in the occupation, particularly weapons makers and tech giants like Google, Amazon and Microsoft. They wanted universities to cut joint programs with Israeli universities. They also demanded amnesty for students, faculty and staff subjected to disciplinary procedures for protesting, which at Columbia University was 'at least 160 students'.[12] Students made decisions by some form of voting, but would defer to Palestinian–Americans and others directly affected by Israeli–US wars, just as African–Americans usually led the George Floyd protests in 2020.

The Palestinian liberation movement is one of the last national liberation and decolonization struggles. The PSM resembles anti-imperialist, antiwar and solidarity movements since the Vietnam War, but for the first time since the 1930s the Marxist left is not central to organizing it. The PSM is also similar to the George Floyd movement in that it has raised mass awareness and discredited state violence, even as ruling-class interests and institutions struck back with police violence and political and legal repression. The challenge for the PSM is building power to disrupt US support for Israel – just as the antiwar movement did during the Vietnam War, which combined with Vietnamese resistance and armed struggle to defeat the American war effort. This requires organization, leadership and a mass movement that is broad, strategic, disciplined and refuses to compromise on Palestinian national liberation and ending Zionist settler-colonialism. But it also faces the same trap confronting all movements today. PSM protests are highly dependent on social media and can unleash mass disruptive power seemingly out of nowhere. But social media also determines the form of protests, and in particular the ephemeral viral tactics they adopt, making them almost impossible to organize and institutionalize in the very moment when they have the most influence.

THE FIRST LIVESTREAMED GENOCIDE

Media is inseparable from modern US wars and antiwar organizing. If television made Vietnam a living-room war, then smartphones made Gaza a social-media war. Speaking from the Columbia University encampment in April 2024, Darializa Avila Chevalier, an alum, said, 'This is a generation that has witnessed a genocide for the last six months on their phones. Witnessing something this horrific has been incredibly formative. They are really committed to movements for social justice. This will never leave them.'

Social media is a double-edged sword. On 25 May 2020, videos went viral of a cop murdering George Floyd, and of a white woman calling 911 to falsely claim she was being threatened by Christian Cooper, a Black man birding in Central Park. They triggered the largest protests in US history, with more than 15 million people demonstrating in 2,400 towns and cities.[13] But the far right found social media useful, too. *The Washington Post* reported that right-wing militias 'often coordinated on Facebook' to threaten protestors. In rural Oregon, 'of the more than 60 actions … virtually all of them have encountered backlash from armed groups, whether in the form of intimidation on social media or actual boots on the ground'.[14] Social media put millions in the streets, but they outran attempts at coordination. The response to protests against police violence was more police violence, including 'mass arrests, indiscriminate use of projectiles and chemical weapons (e.g., rubber bullets, tear gas, pepper spray), and driving police vehicles into crowds of protestors'.[15] State violence squashed protests by millions because there was little organization, strategy, leadership or discipline.

A month later, the George Floyd protests had petered out in nearly every city. In Portland, demonstrations had dwindled to a few hundred people per night until Trump sent in a Border Patrol military force. His strategy was to 'amplify strife in cities' so as to generate 'viral online content' that could be used in his re-election campaign.[16] Trump was borrowing a trick from Portland. A few years earlier, provocateur Andy Ngo had gained notoriety for deceptively editing videos to drive a narrative that antifa hordes were destroying Portland and threatening white residents. Far-right gangs like the Proud Boys and Patriot Prayer would point to the videos to justify invading Portland to attack antifascists, often with the complicity of the Portland police. The gangs would then use video clips of their own violence to build their profile and attract new recruits. In fact, they used Portland as a proving ground to grow their ranks and develop the tactics they employed during the January 6 insurrection in Washington, DC.[17]

On the left, savvy individuals can quickly build a mass social media audience that they can use to shape protests. Even if they are well intentioned, there is a lack of accountability and democratic decision-making, temptations for personal and financial gain, and no mechanism to create lasting institutions, along with pervasive maximalism, call-out culture, and the burning and burning out of those who join protests as a result of the scant legal support for arrestees. Organizers can't ignore social media since it is a primary form of communication and recruitment. But for Palestinians and solidarity groups this comes at the cost of systematic censorship by Instagram and Facebook, owned by Mark Zuckerberg, and X (formerly Twitter), owned by Elon Musk, the two wealthiest men on the planet.[18] Many groups have also been 'deplatformed'. Before the start of the fall 2024 semester, Instagram erased the Columbia University chapter of Students for Justice in Palestine's account of 124,000 followers and 'permanently deleted' all the information associated with it, erasing years of work.[19] The far right has also become adept at using social media to incite violence against the left. On 30 April 2024, a social-media organized gang of extremists funded by Zionist celebrities assaulted a student encampment at UCLA for five hours – sending 25 people to hospitals with injuries – while police watched.[20]

Despite these obstacles, the students put Washington and Tel Aviv on the defensive. Global support for the students reached Palestinians in Gaza, who wrote messages of gratitude on their tents.[21] At the same time, solidarity activists were unable to meaningfully fracture the US relationship to Israel. Instead, the aggression got worse. One year after the genocide began, Israel invaded Lebanon with US support, repeating the tactics it was using in Gaza: killing thousands, targeting healthcare workers and hospitals, destroying residential areas and civilian infrastructure, and displacing more than a million civilians.[22] Reflecting on organizing against the US-Israeli wars, Rabbi Alissa Wise, founder of Rabbis for Ceasefire and co-author of *Solidarity Is the Political Version of Love: Lessons from Jewish Anti-Zionist Organizing*, said, 'I think one of the things that's really hard right now is that we've had a year of sustained protest where we've demonstrated mass public grassroots refusal of Israeli genocide. In the US and across the world, we've seen the highest level of Palestine solidarity probably ever. And yet there's nothing to show for it in terms of stopping the genocide.'[23]

THE ORIGINS OF SPONTANEOUS PROTEST

Spontaneous internet-driven protest goes back to the GJM, when thousands of nonviolent protesters gathered in Seattle to shut down the World Trade Organization Ministerial on 30 November 1999.[24] The protest outside emboldened countries from the Global South on the inside to reject a US-led pact to institute neoliberal trade and finance policies worldwide. The success made 'summit-hopping' a fad. Protesters dogged world leaders from city to city – Prague, Quebec City, Washington, DC, Genoa, Miami, Cancun – trying to create enough chaos to prevent them from advancing policies and trade deals that primarily benefit powerful countries and corporations.

The theory of change was to get enough people in the streets, and to shape actions in 'spokescouncils', which could gum up the gears of power and cause capitalism to grind to a halt. The theory valorized action while eschewing any real politics beyond sloganeering.[25] There was no shared vision of what participants were fighting for, who was the agent of change or the form of counter-hegemonic power (such as vanguard formations, industrial unionism or political parties). Slogans and buzzwords filled in for politics: 'horizontalism', 'consensus' and 'another world is possible'. Months after Seattle, Naomi Klein – who shot to fame after her first book, *No Logo*, was published days after the failed WTO ministerial and became the movement bible – likened summit hopping to nomadic followers of the Grateful Dead.[26] She warned that mobilizing tens of thousands of people to trek from protest to protest was sucking up all the organizing energy and losing sight of the need to connect globalization to local issues. Additionally, capital had many ways to respond. Trade meetings retreated to fortress resorts in Qatar and Switzerland. Legal repression intensified, as did violence. Police fired more than 5,000 canisters of tear gas in Quebec City and killed a protester in Genoa, Italy.[27]

At the same time, the GJM did achieve results. The opposition it crystallized killed the Doha Round, the WTO's attempt at a global trade deal. Reverberations continued for years with the collapse of the Free Trade Area of the Americas in 2005 and the Transpacific Partnership in

2017.[28] Also, the protests did succeed on their terms – but no one knew it. In September 2001, nonviolent direct action was planned to shut down the semi-annual IMF and World Bank meetings in Washington, DC. Demonstrations in the spring drew 20,000 activists who blocked streets and intersections, but failed to stop the talks. By the fall, the AFL-CIO signed up to protest. Police estimated 100,000 people would be in the streets. A source in the IMF claimed police warned the agency that they could not guarantee the summit's protection. The IMF quietly cancelled the meeting weeks in advance. But the September 11 attacks saved their hide as organized labour and major NGOs withdrew from protests, leaving only 5,000 hardcore activists who were brushed aside by police.

At heart, the GJM was anarchist. Many activists were influenced by the Zapatista movement in Chiapas, which launched a 12-day war against the Mexican government on 1 January 1994, the day NAFTA went into effect. The Zapatistas practiced bottom-up and horizontal decision-making.[29] They contrasted themselves to the top-down Marxist-Leninist guerrilla armies that had led many anticolonial revolutions in the 20th century. The Zapatistas lived mainly in peasant communities on the fringes of capitalism. Since they shared social, cultural and economic life, it was possible to make decisions collectively, enforce them and punish those who violated the rules.

The GJM was based on 'affinity groups', modeled on the Spanish Civil War.[30] US-based activists often had anarchist credentials such as Earth First!, Ruckus Society, Direct Action Network, the IWW, forest defense, United Students Against Sweatshops, and art and music collectives, alongside members of labour unions, 'fair trade' advocates, indigenous people, environmentalists and farmers.[31] Prior relationships enabled some accountability, but nothing like the Zapatistas could impose. However, activists in movements the GJM influenced, such as OWS, formed relationships after joining a camp, meaning there was no meaningful accountability. From there, OWS influenced Black Lives Matter in Ferguson, Missouri, in 2014, the Standing Rock oil pipeline blockade in 2016, Occupy ICE in 2018, the George Floyd movement in 2020 and the student movement for Gaza in 2023–2024. These were spontaneous, digital media protests that captured lightning in a bottle. Standing Rock and the student movement for Gaza both lasted more than a year because there was pre-existing organization and leadership. But the others rarely lasted more than a couple of months, collapsing as numbers dwindled, and activists often flailed about after the glow had faded trying to recapture the magic.

Precisely because anarchists lack state-recognized institutions such as nonprofits, they are free of constraints such as the need to follow the dictates of funders, legal restrictions on political activity, institutional fears of state repression, the safety or job security of workers, public image, or the imperative to ensure institutional reproduction. This allows a high degree of creativity and risk-taking, as well as ignominious flame-outs. The initial spark is based on an innovative tactic that reconfigures public space, such as horizontalist direct action in Seattle, encampments in OWS, social media-initiated protests for the George Floyd movement and campus encampments for Gaza. Once the movement spreads, activists have little control over what happens next. Anarchist-style network organizing is decentralized, which makes them resilient and hard to crush, but innovation fossilizes quickly. The absence of leaders and strategy leads to sclerotic decision-making. Meetings tend to be formalistic, long and spiked with jargon, which creates barriers to those who lack time or academic backgrounds. When social conditions change, the organizing often dissipates. The GJM, for example, was blindsided by the 9/11 attacks. The Direct Action Network was incapable of figuring out how to reorient and voted to dissolve. One wing of the movement in San Francisco reconstituted as 'Direct Action to Stop the War' after the US invaded Iraq on 20 March 2003. They disrupted the city for several days and carried out mass actions for ten weeks, but 'lacking a strategy', the energy dissipated.[32]

PAST IS PROLOGUE

If anarchists were not up to mobilizing growing discontent with the war on terror, Marxists were. By the time US forces invaded Iraq in March 2003, antiwar groups had proliferated. The Iraq antiwar movement offers important lessons as it was the last mass antiwar, anti-imperialist movement prior to the 2023 Palestine solidarity movement. One significant commonality was that leaders of the Iraq antiwar movement came from Marxist parties. United for Peace and Justice (UFPJ), a coalition of 1,300 organizations, was led by individuals affiliated with the Communist Party USA and the Committees of Correspondence for Democracy and Socialism, which had broken with the former in 1992, but later reconciled with it (some UFPJ leaders had also been in the 1970s-era Line of March).[33] UFPJ represented the peace and social justice left, and organized major protests on the East Coast from 2003 to 2007. UFPJ was rivaled by International ANSWER (Act Now to Stop War and End Racism), initiated by the Workers World Party (WWP) after the 1991 Persian Gulf War. WWP had a Third World nationalist approach that veered into 'campism', meaning it claimed repressive states were anti-imperialist solely because they were on Washington's hit list.[34] The main antiwar group on the West Coast, ANSWER broke away from

WWP in 2004 and its leaders set up the Party for Socialism and Liberation (PSL). The now-defunct International Socialist Organization (ISO) set up the Campus Antiwar Network (CAN) in 2001, which succeeded a student antiwar group it had organized during the first Gulf War.[35] Finally, the Revolutionary Communist Party employed a grab bag of front groups for antiwar organizing like Not In Our Name, the World Can't Wait and Refuse and Resist. Starting in 2002, protests attracted huge numbers, such as the historic 15 February 2003 protests that drew half-a-million in New York City and tens of millions more in nearly 800 cities around the world one month before the US invasion.[36] The three main formations and leaders during the Iraq War – UFPJ, ANSWER and CAN – were a reboot of the antiwar movement during the Gulf War.

Theory and organization explain why Marxists have been prominent in antiwar organizing. Marxism is internationalist – it holds that the proletariat exists without national or ethnic distinctions, and as the revolutionary class it is the agent of change. As such, Marxists place a high value on solidarity with those staring down the barrel of Western power, which is reinforced by Lenin's work, *Imperialism, the Highest Stage of Capitalism*. There are historical elements, too. US power reached its nadir in the 1970s as defeat in Vietnam loomed. Anticolonial movements were sweeping the global South, and Western youth were intoxicated with revolutionary fervour. Because wars of aggression are brutal, costly and dramatic, Marxists view the passion and dissent they stir as opportunities to act on their politics and build power. Marxists also punch above their weight. Having committed cadres and operating by democratic centralism, in theory if not in practice, enables them to react quickly to new developments and deploy disciplined members to do the necessary leg work. After Iraq invaded Kuwait in August 1990, the Workers World Party set up the Coalition to Stop US Intervention in the Middle East within a few weeks. Others on the left who criticized WWP as opportunists for acting quickly and alone later formed the National Campaign for Peace in the Middle East.[37] Many found the WWP unpalatable because of its history of supporting repression by Communist states, back to the 1956 Soviet invasion of Hungary and Czechoslovakia in 1968.[38] But WWP also opposed US sanctions, which it criticized as 'financial weapons of mass destruction', while the National Campaign supported these, and the Coalition called for ending the Israeli occupation of Palestine, which the more liberal National Campaign swept under the rug.

A decade later, the same tensions surfaced during the Iraq War. In 2003, UFPJ coordinated actions in 11 cities against Israel's 'separation wall', thus recognizing that the occupation of Palestine was central to Middle

East politics. But downplaying the 'apartheid wall', as Palestinians called it, was symptomatic of UFPJ's approach to favouring political expediency over principle. Soft Zionists in UFPJ, such as *Tikkun* publisher Michael Lerner, scoffed at the idea Israel was racist. In 2001, Lerner called it 'one of the most multiethnic societies in the world'.[39] UFPJ leaders argued that trying to keep 1,300 groups on board and focusing on the Iraq War necessitated avoiding divisive issues. However, this meant pushing other groups overboard if they advocated for Palestinian liberation or against the US war on Afghanistan, two 'controversial' issues at the time. Many activists felt sacrificing Palestinians for numbers weakened the movement. ISO cadre in the Campus Antiwar Network pushed student chapters to oppose the Israeli occupation of Palestine. The ISO also helped organize the first protest against the Afghanistan War, in Times Square, right after US bombing began on 7 October 2001.

UFPJ's expediency surfaced in other ways as well. In 2004, it agreed to NYPD demands that a demonstration avoid the Republican National Convention (RNC) at Madison Square Garden and end on a shadeless, isolated highway at the hottest time of summer. A grassroots outcry forced UFPJ to renegotiate, and 500,000 marched past the RNC without a hitch. But the protest itself was fatally flawed. It was billed as an action to 'Say No to Bush's War on Iraq', thus turning a principled movement into a partisan effort. UFPJ let Democratic presidential nominee John Kerry off the hook, even though he wanted to escalate the Iraq War by sending more troops. In focusing on Bush, UFPJ staff said they were seeking to enlist the support of unions like the United Auto Workers (UAW). They claimed if the RNC protest was nonpartisan, adopting a slogan such as 'No to the war', they would have mobilized only a hundred thousand protesters. When asked how the strategy worked, the staffers admitted it did not. The UAW never signed on. When voters angered by the botched war gave Democrats control of Congress in 2006, UFPJ rejected pressuring the party to cut funding for the war, summed up as 'the power of the purse'. In early 2007, a UFPJ leader told a group of activists in New York City, 'We don't need the power of the purse. We are not on the outside shaking our fists. We are on the inside, meeting with them [Democrats] every week.' When activists asked what they should do, the leader said write and call their representatives. In other words, the strategy was to demobilize activists.

Social theorist and historian Stanley Aronowitz argued UFPJ was practicing clientelism. Their clients were protesters, and UFPJ sought to leverage those numbers with Democrats. Not only did 'accommodationism' fail, but the antiwar movement had made imperialism a partisan issue, and the movement evaporated after a final big march in January 2007. Barack Obama co-opted antiwar sentiment in his 2008 victory, won the Nobel Peace Prize and went on to illegally bomb seven countries without any liberal dissent: Libya, Somalia, Iraq, Syria, Afghanistan, Pakistan and Yemen.[40] There is a question of whether it was inevitable that the antiwar groups would collapse around 2007, when US casualties dropped dramatically and the war disappeared from the headlines. UFPJ withered at this time, as did CAN a few years later. The loss of a principled antiwar movement meant there was little organized resistance to Obama's wars. It also meant the loss of forums to educate new activists on how both parties supported imperialism, with the difference being their tone and tactics of managing empire.

While the 15 February 2003 antiwar march has become renowned for its size and global scope, there was a protest the previous year that, in retrospect, was just as important. In early 2002, the US left was on its back foot. It was unsure how to respond to the 'war on terror' in a time of vengeful, 'either you are with us or against us' nationalism.[41] Several rallies were planned in Washington, DC, for 19 April 2002, incorporating causes from anti-globalization to antiwar.[42] ANSWER organized the first national protest against the war on terror that day. Weeks before, then-Prime Minister Ariel Sharon reinvaded the West Bank, destroying towns and killing scores of Palestinians. The rally shifted focus to the Israeli occupation, and organizing turned out thousands of Palestinian- and Muslim-Americans to protest. At that point it was the largest pro-Palestine march ever, drawing up to 100,000 people.[43] Speaker after speaker denounced Israel's occupation and called for a free Palestine.[44] At the rally, on the National Mall, amid a drum circle hundreds strong, young women in hijabs danced next to dreadlocked hippies. It was an enticing glimpse of the possibilities of multiracial and multifaith organizing. But a deep freeze set in. Whether it was coincidence or causation, the Bush administration ramped up repression of Muslim-Americans. The FBI went on to recruit a staggering number of informants in Muslim communities, tens of thousands by one estimate, to infiltrate, surveil and, eventually, manufacture more than 200 terrorism cases. This pushed many Palestinian- and Muslim-Americans away from activism.[45]

This history is not an endorsement of WWP, PSL or ANSWER, nor of their approach. Many on the left describe them as authoritarian, sectarian, manipulative and Stalinist. But their influence cannot be wished away. When movement leaders avoid hard issues like Palestine, the issue doesn't disappear. Opportunistic elements hammer those who fail to live up to their ideals. The conflict ends up creating divisions that are messier and more toxic than if the issue had been dealt with in a principled manner in the first place.

All this has shaped the context in which the Palestine solidarity movement emerged in 2023. While there is little direct organizational continuity between the two movements, electoral politics has bedeviled PSM organizing just as it did the Iraq antiwar movement.

OCCUPY WALL STREET

The student movement for Gaza is indebted to OWS, having modeled the campus encampments on it. One student at Columbia University said of Occupy, 'we are in awe of you guys'. Occupy was part of a global outburst of protests from 2010 to 2020, as Vincent Bevins details in *If We Burn: The Mass Protest Decade and the Missing Revolution*.[46] Occupy was a mass uprising, with more than 300 encampments around the country and thousands of groups in towns and cities, and it went global. Frances Fox Piven told me in early 2012 that 'Occupy Wall Street is the beginning, I think, of a great movement. One of a series of movements that has episodically changed history.' OWS, Black Lives Matter and the George Floyd movement all influenced US-based Palestine organizing. Ryna Workman, who as a third-year student at the NYU School of Law participated in its pro-Palestine movement, says, 'a lot of people were radicalized by the George Floyd movement'. Lara Deeb, professor of anthropology at Claremont Colleges, says that climate justice provided a path for many activists to join the PSM: 'Students make connections between environmental justice around the world including with Palestine.' Palestine solidarity also 'dovetailed with the abolition movement over detention and incarceration'.

The Occupy movement built on GJM-style protests that are spontaneous, emotional, reactive and facilitated by digital media. OWS was a reaction to dull and futile traditional protests. If all protests are theater, then the Iraq antiwar movement was boring theater. It was scripted with protesters passively listening to the same speeches, holding the same signs and reciting the same chants. Occupy was exciting theater – dynamic, chaotic, disruptive and an open-air social experiment. The student movement for Gaza was likewise dramatic and exciting. OWS grew out of the Arab Spring – popular revolts in Tunisia in late 2010 followed by Egypt in early 2011 that ousted dictatorial regimes. They were followed by the 'Wisconsin Uprising', protests against an anti-union governor imposing austerity, as well as anti-austerity movements in Spain, known as the 'indignados', and Greece that took over public squares in the spring of 2011.[47] In the United States, there were multiple calls for an occupation in the Wall Street area, and a few attempts, before dozens of protesters set up the first Occupy camp in Zuccotti Park in New York City on 17 September 2011. Two weeks later police kettled and arrested more than 700 peaceful protesters marching across the Brooklyn Bridge. Viral video of the arrests inspired hundreds of Occupy camps across the country and around the world. The free-wheeling spontaneity and popular enthusiasm created the kind of moments that grizzled Marxists dream about. Occupy Oakland pulled off a one-day general strike that shut down much of the city and its bustling port.[48] In New York City, about a month after the camp began, mass resistance thwarted plutocrat mayor Michael Bloomberg's first attempt to evict the camp by sending in the NYPD, which he boasted was 'the seventh biggest army in the world'.[49]

The anarchic elements that birthed OWS doomed it as well. In many cities, the biggest protest was the day the camp was set up. From there, movements dwindled. Maintaining camps was the end. Many became social-service sites, feeding and housing homeless who flocked to safe spaces, as in Detroit or Austin. A few, like San Francisco, became open-air drug dens or were beset by low-level violence, as in New Orleans. By mid-November, Occupy camps in Oakland and New York had been violently ejected. In other cities, activists were paralyzed. They waited weeks or months for the inevitable police sweep with no strategy to build on the organizing. Notable campaigns did emerge, such as 'Occupy Our Homes', which fought home foreclosures, labour organizing efforts with bakery workers and locked-out Teamsters at Sotheby's in New York City, and the groundbreaking Debt Collective that made student debt a national issue and won limited relief under President Joe Biden.[50]

But attempts to shift course, such as 'Occu-Evolve', attracted few activists.[51] Instead, activists attempted for a year to create new camps that were crushed by massive deployments of police, who weren't going to be caught flat-footed twice. In New York City, post-occupation meetings that drew hundreds were drained of energy and numbers by a few people with socialization issues. The problem was that the consensus, horizonalist model had become a pathology.[52] Trying to include everyone no matter how disruptive chased away 99 per cent of supporters. By 2012, days of actions against NATO and corporations that fund the American Legislative Exchange Council, and a May Day general strike, were similar to GJM convergences, but too small and diffuse to have any impact. Meanwhile, liberal outfits like MoveOn, Van Jones' 'Rebuild the Dream' and the Service Employees International Union co-opted the ideas and language of Occupy to boost Obama's 2012 re-election bid.[53] In October 2012, after Superstorm Sandy thrashed the Northeast, OWS activists created Occupy Sandy to provide vital emergency relief in the first days, as the state was slow to respond.[54] Activists said it was 'mutual aid', not charity. The efforts went on for months with little protest and no strategy, with activists filling the role of relief services like the Red Cross and renovating private property for free. It was charity.

FREE PALESTINE

Palestine solidarity in the US goes back to the 1960s, according to Lara Deeb and Jessica Winegar, professor of anthropology at Northwestern University. They write that it originated with the Student Nonviolent Coordinating Committee and Students for a Democratic Society in the 1960s, which 'galvanized anti-racist and anti-war student organizing in the US and included support for Palestinians'. Palestinian-American scholars such as Edward Said, Walid Khalidi and Ibrahim Abu-Lughod put '"the Palestinian narrative before college campuses" and broader audiences'. During its lightning war against Arab states in 1967, Israel illegally occupied the West Bank, Gaza, East Jerusalem and the Golan Heights, and solidified US support and backing from Jewish communities in the West. But the 1967 war also 'consolidated the alliance between Black radical internationalism (and its understanding of a global anticolonial struggle against racial capitalism) with Palestinian liberation movements', write Deeb and Winegar.[55] By the 1980s, the anti-apartheid movement boosted support for Palestinians, given parallels between South African and Israeli colonialism. In 1987, the eruption of the First Intifada garnered global solidarity for Palestinian resistance, overwhelmingly nonviolent for the first few years.[56]

Huwaida Arraf argues that the lack of unified Palestinian leadership like the African National Congress hurt organizing: 'I've thought if only we had a political leadership that was respected and legitimate in the eyes of the Palestinian people things would be a lot different. The movement is saying one thing and the Palestinian official representatives are saying another.' Arraf, a Palestinian-American human rights attorney and co-founder of the International Solidarity Movement, which recruits activists to support and document nonviolent resistance to Israeli colonization in the West Bank, says the 1993 Oslo Peace Accord was 'a very devastating time'. Edward Said called the accords 'an instrument of Palestinian surrender', which established the Palestinian Authority as 'Israel's enforcer'.[57] Arraf notes that the Oslo Accords 'broke down a lot of the community structures. It saw the PA usurp the right to represent the people. For Palestinians in the diaspora, I don't think anyone feels represented by the Palestinian Liberation Organization.'

When the Second Intifada began in September 2000, Israel fired '1,300,000 bullets ... during the first few days', wounding and killing thousands and foreclosing the possibility of nonviolence.[58] PLO factions responded with armed attacks, and Hamas and Islamic Jihad with suicide bombers, which, after 9/11, tarnished the Palestine struggle internationally. Alissa Wise told me that 'The Palestine solidarity movement faces repression much more than other movements. A lot of Palestinian-led groups took a big hit from the US government targeting those communities in the eighties and nineties'. She says repression after 9/11 and Islamophobia 'by design had a chilling effect'.

Nonetheless, past organizing laid the groundwork for 2023. Wise, who co-led Jewish Voice for Peace (JVP) in the 2010s, says while the 'Palestine solidarity movement is amorphous, it has grown tremendously' since the 1990s. Students for Justice in Palestine, founded in 1993, and JVP, started in 1996, have been in the forefront in organizing against the Israeli genocide, especially on campuses. Other leading groups include the Palestinian Youth Movement and American Muslims for Palestine. There is also Al-Shabaka, the Palestinian Policy Network, the US Campaign for Palestinian Rights, the US Palestinian Community Network and Jewish-led organizations such as If Not Now and Jews for Racial and Economic Justice. Wise says veteran antiwar groups active in the movement include the American Friends Service Committee and Fellowship of Reconciliation.

Arraf contends that 'Students for Justice in Palestine has been transformative, it's a critical part of the movement. That's because students and universities are usually at the forefront of social change.' She says the Palestinian Youth Movement, founded in 2008, is spurred by 'youth picking up the mantle and not waiting for anyone to pass it on to them and carve out their own space. PYM has been particularly good with taking on our own struggle with deep history and context and not just slogans, and building solidarity with other groups.' Many activists point to JVP as essential. Wise explains, in Solidarity Is the Political Version of Love, that JVP made 'crucial political decisions' in the 2010s, 'including to move further left by endorsing the Boycott, Divestment, and Sanctions (BDS) movement and becoming officially anti-Zionist, even as JVP grew larger and more powerful'.[59] One JVP member said, 'The mere existence of a group of a hundred thousand Jews who are explicitly anti-Zionist is a huge breakthrough. It challenges the idea that Zionism is the national aspirations of the Jewish people.' Arraf adds with regard to If Not Now that because it 'is not fully anti-Zionist', it serves as 'an important bridge between Zionists and the JVP'.

In 2005, Palestinian civil society issued a call for 'boycott, divestments, and sanctions against Israel until it complies with international law and universal principles of human rights'.[60] Wise says that the BDS movement 'has been a real focal point for global solidarity'. The prior year the Palestinian Campaign for the Academic and Cultural Boycott of Israel was initiated, and

British educators were among the first to push their universities to cut ties with Israel. Then in 2011, Pink Floyd co-founder Roger Waters shined a spotlight on the BDS campaign by backing a cultural boycott of Israel.[61] In 2014, the one million-member Presbyterian Church (USA) became the first major church to divest from companies profiting off the Israeli occupation, and has since denounced Christian Zionism, declared Israel an apartheid state, and, in July 2024, voted to divest from Israeli bonds.[62] At the same time, there has been a concerted attack on BDS, with 27 US states passing anti-BDS laws by 2019 that penalize companies that cut ties with companies doing business with Israel – even in illegal West Bank settlements.[63] Lara Deeb says the backlash is a sign of the effectiveness of BDS: 'The amount of money spent by the US and Israeli state to try to thwart boycotts wouldn't be happening if boycott wasn't considered a threat.'

It turns out, then, that the spontaneous outburst of the PSM in October 2023 was not entirely spontaneous. In the month after the genocide began, probably more than a million Americans protested in streets and on campuses, as did millions more around the world. Deeb says groups that have facilitated the growing movement include JVP, If Not Now and Open Hillel, the latter an alternative to pro-Zionist Hillel houses on college campuses.[64] She comments:

> There are anti-Zionist groups on and off campus that are creating space for Jewish students to ask and think about where they stand on issues without having to abandon their faith and where they can still be in community. Anti-Zionist Jewish students have been in the lead and that has been a crucial change. You have students who have been questioning the Israeli narrative they grew up with. They're saying, 'We don't want these crimes of genocide and apartheid committed in our name'.

Since October 2023, 'there have been three or four big mobilizations in DC', says Arraf, which 'took a lot of people working together'. The Free Palestine March in Washington, DC, on 4 November 2023, drew more than 100,000 people.[65] Arraf says that in the last 20 years, 'One of the most important developments is groups are working together a lot more. If there is a big mobilization in DC there will now be hundreds of co-sponsoring organizations.' For its part, JVP has non-violently shut down Grand Central Station, occupied the rotunda on Capitol Hill and blocked the New York Stock Exchange. Despite these successes, Wise says the movement is battling an array of powerful forces: 'Jewish communal support for Israel is one of the main pillars, but it's not the only one and ending it will not topple it.

There is also Christian nationalism, Christian Zionism, the military-industrial complex and Islamophobia.' The corporate media is another pillar, which repeats Israeli propaganda with minimal qualifications.

STUDENTS IN THE LEAD

College students were quick to protest the unfolding genocide and bore the brunt of legal and extralegal repression. As soon as the Palestine movement at Columbia emerged, it was attacked. In October 2023, 'doxxing trucks' circled Columbia and Harvard, displaying electronic images of students with their names.[66] Accuracy in Media, which peddles disinformation, dispatched the trucks and published websites labeled 'Columbia Hates Jews', naming dozens of students. Many were inundated with online harassment and death threats.[67] One student said Columbia amplified the hostility as it 'suppressed and harassed students who voiced their support for the Palestinian people'. On 10 November 2023, Columbia suspended the SJP and JVP chapters on thin grounds.[68] Students kept protesting, and Columbia kept punishing them. In January 2024, students at a divestment rally alleged two individuals sprayed them with a chemical while calling them 'Jew killers' and 'self-hating Jews'. Palestinian students claimed the chemical was 'Skunk', a weapon used by Israeli forces that smells like sewage and rotting flesh.[69] The university chastised the students for holding an 'unsanctioned' rally.[70] On 3 April 2024, Columbia suspended four students and evicted them from housing for holding a webinar entitled 'Resistance 101' with a Palestinian activist whom Zionists accused of being affiliated with a US-designated terrorist organization, which the speaker denied.[71]

The spark for the student camps began when the University of Southern California cancelled the commencement speech of student valedictorian Asna Tabassum over 'safety' concerns on 15 April 2024.[72] The real reason for the cancellation seems to be that she was smeared as antisemitic for being pro-Palestine.[73] Two days later, Columbia University President and Baroness Minouche Shafik testified at Congressional hearings on antisemitism.[74] Before the hearing, 23 Jewish faculty at Columbia and Barnard warned that she would be joining in the 'political theater of a new McCarthyism' seeking to destroy intellectual inquiry.[75] Hours before the hearing, Columbia students erected a Gaza Solidarity Encampment on campus.[76] Once back on campus, Shafik authorized a 'notoriously violent' NYPD force on 18 April to arrest more than 100 students. Perhaps Shafik thought she had put a lid on the simmering anger.[77] It blew up in her face.

Columbia students revived the camp within 24 hours. That day, senior Sebastian Gomez joined the camp. He said it was 'a beautiful place with students from every walk of life supporting each other. We have seminars, teach-ins, and I am learning about so many things. People are bringing us wonderful food every day. I've eaten better than I have in months.' Students countered the media drama of 'administration vs. protesters' by highlighting the role academia plays in genocide. They created a chart that listed wealthy trustees at Columbia who oversee a $13.6 billion endowment fund that invests in 'war profiteers', such as Lockheed Martin and Google.[78] Students said at least five trustees are tied to military contractors, the NYPD and Zionist organizations that 'manufacture consent' for Israel.[79] For the students, Shafik was a hatchet-man 'intimidating' faculty and staff, calling in the NYPD to 'punish' students and doing the bidding of far-right politicians.

Some universities didn't wait to send in police. On 22 April, in front of the NYU Stern School of Business, the NYPD arrested more than 130 people, including students and faculty, at a protest camp just hours old.[80] On 30 April, walls of riot police blocked off Columbia and City College of New York while hundreds of cops swept in using pepper spray to arrest 282 people at the campuses.[81] On 1 May, New York City's Mayor Eric Adams exposed the web tying together Israel, academia and policing. At a press conference, Adams said, 'I really want to thank' Rebecca Weiner, the NYPD deputy commissioner of intelligence and counterterrorism, for 'monitoring the situation'. Weiner, who teaches at Columbia's School of International and Public Affairs, accused Columbia students of the 'normalization and mainstreaming of rhetoric associated with terrorism that has now become pretty common on college campuses'.[82]

Like Occupy Wall Street, repression often triggered more protest. After being ejected from Stern, NYU students resettled two blocks away for a week before the police raided the new camp. At the New School, after police squashed a student protest on 5th Avenue, teachers initiated the first faculty-led encampment on 8 May.[83] At MIT, students tore down fencing to retake their camp despite threats of suspension.[84] At Harvard University, the suspension of a student group spurred a takeover of the historic Harvard Yard.[85] Students at the University of Texas at Austin kept protesting after police attacked a peaceful gathering with chemical spray, beatings and stun grenades that can maim and kill.[86] By 6 May, Wikipedia tallied pro-Palestine protests and camps at almost 140 universities in 45 of 50 states, and in 29 countries from Argentina to Yemen.[87]

Violence was not inevitable. At least six university administrations agreed to some demands of students without going from zero to police batons in an instant. The president of Wesleyan University wrote in *The New Republic* why he declined to send in police.[88] Students at Rutgers University dismantled their camp after the administration agreed to 8 of their 10 demands, although not divesting from Israel or cancelling plans to open a branch of Tel Aviv University in New Jersey.[89] In Philadelphia, progressive district attorney Larry Krasner helped keep police at bay from the University of Pennsylvania for more than two weeks. Visiting the camp on 3 May Krasner said, 'we don't have to do stupid like they did at Columbia'.[90]

Over the summer of 2024 university administrators introduced new codes covering more than 100 campuses that 'impose severe limits on speech and assembly that discourage or shut down freedom of expression', according to the American Association of University Professors.[91] As the fall 2024 semester began, administrators turned the screws to some pushback. NYU designated Zionism, a political ideology, as a protected category like Black people or women.[92] At Harvard University, at least 12 students were suspended for two weeks from a library after holding a silent 'study-in' there while wearing keffiyehs and with signs on their computers reading, 'imagine it happened here'. Following the students' suspension for violating 'guidelines on free expression', 25 Harvard faculty upped the ante by holding their own silent study-in at the same library. They, too, were suspended but that was met with four more library protests, including one where faculty displayed blank papers in reference to Hong Kong activists in 2020 who waved blank sheets of paper in defiance of laws criminalizing speech.[93] At Rutgers University, students wearing keffiyehs were blocked from a library and threatened with arrest. Cornell University suspended Momodou Taal, a British-Gambian PhD student, for participating in a protest, which would have resulted in his immediate deportation. After a spirited defense campaign, Cornell retreated, allowing Taal to continue his program but barring him from campus and teaching duties.[94] Deeb says, 'The effect of those policies, the lingering effect of arrests, the limiting of academic freedom has created a chilling effect on campuses for many people as it is intended to do.'

In August 2024, protests took place for five days straight at the Democratic National Convention in Chicago. The largest march drew about 4,000 people, mainly from 'Little Palestine', the largest Palestinian-American enclave in the country. The DNC protests were less than 1 per cent of the turnout at the 2004 RNC protests, despite one poll in June 2024 that showed 64 per cent of respondents backed a complete ceasefire, while only 26 per cent opposed it. In a CBS News poll the same month, 61 per cent supported stopping US arms shipments to Israel.[95]

By the time of the DNC protests, the Palestine solidarity movement had run into the buzzsaw of electoral politics. A campaign to cast 'uncommitted' ballots in the Democratic primary instead of voting for Joe Biden gained more than 700,000 votes and sent 30 delegates to the DNC in protest of the genocide.[96] After being repeatedly sidelined by the Harris campaign, the Uncommitted National Movement conducted a sit-in outside the convention hall demanding a Palestinian-American speak at the convention. But Harris's campaign nixed a long list of speakers, including Ahmed Fouad Alkhatib, who is a member of the pro-Israel Atlantic Council and says he is 'anti-Hamas'. Alkhatib says he was rejected despite offering to bring along the family of an Israeli hostage and 'share a message of healing and unity… and confronting hate and extremism'.[97]

I am writing two weeks after Trump won a race defined by high inflation. Facing headwinds of rising grocery and energy bills, Harris flubbed the contest with the 'Fyre Festival of Campaigns': heavy on billionaire celebrities, backed by neocons like Dick Cheney, and bearing a 'Wall Street-approved economic pitch'. Nonetheless, Gaza was a significant factor in Harris's loss, as she spent months antagonizing Palestinian, Lebanese and Muslim voters. She closed ranks with Israel's rampage by repeatedly declaring her support for 'Israel's right to defend itself'. She implied protesting genocide was worse than committing it by telling demonstrators denouncing her embrace of Israel, 'You know what? If you want Donald Trump to win, then say that. Otherwise, I'm speaking.' She dispatched Bill Clinton to Michigan, where he outraged voters by claiming Palestinians 'force [Israel] to kill civilians'. Muslim and Arab voters refused to bend, and it was Harris who capitulated. Two days before the election, Harris vowed to 'do everything in my power to end the war in Gaza'. It was a victory for the Palestine solidarity movement, but the last-minute flip-flop reeked of desperation. Returns showed a staggering drop in the Muslim vote for Democrats, as much as 50 points from 2020 to 2024. That alone cost Harris Michigan. She was also abandoned by young voters, who were most active in Gaza protests. 'Big liberal college counties' trailed the 'Democratic ticket by a point or two'. Those three factors could have cost her Wisconsin, given Trump won by less than 30,000 votes.[98]

Genocide is like global warming and the Covid-19 pandemic: they all spread unless aggressive measures are taken to stop them. After a year of genocide, Israeli forces began liquidating North Gaza, massacring and ethnically cleansing the 400,000 remaining residents. It was at the same time ethnically cleansing in the West Bank, as part of a killing spree and unprecedented land grab. It extended its genocidal war to Lebanon, with indiscriminate bombing that killed thousands and a land invasion. It was bombing Yemen, Syria and Iran. Even the corporate media, which had claimed for a year that Biden was working hard for a ceasefire, no longer seemed to believe its own lies.

The trends shaping politics and protest that emerged in Seattle 25 years earlier had become more pronounced since then. Digital media delivered a new unimaginable horror every day, from hospitalized patients burning to death in beds from an Israeli air strike, to prisoners being gangraped by Israeli soldiers, to parents carrying dismembered toddlers in plastic bags. These images pushed Palestinian voters, Muslim voters, young voters and left voters away from Harris. Israel's wars played into Trump's strongman appeal. He presented himself as a peace candidate who would end the wars and chaos in the Middle East and Ukraine wrought by the Democrats.

A second trend was the disintegration of the Marxist left. Its demise left few spaces to educate and train new activists in the fundamentals of organizing and the history of the left. Social media replaced solidarity, stoking grandstanding, circular arguments and undermining rather than building collective analysis and power. Solidarity means seeing the world through the eyes of the people you support and putting the needs of oppressed peoples before our own. Leftists might protest for Palestine, but fewer and fewer were in solidarity with them. Huwaida Arraf explained the election from a Palestinian perspective:

We are in a very shitty place. You know Trump is horrible and will not be good for you, and may be worse, so you definitely don't want Trump. But at the same time Palestinians and a lot of other people are done with accepting crumbs from the Democratic Party ... It is dangerous to give your vote to a party that is not only actively involved in the commission of genocide but that is gaslighting and dehumanizing Palestinians and Palestinian-Americans, and shunning us, our needs, and our humanity at every turn. It is also belittling our community by thinking that they don't have to do anything except scare us into believing that the other guy will be much worse. They are literally making us watch our families get slaughtered, paid for with our own money. If you, in the end, turn around and give your vote to the party that has done and continues to do this, then what can't they do to you and you'll still vote for them?

Rather than working to end the genocide, which would have improved the Democrats' chances of winning, many leftists muted criticism and got the worst of both worlds: Trump and genocide. They claimed Trump would be worse for Palestine, meaning they were more opposed to a hypothetical genocide than an actual genocide. They baselessly claimed Harris would end the genocide if elected. Left supporters for Harris vowed, 'we will hold her accountable when she is in office'. History does not bear this out. Liberals or the left never held Biden, Obama or Clinton accountable. That was done by spontaneous movements with few prior ties to left organizing (other than the GJM).

Most egregious, voting for Harris without making demands was a negation of power. The most power over a candidate is before an election, not after it. A concerted effort might have turned out 50,000 protesters at the DNC, given protests at past conventions and the number of people who had been marching for Gaza. That could have forced Democrats to end the genocide. An uncommitted vote two or three times higher might also have had the same result. Experienced organizers bemoaned the lack of an organizing umbrella like UFPJ, or Marxist groups that could provide strategic direction and education. I spoke with three long-time Marxist organizers who asked not to be identified. One organizer, who was not in the ISO, said, 'If the ISO was still around the movement would look different'.

Another organizer noted, 'The PSM is suffering from not having a collective space to strategize, to talk about what are we doing, how are we getting there. We can't just keep calling actions and expecting it to turn out different. They haven't figured out a way to talk together. There are no summits, no regular coordinating meetings.'

In the absence of any such mechanisms, Jewish anti-Zionist groups 'picked a lane'. JVP chose to engage in direct actions because they face fewer legal risks than Muslim or Palestinian activists. This is not to imply ISO would have been a silver bullet. On top of imploding in 2019, the ISO was often faulted by antiwar activists for sectarianism, and I have seen ISO cadre acting needlessly divisive in trying to 'sharpen the line'.

Into this void stepped the Party for Socialism and Liberation. Two organizers said the PSL is allied with the Palestinian Youth Movement, which provides national leadership for Students for Justice in Palestine, and that the PSL also works closely with American Muslims for Palestine. The sources claim the PSL does not collaborate with left organizations outside its umbrella, hampering movement building. One headline-making Palestinian-led organization, the Brooklyn-based Within Our Lifetime (WOL), has been called a 'one-woman show'. One organizer accurately described what I have also witnessed: 'WOL doesn't want to have any plan for an action. They throw themselves against the wall and the protest ends when the police attack.' WOL marches are frequent and go on for hours. In late 2023, they attracted ten thousand youths, mainly Arab and Muslim. By the spring of 2024, it was hundreds, in part because they provided no legal support. A third organizer grimly described student organizing on some campuses. It matches my experience of OWS, Occupy ICE and the George Floyd movement. They said:

Whoever says the most strident thing, is the most radical. A lot of it is super-performative. They don't want to build alliances with faculty and staff. They're the revolutionary agent and everyone else is a sellout. They are not open to a welcoming process where people may come in with a mix of ideas, good and bad, and engage in political education. It's sectarian, it's alienating, it's juvenile.

In many ways, the moment was made for the Democratic Socialists of America (DSA). But the DSA was not made for this moment. The DSA has around 80,000 dues-paying members, but active members are far fewer. It is not a cadre organization, it is opposed to democratic centralism and it focuses mainly on electoral politics. One organizer said, 'the DSA flubbed the George Floyd movement, and then flubbed the Gaza movement'. Having a diffuse structure where chapters have considerable freedom to take positions and decide on campaigns has enabled productive organizing, particularly around labour. One DSA activist points out that its 'internal life' is complicated, with different caucuses ranging from Marxists on the left to social democrats on the right. The DSA could have expanded the PSM by mobilizing the white left and progressives, but its bureaucratic structure makes it very hard to move the entire organization into non-electoral work. The organizer claimed, 'most of the people who are interested in building movements and building struggles have left the DSA', although other DSA organizers dispute this. Organization is the Achilles heel of the Palestine solidarity movement. There is a lack of national student leadership, a lack of overall national leadership and a lack of unifying Palestinian leadership in the Occupied Territories and worldwide.

Empires are defeated not only on the battlefield but primarily on the balance sheet. Israeli bonds have been downgraded multiple times, its economy is shrinking, and tens of thousands of well-educated young people who power its high-tech economy have fled abroad.[99] Turkey, a major economic partner, has axed some trade with Israel, while activists have been staging sit-ins and blockades at Turkish ports targeting Israel-bound cargo ships.[100] Colombia, Israel's top supplier of coal, has stopped exports of the fuel that accounts for 20 per cent of Israel's electricity supply.[101] Belgium, Spain, Canada, the Netherlands, Italy and Britain have banned or restricted weapons sales.[102] Foreign investors have dumped nearly $13 billion in Israeli stocks and bonds, and Israeli weapons makers were banned from or skipped trade shows.[103] Pret A Manger dropped plans to open 40 stores; in a huge blow, Intel suspended work on a $25 billion chip plant; and Starbucks and McDonald's admitted pro-Palestine boycotts against them have contributed to declining profits.[104] Brutal regional powers don't just disappear on their own, however. In the case of South Africa, the ANC marshalled wide support to guide an internal mass struggle that was largely nonviolent, a guerrilla war with crucial support from the Cuban military and other revolutionary movements in Southern Africa, and an international solidarity movement that chipped away at the apartheid state economy through divestment and boycotts until the regime crumbled. At best, the PSM has only fragments of these components and Israel is far more integrated into the Western ruling order than South Africa ever was.

Israel's genocide in Gaza serves the function of papering over a society at war with itself, between secular Jews and fanatical religious settlers, between Jews and second-class Israeli Arabs, between those who serve in the army and the poorly educated Orthodox who refuse to enlist. Foremost, Zionism has reached its historic conclusion as a genocidal racist ideology. There is no redeeming it, and modern states based in these ideas never last long.

NOTES

1   I have been involved in left social movements for more than 30 years both as a reporter and participant. I have reported on every movement discussed in this essay, and have been privy to significant events and conversations that have rarely been discussed openly if at all. My focus is the US Palestine solidarity movement and historicizing it – particularly the campus protests in the spring of 2024 that captured national and global attention. I offer my perspective informed by others whom I have interviewed to try to provide an accounting that is forthright, though hardly complete, of left movements over the last three decades. Quotations without endnote citations are from interviews I conducted. All opinions and errors are mine.

2   'Lessons Learned: City's Response to Protests Exposed Vulnerabilities in Portland's Police Accountability System', 2022, available at: www.portland.gov.

3   Aparna Gopalan, 'After the Encampments', Jewish Currents, 26 September 2024, available at: www.jewishcurrents.org.

4   Jo Freeman, 'The Tyranny of Stucturelessness', 2019, available at: www.jofreeman.com.

5   Robert Young, 'One Big Union, One Long Fight', Monthly Review, 1 November 2017, available at: www.monthlyreview.org.

6   'Industrial Workers of the World', New World Encyclopedia, available at: www.newworldencyclopedia.org.

7   Arthur J. Miller, 'Building a New World from the Shell of the Old; the Old Time Wobblies,' 2024, available at: www.iww.org; Jeet Heer, 'Welcome to the Time of Monsters', 21 April 2021, available at: jeetheer.substack.com.

8   Various Contributors, 'What Occupy Wall Street Organizers Would Do Differently', The Nation, 17 September 2021, available at: www.thenation.com.

9   Zachary A. Goldfarb, 'Liberals Didn't Kill Obama's Social Security Cuts. Republicans Did', The Washington Post, 21 February 2014.

10   Arun Gupta, 'Fight for 15 Confidential', *In These Times*, 11 November 2013; Pew Research Center, 'Modest Declines in Positive Views of "Socialism" and "Capitalism" in US', 19 September 2022.

11   CUAD, 'Gaza Solidarity Encampment Negotiations Update', 28 April 2024, available at: cuapartheiddivest.substack.com; Dan Primack, 'Endowment Secrecy Complicates Campus "Divestment" Demands', *Axios*, 30 April 2024; Sidney K. Lee and Thomas J. Mete, 'Critics Says Harvard's Endowment Is Underperforming and Overly Secretive. Is It?', *The Crimson*, 2023.

12   Sarah Huddleston, 'Inside Columbia's Surveillance and Disciplinary Operation for Student Protesters', *Columbia Daily Spectator*, 12 September 2024.

13   Larry Buchanan, Quoctrung Bui and Jugal Patel, 'Black Lives Matter May Be the Largest Movement in US History', *The New York Times*, 3 July 2020.

14   Isaac Stanley-Becker, 'As Protests Spread to Small-Town America, Militia Groups Respond with Armed Intimidation and Online Threats', *The Washington Post*, 18 June 2020.

15   Sandhya Kajeepeta and Daniel Kent Neil Johnson, 'Police and Protests: The Inequity of Police Responses to Racial Justice Demonstrations', Thurgood Marshall Institute, November 2023, available at: www.tminstituteldf.org.

16   It worked but not in the way Trump planned. Videos of federal police beating, disappearing and shooting peaceful protesters in the head went viral and ignited weeks of nightly protests by thousands of residents geared up in helmets, body armor and gas masks. Portland police recorded 6,249 uses of force against the public in a six-month period in 2020, a 20,000 per cent increase annualized over 2019. That does not include violence from federal forces. Portland may be the only instance of a mass white, middle-class revolt against police in US history. Trump withdrew most forces in defeat weeks later, while the left fell into tragic-comic levels of infighting and disintegrated. Sarah Sicard, 'Federal Officers in Portland Break Former Navy Seabee's Hand', *Military Times*, 20 July 2020; Jonathan Levison et al., 'Federal Officers Use Unmarked Vehicles to Grab People in Portland, DHS Confirms', *NPR*, 17 July 2020; Conrad Wilson, 'US Justice Department Defends Use of Force Against 2020 Protester Struck in the Head as "Reasonable and Privileged"', *OPB.org*, 15 May 2024; Alex Zielinski, 'Portland Police Have Used Force Against Protesters More Than 6,000 Times in 2020', *Portland Mercury*, 16 November 2020.

17   Arun Gupta, 'Portland's Andy Ngo Is the Most Dangerous Grifter in America', *Jacobin*, 16 August 2019; Arun Gupta, 'Riotlandia: Why Portland Has Become the Epicenter of Far-Right Violence', *The Intercept*, 16 August 2019.

18   'Meta's Broken Promises', Human Rights Watch, 21 December 2023, available at: www.hrw.org; Dali Hatuqa, 'Twitter under Fire for Censoring Palestinian Public Figures', *Al Jazeera*, 28 February 2023.

19   Kevin Reed, 'Instagram Shuts down Accounts of Anti-Genocide Student Groups before Start of Fall Classes', World Socialist Web Site, 28 August 2024, available at: www.wsws.org.

20   Kate Briquelet, 'Jessica Seinfeld and Bill Ackman Fund Pro-Israel Counterprotests at Colleges', *The Daily Beast*, 1 May 2024; Piper French, 'UCLA: Whose Violence?', *The New York Review of Books*, 11 May 2024; Neil Bedi et al., 'How Counterprotesters at U.C.L.A. Provoked Violence, Unchecked for Hours', *The New York Times*, 3 May

2024; Blake Ellis et al., 'Unmasking Counterprotesters Who Attacked UCLA's Pro-Palestine Encampment', *CNN*, 16 May 2024.

21   'Palestinians in Rafah Express Thanks to US University Protesters', *Al Jazeera*, 28 April 2024.

22   Hafiz Rashid, 'How Biden Officials Secretly Greenlit Israel's Attack on Lebanon', *The New Republic*, October 2024.

23   Rebecca Vilkomerson and Alissa Wise, *Solidarity Is the Political Version of Love: Lessons from Jewish Anti-Zionist Organizing*, Chicago: Haymarket Books, 2024, p. 13.

24   'WTO Seattle Collection', University of Washington University Libraries, available at: content.lib.washington.edu/wtoweb/index.html.

25   Seeds for Change, 'The Spokescouncil (or Delegates' Meeting)', available at: www.seedsforchange.org.uk/spokescouncil.

26   Naomi Klein, 'Not Like a Deadhead Odyssey', 11 April 2011, available at: www.naomiklein.org.

27   Raymond Parker, 'The Riot That Rocked Quebec City, 2001', 9 December 2019, available at: www.raymondparkerphoto.com; Luana Ruscitti, 'A Gunshot, and a Protester Falls: Genoa G8 Death Still Divides Italy', *Liberties*, 5 August 2016, available at: www.liberties.eu.

28   Lori Wallach and Deborah James, 'Why the WTO Doha Round Talks Have Collapsed — and a Path Forward', Public Citizen, 14 August 2006, available at: www.laborrights.org; Michele de Mello, 'No to FTAA 15 yrs on: Overcoming Capitalism Still Best Alternative for Latin America', translation Ítalo Piva, *Brasil de Fato*, 24 November 2020, available at: www.brasildefato.com; Reihan Salam, 'Why the Trans-Pacific Partnership Failed', *Slate*, 25 January 2017.

29   Leonidas Oikonomakis, 'Why We Still Love the Zapatistas', *ROAR Magazine*, 2015, available at: www.roarmag.org/wp-content/uploads/2015/12/ROAR-Issue-0.pdf.

30   Chandler Dandridge, 'The Legacy of the "Battle of Seattle"', *Jacobin*, 5 June 2024.

31   Chris Dixon, 'The Shutdown WTO Organizers History Project', available at: www.shutdownwto20.org.

32   Tristan Savatier, '"Stay Strong, This War is Long!" The Battle of San Francisco', Found SF, available at: www.foundsf.org/index.php?; Scott Parkin, 'Direct Action to Stop the War - the Understory - Rainforest Action Network', Rainforest Action Network, 27 January 2008, available at: www.ran.org.

33   Paul Krehbiel et al., 'Committees of Correspondence for Democracy and Socialism', 12 July 2018, available at: upr-info.org/sites/default/files/documents/2019-01/ccds_upr32_vnm_e_main.pdf.

34   On the eve of Russia's illegal invasion of Ukraine in 2022, the United National AntiWar Coalition claimed Russia's military moves were a 'defensive move ... to counter the threat of the US and NATO'. The problem with this position, and the opposing one held by leftists who lined up with the Pentagon, is two seemingly contradictory facts can be true at once: Ukrainian resistance to Russian imperialism is completely legitimate, and Washington turned the conflict into a proxy war by advocating for a 'strategic defeat' of Russia, as US Secretary of State Antony Blinken stated two weeks into the war. United National AntiWar Coalition, 'US and NATO Aggression Towards Russia – Danger at the Ukrainian Border', 8 December 2021, available at: www.nepajac.org/USrussia.htm; 'Blinken: Putin Will Lead Russia to

Strategic Defeat in Ukraine', *The Guardian*, 9 March 2022, available at: youtube.com/watch?v=frheRl9oO1Y.

35   Liberation School, 'Founding Statement of the Party for Socialism and Liberation', Party for Socialism and Liberation, 1 August 2004, available at: www.liberationschool.org.

36   Phyllis Bennis, 'February 15, 2003: The Day the World Said No to War', 15 February 2013, available at: www.ips-dc.org.

37   Peter Drucker, 'The Peace Movement Responds', *Against the Current*, No. 29, November/December 1990, available at: www.againstthecurrent.org.

38   Todd Chretien, 'Tiananmen Square: Which Side Are You On?', *Socialist Worker*, 17 June 2009, available at: www.socialistworker.org.

39   Michael Lerner, 'The Danger of Walking Out of Durban', *The New York Times*, 5 September 2001.

40   Heather Saul, '"Peace" President? How Obama came to bomb seven countries in six years', *Independent*, 27 September 2014.

41   The White House, 'Address to a Joint Session of Congress and the American People', 20 September 2001, available at: georgewbush-whitehouse.archives.

42   Megan Garvey and Bob Drogin, 'Causes Merge in Support of Palestine', *Los Angeles Times*, 21 April 2002.

43   Manny Fernandez, 'Demonstrators Rally to Palestinian Cause', *The Washington Post*, 20 April 2002.

44   C-SPAN, 'International A.N.S.W.E.R. Rally', 20 April 2002.

45   Trevor Aaronson, 'The Informants', *Mother Jones*, 29 July 2011; 'Targeted and Entrapped: Manufacturing the "Homegrown Threat" in the United States', *Jadaliyya*, 18 May 2011, available at: www.jadaliyya.com.

46   Vincent Bevins, *If We Burn: The Mass Protest Decade and the Missing Revolution*, Public Affairs, 2023.

47   Eric Touissaint, 'From the Arab Spring to the Indignados Movement to Occupy Wall Street', CADTM, 10 January 2012, available at: www.cadtm.org.

48   Davey D, 'Thoughts on Occupy Oakland's Historic General Strike: Celebration & Sobering Lessons', *The Progressive Magazine*, 5 November 2011.

49   Mike Riggs, 'Michael Bloomberg: "I have my own army in the NYPD, which is the seventh biggest army in the world"', *Reason*, 30 November 2011.

50   Ryan Devereaux, 'Occupy Our Homes: Protesters Bid to Move Families Into Foreclosed Houses', *The Guardian*, 7 December 2011; Mark Brenner and Jenny Brown, 'At Sotheby's and Beyond, "Occupy" Movement Boosts Unions', *Labor Notes*, 10 November 2011; Jana Kasperkevic, 'The Hand That Feeds: How Undocumented Workers at a New York Bakery Chain Won Higher Wages', *The Guardian*, 15 April 2015; Guillem Casasús, 'The Fight for Student Debt Relief Started a Decade Ago—at Occupy Wall Street', *Mother Jones*, July/August 2022.

51   Nathan Schneider, 'Breaking Up with Occupy', *The Nation*, 11 September 2013.

52   Arun Gupta, 'The Philadelphia National Gathering Reveals Occupy's Law of Entropy', *The Guardian*, 5 July 2012.

53   Arun Gupta, 'How to Rebrand Occupy', *Truthout*, 1 May 2012.

54   Ari Paul, 'Storm Troopers: The Legacy of Occupy Sandy', *Brooklyn Rail*, September 2013.

55   Lara Deeb and Jessica Winegar, 'Resistance to Repression and Back Again: The Movement for Palestinian Liberation in US Academia', *Middle East Critique*, 15 July 2024.

56   'Fatalities in the First Intifada', The Israeli Information Center for Human Rights in the Occupied Territories, B'Tselem, 2019, available at www.btselem.org.

57   Edward Said, 'The Morning After', *London Review of Books,* 21 October 1993.

58   Reuven Pedatzur, 'More Than a Million Bullets', *Ha'aretz*, 29 June 2004.

59   Vilkomerson and Wise, *Solidarity Is the Political Version of Love.*

60   'Palestinian Civil Society Call for BDS', Palestinian Civil Society, 9 July 2005, available at: www.bdsmovement.net/call.

61   Roger Waters, 'Tear Down This Israeli Wall', *The Guardian*, 11 March 2011.

62   'By Slim Margin, Assembly Approves Divestment from Three Companies Doing Business in Israel/Palestine', Presbyterian Church (USA), 20 June 2014, available at www.pcusa.org.

63   'US: States Use Anti-Boycott Laws to Punish Responsible Businesses', Human Rights Watch, 23 April 2019, available at: hrw.org.

64   Open Hillel is now known as Judaism On Our Own Terms, available at: www.jooot.org.

65   'Voices from Largest Pro-Palestinian Protest in US History: Stop the Siege on Gaza Now!', *Democracy Now!*, 6 November 2023.

66   Esha Karam, '"Doxxing Truck" Displaying Names and Faces of Affiliates It Calls "Antisemites" Comes to Columbia', *Columbia Daily Spectator*, 25 October 2023.

67   Gaby Del Valle, 'Columbia University Has a Doxxing Problem', *The Verge*, 26 April 2024.

68   Sarah Huddleston, 'Columbia Updated Its Event Policy Webpages. Seventeen Days Later, It Suspended SJP and JVP', *Columbia Daily Spectator*, 17 November 2023.

69   Chris Mendell, 'Protesters Allegedly Sprayed With Hazardous Chemical At Pro-Palestinian Rally, Nearly Two Dozen Report', *Columbia Daily Spectator*, 22 January 2024.

70   Prem Thaker, 'Columbia Scolds Students for "Unsanctioned" Gaza Rally Where They Were Attacked With Chemicals', *The Intercept*, 22 January 2024.

71   Sarah Huddleston, Maya Stahl and Chris Mendell, 'Four Columbia Students Suspended, Evicted from University Housing Following Unauthorized "Resistance 101" Event', *Columbia Daily Spectator*, 4 April 2024.

72   Sara Hoffman, 'Important Update on 2024 Commencement', USC Office of the Provost, 15 April 2024, available at: provost.usc.edu.

73   Ramon Antonio Vargas and Abené Clayton, 'Backlash as USC Cancels Valedictorian's Speech Over Support for Palestine', *The Guardian*, 16 April 2024.

74   'Experience for Baroness Shafik', UK Parliament, available at: members.parliament. uk; Nicholas Fandos, Stephanie Saul and Sharon Otterman, 'Columbia's President Tells Congress That Action Is Needed Against Antisemitism', *The New York Times*, 17 April 2024.

75   Hank Reichman, 'Open Letter from Jewish Faculty to Columbia University President Minouche Shafik', *Academe Blog*, 15 April 2024, available at: www.academeblog.org.

76   Maya Stahl, 'Hundreds of Protesters Occupy South Lawn, Call for Divestment from Israel During Shafik Testimony', *Columbia Daily Spectator*, 17 April 2024.

77   'Inside the Special NYPD Unit That's Brutalizing Protesters', NYCLU, 19 October
      2023, available at: www.nyclu.org; Maya Stahl, Sarah Huddleston and Shea Vance,
      'Shafik Authorizes NYPD to Sweep "Gaza Solidarity Encampment," Officers in Riot
      Gear Arrest over 100', *Columbia Daily Spectator*, 18 April 2024.

78   Adam Tooze, 'Chartbook 279: Columbia University's "Crisis" – a Political Economy
      Sketch Map', *Chartbook*, 26 April 2024, available at adamtooze.substack.com; Asheesh
      Kapur Siddique, 'The Modern American University Is a Right-Wing Institution',
      Teen Vogue, 19 May 2021.

79   Mona Chalabi, 'Meet Some of the Board of Trustees at Columbia University',
      Instagram, 2 May 2024, available at: instagram.com/monachalabi/p/C6eikmouK51.

80   Kiara Alfonseca et al., '150 Arrested at New York University amid Pro-Palestinian
      Protests, NYPD Says', *ABC News*, 24 April 2024.

81   Elizabeth Wolfe et al., 'Live Updates: Pro-Palestinian University Protests at Columbia,
      UCLA, UT, Campuses amid Israel's War in Gaza', *CNN*, 1 May 2024.

82   'LIVE: New York Mayor Eric Adams speaks after police cleared Columbia University
      protest encampment', *Reuters*, 1 May 2024, available at: youtube.com/live/
      B8YGRzarLjM?t=1546s; Maria Cramer, 'N.Y.P.D.'s New Intelligence Chief Takes
      Reins of Secretive Unit', *The New York Times*, 13 August 2023.

83   Charles Lane, Catalina Gonella and Christian Santana, 'Faculty establish pro-
      Palestinian encampment in Manhattan's New School', *Gothamist*, 8 May 2024.

84   Yaakov Aldrich, 'Students at Harvard and MIT Continue Protests Despite School
      Warnings, But So Far Avoid Arrests', *Cambridge Day*, 7 May 2024.

85   Nicholas Bogel-Burroughs, 'Hundreds at Harvard Protest Suspension of Pro-
      Palestinian Group', *The New York Times*, 24 April 2024.

86   Stephen Simpson, Sneha Dey and William Melhado, '79 Arrested amid Second
      Crackdown on UT-Austin Campus', *The Texas Tribune*, 30 April 2024; Julia Angwin
      and Abbie Nehring, 'Hotter than Lava', *ProPublica*, 12 January 2015.

87   'List of pro-Palestinian protests on university campuses in 2024', Wikipedia.

88   Michael S. Roth, 'Why I'm Not Calling the Police on My Students' Encampment',
      The New Republic, 7 May 2024.

89   Carly Baldwin, 'Rutgers Agrees to 8 Demands from Pro-Gaza Protesters', *New
      Brunswick, NJ Patch*, 6 May 2024, available at: www.patch.com.

90   Elea Castiglione, '"We Don't Have to Do Stupid" Like Columbia: Philadelphia
      District Attorney Visits Penn Encampment', *The Daily Pennsylvanian*, 1 May 2024.

91   Odeya Rosenband, 'How Universities Have Changed Their Policies on Protest because
      of the War in Gaza', *The Forward*, 28 August 2024; Alice Speri, '"A Police State": US
      Universities Impose Rules to Avoid Repeat of Gaza Protests', *The Guardian*, 17 August
      2024; AAUP Updates, 'AAUP Condemns Wave of Administrative Policies Intended to
      Crack down on Peaceful Campus Protest', 14 August 2024, available at: www.aaup.org.

92   Natasha Lennard, 'College Administrators Spent Summer Break Dreaming up Ways
      to Squash Gaza Protests', *The Intercept*, 27 August 2024.

93   Michelle N. Amponsah and Joyce E. Kim, 'Pro-Palestine Students Banned From
      Widener Library for 2 Weeks After "Study-In" Protest', *The Harvard Crimson*, 3
      October 2024; Tilly R. Robinson and Neil H. Shah, 'Harvard Faculty Hold Widener
      Library "Study-In" to Protest Student Activist Bans', *The Harvard Crimson*, 17
      October 2024; Max L. Krupnick, 'Silent Study-Ins', *Harvard Magazine*, 14 November

2024; Tilly R. Robinson, 'No ID Checks, but Harvard "Determining Next Steps" After Second Faculty Study-In', *The Harvard Crimson*, 9 November 2024.

94   Azad Essa, '"Under House Arrest": Cornell University "Modifies" Suspension of International PhD Student', *Middle East Eye*, 10 October 2024.

95   Prem Thakker, 'New Poll Suggests Gaza Ceasefire and Arms Embargo Would Help Dems with Swing State Voters', *Zeteo*, 14 August 2024; 'CBS News Poll — June 5-7 2024', *CBS News/YouGov*, 9 June 2024, available at: d3nkl3psvxxpe9.cloudfront.net/documents/cbsnews_20240609_1.pdf.

96   Melissa Hellmann, 'Uncommitted Movement Declines to Endorse Harris – but Warns Against Trump Presidency', *The Guardian*, 19 September 2024.

97   Ahmed Fouad Alkhatib, Twitter, 22 August 2024, available at: x.com/afalkhatib/status/1826641076322795622.

98   Nnamdi Egwuonwu, Jillian Frankel and Gabe Gutierrez, '"I am speaking now": Harris Responds After Michigan Rally Interrupted by pro-Palestinian Protesters', *NBC News*, 8 August 2024; Adam Gabbatt, 'Harris Vows at Michigan Rally to "Do Everything in My Power to End the War in Gaza"', *The Guardian*, 3 November 2024; Nicholas Nehamas and Andrew Duehren, 'Harris Had a Wall Street-Approved Economic Pitch. It Fell Flat', *The New York Times*, 9 November 2024; Stephen L. Miller, 'Kamala Harris Ran the Fyre Festival of Campaigns', *The Spectator World*, 11 November 2024; Liz Crampton, 'Dearborn's Arab Americans Feel Vindicated by Harris' Loss', *Politico*, 10 November 2024; Charlie Mahtesian, 'What the Electoral Map Tells Us About Kamala Harris' Loss', *Politico*, 6 November 2024; Ismail Allison, 'CAIR Exit Poll of Muslim Voters Reveals Surge in Support for Jill Stein and Donald Trump, Steep Decline for Harris', CAIR, 8 November 2024, available at www. cair.com; Arun Gupta, 'How US Sanctions Torpedoed Kamala Harris', *Jacobin*, 19 November 2024.

99   Steven Scheer, 'More Ratings Cuts Feared After Moody's Downgrades Israel Two Notches', *Reuters*, 1 October 2024; Shlomo Maoz, 'Israel Faces Record Emigration as Thousands Leave the Country', *The Jerusalem Post*, 13 October 2024.

100 Gulsi Harman et al., 'As Turkey Cuts Trade Ties, Israel's Isolation Grows', *The New York Times*, 3 May 2024; 'Activists Continue to Protest Docking of Israeli Ships at Turkish Ports', *Turkish Minute*, 7 November 2024.

101 Oscar Medina, 'Colombia to Ban Coal Sales to Israel to Seek War's End', *Bloomberg*, 8 June 2024.

102 Oliver Holmes, 'Which Countries Have Banned or Restricted Arms Sales to Israel?', *The Guardian*, 3 September 2024.

103 John Irish, 'In Widening Dispute, Israel Lashes Out at France After Firms Barred from Arms Show', *Reuters*, 16 October 2024; Alexander Cornwell, 'Israel Weapons Makers Leave Stands Empty at Dubai Airshow', *Reuters*, 13 November 2023.

104 'British Sandwich Chain Pret Abandons Plan to Open in Israel', *Reuters*, 3 June 2024; 'Chipmaker Intel to Halt $25-Billion Israel Plant, News Website Says', *Reuters*, 10 June 2024; Jonah Valdez, 'Boycotts Against Israel Are Hurting Starbucks and McDonald's Sales Worldwide', *The Intercept*, 30 July 2024.